Thorburn, Thomas James. The mythical interpretation of the Gospels (Bross library) N. Y. Scribner, 1916. 356p. $1.50 net.

An able and scholarly refutation of the mythical interpretation of the Gospels, directed specially against the myth theories of Andrew Drews, W. B. Smith, and J. M. Robertson. Based on a detailed critical and comparative study of the New Testament narratives and the mythical episodes from which they are supposed to be derived. Awarded the Bross prize, 1915.

226 Bible—New Testament—Gospels ‖ Bible—New Testament—Criticism and interpretation   16–21563/4

THE BROSS LIBRARY

VOLUME VII

226
T

THE
MYTHICAL INTERPRETATION
OF THE GOSPELS

CRITICAL STUDIES IN THE HISTORIC NARRATIVES

BY

THOMAS JAMES THORBURN, D.D., LL.D.

NEW YORK
CHARLES SCRIBNER'S SONS
1916

TO

THE PRESIDENT, TRUSTEES, AND FACULTY

OF

LAKE FOREST COLLEGE, U. S. A.

THIS WORK IS GRATEFULLY DEDICATED

BY

THE AUTHOR

Οὐ γὰρ σεσοφισμένοις μύθοις ἐξακολουθήσαντες
ἐγνωρίσαμεν ὑμῖν τὴν τοῦ Κυρίου Ἰησοῦ Χριστοῦ
δύναμιν καὶ παρουσίαν, ἀλλ' ἐπόπται γενηθέντες
τῆς ἐκείνου μεγαλειότητος.

—II Peter 1 : 16.

THE BROSS FOUNDATION

THE BROSS LIBRARY is an outgrowth of a fund established in 1879 by the late William Bross, lieutenant-governor of Illinois from 1866 to 1870. Desiring some memorial of his son, Nathaniel Bross, who died in 1856, Mr. Bross entered into an agreement with the "trustees of Lake Forest University," whereby there was finally transferred to them the sum of forty thousand dollars, the income of which was to accumulate in perpetuity for successive periods of ten years, the accumulation of one decade to be spent in the following decade, for the purpose of stimulating the best books or treatises "on the connexion, relation, and mutual bearing of any practical science, the history of our race, or the facts in any department of knowledge, with and upon the Christian Religion." The object of the donor was to "call out the best efforts of the highest talent and the ripest scholarship of the world to illustrate from science, or from any department of knowledge, and to demonstrate the divine origin and the authority of the Christian scriptures; and, further, to show how both science and revelation coincide and prove the existence, the providence, or any or all of the attributes of the only living and true God, 'infinite, eternal, and unchangeable in his being, wisdom, power, holiness, justice, goodness, and truth.'"

The gift contemplated in the original agreement of 1879 was finally consummated in 1890. The first decade of the accumulation of interest having closed in 1900, the trustees of the Bross Fund began at this time to carry out the provisions of the deed of gift. It was determined to give the general title of "The Bross Library" to the series of books purchased and published with the proceeds of the Bross Fund. In accordance with the express wish of the donor, that the "Evidences of Christianity" of his "very dear friend and teacher, Mark Hopkins, D.D.," be purchased and "ever numbered and known as No. 1 of the series," the trustees secured the copyright of this work, which has been republished in a presentation edition as Volume I of the Bross Library.

The trust agreement prescribed two methods by which the production of books and treatises of the nature contemplated by the donor was to be stimulated:

1. The trustees were empowered to offer one or more prizes during each decade, the competition for which was to be thrown open to "the scientific men, the Christian philosophers, and historians of all nations." In accordance with this provision, a prize of six thousand dollars was offered in 1902 for the best book fulfilling the conditions of the deed of gift, the competing manuscripts to be presented on or before June 1, 1905. The prize was awarded to the late Reverend James Orr, D.D., professor of apologetics and systematic theology in the United Free Church College, Glasgow, for his treatise on "The Problem of the Old Testament," which was published in 1906 as Volume III of the Bross Library.

The second decennial prize of six thousand dollars was offered in 1913, the competing manuscripts to be submitted by January 1, 1915. The judges were President William Douglas Mackenzie, of Hartford Theological Seminary; Professor Rufus M. Jones, of Haverford College; and Professor Benjamin L. Hobson, of McCormick Theological Seminary. The prize was awarded by the judges to a manuscript entitled "The Mythical Interpretation of the Gospels," whose author proved to be the Reverend Thomas James Thorburn, D.D., LL.D., St. Helen's Down, Hastings, England. This essay is now issued as Volume VII of the Bross Library.

The next Bross Prize will be offered about 1925, and will be announced in due time by the trustees of Lake Forest University.

2. The trustees were also empowered to "select and designate any particular scientific man or Christian philosopher and the subject on which he shall write," and to "agree with him as to the sum he shall receive for the book or treatise to be written." Under this provision the trustees have, from time to time, invited eminent scholars to deliver courses of lectures before Lake Forest College, such courses to be subsequently published as volumes in the Bross Library. The first course of lectures, on "Obligatory Morality," was delivered in May, 1903, by the Reverend Francis Landey Patton, D.D., LL.D., president of Princeton Theological Seminary. The copyright of the lectures is now the property of the trustees of the Bross Fund. The second course of lectures, on "The Bible: Its Origin and Nature," was delivered in May, 1904, by the late Reverend Marcus Dods, D.D., professor of exegetical theology in New College, Edinburgh. These lectures were published in 1905 as Volume II of the Bross Library. The third course of lectures, on "The Bible of Nature," was delivered in September and October, 1907, by J. Arthur Thomson, M.A., regius professor of natural history in the University of Aberdeen. These lectures were published in 1908 as Volume IV of the Bross Library. The fourth course of lectures, on "The Religions of Modern Syria and Palestine," was delivered in November and December, 1908, by Frederick Jones Bliss, Ph.D., of Beirut, Syria. These lectures were published in 1912 as Volume V of the Bross Library. The fifth course of lectures, on "The Sources of Religious Insight," was delivered in November, 1911, by Professor Josiah Royce, Ph.D., of Harvard University. These lectures were published in 1912 as Volume VI of the Bross Library. The sixth

course of lectures, on "The Will to Freedom, or the Gospel of Nietzsche and the Gospel of Christ," was delivered in May, 1915, by the Reverend John Neville Figgis, D.D., Litt.D., of the House of the Resurrection, Mirfield, England. These lectures will be published as Volume VIII of the Bross Library.

JOHN SCHOLTE NOLLEN,
President of Lake Forest College.

LAKE FOREST, ILLINOIS,
    January, 1916.

PREFACE

It is but fitting that the writer of this volume should introduce his work, which has gained the Bross Prize for 1915, with an expression of gratitude to the memory of the founder of that bequest, to the present trustees of Lake Forest College, and also to the judges for their courtesy and the trouble involved in dealing with the manuscript submitted for their consideration. He may add, however, that the work was not commenced with a view to competing for the Bross, or indeed any, prize; it had been in hand for about two years, and had already progressed considerably towards taking a final shape, when he bethought him that, perhaps, it might be a suitable book for the purpose which the late William Bross, formerly lieutenant-governor of the State of Illinois, had in view when he established the trust.

The subject of this treatise, "The Mythical Interpretation of the Gospels," as it may be termed, is, it should be widely known, nothing more nor less than the theory that our present four canonical Gospels are in no sense whatever what we nowadays mean by the term "historical documents." This is, in truth, a most serious proposition to fling down before the world after close upon nineteen centuries of Christian teaching which has been throughout based upon the contrary affirmation. For, if any such theory be a true one, and can be so established to the satisfaction not only of scholars but to that of the world at large, then the documents referred to must be in effect probably nothing more than a mere congeries of ancient nature-myths, and their Central Figure also can only be an embodiment of one or more

of the various cult-gods or nature-spirits (demons) with
which the imagination of the ancient races who formerly
dwelt in the southern parts of western Asia and eastern Europe, with Egypt and Arabia, peopled those lands
for many centuries before and subsequent to the Christian era.

The subject, the present writer repeats, is one of the
utmost importance when viewed from the religious standpoint; and it has hitherto, in his opinion, been somewhat too hastily set aside without examination, and even
quietly snubbed by critical as well as by dogmatic theologians. It is not thus that any theory, however wrong-
headed it may be, is checked, nor by these means are
genuine seekers after truth ever convinced of its errors.
On the contrary, such theories and assertions should be
challenged freely and criticised, and their mistakes and
assumptions frankly and systematically pointed out.

After making the above prefatory statement, it may
not be inopportune or superfluous here to give, for the
benefit of such readers to whom it will be welcome, a
brief sketch of the chief mythical and non-historical explanations of the origin and nature of Christianity which
have been put forth from time to time during the period
covered by the past one hundred and twenty years.

Previously to the end of the eighteenth century the
mythical hypothesis of Christianity was, for all practical
purposes, wholly unknown. Going still further back, in
the earlier centuries of the Christian era, we find the various fathers of the church and other contemporary writers, secular as well as ecclesiastical, distinguishing most
carefully and emphatically the historical Gospel narratives, as they had received or examined them, and above
all the personality of Jesus Christ, from the nature-
myths and the deities of various classes and grades,
whether Olympic gods or cultual nature-spirits (demons),
which were held in awe or honour by the peoples in whose

very midst Christianity had but recently been introduced
and established. This is, indeed, an indisputable and
accepted fact.

Much the same, too, may be said of the Jewish rabbins
and others who contributed to that body of authoritative Jewish teaching, mingled with fact and fancy, which
at an early period took shape and became known as the
two *Talmuds*. To the Christian fathers and the Jewish
rabbins alike both Jesus Christ and the records of his
life and teaching had an undoubted historical basis.
Even his miracles were in general admitted by the Jews,
but were attributed by them either to the agency of demons or to the magical arts which he was supposed to
have learned in, and brought from, Egypt. Neither early
Christian nor Jew of any period felt the smallest doubt
as to the historic character of either Christianity or its
Founder, whilst even the pagan Romans and Greeks always refer to both in professedly historic terms. Indeed, the educated Gentiles of all races included within
the Roman Empire of that period regarded the Christian
system as wholly unlike, and in every respect totally
opposed to, the stories told of the cult-gods and divine
heroes of their myths. These three primary facts are
beyond dispute, and all three taken together form, in
the opinion of the present writer, a great and *a priori*
obstacle to any modern scheme that can be devised for
the mythicising of the story of the Christian religion or
the person of its Founder.

With the period of the great French Revolution, at
the end of the eighteenth century, a great change was
obviously impending. Its advent was heralded by the
publication, in 1794, of the notorious work of Charles
François Dupuis (1742–1809), entitled *L'origine de tous
les Cultes, ou la Réligion Universelle*, which had followed
close upon Volney's *Les Ruines, ou Méditation sur les
Révolutions des Empires*, a thinly veiled and *dilettante*

attack upon all religion, and especially upon the historical character and evidences of Christianity. In the work
of Dupuis all primitive religion is connected with a system of astral mythology, and the origin of astral myths
is traced to Upper Egypt. This book excited some interest at the time of its publication, though it had only
a small sale; it is said, however, to have been largely
instrumental in bringing about the expedition organised
by Napoleon Bonaparte for the exploration, or exploita-
tion, of that country. Regarding this book, it will suffice
here to say that a distinguished modern astronomer[1] has
(March 20, 1914) informed the present writer that Dupuis's "method led him to the conclusion that the constellations must have been devised when the sun was in
the constellation Aries at the autumnal equinox, *i. e.*,
about 13000 B. C. The evidence afforded by the unmapped space round the south pole proves that he was
ten or eleven thousand years wrong; in other words,
nearly as wrong as he could be"![2] Any system which
is based upon such a huge and primary error as this
stands self-condemned at the outset.

The method of Dupuis soon fell into disrepute, but in
spite of this fact it has been revived in our own day in a
somewhat modified form by certain modern mythicists,
notably A. Niemojewski (*Bog Jezus*, 1909, and *Gott Jezus
im Lichte fremder und eigener Forschungen, samt Darstellung der evangelischen Astralstoffe, Astralszenen, und Astralsysteme*, 1910) and Fuhrmann (*Der Astralmythen von
Christus*), who have used this once much-vaunted "key"
to the origin of religions in a manner regardless not only
of astronomical facts but even, at times, of common sense.

With the downfall, in the early nineteenth century,
of the astral theory of Dupuis, which in speculative
theology was largely superseded by the unimaginative

---

[1] Mr. E. Walter Maunder, F.R.A.S.
[2] See also *Encyclopædia Britannica*, 11th ed., art. "Dupuis."

rationalism of Paulus (1761-1851), the next generation
were confronted with a revival of the mythic theory in
a new and improved form.   David Friedrich Strauss
(1808-74) issued in 1835-6 his famous work, *Das Leben
Jesu*, based to a great extent upon the dialectical method
of the then fashionable Hegelian idealistic philosophy,
in which, while he acknowledged the actual existence of
an historical Jesus who formed the subject of the Gospel
memoirs, Strauss maintained had had such a complete
halo of myth thrown around him that for all practical
purposes his life was entirely unknown to us.   This work
created a great sensation almost throughout Europe,
and a fourth edition of it, translated by George Eliot,
appeared in England in a popular form under the English title of *The Life of Jesus Critically Examined* (1846).
Finally the work was entirely recast and rewritten as
Das Leben Jesu für das Deutsche Volk bearbeitet (1865); in
this new form Strauss declared that he viewed the Gospel
stories rather as conscious *inventions* than as poetic myths,
as he had maintained in the original *Das Leben Jesu*.

This non-historical and later view of the Gospel records and the person of Jesus was next taken up by Bruno
Bauer (1809-82), a critic belonging, like Strauss, in the
earlier part of his career, to the Hegelian "Left Wing,"
and who differed from Strauss chiefly in denying that
the Judaism antecedent to the rise of Christianity har-
boured any potent Messianic expectations.   The Messiah,
Bauer maintained (*Kritik der Evangelischen Geschichte der
Synoptiker*, 1841), was the product of the Christian consciousness, and was rather carried back from the Christian system into that of Judaism than borrowed by the
former from the latter source.   As for the Gospels, they
were, he thought, abstract conceptions turned into history, probably by one man—the evangelist Mark.

Before, however, dismissing Jesus as a wholly fictitious
character in history, Bauer decided to make a further

critical examination of the structure and contents of the
Pauline epistles (*Kritik der Paulinischen Briefe*, 1850–1).
As an outcome of these combined investigations he at
last decided that an historical Jesus never existed—a
result little, if at all, removed from the final conclusions
of Strauss.

With the death of Bauer the mythical hypothesis may
be said to have entered upon a new phase. In 1882 Rudolf
Seydel published his *Das Evangelium von Jesu in seinen
Verhältnissen zur Buddha-Sage und Buddha-Lehre*, which
was followed not long afterwards by his *Die Buddha-
Legende und das Leben Jesu nach den Evangelien* (2d ed.,
1897), and *Buddha und Christus* (1884), in which the
avowed object was to demonstrate that the life of Jesus,
as related by the compilers of the synoptic Gospels, was
almost wholly derived from similar anecdotes related of
the Buddha in Buddhist legend and myth. The reader
of the present book will find the greater number of these
stories quoted and compared with their (so-called) Christian "parallels" and "derivatives." This theory had
been, however, already effectively criticised by Bousset
in the *Theologische Rundschau* for February, 1889.

At the opening of the twentieth century another Oriental "source" was proposed by Mr. J. M. Robertson
(*Christianity and Mythology*, 1900; *Pagan Christs: Studies in Comparative Hierology*, 1903, 2d ed., 1912). This
author, whose excursions into the field of theology all
bear the marks of great haste and extreme recklessness
of statement, has been very largely dealt with in the present volume. It will suffice, therefore, to add here that
he traces the portrait of Jesus, as drawn by the synoptic
writers, to a syncretism of mythological elements derived primarily, perhaps, from early Hebraic tradition
and myth combined (later on) with various pagan myths,
European as well as Asiatic, and especially the stories
told about the early life of Krishna and, in some cases,

those recorded of the Buddha. Indeed, the *idea* contained in the story of Jesus is, in the main, for him, very largely a recension of the myth of an old Ephraimitic sun-god "Joshua," which, when historicised, gave rise to a legend regarding a northern Israelite Messiah, Joshua ben Joseph.

This last-mentioned view of Christianity and its Founder, again, does not differ very greatly from that of Professor W. B. Smith, of Tulane University, New Orleans, U. S. A., who (*Der Vorchristliche Jesus*, 1906) derives the "Christ-myth" from certain alleged "Jesus-cults," dating from pre-Christian times. Jesus is, he thinks, the name of an ancient Western Semitic cult-god, and he finds a reference to the doctrines held by the devotees of this deity in Acts 18 : 25. He also further maintains that "Nazareth" was not in pre-Christian times the name of a village in Galilee (since no such village then existed), but is a corruption of Nazaraios (Ναζαραῖος), meaning "guardian" or "saviour"—a word identical in its signification with "Jesus," the name of this ancient cult-god. "Christ," also, in like manner has reference to the same deity, for Χριστός is equatable with χρηστός, found in the LXX version of Psalm 34 : 8.

The above views Professor Smith subsequently developed more fully in a later work (*Ecce Deus*, 1912), in which he maintains, contrary to the commonly accepted view, that Jesus is presented by the evangelist Mark wholly as a god (*i. e.*, a cult-deity) in an anthropomorphic guise.

We may, perhaps, here also briefly note another variant form of the mythical theory which has been proposed by the German Assyriologist, P. Jensen.

Doctor Jensen states (*Das Gilgamesch-epos in der Weltliteratur*, 1906; *Moses, Jesus, Paulus: drei Varianten des Babylonischen Gottmenschen Gilgamesch*, 1909; *Hat der Jesus der Evangelien wirklich gelebt?* 1910) that Jesus may be identified with not merely one but several of the mythical heroes in the Babylonian Gilgamesh epic, and a series of so-called parallels found in that work and the Gospels are set forth in his *Moses, Jesus, Paulus*, as establishing the truth of his *thesis*. His theory, however, has been rejected by the almost unanimous consent of scholars, and one American theologian has even gone so far as to pronounce the whole hypothesis "elaborate bosh."

But the hypothesis of the mythical origin and nature of Christianity and the unhistorical character of the Gospel narratives reaches its culminating point in two recent works of Professor Drews, of Karlsruhe, who, abandoning for a time the exposition of philosophy, appears as the strenuous advocate of a mythical Christianity (*Die Christusmythe*, 1910, English translation *The Christ Myth;* and *The Witnesses to the Historicity of Jesus*,[1] 1912). His method and conclusions may be briefly summarised as follows: From Robertson and W. B. Smith he borrows the general mythical view of the Gospel narratives, and in particular the identification of Jesus with an ancient Hebrew cult-deity, Joshua, and an old Greek divine healer-hero, Jason—equating Jason = Joshua = Jesus (Joshua forming the intermediate link) as all representing the sun.

Further, from Professor W. B. Smith he adopts the theory that the members of these cults had been termed "Nazoraeans" (Nazaraioi). Christianity, he maintains, is primarily and mainly a syncretism of these elements together with (orthodox) Jewish Messianism *plus* the pagan (Greco-Roman, etc.) idea of a "redeemer-god," who annually "dies" and "rises," and thereby promotes the welfare of mankind. This synthesis, he thinks, was effected in the mind of St. Paul, who "knew no historical Jesus" (II. Cor. 5 : 16). This explains, he surmises, the great change which took place in the views and actions

[1] An amended version of the second part of *The Christ Myth.*

of St. Paul. At first, he says, Paul, as a legalist, violently opposed the gospel because the law pronounced cursed every one who had been "hanged upon a tree." But suddenly he became "enlightened," and a reconciliation became possible. He found that he could combine the *idea* of the expected and orthodox Jewish Messiah of the first century with the older and self-sacrificing god of the ethnic nature-cults, which latter were closely akin to the pre-Christian Joshua or Jesus cults. "This," concludes Professor Drews, "was the moment of Christianity's birth as a religion of Paul." [1]

To sum up: Professor Drews has himself stated his position in the following terms: The Gospels do not contain the history of an actual *man*, but only the myth of the god-man Jesus clothed in an historical dress. Further, such important, and for religious purposes significant, events in the Gospels as the Baptism, the Lord's Supper, the Crucifixion, and the Resurrection of Jesus are all borrowed by St. Paul from the cult-worship of the mythical Jesus, being embodied in ancient and pre-Christian systems of religious ritual.

Yet further: The "historical Jesus" of modern critical theology has now become so vague and doubtful a figure in both religion and history that he can no longer be regarded as the absolutely indispensable condition of salvation. Doctor Drews likewise believes that his own works are written in the true interests of religion, for which *ideas* alone—not personalities—have value, and, by reason of his convictions, that the forms of Christianity which have hitherto prevailed are no longer sufficient for modern needs. Not the *historical Jesus*, he urges, but Christ *as an idea*—as an idea of the divine humanity—must henceforth be the ground of religion. And he adds that "when we can and will no longer believe on acci-

[1] We have here an example of the application of the three "moments" of the Hegelian dialectic—thesis, antithesis, synthesis; see Hegel's *Logic*.

dental [!] personalities, we can and must believe on ideas." [1]

It is not our purpose here to deal with this complex mass of crude theories, suppositions, and assumptions, but we may, perhaps, in this place appropriately quote the apposite remarks thereupon of Doctor A. Schweitzer (*Paul and His Interpreters*, pp. 193 and 239): "In particular, these [mythical] works aim at getting hold of the idea of a Greek redeemer-god who might serve as an analogue to Jesus Christ. No figure of this designation occurs in any myth or in any mystery religion; it is created by a process of generalisation, abstraction, and reconstruction."

Again: "These writers make a rather extravagant use of the privilege of standing outside the ranks of scientific theology. Their imagination leaps with playful elegance over obstacles of fact, and enables them to discover everywhere the pre-Christian Jesus whom their souls desire, even in places where an ordinary intelligence can find no trace of it." [2]

This is true; and it is also true that any discussion of a general nature which may be carried on with reference to these "generalisations, abstractions, and reconstructions" is seldom a fruitful one. Let us, therefore, put the results of the above mental operations to a more concrete test, viz., that of an actual comparative study in detail. In other words, let us analyse and compare carefully the stories told by the evangelists with the mythic episodes from which the former are said to be derived, or which they are confidently stated to resemble. If they fail in this final and supreme test, then we may safely dismiss the whole theory of the mythical interpretation of the Gospels, with its "generalisations, abstrac-

[1] See the *Berliner Religionsgesprach*, 1910, pp. 94 *f.*; and *cf. Die Christusmythe*, p. xi.

[2] See also Doctor F. C. Conybeare, *The Historical Christ*, p. 29.

tions, and reconstructions," as an interesting but empty dream. This is, indeed, the practical and only true method of testing all theories in almost every department of knowledge, and it is the one which the present writer has endeavoured to set before his readers in the following pages.

Further, the author wishes to express his great obligations and sincere thanks to a number of eminent scholars who have kindly furnished him with expert information upon various special or obscure points where his own knowledge was either wanting or defective. Amongst these the following gentlemen may be specially mentioned: Doctor E. M. Wallis Budge, keeper of the Assyrian and Egyptian antiquities in the British Museum, London; Doctor A. A. Macdonell, Boden professor of Sanscrit in the University of Oxford; Doctor L. H. Mills, professor of Zend philology in Oxford University; and Doctor W. M. Flinders Petrie, F.R.S., F.B.A., Edwards professor of Egyptology in University College, London University. His friend the Reverend F. B. Allison, M.A., F.R.A.S., formerly fellow of Sidney Sussex College, Cambridge, and E. Walter Maunder, Esq., F.R.A.S., late superintendent of the Solar Department in the Royal Observatory, Greenwich, also gave him valuable assistance on astronomical questions, which he acknowledges with gratitude.

Finally, the author's thanks are due to his son, Charles E. A. Thorburn, for his kindness in typing the three copies of the original manuscript which were required by the conditions of the trust.

CONTENTS

xxiii

THE MYTHICAL INTERPRETATION
OF THE GOSPELS

The Mythical Interpretation of the Gospels

CHAPTER I

MARY AND JOSEPH

IT is an almost primary necessity of every theory of a mythical interpretation of the Gospels to demonstrate that Mary and Joseph are ancient deities, the former in particular being identical with the mother-divinities of the pagan nature-cults, who were worshipped under one form or another, and under different names, by the various nations and races which occupied the countries situated round about the eastern end of the Mediterranean Sea.[1] We will, therefore, begin our study of this complex question with the statements of this *thesis* as they are set forth by two of the leading exponents of the theory, and for the most part in their own words.

"The whole birth-story," writes Mr. J. M. Robertson (*Christianity and Mythology*, p. 319), "is indisputably late, and the whole action mythic; and the name [Mary] is also to be presumed mythical. For this there is the double reason that Mary, or Miriam, was already a mythic name for both Jews and Gentiles. The Miriam of Exodus is no more historical than Moses; like him and Joshua she is to be reckoned an ancient deity evemerised, and the Arab tradition that she was the mother of Joshua (= Jesus) raises an irremovable surmise that a

---

[1] Similarly, the patriarch Joseph is regarded by Doctor Winckler and others as a form of the sun-god.

3

Mary, the mother of Jesus, may have been worshipped in Syria long before our era."

But Mr. Robertson further continues: "It is not possible, from the existing data, to connect historically such a cult with its congeners; but the mere analogy of names and epithets goes far. The mother of Adonis, the slain 'Lord' of the great Syrian cult, is Myrrha; and Myrrha, in one of her myths, is the weeping tree[1] from which the babe Adonis is born. Again, Hermes, the Greek Logos, has for mother Maia, whose name has further connexion with Mary. In one myth Maia is the daughter of Atlas (Apollod., III, 10, 2), thus doubling with Maira, who has the same father (Paus., VIII, 48) and who, having died a virgin (*ibid.*, X, 30), was seen by Odysseus in Hades. Mythologically, Maira is identified with the dog-star, which is the star of Isis.

"Yet again, the name appears in the East as Maya, the virgin mother of the Buddha, and it is remarkable that, according to a Jewish legend, the name of the Egyptian princess who found the babe Moses was Merris (Euseb., *Præp. Evan.*, IX, 27). The plot is still further thickened by the fact that, as we learn from the monuments, one of the daughters of Rameses II was named Meri (Brugsch., *Egypt Under the Pharaohs*, II, p. 117)."

Further: "In the matter of names, it is of some though minor interest to recall that Demeter is associated in Greek mythology with one Jasios, or Jasion, not as mother but as lover (*Od.*, V, 125; Hesiod, *Theog.*, 960). Jason, as we know, actually served as a Greek form of the name Joshua, or Jesous (Jos., *Ant.*, XII, 5, 1); and Jasion, who in one story is the founder of the famous Samothracian mysteries (Preller, *Griech. Myth.*, I, 667), is, in the ordinary myth, slain by Zeus. But the partial parallel of his name is of less importance than the possible parallel of his mythical relation to the goddess-mother.

---

[1] *I. e.*, it exudes a resinous gum. See σμύρνα (Greek lexicon).

"In many if not all of the cults in which there figures a nursing mother, it is found that her name signifies the nurse,[1] or that becomes one of her epithets. Thus, Maia stands for 'the nurse,' τροφός (Porphyr., *De Abstin.*, IV, 16); Mylitta means the child-bearing one (Bahr, *Symbolik des mosaïsch. Cult.*, I, 436); both Demeter and Artemis were styled child-rearers, and Isis was alternately styled 'the nurse' and 'the mother' (Plut., *De Is. et Osir.*, 53, 56).[2]

"Now one of the most important details of the confused legend in the Talmud concerning the pre-Christian [?] Jesus Ben Pandira, who is conjoined with Ben Stada,[3] is that the mother is in one place named Miriam Magdala, Mary the nurse, or the hair-dresser (Jastrow, *Dict. of the Targ. and the Midr. Lit.*, part 2, p. 213, 1888). As Isis, too, plays the part of a hair-dresser (Plut., *De Is. et Osir.*, 15),[4] it seems clear that we are dealing here also with myth, not with biography. In the Gospels we have Mary the Magdalene, that is, of the supposed place Magdala, which Jesus in one text (Matt. 15 : 39, A. V.) visits. But Magdala at most simply means 'a tower,' or 'high place' (the same root yielding the various senses of nursing, rearing, and hair-dressing); and, in the revised text, Magdala gives way to Magadan, thus disappear-

---

[1] So (in Homer) μαῖα applied, in familiar sense, to old women, "mother."

[2] Plutarch says (53) that Isis is the *female principle* of nature, and is, therefore, styled by Plato the "Nurse" and "All-receiving"; but, by the generality of mankind, the "One of numberless names." In 56 he further remarks that Plato calls *matter* "mother" and "nurse," while *idea* is termed "father." This is not quite the same thing as the above. Isis, however, was a special form of the great *Mater Nutrix*, though it is not directly so stated here.

[3] It is highly uncertain whether these "Jesuses" are one and the same or not. Mr. Robertson is making an assumption here.

[4] Plutarch, again, says here that Isis, having come to Byblus, made friends with the servants of the queen of that place by dressing their hair for them. This is hardly being a professional hair-dresser, as implied above, and savours somewhat of special pleading. Moreover, there is a confusion of Marys.

ing entirely from the Gospels. There is no documentary trace of it save as a citadel so named by Josephus.

"Mary Magdalene, finally, plays in the Gospels a purely mythical part, that of one of the finders of the risen Lord. The interpolated text in Luke (8 : 2) baldly describing her as having seven devils cast out of her by Jesus is equally remote from history; but it points towards the probable mythic solution. Maria, the Magdalene, who in the post-evangelical myth becomes a penitent harlot, is probably cognate with the evemerised Miriam of the Mosaic myth, who is morally possessed by devils [!], and is expressly punished for her sin before being forgiven. Something else, evidently, has underlain the pseudo-historical tale; and the Talmudic reference, instead of being a fiction based on the scanty data in the Gospels, is presumptively an echo of a mythic tradition, which may be the real source of the Gospel allusions. In Jewry the profession of hair-dressing seems to have been identified with that of *hetaira* [courtesan], the character ultimately ascribed in Christian legend to Mary Magdalene."

Thus far Mr. Robertson. The remainder of his section on the "Mythic Maries" deals chiefly with the *rôle*, in which he thinks they figure in finding the risen Saviour, and which, in his view, is comparable to the parts played by the various representatives of the mother-goddess.

This *thesis* of Mr. Robertson is practically accepted in its entirety by Professor Drews, who says (*The Christ Myth*, p. 239): "That the parents of Jesus were called Joseph and Mary, and that his father was a carpenter, were determined by tradition." And, again, he writes (*ibid.*, pp. 116 and 117): "Mary, the mother of Jesus, was a goddess. Under the name of Maya she is the mother of Agni.[1] . . . She appears, under the same name, as

---

[1] The Vedic fire-god. He was born, according to the *Yajur-Veda*, from the mouth of a divine being (Prajapati), Muir, *Sanscrit Texts*, 2d ed., I, p. 16.

the mother of Buddha, as well as of the Greek Hermes.
She is identical with Maira (Mæra), as, according to
Pausanias (VIII, 12, 48), the Pleiad Maia, the wife of
Hephaistos, was called.[1] She appears among the Persians as the 'virgin' mother of Mithras. As Myrrha, she
is the mother of the Syrian Adonis; as Semiramis, mother
of the Babylonian Ninus (Marduk). In the Arabic legend she appears under the name of Mirzam, as mother
of the mythical saviour, Joshua, who was so closely related to Moses; and, according to Eusebius, Merris was
the name of the Egyptian princess who found Moses in a
basket and became his foster-mother."

Finally, in *The Witnesses to the Historicity of Jesus*
(1912), p. 164, Doctor Drews complains that Weiss[2] is
unable to recognise in Mary Magdalene and the other
Marys at the cross and the grave of the Saviour the
Indian, Asiatic, and Egyptian mother of the gods—the
Maia, Mariamma, or Maritala, as the mother of Krishṇa
is called, the Mariana of Mariandynium (Bithynia),
Mandane, the mother of the Messiah, Cyrus (Isaiah
45 : 1), the "great mother" of Pessinunt,[3] the sorrowing
Semiramis, Miriam, Merris, Myrrha, Maira (Mæra), and
Maia, "beloved of her son," as the more enlightened
mythical school have done.

We have given in the above extracts, as far as possible, the *ipsissima verba*[4] of these writers in order to preclude any possibility of a misstatement of their views and

[1] Drews points out (*The Witnesses to the Historicity of Jesus*, p. 169, note 2)
that Augustus was called the "World Saviour," and referred to by Horace
as Maia's winged child. But the former title is used only in a secular sense
—saviour of the world from anarchy and bloodshed; and the latter is
merely a fulsome compliment paid by Horace. This really shows that historical personages were thus complimented. His actual mother was Atia,
niece to Julius Cæsar, as Horace knew very well. But see also Suetonius,
Div. Aug., 94; Dio Cassius, XLV, 1, 2.

[2] In his *Jesus von Nazareth: Mythus oder Geschichte?*

[3] See *The Christ Myth*, pp. 53 and 78.

[4] The last two from authorised translations.

meaning. We will now proceed to examine, as concisely
as may be, these "second-hand statements," as they are
truly termed by Doctor Cheyne, who adds: "Even if they
were always correct, and had no need of verification, the
inferences are impossible."[1]

It will have been gathered from these quotations that
both Mr. Robertson and Doctor Drews, admitting the
silence of history upon these points, very largely base
their hypothetical identifications of all the Marys with
the mother-goddesses upon analogy and the etymologies
of their numerous local appellations. This is—within
limits—justifiable, and a salutary check upon wild speculation; let us, therefore, in the present chapter apply
this important test, so far as it is applicable, and see what
results we get from it.

The Goddess-Mothers

Speaking broadly and generally, it may be affirmed that
in the various localised forms of the goddess-mother the
root *ma* ("bring forth") forms part of the name. This
is especially evident in that very primitive form, *Amma*[2]
(*Ma*), the Hittite name of the mother. But this root
certainly cannot be found in all the names enumerated
by Professor Drews, who, along with Mr. Robertson,
appears to think that because an Oriental female name
begins with M, or contains a syllable in which that consonant forms the initial letter, it is a sure indication that
we are dealing with some form of the universal mother.[3]

[1] See his review of *The Christ Myth* in the *Hibbert Journal*, April, 1911,
p. 60.

[2] Probably akin to Assyr., *alittu*, "the begetting one," fem. part. of *alâdu*,
"to give birth." Thus we get the form *mulitta* (*cf.* Herod., I, 199) from
valid-tu, the *m* reproducing the semi-vowel *y* and *a* becoming *u* through the
influence of the labial *m*.

[3] It will be impossible here to take all these names in detail. Amongst
the striking exceptions to the rule laid down by Drews we may mention
Mandanê. According to Doctor Mills, professor of Zend philology at Oxford, Mandane may be derived from any of the following: (1) *mad* (*cf.*

Mary, or Mariam (Miriam)

But it is when we turn to the alleged connexion of the name "Mary" ("Mariam") with that of the goddess-mothers that this theory is seen to be wholly untrue to fact.

With regard to the derivation and meaning of the Hebrew name "Mariam," Doctor Schmiedel says (*Enc. Bib.*, art. "Mary," sec. 1): "There are but two alternative roots that can be seriously considered, מרה, 'to be rebellious,' and מרא, 'to be fat.' The א of the מרא might before the *a* of -*ām* pass into י, which in the case of מרה is already the third consonant. The termination -*ām* indicates substantives as well as adjectives, and is especially common in the case of proper names. Mariam, then, might mean either 'the rebellious' (*cf.* Num. 12 : 1-15), or 'the corpulent.'"

Finally, he decides in favour of the latter meaning as according excellently with the whole analogy of Semitic names; it is associated, he adds, with the Semitic idea of beauty.

Doctor Boyd, on the other hand, thinks (Hastings' *D. B.*, vol. I, art. "Miriam") that the name "is probably of Egyptian derivation," and explains it thus: Miriam = *mer Amon* (*Amun*), "beloved of Amon"[1]—an explanation equally remote with that of Doctor Schmiedel from the one sought to be established by the mythicists. It is clear, therefore, that in the name Mary there is absolutely no trace of a meaning "begetter," or "nursing mother," which is often found in the names of the mother-goddess.

Sansc., *mad* and *mand*), "to delight," "the winsome one." (2) *man + dha*, "the prudent (*i. e.*, "exercising") mind." (3) A form from *mana*, "house," *i. e.*, mānadha, "house-mistress." There can be but little doubt that she is an historical character.

[1] Similarly, Moses has been connected with *mes, mesu*, "son." *Cf. Ramesu* (Rameses), "son of Ra," etc. (so Sayce).

Mr. Robertson, however, at this point attempts to affiliate directly the Mariam (Mary) of the Gospel story with the Miriam of Exodus, who is, he adds with dogmatic self-confidence, "no more historical than Moses." This latter theory has, it is true, been somewhat fashionable of late, and it is zealously advocated by Doctor Hugo Winckler in his *Geschichte Israels in Einzendarstellungen* (1900). But, after all, it is still a mere hypothesis, and very far from being an established fact upon which an argument may be based. In short, the entire non-historicity of both Miriam and Moses has yet to be proved. Yet, he insists: "She is to be reckoned an ancient deity evemerised." *Men*, not deities—we may remark here—are evemerised by being raised to the rank of gods. Very probably there has been some evemerism at work here, and Moses and Miriam were subsequently deified by the polytheistic Arabians and other neighbouring races. This, however, would be a more conclusive argument for their historicity, though of course it would not prove that various mythic stories had not gathered round them and their exploits. In any case, Mr. Robertson's "irremovable surmise" that Mary the mother of Jesus "may [he is less dogmatic here!] have been worshipped in Syria as a form of the goddess-mother, long before our era," is nothing but a pure guess unsubstantiated by any admitted facts.

We may at this point deal with Mr. Robertson's reference to the Talmud in connexion with this question. There is an evident confusion in this work between Mary the mother of Jesus and Mary Magdalene, and the imputation implied in the term "hair-dresser" was no doubt connected with the birth-slanders of which Origen (*Cont. Cels.*, I, 25, 32) speaks.

Now Mary Magdalene is said (Luke 8 : 2) to have been formerly possessed of "seven demons." But the demoniacal possession of a woman would not of necessity imply harlotry as one of its effects. "Possession" frequently resulted in nothing worse than a morose disposition and violent and mischievous acts (*cf.* Matt. 8 : 28).

Again, Miriam (Mariam) is stated (Num. 12 : 10; *cf.* Deut. 24 : 9) to have been smitten with leprosy for contempt of Moses. But this "contempt" in no way indicates "moral possession by devils." It is true that in those times, and long previously, disease of all kinds was commonly attributed to malicious demons, and in Babylonian and other literature many *formulæ* exist for the expulsion of these intruders. But the act is referred by the writers of both Numbers and Deuteronomy to Jahveh, and the treatment of that disease was not exorcistic (see Lev. 13 and 14). Moreover, Miriam's leprosy (צָרַעַת) seems to have been only some transient skin affection, simulating perhaps the graver disease, and not the true leprosy (*elephantiasis Græcorum*). Neither is there any evident connexion between the story of Miriam and the story of the Magdalene; still less is there any with that of Mary the mother of Jesus. The "myths"—if myths they be—are apparently quite unconnected.

Again, Mr. Robertson's contention that the root of the Hebrew word מִגְדָּל (*Migdal*, "tower"), from which *Magdala* is commonly derived, and which yields also the various senses of "nursing" ("rearing"), and especially "hair-dressing," connects Mary Magdalene (who thus becomes a reduplication of Mary the mother of Jesus) with the pagan goddess-mother, is founded upon the slenderest possible grounds, and really proves nothing. It is true that *Migdal* has been—more or less plausibly —derived from a root גדל, which has various meanings. Amongst these, in the *Piel* voice, it signifies intensively "to cause or take care that anything shall grow," etc.; hence "to nourish," "to cultivate," "to bring up children" (II Kings 10 : 6; Isaiah 1 : 2; 23 : 4); "to train the hair" (Num. 6 : 5), *i. e.*, not to cut it. But there is great

uncertainty here. Apart from doubt as to the real derivation, *Magadan* is a better reading. This, however, has
been conjectured to be a "possible corruption of an original Magdala." It is really impossible to frame any trustworthy hypothesis upon such meagre *data*. And in any
case the existence of a town—whatever the derivation
and meaning of its name may be—called Magdala is
amply proved by its mention in the *Jerusalem Talmud*
('Erūbīn, 5, 1) which places it within a Sabbath day's
journey of Tiberias. The same authority (Ta'anith, 4, 8)
states that it was a place of some wealth, and in the
Midrash 'Ēkkāh, 2, 2, it is said to have been destroyed
"because of licentiousness," which statement may have
some connexion with the sinister post-evangelical reputation of Mary Magdalene.

It is much more probable, therefore, that this Mary
derived her designation from the *town* of her origin than
from any practise of *hair-dressing*, of which there is no
trace in Christian tradition.

Neither is there any evidence for the theory of her identity with Mary the mother of the Lord further than the
confusion between them which is shown in the Talmud;
nor for the concomitant idea of her name indicating
"begetting" or "nursing," for, as we have already shown,
of this the name Mary (Mariam) contains no trace
whatever. In short, Mr. Robertson's excursion into
philology is a very precarious one, and proves nothing.
Probability points to the reputation of the town in Jewish tradition as having later adversely affected that of
its townswoman,[1] and to a Talmudic misstatement—in-
advertent or deliberate—as having helped to formulate
the confused and scurrilous birth-stories so common in
the Jewish synagogues of the second century.

[1] *I. e.*, the "seven demons" were supposed to cause licentiousness of life.
But she is an ἁμαρτωλός, *not* a πόρνη (Luke 7 : 37).

The "Virginity" of the Goddess-Mothers

In order to understand rightly the term "virgin" as used in mythical literature, it must be remembered that it means no more than that the goddess in question had no recognised *male partner*, or, as Doctor Cheyne euphemistically states it (*Bib. Probs.*, p. 75), that she was not "bound by the marriage-tie."[1] The mythical idea was wholly sexual and "unmoral." In the Gospels, on the contrary, the idea is purely parthenogenetic and has no implications of license.

In addition, however, to overlooking this important and fundamental distinction, Professor Drews makes various assumptions and falls into divers errors in connexion with several of his "mythic mothers." Thus, he refers to *Maera* as "the virgin mother of Mithra." Now the actual Mithra-myth is lost; we gather, however, from other sources that Mithra was variously described as having sprung from the incestuous intercourse of Ahura-Mazda with his own mother, and as being the ordinary offspring of a common mortal.

Moreover, the extant Mithraic sculptures depict the god as originating from a rock (*Petra genetrix*) at birth (Justin Martyr, *Dial. c. Try.*, 70). Furthermore, Mr. Robertson's assertion (*Pagan Christs*, p. 339) that "the virginity" of the mother of Mithra was admitted by cer-

---

[1] Franckh says emphatically ("Geburtsgesch. Jes. Chr. im Lichte der altorientalisch. Weltansch," *Philostia*, 1907, pp. 213 *f.*): "None of these personages that play the part of a mother-goddess is thought of as a *virgin*. . . . As mother-goddess Ishtar has no male god who permanently corresponds to her. This is the reason why she is vaguely spoken of as virgin Ishtar." In the Babylonian liturgies, as well as in the incantations, the "divine harlot" *Lilitu* (Heb., ליליח) is especially described as a *virgin* (*Babyloniaca*, IV, 188, 4 *f.*, translated by S. Langdon). We also meet with the term "virgin-harlot" (*iš-ta-ri-tum*). See Haupt, *Akkadische und Sumerische Keilschrifttexte*, 126. 18. According to Epiphanius (*Hær.*, LI) the mother of Dusāres (the N. Arab. equivalent for Tammuz, etc.) was adored as "the Virgin" (παρθένος, κόρη), while her son was worshipped as μονογενὴς τοῦ Δεσπότου.

tain Christian bishops of Armenia in the fourth and fifth centuries A. D. is wholly incorrect. The Armenian historian Elisaeus says (*Concerning the Vardans and the Armenian War*, II, 53, 57) the bishops stated that "The god Mithra was born of a woman"; and again: "The god Mithra was incestuously born of a mortal mother."

A similar error is perpetuated by Doctor Drews when he represents (*The Christ Myth*, p. 39) Saoshyant as the "virgin's son." According to the mythic story the "seed" of Zarathustra was miraculously preserved in water in which three maidens bathed at different times. Each of them in succession became pregnant in consequence, and they severally afterwards gave birth to Saoshyant and his two precursors. It is in the highest degree absurd to classify stories of this type as "virgin births" in the Biblical sense of the term. But the most glaring error committed by him is one into which he falls in common with many other modern writers. It is a defiance of all ancient authority to term the mother of the Buddha "the virgin Māyā." Not only the older Pāli texts, but the Chinese version of the *Abhinishkramana Sūtra*, and even the later *Lalita vistāra*,[1] of the Northern or Tibetan canon, plainly state that Māyā was a married woman and lived with her husband after the usual manner. A similar remark applies to the statement that "the virgin mother of Krishṇa" was named "Mariamma," or "Maritala." The *Purāṇas* (circ. 1000 A. D.), from which we derive our principal knowledge of the family affairs of Krishṇa, affirm that the name of his mother was Dēvakī, and that so far from being a "virgin" she had had, before the birth of Krishṇa, seven children by her husband Vasudēva.

[1] A life of the Buddha.

The Virgin of the Zodiac

Finally, the attempt made by several German scholars to identify or connect Mary the mother of Jesus with the "Virgin" of the zodiac is equally futile. This astral concept, if it be a reflection of the great mother-goddess idea, has a very different connotation from the Christian use of the word "virgin" ($\pi\alpha\rho\theta\epsilon\nu\sigma$), as we have already shown.

Again, when Jeremias (*Babylonisches*, p. 48) and Cheyne (*Bib. Probs.*, pp. 242 *f.*) point out that Mary, according to Epiphanius (fourth century A. D.), was at a later period identified with the mother-goddess, Professor Carl Clemen very properly replies that this fact proves nothing for earlier times. "Still less," he adds, "does the fact which the former scholar adduces (following Dupuis), viz., that on a side door of Notre Dame, in Paris, Mary is associated with the signs of the zodiac" (*Prim. Christ. and Its Non-Jewish Sources*, p. 292, note 9).[1]

A consideration of the various facts set forth in the above analysis of this question point, we think, very strongly to the following conclusions upon the matter: (1) That Mary the mother of Jesus has no connexion whatever, linguistically or analogically, with the great mother-goddess of the ancient world. (2) That the term "virgin" is applied to her in quite a different sense to that which it bore in relation to the various local representatives of the mother-goddess. Further, this last-named conclusion is supported by the additional fact that nowhere in the New Testament is Mary the mother of Jesus regarded as in any sense *divine* (*cf.* Mark 3 : 33 and 34). This fact alone, indeed, would form the greatest possible

---

[1] According to Jensen (*Die Kosmol. der Babylonier*, p. 67) the earlier Babylonians, and the Eastern nations generally, had no such name as "Virgin" for the sign which was later known as *Virgo*.

bar to any identification of her with the pagan goddess-mothers, which forms the basis of the mythical theory.

Joseph

"The myth of Joseph," writes Mr. Robertson (*Christianity and Mythology*, pp. 236 f.), "arose as a real accessory to the cult [of the mother]. Once introduced, he would naturally figure as an elderly man, not only in the interests of the virgin birth, but in terms of the Hebrew precedent adopted in the myth of the parentage of John the Baptist." [1] And then he proceeds to state that this, together with the story of "the leading of the laden ass by Joseph in the journey of the 'holy family,' was suggested by old religious ceremonial." This ceremonial turns out to be a sacred procession in the cult of Isis, as described by Apuleius (*Metamorphoses*, book XI), wherein there figures "a feeble old man leading an ass." [2] The great Isiac cult, he argues, would be unlikely to adopt such an episode from a new system like Christianity. The antiquity of this symbolism may next be traced to Plutarch's statement (*De Is. et Osir.*, 32) that "in the forecourt of the temple of the goddess at Sais there were sculptured a child, an old man, and some animal figures." Lastly: "The Egyptians held that all things came from Saturn (*ibid.*, 59), or a similar Egyptian god, who signified at once time and the Nile (*ibid.*, 32), and was always figured as aged." In short, "the Christian system is a patchwork of a hundred suggestions drawn from pagan art and ritual usage."

But Mr. Robertson has a further and more important source. Let us hear him patiently a little further (*Chris-*

---

[1] Referring here to the *Hist. of Joseph the Carpenter*, IV and VII, and the *Gospel of the Birth of Mary*, VIII. "This is the view," he adds, "of Christian tradition."

[2] Apuleius says: "An ass, on which wings were glued, and which walked near a feeble old man." "These were supposed to represent Pegasus and Bellerophon" (Budge, *Osiris*, etc., vol. II, p. 297).

tianity and Mythology, pp. 326 *ff*.): "The first presumption of the early Judaic myth-makers evidently was to present the Messiah as Ben David, son of the hero-king, himself clothed about with myth, like Cyrus. For this purpose were framed the two mythic genealogies. But it so happened," he proceeds, "that the Palestinian tradition demanded a Messias Ben Joseph—a descendant of the mythic patriarch—as well as the Messias Ben David." He declines to enter into the origin of the former doctrine, which, he says, "suggests a partial revival of the ancient adoration of the god Joseph, as well as that of the god Daoud [*sic*], though it may have been," he concludes, "a tribal matter."

We have not space to follow out in further and minute detail this argument, which the reader will find in Mr. Robertson's work, but we will here merely add his summary taken from *Fragments of a Samaritan Targum* (Nutt, 1874), p. 70, where the author writes: "Messiah the son of Joseph will come before Messiah the son of David, will assemble the ten tribes in Galilee and lead them to Jerusalem; but will at last perish in battle against Gog and Magog for the sins of Jeroboam." This passage, however, he adds, "overlooks the circumstance that in two Talmudic passages the Messiah Ben David is *identified* with the Messiah Ben Joseph, or, as he is styled in one case, Ben Ephraim."[1]

Professor Drews, to whom we will now turn, in general accepts the above presentation of the case and adds various details of his own. Thus, he says (*The Christ Myth*, pp. 115–117): "As is well known, Jesus, too [like Agni], had three fathers [*sic*], viz., his heavenly Father Jahwe, the Holy Spirit, and also his earthly father Joseph. The latter is also a workmaster, artisan, or car-

---

[1] References to *Tract. Succa*, folio 52, 1; *Zohar Chadash*, folio 45, 1; and *Pesikta*, folio 62, quoted by F. H. Reichardt, *Relation of the Jewish Christians to the Jews* (1884), pp. 37 and 38.

penter, as the word *tekton* indicates.[1] Similarly, Kinyras, the father of Adonis, is said to have been some
kind of artisan, a smith or carpenter. That is to say,
he is supposed to have invented the hammer and the
lever, and roofing as well as mining. In Homer he appears as the maker of the ingenious coat of mail which
Agamemnon received from him as a guest-friend (*Il.*,
XI, 20; *cf.* Movers, *Die Phön.*, 242, s.). The father of
Hermes is also an artisan." And in a foot-note he adds
(p. 116): "According to the Arabian legend, Father
Abraham, also, who plays the part of a saviour [!],
was, under the name of Thare[2] [? Terah], a skilful mas-
ter-workman, understanding how to cut arrows from
any wood, and being especially occupied with the preparation of idols (Sepp, *Das Heid. u. dess. Bedeut. für das
Christent.*, 1853, III, 82)."

Finally, he asserts that "Joseph, as we have already
seen, was originally a god . . ."; and "In reality, the
whole of the family and home life of the Messiah, Jesus,
took place among the gods. It was only reduced to
that of a human being in lowly circumstances by the
fact that Paul described the descent of the Messiah upon
the earth as an assumption of poverty and a relinquish-
ment of his heavenly splendour (II Cor. 8 : 9). Hence"
—and this is the crucial point in the whole of Drews's
hypothesis—"*when the myth was transformed into history*,[3] Christ was turned into a poor man in the economic
sense of the word, while Joseph, the divine artificer, and
father of the sun [!], became an ordinary carpenter."

We will now subject this complex mass of confident

---

[1] All clean handicrafts were looked upon by the Jews as honourable occu-
pations. Even the high priest might be a carpenter. This is quite a Semitic view.

[2] See *Koran* (Sale's translation), pp. 95, 96, and notes. In Jewish records
Terah is the *father* of Abraham. Arab traditions are very inaccurate and
untrustworthy.

[3] Italics ours.

assertions, unproved theories, and plausible identifications to as detailed an analysis as is here possible.

It would be interesting to learn, in the first place, why
the myth of Joseph arose as a real accessory to the cult
[of a divine and virgin mother]. At the outset it is foreign to the pagan myths, and his presence in a story of
that type would rather tend to discount it. But that
is the reason, Mr. Robertson thinks, why he must be
"elderly." The canonical Gospels, however, which contain by far the oldest version of the story, nowhere describe, or appear to regard, him as being elderly. Matthew, indeed (1 : 18, 25—in the latter verse especially),
indirectly negatives that view. It is only in the very late
Apocryphs (and in popular Christian art, derived from
them) that Joseph is so depicted. And the motive for
this newer view is plain. The church had then become
less Jewish, and the normal Hebrew ideal of faithful
wedlock had largely given place to an alien and ultra-
ascetic Gentilism in which perpetual virginity was held
up as the model virtue for both men and women. This,
however, was really in flat contradiction to the teaching
of the earliest church, as well as that of the synoptic
Gospels, which were the expression and the outcome of it.

But having got the elderly man (from the late and un-
canonical gospels), Mr. Robertson proceeds to make the
most of him. He is (apparently) identified with the
feeble old man "leading an ass"[1] in the sacred procession of Isis, described by Apuleius in his *Metamorphoses*.
How, may we ask, does Mr. Robertson know this?
Apuleius does not explain the symbolism of this procession, and Plutarch, to whom Mr. Robertson would seem
to appeal, merely says that in the court of the temple
at Sais there were graven figures of "a child and an old
man," together with those of a hawk, a fish, and a hip-

[1] For the symbolism of the *ass*, see Budge, *The Gods of the Egyptians*,
vol. II, pp. 246 and 367.

popotamus, and adds that the two first-named stood for "the beginning and end of life." Here we certainly get the elderly man (together with what Plutarch thought he symbolised); but what both of these examples have to do with the story of Joseph it is impossible to see. Apparently Mr. Robertson thinks that because an old man and a donkey figure, in some connexion or other, in a pagan cult, this fact constitutes an origin or source for either the story of the journey of Joseph to Bethlehem, or perhaps that of his subsequent flight with Mary and the Child upon an ass to Egypt. This connexion here, as the reader will see, is both highly obscure and extremely precarious.

The parallel suggested by the aged Zacharias is more plausible. But even here the circumstances and details are very different. Both Zacharias and Elisabeth are aged married people, who, it would seem, greatly desired a son, because barrenness was a subject of reproach amongst the Jews as a mark of God's displeasure. Moreover, the Matthæan and Lucan stories came from different sources,[1] and the Lucan is later. In any case, it is most unlikely that it has influenced the story of Matthew or in any way suggested an elderly Joseph as an accessory to the virginal (parthenogenetic) conception of Mary. The whole of Mr. Robertson's argument here, in short, is *nil ad rem*—it is beside the mark whether these stories are in any way historical or not.

As regards the *genealogies*, it will be impossible here to deal with them in any detail. But we may advert to two important points which tend to throw some light upon them. Mr. Robertson has pronounced them both to be, like the birth-stories, mythic, late, and artificially concocted in support of the tradition of a future Messias Ben David.

It so happens, however, that in the Jerusalem Talmud

[1] This is shown, *inter alia*, by its difference of treatment and standpoint.

(*Mishna*, Jabamoth, 49*a*) there is a mention of an official record of the birth of Jesus, with apparently a reference to some genealogy. It runs thus: "Simeon ben-Azzai[1] has said: I found in Jerusalem a book of genealogies; therein was written that 'So and So'[2] is an illegitimate son of a married woman (*mamser*)."

Now, it is well known that very soon after the fall of Jerusalem (A. D. 70) and the destruction of the Jewish state the interest in the Davidic descent of the Messiah rapidly declined; to *invent* such documents, therefore, *after* that date, would have been ill-timed and practically useless. It may also be suggested that our present genealogies seem to be designed rather with a view to tracing the descent of Jesus respectively from Abraham, "the Father of the Jewish race," and from Adam, "the father of all men." But the genealogy of the Messiah was, in any case, more a matter of interest to the Jew than to the Gentile. Our present lists, too, are very artificial documents, and show signs of redaction and adaptation.

Finally, as to Mr. Robertson's theory of a rival, and perhaps contemporary, Messias Ben Joseph, it must suffice here to reply in the words of Doctor Cheyne (*Enc. Bib.*, art. "Messiah," sec. 9): "The developed form of this idea is almost certainly a product of the polemic with Christianity in which the rabbins were hard pressed by arguments from passages, which their own exegesis admitted to be Messianic."

There is certainly, we may add, no evidence of its existence until after the time of Christ. That the Samaritans, after their rejection by the Jews (Ezra 4 : 3), may have hoped for a non-Jewish Messiah is another matter,

---

[1] Flourished end of first century A. D.

[2] Or "that man," a common Talmudic and cryptic reference to Jesus, used to avoid suppression by the Christian censor. Herod I is said (Eusebius, *H. E.*, I, 7; *cf. Talmud*, Pesachim, 62b), to have burnt all genealogical registers in order to conceal traces of his humble birth.

and not improbable. At the same time, the Samaritan doctrine of the *Tāḥēb* ("he who returns," or "he who restores") is founded entirely upon Deut. 18 : 15, where it has no Messianic application whatever. Moreover, in the Gospels, Joseph is not a rival Messiah but the foster-father of the Messias Ben David (Jesus).

The additional and special points added to this argument by Professor Drews must be briefly noticed. The comparison which he draws with Agni and his "three fathers"[1] is almost too absurd to be taken seriously. The reference, in the case of Agni, is to his three successive *births*—a concept wholly different from the one with which we are dealing here. Jahveh, too, in the Gospels, is called the Father of Jesus, especially in the sense of source or origin of his divine nature (Πηγὴ Θεοτήτος). Joseph is placed in the capacity of foster-father and guardian of the young Child and his mother. The Holy Spirit alone is regarded by "Matthew" as bringing about the conception of Jesus Christ.

As to Kinyras, he is stated to have been a son of Apollo, and a king of Cyprus, as well as priest of the Paphian Aphrodite. But Homer says distinctly that Kinyras, "the man (or 'god') of the harp," *gave* the breastplate to (not made it for) Agamemnon.[2] This would seem to indicate that he was not considered by Homer to be an artisan of any kind, and therefore not at all comparable with Joseph, the carpenter.[3] The real difficulty, in regard to Joseph, lies in none of the points noticed above. It arises rather out of the meagre refer-

---

[1] Savitar (sky), Tvashtar (smith), and Matarishvan (wind-god).

[2] θώρηκα περὶ στήθεσσιν ἔδυνεν
τὸν ποτέ οἱ Κινύρης δῶκε ξεινήϊον εἶναι.
—*Il.*, XI, 20.

[3] The concepts underlying the Greek god Hermes, next referred to by Drews, are too complex and difficult for treatment here. If, however, his nature and character are carefully studied in the light of comparative mythology, it will be seen that he represents no real parallel whatever with Jesus, as the son of an "artisan."

ence that is made to him in the New Testament generally, and, above all, from the fact that he is not even
named in the earliest Gospel (Mark). He is mentioned
just fourteen times in all, and only by Matthew and
Luke.[1] Mark, having no birth-story, does not allude to
him, though this does not necessarily imply, as some
critics would have it, that he knew nothing of Joseph.
Certainly, had Mark been historicising a myth, he must
have heard of a birth-story of some kind, and, in that
case, he would probably have tried his hand at a trans-
position of it into history.

Whatever conclusion, therefore, we may reach with
regard to the nature of these narratives, which are not
so late in their origin as Mr. Robertson confidently assumes, it will be well to remember the caution of Doctor
Cheyne (a critic who, as it is well known, is strongly disposed to discount a great deal for myth) when he says
(*Enc. Bib.*, art. "Joseph"): "It would, however, be hasty
to assert that there is no element of truth in the expression, 'Joseph, the husband of Mary, of whom was born
Jesus, who is called the Christ (Matt. 1 : 16).'"[2]

---

[1] *I. e.*, in Matt. 1 and 2 seven times, in Luke 1–4 also seven times, the references in both cases being in the introductory sections of the two Gospels.
The *Sin. Palimp.* has "son of Joseph" (for "carpenter's son") in Matt. 13 :
55. The phrase בַּר נַגָּר (Bābā Bathrā, 73*b*), however, simply means "a carpenter," בַּר נַגְּרִין, and it has been suggested that, as used in the tradition, it
may mean no more than this (see *Enc. Bib.*, art. "Joseph," 9).

[2] Doctor Cheyne suggests, in the above article, that "Jesus, son of Joseph,"
may mean Jesus a member of the house [clan] of Joseph (Zech. 10 : 6).

CHAPTER II

THE ANNUNCIATION, CONCEPTION, AND BIRTH

The Annunciation and Conception

THE narratives describing the annunciations to Mary and Elisabeth, the nature of the conception of Jesus and his birth at Bethlehem have commonly been wholly ruled out of history not merely by the mythicists but also by many scholars who frankly accept an historical Jesus. The latter, while holding the undoubted historicity of Jesus, have been accustomed to regard Matt. 1 : 16–2 and Luke 1 and 2 as popular stories relating to an actual man which have undergone in places a supernaturalising modification at the hands of pious and well-meaning, but ill-informed, copyists;[1] whereas the former, who regard the person of the Jesus set forth in the Gospels as purely mythical, have looked upon these records as substantially variants of well-known myths containing no substratum whatever of historical fact. The birth-stories, they assert, are nothing but old myths, and as such have a meaning, though this meaning is not historical; it is connected with an explanation of the universe, and the gods and mankind.[2]

[1] *E. g.*, Matt. 1 : 16 is said to have had an original reading: "And Joseph begat Jesus, who is called Christ" ('Ιωσὴφ δὲ ἐγέννησε 'Ιησοῦν τὸν λεγόμενον Χριστόν), which was altered to the various readings now found in the MSS.; Luke 1 : 34 and 35, and also the "as supposed" (ὡς ἐνομίζετο) of 3 : 23, are later interpolations in the interests of a supernatural birth. The present writer has discussed these questions at considerable length in a former work (*A Critical Examination of the Evidences for the Doctrine of the Virgin Birth*, 1908), to which the reader is referred for details.

[2] Dupuis (1742–1809 A. D.) is the real "father" of the more modern form of mythicism. See *L'origine de tous les cultes* (1794).

The criticism of Strauss dealing with the annunciations and the conception, which we will take first, is, however, less concerned with any explanation. It is chiefly concentrated on the impossibility of the supernatural character commonly ascribed to these two events. It may be summed up as follows: The announcement to the priest Zacharias, by the angel Gabriel, that a son will be born to him, is described as "the first point which shocks all modern conceptions" (*The Life of Jesus*, English translation, 1838, chap. 1, p. 98). By this he means that the thought of the age rejects "the reality of angels," who were unquestionably accepted by the Jews (with the exception of the Sadducees) and the early Christians as actual beings existent in a spiritual world, but also occasionally manifesting themselves in this material sphere. He finds, too, the "dumbness" which fell upon Zacharias "unreasonable," and the other details of the vision inconsistent and incredible. The previous proposals of Paulus to rationalise these stories are also rejected.[1]

Similar objections are taken to the story of the annunciation to Mary. Moreover, the accounts of Matthew and Luke are, in several respects, held to be mutually inconsistent and even contradictory. Thus: (1) in the former the "apparition" is merely an "angel of the Lord" (ἄγγελος Κυρίου); in Luke he is specifically called "the angel Gabriel" (ὁ ἄγγελος Γαβριήλ); (2) this angel appears to Joseph in Matthew; to Mary in Luke; (3) in Matthew the appearance takes place in a dream; in Luke it occurs in the wakeful state; (4) in Matthew the communication is made after pregnancy; in Luke before it; (5) according to Matthew its object was to tranquillise Joseph; according to Luke it was to anticipate all

---

[1] Paulus (1761–1851) has rationalised the apparition in Matthew as a natural dream, while the appearance to Mary (recorded in Luke), he thought, was that of some human being who announced what was a very probable event—the birth of a son. A recent work (1915) on the subject is *The Virgin Birth of Jesus in the New Testament*, G. H. Box, M.A.

offense by a preliminary announcement to Mary (chap. 3, pp. 141 and 142).[1]

As regards the actual conception, Strauss freely admits (chap. 3, pp. 156 and 157) that "the expression of Matthew, 'that which is conceived in her is of the Holy Ghost,' and the word 'overshadow'[2] employed by Luke, clearly puts divine virtue in the place of the fecundating principle . . . nevertheless" he maintains that "the serious difficulties which surround it scarcely allow us to follow out that idea."[3]

The chief difficulty in the narrative, however, is summed up on the same page (157) in the following sentence: "It is physiologically certain," says Strauss, "that the concourse of two human bodies, of different sexes, is necessary to generate and develop the germ of a new human being." Furthermore, it [the parthenogenetic birth] would involve the suspension of a natural law; "but to suspend a natural law, established by himself, God could not have a motive sufficient to show

[1] It is more strictly correct to say that the Matthæan and Lucan narratives here are intended by their compilers to be complementary, Luke dealing generally with the incidents of the annunciation and conception from a different standpoint, and also, in general, inserting much that Matthew omits.

[2] Doctor F. C. Conybeare (*Myth, Magic and Morals*, 1909, pp. 204 and 205), while admitting that the word ἐπισκιάζω ("overshadow") is generally interpreted as signifying an impregnation [!] of the Virgin by the Holy Spirit [though in such a case there would be no *true* virginal birth, or *parthenogenesis*], adds that it usually signifies no more than "to hide," or "conceal." Among the Jews, "it was a common belief," he says, "that women with child were peculiarly liable to the assaults of demons" (refer to Rev. 12); accordingly, "by the Holy Spirit coming upon the mother Luke may have meant no more than that the child, conceived as usual, received a peculiar sanctity before it was born, just as John the Baptist also (Luke 1 : 15) was 'to be filled with the Holy Ghost even from his mother's womb.'"

[3] Professor C. Clemen (*Primitive Christianity and Its Non-Jewish Sources*, p. 296) argues that if the Gospel idea had been derived from *Greek* mythical influences one would have expected to find "an act of divine procreation" here. But we do not find this; and the overshadowing of Mary is, therefore, comparable to that referred to in Mark 9 : 7 and parallels; *cf.* also Acts 5 : 15.

that such a suspension was indispensable to the obtaining of results worthy of him."

Finally, after noticing various alleged pagan analogues referred to by some of the Christian fathers and others, and noting that Isaiah 7 : 14 was applied to Jesus in the early Christian church: "Jesus, as the Messiah," said they, "*ought*, agreeably to that passage, to be born of a virgin by a divine operation," and "that which ought to be," they took for granted, "had really taken place"; thus, from the influence of the above tendency, and the supposed necessity of the doctrine, he concludes that there was developed dogmatically "a philosophic myth upon the birth of Jesus."[1]

The critical attitude of Strauss, if not very profound, or characterised by deep spiritual insight, is at least generally sensible, and merits even at this time careful attention. It is, however, nowadays to some extent obsolete, and, moreover, has from time to time been effectively dealt with by various writers. We will, therefore, here only briefly discuss the above summary of his objections, and then turn to the more important and deeper-reaching criticism of our own day.

His difficulty with the question of the apparition is thoroughly characteristic of the man and his thought, and no doubt of the age in which he wrote. The great idealist philosophers of Germany—Kant[2] and Fichte and, above all, Hegel—had passed away. Schelling alone remained, still striving to build up an ideal system which

---

[1] Strauss (p. 160) declares that "when the Apostle Paul says that he [Jesus] was *born of a woman* (Gal. 4 : 4) he could not desire to convey in that expression a denial of the masculine participation." But the phrase γενόμενον ἐκ γυναικός is more correctly translated "*descended from a woman*," which seems indirectly to imply an absence of male participation. And a great deal would also depend upon whether our present birth-stories were current in St. Paul's time and known to him. Further, it will be remembered that the rabbinical physiology of the period admitted both the possibility and the existence of abnormal conceptions.

[2] Kant was a *critical* idealist.

would be permanent. Their systems of thought were everywhere yielding to newer ones based upon inductive reasoning and the modern scientific method, a fitting prelude to the dawn of an era of great invention and material prosperity throughout the world.[1] The influences of this coming change are discernible throughout the *Leben Jesu*. This fact, indeed, explains the "shock" which the idea of an "apparition" of any kind produces in his mind. Such a concept is wholly outside his ken and quite beyond the horizon of nineteenth-century materialism. Had he lived a hundred years later, or in our own days, for example, and been able to consult, and even verify, the carefully sorted records of the Society for Psychical Research, the shock might have been less, and his views upon such subjects might have been somewhat modified, or at least expressed with greater caution. If there be a spiritual world behind the mere phenomena of matter, which makes up the visible universe, is it incredible that it should have spiritual inhabitants—high intelligences, who are capable, at times, of manifesting themselves to, and communicating with, man?[2]

Again, as regards the Jewish scheme of angels, we are not of necessity committed to it, especially in detail. We have no certain knowledge of the matter, and, therefore, may wisely defer judgment. Gabriel (גַּבְרִיאֵל, "man of God," *cf.* Dan. 8 : 16; 9 : 21) may be one of those high spiritual beings; he may, on the other hand, be merely

---

[1] The disintegrating influences of the "Left-Wing" Hegelianism, which Strauss at that time professed, must be added to the influence of the new scientific method. Strauss, in the end, died a materialistic monist of a pessimistic type.

[2] It is at least worth noting that so distinguished a mathematician and acute a lawyer as the late Professor Augustus de Morgan could write: "I am perfectly convinced, in a manner which should make unbelief impossible, that I have seen things called spiritual, which cannot be taken by a rational being to be capable of explanation by imposture, coincidence, or mistake." (*From Matter to Spirit*, S. E. de Morgan, preface by Professor de Morgan, p. v.).

the *symbol* expressive of a divine communication to man.
The question of the "reality" (as we would say), and the
objectivity of apparitions of all kinds, is still one which
awaits a final solution.   Are they objective facts, of a
spiritual or psychical kind, or are they, mainly, or merely,
subjective phenomena, wholly hallucinatory, perhaps, in
their nature?   And even if these phenomena be ultimately classed under the latter category, they may—in
some cases at least—retain an element of objectivity;
they may yet prove to be the symbolic reflexes of a
thought, or message, projected to our minds from the
mind of the Eternal, a thought which, in the process
of reception, we have pictorialised and posited without
our consciousness, subject to the universal forms of time
and space, under which all our concepts must be sub-
sumed in order to be comprehensible by our sense-
regulated intellects.   Strauss does not even contemplate
these possibilities; he is already practically hidebound
in a crude system of materialism, and, therefore, imper-
vious to all impact of any spiritual world.

The "dumbness" of Zacharias, again, is after all a common experience of many who have found themselves—or
thought that they have found themselves—in the presence of the preternatural.   The fear, the paralysis of
speech, the trembling of the limbs, common in every
such situation, have been universally borne witness to
in all ages and in all lands.   We find those phenomena
vividly described in the words of Eliphaz the Temanite
by the writer of the book of Job (4 : 14–16):

> "Fear came upon me and a trembling,
> Which caused all my bones to shake.
> Then a spirit (רוּחַ) passed before my face;
> The hair of my flesh rose up;
> One stood [before me] whose form I could not discern;
> A shape was before mine eyes;
> There was silence; and I heard a voice."

Such experiences, whether objective or subjective, may be "unreasonable"; no doubt they are. But they require sufficient explanation, and mere human reason (as Kant has shown) is perhaps hardly equal to the task of dealing adequately with the things of a supersensual world. It can, however, observe, and analyse, and record its experiences.

The divergencies between the Matthæan and Lucan narratives at this point are trivial matters in comparison, and doubtless are (assuming the narratives to have some historic basis) largely due to the difficulty, always felt in such cases, of securing full and accurate reports of abnormal experience, and to the difference in the apprehensive powers during the sleeping and the waking states respectively. Some harmonisation, however, is possible here.

The difficulty arising out of the affirmed parthenogenetic nature of the conception is a much greater and more serious one, and Strauss, speaking from a purely scientific point of view, is but stating a truth when he says that human parthenogenesis is unknown in the annals of science. But when he adds that, in order to bring it about, God would have to suspend a natural law established by himself, he oversteps the mark. For, in the first place, the use even of the term "law" in the theoretical sciences is in reality improper. There is no such *law* involved in the genesis of creatures, as the frequent examples of parthenogenesis in many groups of beings below the vertebrates in the scale of development clearly show. All we are entitled to affirm on this subject is that, so far as careful observation has extended among the higher orders of creation, *gamogenesis* appears to be the invariable rule. This fact, however, is something quite different from the dogmatic assertion that it is an absolute law even for mankind.

The Birth

In his statement of the mythical interpretation of the birth-story, Professor Drews is remarkably clear. He instances (*The Christ Myth*, p. 96) such gods as *Mithra*, "the *sol invictus* of the Romans"; *Dionysus*, "closely related to the season gods of nearer Asia," who was honoured as "Liknites," the infant in the cradle (the winnowing fan). At the annual celebration of the birth of *Osiris*, on the 6th of January, "the priests produced the figure of an infant from the sanctuary, and showed it to the people, as a picture of a new-born god." He then further proceeds as follows (*op. cit.*, pp. 100 and 101):

"There is no doubt that we have before us in the Vedic Agni-cult the original source of all the stories of the birth of the fire-gods and sun-gods. These gods usually enter life in darkness and concealment. Thus the Cretan Zeus was born in a cavern, Mithras, Dionysus, and Hermes in a gloomy grotto, Horus in the stable (temple) of the holy cow (Isis). Jesus, too, was born at dead of night in a lowly stable at Bethlehem.[1] The original ground for this consists in the fact that Agni, in the form of a spark, comes into existence in the dark hollow of the hole bored in the [fire-]stick. The hymns of the *Rig-Veda* often speak of the 'secret birth' and the concealment of Agni. They describe the gods as they set out in order to seek the infant. They make the Angiras discover it lying in concealment, and it grows up in hiding (see *Rig-Veda*, I, 72, 2; V, 11, 6, etc.). But the idea of the fire-god being born in a stable is also foreshadowed in the *Rig-Veda*. For not only are the vessels of milk and butter ready for the anointing compared with cows,

---

[1] In a note he adds: "According to early Christian writers, such as Justin and Origen, Jesus also came into the world in a *cave*, and Jerome complains (Ep. 58) that in his time the heathens celebrated the feast of the birth of Tammuz at Bethlehem in the same cave in which Jesus was born."

but Ushas, the goddess of dawn, who is present at his birth, is called a red milch cow, and of men it is said that they flocked like cows to a warm stable to see Agni, whom his mother held lovingly upon her lap" (*Rig-Veda*, III, 1, 7; X, 4, 2, etc.).

Again (p. 102): "The metaphorical name of stable for the place of sacrifice attains a new significance from the fact that the sun, during a certain epoch of the world (something between 3000 and 800 B. C.), at the beginning of spring passed through the constellation of the Bull and at the time of the winter solstice commenced its course between the Ox (Bull) and the Great Bear, which anciently was also called the Ass.[1]   The birth of the god is said to have been in secret because it took place at night.   His mother is a virgin, since at midnight of the winter solstice the constellation of the Virgin is on the eastern horizon (Jeremias, *Babylonisches im N. T.*, 35, note 1; *cf.* Dupuis, *L'origine de tous les cultes*, 111 *f.*). Similarly, Mr. Robertson (*Christianity and Mythology*, p. 212): "We should not forget the suggestion of Dupuis and Volney, that the birth of the sun-child between the ox and ass is simply a fable based on the fact that in the zodiacal celestial sphere the sun would come at the winter solstice between the *Bull* and *Ursa Major*,[2] sometimes represented by the ancients as a Boar, sometimes as a Hippopotamus, sometimes as the Ass of Typhon.   But the conception may be older than the zodiac, the fundamental idea of the stable being, as we have seen, the sky as the home of the cloud cows.   The sun-god is, in this

---

[1] *Cf.* Volney, *Die Ruinen*, 1791 (Reclam), note 83 to chap. 13.   "This is the reason why the infant Christ was represented in early Christian pictures lying in his mother's lap, or in a cradle between an Ox and an Ass." But Volney merely represents the constellation on his planisphere as a boar, and labels it "Bear Boar, Ass Typhon."   He appears to have no authority for this!

[2] But see *ibid.*, p. 142, where the sun in the Bull is said to open the spring! Now it is between the Bull and the Bear from May to August.

primary sense, born of two mothers, Earth and Sky, of
the earth in the cave, of the sky in the stable."

Mr. Robertson also maintains (*op. cit.*, p. 257) that
the late Christian myth of the "synchronous birth" of
Christ's cousin John the Baptist is reasonably to be traced
to the Buddhist myth of the synchronous birth of the
Buddha's cousin Ananda rather than to the Kṛishṇaite
motive of Arjuna, or Bala Rama. This course, he thinks,
is reasonable, chiefly because the Kṛishṇaite system gives
an origin to the Buddhist myth.

The general relation which such gods of nature-cults
as Mithra, Dionysus, Osiris, etc., bear to Jesus—if there
be any—will be dealt with from time to time throughout this work. Meanwhile, we may remark here that
the birthday of Mithra, as a solar deity, was celebrated
just after the winter solstice, when the power of the sun
begins to revive again. That Jesus was not a mere equivalent of Mithra is shown partly by the fact that there is
a good deal of evidence to indicate that he was born in
the month of October.[1]

The myth of Zagreus, "the winter Dionysus," seems
to have originated in Crete. The story ran that the hand
of Persephone, daughter of Dēmētēr, the earth-goddess,
had been sought by all the gods. But her mother concealed her in a cave. Zeus, having discovered her re-
treat, and changed his form into that of a serpent, visited her, and the fruit of their union was Zagreus.

The epithet "Liknites," as applied to Dionysus, was
derived from the λίκνον, a broad basket in which the

---

[1] This is founded partly upon what is known of the order in which "the
course of Abia" (Luke 1 : 5) served in the temple. Moreover, in Judæa,
December comes in the height of the rainy season, when cattle and sheep
are not out on the hills, but stabled for the winter. The earliest church
commemorated it at various times from September to March, until in 354
A. D. Pope Julius I assimilated the festival with that of the birth of Mithra
(December 25), in order to facilitate the more complete Christianisation of
the empire.

corn was placed after threshing. It was sacred to Dionysus, and was carried about at his festivals with the sacred
utensils and first-fruits, and the infant Dionysus, represented by a small doll, was sometimes carried in it.[1]

The attempt to find an analogue for this in the manger (φάτνη) of Luke, which Mr. Robertson calls the
"manger-basket," is vain. The one was a *basket* for
corn, the chief of the fruits of the earth-goddess, sometimes used by the country folk as a cradle; the other
was merely a *feeding-trough* for cattle, a totally different
thing, and (unlike the *liknon*) possessing no mythical
significance whatever.

The birth-story found in the Gospels cannot by any
possibility be regarded as an analogue, or an historicised
variant of this sensual myth, which really represents
simply the fecundation of earth by sky, and the production thereby of the various fruits, children of the earth-
mother.

Osiris, again, whose rebirth, celebrated under the form
of the young Horus (the Osiris, or sun, of the next day)
was closely connected with the mysteries of Isis, the
sister-wife of Osiris the father. These Isiac mysteries
were among the *secret* (*i. e.*, sexual) ones, and abounded
in gross superstition, vile juggling, and scandalous inde-
cency. Here, too, a small effigy of Osiris (as Horus) was
shown to the people by the priests of Isis.[2] But it still
remains to be demonstrated that the Bethlehem birth-

[1] For the use of the winnowing-fan as a cradle, and the meaning of the
custom, see "The Golden Bough," *The Spirits of the Corn and of the Wild*,
vol. I, pp. 5 *ff*.

[2] Macrobius, *Saturn.*, I, 18. Perhaps this practise in later ages was imitated by many churches, and doubtless is the origin of the somewhat child-
ish "Bethlehem Tableaux" frequently exhibited at Christmas time. Indeed,
Conrady (*Die Quelle der kanonischen Kindheitsgeschichte Jesu*) derives the
birth-story of Jesus from the *Isis*-myth; that is, from Egyptian in preference to Babylonian, or Hellenistic, sources. The well-known legend cut on
the Metternich Stele says that Isis brought forth her son Horus among the
papyrus swamps of Egypt and reared him there.

narrative bears any real relation to such mythic stories, or that the early Christians had any such *mysteries*, wherein effigies of the infant Jesus, or, indeed, any objects, were exhibited to initiates.   Neither is it in the least degree probable that the first-century Christians recognised any kinship between the story of Christ and these myths; where they mention them it is to contrast, not to identify, a thing which they would gladly have done to gain converts had Jesus been regarded as one of the cult-gods.

The Birth of Agni

We next come to what is the main point in the astral system of Drews—the original source of all the stories of the fire-gods and sun-gods: this is the Agni-cult. The birth of the earthly fire-god (Agni) was celebrated by the ceremony of kindling the spark in the fire-sticks. The spark, produced by friction, was the infant Agni, who grew to be a fire—the earthly manifestation of the god.

Now, Professor Drews emphasises several points: (1) These gods were usually born in darkness or caverns; in the case of Agni in the dark hollow of the wood (the stable) in which the drilling-stick was twirled.   This ceremony is (2) held to be comparable with the birth of Jesus, because in the *Rig-Veda* the vessels of milk and butter[1] near by are compared to cows, and Ushas, the dawn-goddess, who is present, is called a red milch cow; furthermore, it is said that men flocked to see Agni in his mother's lap, "like cows to a warm stable."

---

[1] The butter was for pouring upon the newly kindled fire (Agni).   The *Agni-hotra* was a sacrifice consisting of burnt offerings and libations of butter and milk made every morning, and was one of the five religious duties of the Hindu householder.   The "birth" of Agni, as the earthly fire, was thus celebrated daily.   "Born from the floods of heaven (the Thunder-shower) he first came down to earth as lightning . . . and remained hidden in the recesses of wood until called forth by friction, when he suddenly springs forth into gleaming brightness."

We must confess that we do not see how all this affects the question, or establishes any parallel between the birth of Agni and the birth of Jesus! Jesus was born in the dead of night, says Professor Drews. Whence does he derive this information? The narrative of Luke merely says that the shepherds were informed of the fact during the night. The event might, therefore, have taken place during the day, or earlier in the evening. (See Luke 2 : 8 and 11.) Neither can we say that it happened in darkness, or that the stable was a cave. It is true that caves were then often used as stables; also that Justin and Jerome say that it was a cave. But their information seems to have been derived from later legends, which, largely following the pagan myths, are all for a cave.[1] There is much assumption in this hypothesis of Doctor Drews, and much is quoted from dubious sources. The mythical additions to the original story are elaborately worked up in the Apocryphs,[2] which differ *toto cœlo* both in style and matter from the canonical Gospels.

Lastly, as regards the details in the story as thus developed, the idea that the birth of Jesus took place in the midst of the stabled animals is certainly inconsistent with Luke's definite statement that these were out on the hills, and being watched by shepherds. The ass[3]

[1] Doctor Plummer says (*St. Luke*, "Critical Commentaries"): "In Origen's time the cave was shown, and the manger also (*Cont. Cels.*, I, 51). One suspects that the cave may be a supposed prophecy turned into history. . . . Isaiah 33 : 16, LXX version (οὗτος οἰκήσει ἐν ὑψηλῷ σπηλαίῳ πέτρας ὀχυρᾶς) was supposed to point to birth in a cave, and then the cave may have been imagined in order to fit." It is very probable.

[2] These, however, declare that there was *a great light* suffusing the cave!

[3] The statement, borrowed by Robertson and Drews, that the *Great Bear* was anciently called "the Ass," is more than highly questionable, and the authorities cited (Dupuis and Volney) are worthless upon such questions. If it ever were so named it would be found in the Egyptian version of the constellations; but it certainly does not occur there or in the Chaldean and Greek lists. On the planisphere of Dendera, however (our chief authority for Egypt), near the place of the Great Bear, a figure usually called "The Thigh" is shown, and close by it is another one, erect and supposed

might, of course, be regarded as the beast of some travel-
ler; but the ox would not be in his stall at night at that
time of the year. As for the scene, represented in much
later Christian art, of the Holy Family grouped together
amidst these animals, this concept was derived wholly
from the fifth-century apocryphal *Gospel of the Pseudo-
Matthew*, chap. 14, and the passage so often quoted from
Hab. 3 : 2 (M. T.)—"O Jahveh, revive thy work in the
midst of the years; in the midst of the years make it
known"—in the LXX version reads, "in the midst of two
animals thou shalt be known";[1] being in this version apparently derived from Isaiah 1 : 3—"The ox knoweth his
owner, and the ass his master's manger; but Israel doth
not know, my people doth not consider"—a passage void
of all Messianic implications. The LXX version here is
really a mere misreading of the older Hebrew text and of
no critical value.

Professor Drews's further explanation that the mother
of Jesus was termed a "virgin" because at midnight of
the winter solstice the constellation of the Virgin is on
the eastern horizon cannot be upheld, since, as we have
seen, it is practically certain that the birth of Jesus did
not take place at that time of the year, and was not even

to be a *Hippopotamus*. This latter was probably merely an Egyptian variant of the Great Bear of the Greeks; for the Hippopotamus was familiar
to the Egyptians, whereas the Bear was not. The Dendera planisphere
occurs in a temple, erected about the time of Hadrian (early second century A. D.), and is, therefore, late. Moreover, it is also merely an Egyptian
variant of the ancient constellations preserved for us in the writings of
Aratus, Hipparchus, and Ptolemy. It will be found figured on Plate III of
Boll's *Sphæra*, and may be compared with the Farnese globe of about A. D.
300. Doctor Budge says (*The Gods of the Egyptians*, vol. II, p. 312) that the
Egyptian equivalent of our Great Bear was the Bull *Meskheti*.

[1] *I. e.*, שָׁנִים חָיִים (ἐν μεσῷ δύο ᎏῴων) for שָׁנִים חַייהוּ. This latter reading
is, according to Driver, the older and the true one. See an able article on
the subject by A. Frost, *Contemp. Rev.*, December, 1903, pp. 873 *ff*. Professor Weber, the eminent Sanscritist, states that the *ox* and the *ass* figuring
in the Kṛishṇa birth-ritual are borrowed from debased Christian sources,
doubtless the very late apocryph referred to above.

commemorated then until the fourth century.[1] Indeed, the whole set of correspondences which are worked out between the earthly celebration of the birth of the sun (or fire) god, regarded as a reflexion of the same drama enacted mystically in the heavens, and the birth of Jesus, though it is an ingenious speculation, and its working out a clever piece of special pleading, is thoroughly unreal. The entire theory, in short, when carefully examined, is full of flaws, and, as a consequence of this, it is unconvincing to the thoughtful reader.

But we have, besides all this, the usual parallels drawn from India. Both Mr. Robertson (*Christianity and Mythology*, p. 319) and Professor Drews (*The Christ Myth*, p. 105)—not to mention other writers—have laid great stress on the older legend of Krishna. The former, in particular, regards the bringing forth of the god-child on a journey as an incident quite common in this type of myth.

But other men besides "god-children" have been born on a journey, and Mr. Robertson's half-dozen examples, when carefully examined, are not always quite apposite. Neither can Jesus be correctly termed a "god-child," in the pagan sense of the term. In the myths, the gods when desirous of becoming the fathers of children by mortal women usually presented themselves in mortal or animal guise to the prospective mothers, sometimes even as duplicates of the women's husbands.[2] Neither, again, were the mothers of such god-children as Krishna, Cyrus, etc., "virgins" in the Biblical sense of that term.[3] Both Dēvakī and Mandānē, and indeed all the mothers that have been quoted in this connexion,

[1] "To adapt Christian festivals to pagan ones" (Chrysostom, *Homily* XXXI).

[2] The credulity formerly displayed by many, even educated, women in matters of this kind is well illustrated by the disgraceful story told by Jos., *Ant.*, XVIII, 3, 4.

[3] The term "virgin," as used in pagan cults, meant only an "independence of the marriage-tie"; *i. e.*, that the goddess had no recognised male partner.

were married women, and, therefore, the births of their sons cannot in any sense be termed parthenogenetic.

The Birth of Krishna

It is true, as he states, that, according to one account, Krishna was born in a cow-shed, or stable; but the Purāṇic version of the event locates it in Kansa's fortress. A careful survey, indeed, of the whole of Krishna's birth-story in its later form points to the Apocryphs as its real source.[1]

Professor Drews also mentions several points which confirm the above view: the dungeon is filled with light; the parents, as well as others, fall down before the child; and additional marvels not found even in the most debased Christian writings. The marvellous powers of the apocryphal infant Jesus are likewise quite outdone by the babe Krishna, who, like Herakles, strangled a deadly snake with his own hand.[2]

The Birth of Gautama

From this we pass on to the birth of Gautama. Here, again, the mother is no "virgin," as De Bunsen (*The Angel Messiah of Buddhists, Essenes, and Christians*, p. 33) asserts.[3] The *Lalita vistāra* says that the mother of a

---

[1] It may be added that the ritual for Krishna's birthday is drawn largely from Christian sources, for it differs from the early Hindu stories precisely in the points where it approximates to the accounts of the nativity of Jesus.

[2] We may add here that the "taxing-motive" of Vasudeva's journey is plainly a borrowing of the mistranslation of the Lucan ἀπογράφεσθαι (2 : 1–5), which word means not *taxing* (as in A. V.), but "*enrolment* in a census of the population." This is mere ignorant copying, apparently from the A. V.

[3] The *Abhinishkrāmana Sūtra*, in the Chinese version, says that Māyā was married and lived with her husband. So also does the *Lalita vistāra*. Mr. de Bunsen, however, speaks of the Buddha as "conceived of the Holy Ghost and born of the virgin Māyā"; and says again that, according to Buddhist authorities: "It was the Holy Ghost, or *Shing-Shin*, which descended upon the virgin Māyā." But he gives no authority for the statement, and we may add that Buddhism recognises no "Holy Ghost"! Mr.

Buddha must have thirty-two special marks, and the thirty-first of these must be "faithfulness to marriage vows." Māyā, again, like Dēvakī, does not accompany her husband, for the same reason as Mary. We are told that she begged permission of the king to return to the town of her own people. To this he consented, and the future Buddha was born, not in a cave or a cow-shed, but under the shelter of the grove Lumbini.[1]

The conception of Māyā, too, though distinctly supernatural, is, again, neither parthenogenetic nor due to divine power. She dreamt, we learn, that she saw the future Buddha approaching her in the form of a six-tusked white elephant, and holding a lotus flower. After making an obeisance he seemed to enter her right side.[2] Thereupon wonderful prodigies happened, far beyond any recorded even in the most extravagant of the Christian Apocryphs. The ten thousand world systems were shaken, a great light appeared in all of them, the blind, deaf, and lame were healed, and all the hungry *manes* (ghosts) were miraculously fed.

Māyā was thenceforward, to the time of her delivery, guarded by four supernatural beings with drawn swords. At the time of the birth, refreshing showers from heaven fell upon the Bodhisat and his mother. Four kings received the babe at the hands of the gods, and as soon as he was born, when set upon his feet, the child walked, and at every seventh step called out: "I am the chief of the world," etc.[3]

Hardy also speaks (*Manual of Buddhism*, 1880, p. 145, note) of the Tibetan scholar Csoma as stating that the Mongolian accounts affirm the virginity of Māyā, but adds that the Tibetan records make no mention of it. Professor Rhys Davids says (*Buddhism*, Hibb. Lects., 1881, p. 183, note 1) that the above reference "has not been confirmed."

[1] So the *Nidāna Kathā;* the *Lalita vistāra* merely mentions a request to go to the grove.

[2] The *Lalita vistāra* affirms that he did enter.

[3] The *Lalita vistāra* may be consulted for these narratives in Rājendral Mitra's translation. The whole system of Buddhist "parallels" is elabo-

In all this silly and bombastic nonsense we may, perhaps, recognise here and there a faint gleam reflected from the birth-stories of the New Testament. But one thing is very clear, viz., that the Gospel stories are neither borrowed from, nor mere variants of, the above accounts. Myths are frequently superposed upon historical stories; historical stories never grow out of myths pruned down and rendered acceptable to thinking people.

The Birth of Saoshyant

Lastly, as regards the birth-parallel in the story of Saoshyant, we have a case of preternatural birth more akin to rabbinical ideas of *agamogenesis*[1] than what is, strictly speaking, termed parthenogenesis. The seed of Zarathustra was said to have been miraculously preserved in the water of a certain pool,[2] in which three maidens successively bathed, and of these one became the mother of this Persian Messiah. It has been surmised that perhaps the author of II Esdras 12 : 3, 25, 51, who imagined that the Jewish Messiah would come out of the sea, thought that the seed of David might be preserved in a similar manner, and the Messiah thus agamogenetically conceived. This, however, is all very problematical, and, in any case, there is no real parallel here with a strictly parthenogenetic conception.

rately worked out in Professor Seydel's *Das Evangelium von Jesu in Seinen Verhältnissen zu Buddha-Saga und Buddha-Lehre* (1882). Also see his *Die Buddha-Legende und das Leben Jesu*, etc. (1889).

[1] Doctor Conybeare holds that Philo's allegorical language in *De Cherubim*, xiii f., respecting the wives of the patriarchs as symbolical characters, implies the belief that their sons were conceived parthenogenetically. In other words, Philo's statement, *e. g.*, that Sepfora (the wife of Moses (= Virtue) finds herself pregnant ἐξ οὐδενὸς θνητοῦ ("by no mortal") = the ἐν γαστρὶ ἔχουσα ἐκ Πνεύματος ἁγίου of Matt. 1 : 18. But this is very doubtful. Angels or demons may be referred to, and the conception regarded as *gamogenetic* (*cf.* Gen. 6 : 2, and see *The Academy*, November 17, 1894, p. 401).

[2] "The triumphant Saoshyans will be born out of the water Kaosya from the Eastern quarter" (*Vendidad*, Fargard XIX, 5).

The conclusion of the whole matter, therefore, up to the present time, may be thus stated: The Gospel story of the conception and birth—whether it be historical or otherwise—presupposes a peculiar case of true parthenogenesis, the idea of which has not been borrowed from either Jewish or Gentile sources.

CHAPTER III

WE have now to consider a number of narratives dealing with the stories related about the birth and childhood of Jesus. The form in which these narratives have reached us suggests that, if they are to be regarded as historical in the true sense of the word, we must look upon them as popularised versions of the incidents in question, which have, in some degree, undergone a change of form in order to adapt them to the intelligence of the simple folk who formed the bulk of the earliest converts to Christianity.

The Shepherds

The episode of the shepherds' visit—an event in itself natural enough but for its connexion with a supernatural apparition—is either ignored or summarily dealt with by the mythicists.

Mr. J. M. Robertson, in particular, quickly rids himself of the whole story. He says: "The shepherds come from the same prehistoric sources as the rest. They belong to the myths of Cyrus and Krishna, and they are more or less implied in that of Hermes, who, on the day of his divine birth, stole the cloud cows[1] of Apollo, himself a divine shepherd and god of shepherds"[2] (*Christianity and Mythology*, sec. "The Cow and Stable Birth," pp. 320 *ff.*).

---

[1] This idea is found in the *Rig-Veda*, where the clouds are called the "cows of Indra."

[2] Strauss (*Life of Jesus*, vol. I, p. 214) attempts to explain the story of the shepherds by the pagan idea that the gods frequently appeared to shepherds. But there is no suggestion of the kind in this story.

The absurdity of this derivation of the story must be patent to every reader who gives real thought to the matter. Whether the story of the shepherds be true or untrue, the connexion of both Cyrus and Krishna with shepherds is wholly different from that of these Jewish shepherds with Jesus. Cyrus, for instance, is carried off by one, in infancy, to be exposed, with a view to his destruction (Herod., I, 107–110); Krishna was exchanged by his father for a shepherd's son, shortly after his birth, in order that he might escape the destructive wrath of Kansa (*Vishnu Purāṇa*, Wilson's translation, p. 502. *Cf.* also the story in the *Bhāgavata Purāṇa*).

In the Lucan narrative the Bethlehemite shepherds merely visit the stable of the inn to see the young child and, perhaps, to attest the fact of his birth. There is here absolutely no reason to suppose that the narrative— whether historical or not—is borrowed either from Indian or Persian sources, as Mr. Robertson dogmatically asserts. As for the fact that shepherds are concerned in all three (or even four) stories, in ancient civilisations of the pastoral type it is only probable that they would be involved in many events connected with the lives and acts of the more important individuals of their respective countries.[1]

The Presentation in the Temple

This ceremony is strictly in accordance with the spirit of the Jewish law (Num. 18 : 15 and 16). It is, however, recorded chiefly on account of the public recognition at the time of the infant Jesus as the future Messiah by Simeon the Levite and Anna a prophetess.

But two Buddhist stories are told which are often supposed to be parallels and sources of the canonical account of the blessing of Simeon, which was given on this occasion.

[1] The *Talmud*, Sanh. 3, disallows the evidence of shepherds.

On the day of Gautama's birth a venerable ascetic named Asita,[1] who, after eating his midday meal, had gone to heaven to rest during the heat of the day, saw the heavenly hosts rejoicing, and learning the cause he immediately hastened down to earth to see the new-born and future Buddha. When the old man came into his presence, Māyā tried to make the child salute him, but the latter insisted on presenting his feet instead of his head to the saint. The old ascetic then took the infant up in his arms, and when Suddhodana urged that the sage must be reverenced, the latter replied: "Say not so, O king; on the contrary, both I and the gods and men should rather reverence him." He then examined the body of the child to see whether the three hundred and twenty-eight marks of a supreme Buddha were upon him. Then follows what has been termed a "blessing" of Gautama by the old saint, who, we are told,

"Began to weep like a broken water-vessel and cried:
    'By grief and regret I am completely overpowered,
    Not to meet him when he shall have attained to supreme
        wisdom!'"

This is all very different from the narrative describing Simeon's blessing (Luke 2 : 25), though it may be a faint echo of that story, modified to suit a different set of tastes and circumstances. On the fifth day the ceremony of naming the child took place.

Later on, during his boyhood, another kind of presentation in a temple occurred, which is still more unlike that described in the Lucan narrative. On this occasion one hundred thousand gods harnessed themselves to the car which conveyed the boy thither; blossoms were showered down upon him by heavenly nymphs; the earth shook as

---

[1] In the *Nidāna Kathā* he is called Kāla Devala. The story will be found in Beal's *The Romantic Legend of Sakhya Buddha*, a translation of the *Fo-pen-hing*, which is a Chinese version of the *Abhinishkrāmana Sūtra*.

he entered the temple; music was heard, played by invisible performers in heaven; the images in the temple descended from their pedestals and came and prostrated themselves before him. Finally, the scene was concluded by a hymn of praise sung by the gods. Kuenen remarks upon the story (*National and Universal Religions*, Hibb. Lects., 1882, p. 326): "The simple scene in the temple at Jerusalem is really no parallel at all to the homage rendered to the Buddha-child."

The story of the prophetess Anna (Luke 2 : 36–38) Seydel derives from the account of the old women who came to wish Gautama good luck, an impossible derivation. (See *The Romantic Legend of Sakhya Buddha*.)

Neither does it seem to be possible to extract a mythical meaning from these narratives.

The Magi

Probably none of the stories told of the childhood of Jesus have given rise to more interest and speculation than this one. The visit to Bethlehem of the "Wise Men from the East" (Μάγοι ἀπὸ ἀνατολῶν), who came to "worship" (προσκυνῆσαι) the new-born "King of the Jews," is unique even among the most touching and vivid of the Biblical narratives. Who were they? what were they? from whence did they come? what was their star?[1] is the story in any sense historical? These are the questions which have exercised the minds of men for generations.

Strauss—writing from the older mythical standpoint —has dealt at some length, and in an unsatisfactory manner, with the story in his *Life of Jesus*, IV, pp. 213–231. His conclusion, wholly predetermined by the natural bias of his mind, practically amounts to this: The prediction of Balaam (Num. 24 : 17) "was not the rea-

[1] There was an interesting correspondence on this subject in *The English Mechanic*, March 17, 1893.

son why the Magi took a star for that of the Messiah, and went to Jerusalem." . . . "But it was the cause why the legend supposed a star would appear at the birth of Jesus, which should be recognised by the astrologers as that of the Messiah."

There are several assumptions here, which we will notice later. Meanwhile, we will turn to a more modern statement of the mythical view, as expressed by Professor Drews at some length in *The Christ Myth* (pp. 93 and 94).

Hadad-Adonis, he observes, is the god of vegetation and fruitfulness, and, like the sun, dies in winter and is born anew in the spring. "Something of the kind," he rather vaguely adds, "may well have passed before the mind of Isaiah when he foretold the future glory of the people of God, under the image of a new birth of the sun from out of the blackness of night" (Isaiah 60 : 1 *ff.*).

"As is well known, later generations were continually setting out this idea in a still more exuberant form. The imagination of the enslaved and impoverished Jews feasted upon the thought that the nations and their princes would do homage to the Messiah with gifts, while uncounted treasures poured into the temple at Jerusalem (*cf.* Psalm 68 : 32 *f.*). This is the foundation of the story of the Magi, who lay their treasures at the feet of the new-born Christ and his virgin mother.

"But that we have here, in reality, to do with the new birth of the sun at the time of the winter solstice appears from the connexion between the Magi, or Kings, and the stars. For these Magi are nothing else than the three stars in the sword-belt of Orion,[1] which at the winter solstice are opposed in the west to the constellations

[1] *I. e.*, *Alnitak* (Arab., nitak al-djanza, "the girdle of the giant"), *Alnilam* (Arab., al-nizham, "a string of pearls"), and *Mintaka* ("a girdle"; Arab. and Pers., *natak*, "to gird"). The Persians seem to have identified Orion with Nimrod, the "mighty hunter before Jahveh" (Gen. 10 : 9). See Gore's *Astron. Essays*, p. 83.

of the Virgin in the east;[1] stars which, according to the Persian ideas, at this time seek the son of the Queen of Heaven—that is, the lately rejuvenated sun Mithras."[2]

The former of these theories, as the reader will see, reduces the figures of the Magi to a mere poetic fiction suggested by ancient prophecies; in the latter the Magi become merely the three central stars in the constellation Orion.

The theory of Strauss must again be pronounced eminently unsatisfactory. It is highly improbable that a wholly untrue story of a recognition by certain (to the legalistic Jewish Christians) heathen astrologers would be attached to a Messianic birth-story of Palestinian origin.[3] It would be utterly foreign to their conceptions derived from Old Testament predictions, and distasteful to all their preconceived ideas. Balaam's prophecy might be accepted as an inspiration of Jahveh; but Balaam's magical, as also his astrological, practises were repugnant to the early Christian mind (cf. Acts 19 : 19). There is no probability whatever in this suggestion.

Neither is it possible to see any connexion between these Magi and the stars in the belt of Orion. Even if we admit the (unproved) tradition that they were kings—a most unlikely supposition—we are nowhere told authoritatively that there were three in number;[4] this was merely inferred later on from the fact that three gifts were offered, and it was supposed that each Magus contributed one.[5]

[1] The constellation of the Virgin is always, at all times of the year, "opposed" to the belt stars, i. e., when she is rising they are setting.

[2] Dupuis, L'origine de tous les cultes, etc. (1795), p. 268.

[3] "Matthew" compiles from that standpoint.

[4] Named respectively Gaspar, Melchior, and Balthasar. This legend is very late and quite worthless. It is probably derived from a misuse of Psalm 72 : 10-15 and Isaiah 60 : 6.

[5] M. Jean Reveille thinks (Études publiées en hommage à la faculté de théologie de Montauban, 1901, pp. 339 ff.) that the adoration of the Magi was suggested by the Mithraic legend. But he admits that he has no proof of this.

Herodotus (I, 101) refers to the Magi as a Median "tribe" (? caste), and in VII, 19, he calls them "soothsayers." Plato, again, speaks of the magianism of Zoroaster (*Alk.*, 1). The "Magi of Chaldea" are mentioned in Daniel 1 : 20; 7 : 11, etc. (*cf.* the Simon Magus of Acts 8 : 9). Of the earlier Fathers, some trace their origin to Persia, others regard them as coming from Arabia.

Professor Clemen says (*Primitive Christianity and Its Non-Jewish Sources*, pp. 298 f.) that the narrative of the visit of these wise men "is beset by so many difficulties[1] that it cannot be regarded as historical." In spite of this judgment from a not unfriendly critic, there would seem to be no valid objection to the existence of a considerable *substratum* of truth in the narrative.[2]

This is the view taken by Doctor Voigt, of Halle (*Die Geschichte Jesu und die Astrologie*, 1912), who thinks that our existing narrative is based upon an earlier and unpopularised version embodying historic facts. His reason for this conclusion will appear when we examine the problem of the star.

Cumont comments upon this view, which is also held by Dieterich (*The Mysteries of Mithra*, p. 195, note): "But I must remark that the Mazdæan beliefs regarding the entrance of Mithra into the world have strangely varied."

[1] Referring to the exhaustive discussion in Strauss's *Life of Jesus*, I, pp. 231 f.

[2] An historical derivation of the story from the recorded visit of Tiridates, King of Parthia (A. D. 66), to do homage to Nero as Mithra, is favoured by some scholars. Pliny (*Nat. Hist.*, XXX, 16) even calls Tiridates a *magus*, and states that *magos secum adduxerat*, from whom the emperor hoped to learn magic. But it is probable that the Christian story was in circulation before that date; and Gruppe (*Mythologie*, 1620), Cheyne (*Bible Problems*, pp. 246 f.), Jeremias (*Babylonisches*, p. 55), Fiebig (*Babel*, pp. 16 f.), and Nestle ("Zu. Matt. 2," *Zeitschr. f. d. Neutest. Wiss.*, 1907, p. 73) for various reasons reject this explanation. It is not wholly improbable that Tiridates was inspired by the previous examples of Magi hailing monarchs and others born under favourable conditions.

The Star

This celestial phenomenon, which is stated by Matthew to have synchronised with the birth of Jesus, and to have been the cause of the visit of the Magi to Bethlehem, has been the subject of much conjecture. It has been variously regarded as a comet—a highly improbable suggestion—a *stella nova*, and an astronomical conjunction of planets.

A remarkable instance of the second of these phenomena occurred in 1572–3, when a new star suddenly flamed out in the constellation *Cassiopeia*, surpassing in brilliancy the planet Jupiter. Theodore Beza interpreted it as heralding the second coming of Christ.

Again, on September 30, 1604, there occurred a triple conjunction of Jupiter and Saturn and (subsequently) Mars, which was accompanied by a new star appearing in the constellation *Pisces*.[1] Kepler then suggested that the natal star of Bethlehem might be a mere conjunction of planets, and calculated that a similar association of Jupiter and Saturn had occurred in 7 B. C. He further surmised that it might have been accompanied by a *stella nova*, which was, perhaps, the star seen by the Magi. This view, however, is open to various objections —amongst others, from the calculations made by the late Doctor Pritchard, of Oxford, it would seem that when the planets Jupiter and Saturn were in conjunction in B. C. 7 they were separated by a space equal to about twice the apparent diameter of the moon. Moreover, there is no reason for supposing that any such temporary star was seen anywhere in that year.

There can be little doubt, indeed, that the solution of this problem must be sought in astrology rather than in astronomy. This is the opinion of Doctor Voigt,

[1] See Kepler's *Judicium de trigono igneo*, dedicated to the Emperor Rudolph II (1603), and his *Stella nova in pede Serpentarii* (1606).

quoted above. He holds that the former "science" had specially connected Jupiter with the God of the Jews, and that his ascendency in Aries, in the spring of B. C. 6, was held to be of good augury for Jewish welfare. The Magi, he thinks, would reason thus: A king is born in Judæa; his destiny, according to the heavens, indicates beneficence and world-wide dominion.

But the date of this phenomenon may prove to be a difficulty, unless we may suppose that the visit was paid when Jesus was somewhat older than Matthew appears to contemplate in his Gospel.[1]

Another objection yet remains. The statement that the star was seen in the east (ἐν τῇ ἀνατολῇ) by the Magi, who nevertheless went westward, preceded, it would seem, by the star, seems to be irreconcilable with all known astronomical phenomena. This question, a short time ago, attracted the attention of Mrs. A. S. Lewis, the discoverer of the Syriac palimpsest of the Gospels at Mount Sinai, when she found that it was quite possible to read the passage otherwise than it is usually translated. We may, she thinks, render the Greek: "We [being] in the East have seen his star,"[2] etc.

To the obvious reply that this rendering is a somewhat strained one, the answer would be that the construction here, as frequently in popular language, is loose when judged by a purely literary standard. But the New Testament Greek, as we now know, represents the ordinary popular and non-literary language of the time.

Lastly, the statement that the "star" went with them and "stood over the place where the young child was" is due, no doubt, to the popularising of the original story—

---

[1] *I. e.*, assuming that the birth took place in B. C. 8, as now seems probable. See Appendix A (1).

[2] Εἴδομεν γὰρ αὐτοῦ τὸν ἀστέρα [ὄντες] ἐν τῇ ἀνατολῇ. It may be also noted that if by the "star" a *constellation* were meant, ἄστρον (ἄστρα) would probably have been used instead of ἀστήρ, which, strictly speaking, means a single star.

unless we may take the whole matter as a purely subjective phenomenon. It is, in fact, discounted at the outset by the narrative itself, which states that the Magi, when they reached Jerusalem, were at a loss how to proceed farther, until they were directed by the priests and scribes to go to Bethlehem. Thus the main difficulties connected with the "star" disappear when the narrative is more carefully examined in the light of modern knowledge.

The Gifts

It is a common practise amongst some modern critics to lay stress upon the fact that the Gentiles had long been expected by the Jews to offer gifts to the Messiah when he appeared, though the idea certainly seems to have been that they would not do so until they had been conquered by him. Isaiah says (9 : 6), "They shall bring gold and frankincense," but myrrh is not mentioned. Again, Fiebig and Jeremias suppose that these gifts were offered to Jesus as the new-born sun-god. Matthew's list of presents, however, differs considerably from those usually presented to that deity. According to Kircher, ambergris and honey were also included. Further, the rebirth of the sun-god could hardly be thought of as announced by a star. It would surely be heralded by the appearance of the sun himself, either immediately after the winter solstice or at the vernal point of the ecliptic.

The gifts here mentioned, we must also remember, merely symbolise the acceptance of Jesus by the "wise men" as the future King of the East, where divinity and priestly office are almost inseparably connected with the monarch.[1]

---

[1] It is also stated in our English versions that the Magi "worshipped him." But it is very doubtful whether we should translate προσκύνησαν (Matt. 2 : 11) in this way. It may mean merely "did obeisance to," *more Orientali*,

This incident has been "paralleled" with a Buddhist story (*The Romantic Legend of Sakhya Buddha*, S. Beal, pp. 65 and 66), from which some would derive it, and which bears a slight general resemblance to the Biblical event. Presents are likewise brought to the young Bodhisat. King Suddhodana and five hundred Sakhyas brought "bracelets for the arms and wrists, for the legs and ankles, necklets composed of every species of precious stones, and cinctures, turbans, and coronels." While these were being put upon him five hundred Brahmans "began in endless laudatory phrases to congratulate the prince"; but the glory of the prince's body eclipsed the glory of the gems, so that their brightness was not seen— "they all appeared dark and black, even as a drop of ink, utterly lustreless."

But of a star, by which all these men were urged to go and pay their respects, there is no mention, though Seydel (*Das Evangelium von Jesu*, etc., 1882, pp. 135 and 298), and Francke (*Deutsche Lit-Zeitung*, 1901, 27, 65), have made great efforts to find one.

The Flight into Egypt

Professor Drews remarks (*The Christ Myth*, p. 94) that Hadad, besides his association with Adonis as a god of vegetation, "is also the name of the sun-god, and the Hadad of the Old Testament returns to his original home out of Egypt, whither he had fled from David. Thus," he continues, "we can understand how Hosea 11 : 1, 'I called my son out of Egypt,' could be referred to the Messiah, and how the story that Jesus passed his early youth in Egypt could be derived from it (Matt. 2 : 14 *f.*)."

Professor Drews's meaning in the above-quoted pas-

and not that the Magi recognised the divinity of Jesus. The probability is that they foresaw in him a future great king, having, like Cyrus (?), a monotheistic faith, and nothing more.

For a recent study of Iranism and Magism, see Professor J. H. Moulton's Hibb. Lects. on *Early Zoroastrianism* (1912).

sage is not very clear. But, if we rightly understand him, he desires to mythicise both the story of Jesus in Egypt and the story of Ader, or Hadad, found in Josephus, *Ant.*, VIII, 6.[1]

Hadad the Edomite, we gather, was saved from a massacre of the Edomites by David, and fled (or was taken as a child) to Egypt. When he heard that David was dead, and Solomon was in a position of some difficulty, he returned to Edom, but was unable to persuade that nation to revolt. He then went to Syria, where he joined a certain Rezon, the captain of a band of robbers, and contrived to be made king of a part of Syria, from whence he invaded Israel and did much damage to Solomon's kingdom.

Now Hadad, the Syrian *god*, is a form of *Tammuz*, a vegetative(-solar) deity, and, if this story be a myth, it would seem that the passage in Hosea is referred by Doctor Drews both to this particular variant form of the sun-myth and to the story of Jesus, which, according to this view, is merely another version of it. But the narrative in the book of Kings professes to be history, and undoubtedly is such in its nature, whatever confusion, or variations, may have been introduced into it before it was recorded in the Bible. Further, we do not believe that the passage in Hosea, referred to above, has any mythical significance whatever, or that the story of Jesus' sojourn in Egypt was suggested by it.[2] The reference is plainly to the stay of the people of Israel in Egypt, who are, according to the prophetical writers, frequently termed "my son" by Jahveh.

---

[1] See also I Kings 11 : 14–25. This story has been carefully examined by Doctor Winckler (*Alttest. Unters.*, pp. 1–15), who thinks that it is made up of two ancient and independent narratives.

[2] "Matthew," it must be granted, introduces the reference in a forced and unnatural manner. Usener derives the idea of the journey to Egypt from the flight of the gods before Typhon (*Zeitschr. f. d. N. T. Wiss.*, 1903, p. 21).

Again, a wide-spread tradition exists among the Jews that Jesus lived for some time in Egypt, though not during the period of his infancy, as stated by Matthew. It was from that country, say both the *Talmud*[1] and the *Toledoth Jeschu*, that he brought the magic by means of which he wrought his mighty works. It would seem probable, therefore, that there is some historical basis for the story of a sojourn in Egypt, and, if the narrative of the visit of the Magi and the subsequent massacre of the infants of Bethlehem be facts, we have the *motif* for the journey to Egypt, where many Jews were settled, as well as for the occurrence of this incident during the childhood of Jesus, as Matthew states.

The Massacre of the Children

Strauss says of this story (*Life of Jesus*, IV, pp. 234–236): "The primitive Christian legend was interested in making Herod commit this crime in order to take away the life of Jesus; for in all times, according to tradition, the birth of great men has been celebrated by murders and persecution. The more danger they ran, the greater they were esteemed, the more unexpectedly they were preserved, the more importance seemed to be attached to their persons by heaven.

"We find this exemplified in the account of the infancy of Cyrus by Herodotus, in that of Romulus by Livy, and, more recently, in the account of the infancy of Augustus by Suetonius. The Hebrew legend gives a similar account of Moses; and it is somewhat singular that this recital concerning Moses is very similar to that given by the evangelists respecting Jesus. In both cases the sentence of death was not passed against the individuals themselves, but against a certain class of children, in which it was thought they would be included.

[1] See Tract. *Shabbath*, 13d, 104, 6.

Thus, in Moses' case, it was against all the *male* children; in Jesus' case it was against *all*[1] children of a certain age. In fact, according to Exodus, the decree of death was not against Moses, for Pharaoh did not then suspect his birth, and he was only accidentally put in danger; but the tradition, which was formed in the bosom of the Hebrew people, did not think the intention sufficiently strong; and in consequence, about the time of the historian Josephus, a turn was given to it which made it much more like the traditions about Cyrus and Augustus, and consequently more like the recital of Matthew." This last-named version is a variant of no authority whatever, as Strauss practically admits.

A similar rabbinical story is related of Abraham and the Chaldean Nimrod. "The Chaldean sages," says Strauss, "whose attention was awakened by a remarkable star, announced to the Babylonian prince that a son would be born to Terah, from whom would spring a powerful people; and upon this declaration Nimrod declared a massacre from which Abraham luckily escaped."

This is, no doubt, a case of astrological prediction so common in ancient, and even modern, history down to quite recent times. It differs from the Biblical story, however, in at least one very important particular: the Magi did not predict that a child *would be*, but believed that he *had been*, born.

Professor Drews, on the other hand, affiliates the story of the massacre with a somewhat similar incident in the life of Kṛishṇa.[2] Like Herod and Astyages, King Kansa,

---

[1] Strauss seems in error here. The MSS. read πάντας τοὺς παῖδας, all the male children. If both sexes had been meant, τέκνα, no doubt, would have been used.

[2] See the story in the later works, the *Bhāgavata Purāṇa* and the *Prem Sāgar*. In the Buddhist variant of this anecdote, King Bimbasāra refuses to kill the youth Gautama, when he is pointed out as a likely rival in the future, and does not massacre any children (see *The Romantic Legend of Sākhya Buddha*, pp. 103 and 104).

in order to prevent any danger arising in the future to himself, or his successor, from his sister's son, against whom he had been warned by an oracle, cast both Vasudeva and Dēvakī into prison. After the former had escaped with the new-born babe, and returned with the child of Nanda the shepherd, Kansa himself came to take the infant away. And when the child had disappeared before his eyes, he gave orders that all the new-born children in his country, under the age of two years, should be slain.

Doctor Cheyne (*Bib. Probs.*, p. 249) regards the story as an analogue of Ex. 1 : 22; *cf.* Ezek. 29 : 30; but the stories are obviously different.

The *critiques* of both Strauss and Drews are founded upon the alleged fact that in Eastern countries the births of all great men are traditionally celebrated by murders and persecution. This is to some extent true, not only in tradition, but in actual history. In barbarous civilisations, where highly placed men and their prospective successors are the centres of intrigue and plot, it is only what we might naturally expect to find. But, at the same time, the fact is not so universal, even in tradition and legend, as Strauss supposes. The examples which are picked out by him from Jewish, Persian, and Roman history, after all, form but a very small number in comparison with the numerous names which could be mentioned concerning whom no tradition, or legend, of an attempted murder exists. This line of argument, indeed, leads to no conclusion and proves nothing.

Neither, again, does the story of Rājah Kansa and the young Kṛishṇa prove anything more than either a mere coincidence or, more probably, one of those numerous borrowings from Christianity with which the later versions of the story of Kṛishṇa, found in such works as the *Bhāgavata Purāṇa*, abound. The true tests for the historical truth, or probability, of stories such as this

are first of all the corroboration which they find elsewhere in contemporary literature, and, secondly, the likelihood of the situation to produce such a crisis. Let us
examine this narrative from both of these points of
view.

It so happens that in the case of the Biblical story
there is some external evidence of an historical character
which tells in its favour. The reference alluded to here
is a passage found in the works of Macrobius, a heathen
writer of considerable repute and a learned collector of
the curiosities of ancient literature, who flourished at
the end of the fourth century A. D. It runs as follows:
"When Augustus [Cæsar] had heard," he says, "that
among the children in Syria, whom Herod the King of
the Jews had ordered to be slain, within the age of two
years, his own son also had been killed, he said: *'It is better to be Herod's hog [ὗν] than his son [υἱόν].'*" [1]

Various objections have been raised against this testimony: *e. g.*, that the original reporter of the story must
have mistaken the reference; that it was much more
likely to have been suggested by the execution, at the
order of Herod, of his two sons Alexander and Aristobulus; or, again, that it refers to the murder of Antipater

---

[1] "Cum audisset Augustus inter pueros, quos in Syria Herodes, rex
Judæorum, intra bimatum jussit interfeci, filium quoque ejus occisum, ait:
'Melius est Herodis *porcum* esse quam *filium*'" (*Saturnalia*, II, 4).

It should be noted that Augustus is reported by Macrobius as having uttered this *bon mot* in Latin. But it was a common custom, in the reign of this
emperor, and subsequently, for the upper and more cultured classes in Rome
to speak in Greek; and, as will be seen, the pun is only appreciable in that
language, where the pronunciation of ὗν (*hūn*) and υἱόν (*whēon*) are sufficiently alike to warrant a fairly good royal jest. The note of Gronovius,
that this seems to be an imitation of an old saying of Diogenes the Cynic
against the Megarians, as caring more for the breeding of their rams than
for their children, does not explain it.

But the jest in the mouth of a Roman, and the reference to the abstinence from pork, which Herod (though not a Jew) was practically obliged
to practise, out of compliment to the scruples of his fanatical subjects,
has in it a sarcasm which is wholly wanting in the remark as attributed to
Diogenes.

two years later; or, once more, that it is improbable that Herod had an infant son at that time.

To the first of these objections we may reply that there is no reason whatever to suspect any misunderstanding; the report, whether true or untrue, is clear and definite. As regards its application to others of Herod's sons, the distinct reference to a massacre of a number of children under the age of two years negatives this explanation.

Again, as Herod was at that time sixty-seven years of age, it is quite possible that he had, by a young wife of his harem, an infant who was (perhaps unknown to him) out at nurse in Bethlehem.[1]

A final objection, that Josephus ignores the incident, is an argument of very trifling value. No historian notices everything that happens, and the fact of a dozen, or even a score, of small children being done to death, by the orders of a cruel and arbitrary despot, was not a matter of sufficient importance to attract much notice at that time from the outside world. Josephus had abundance of matter for his records, all of much greater interest to the Roman people than the sufferings of a few peasant children in an insignificant village of Judæa.

Lastly, as to the probability of such an occurrence, the records of Herod's life supply abundant justification. A man who could deliberately order two of his sons to be strangled, on mere suspicion, and a third son afterwards to be put to death, whilst he himself was upon his death-bed; who, when summoned by Antony to Rhodes, left his best-loved wife Mariamme in charge of one of his friends, with orders that she should at once be put to death, should any misfortune befall him, and actually himself executed her on his return; who, moreover, on his accession massacred all the members of the Sanhe-

[1] It is still more improbable that Macrobius borrowed the story from "Matthew" and invented the jest.

drin but two, and caused the young Aristobulus, brother of Mariamme, whom he had appointed high priest, to be treacherously drowned, and, doubtless, was guilty also of numerous other unrecorded crimes: such a man, we unhesitatingly affirm, was capable of anything.

That a man of this type, if he had heard even the faintest breath of rumour that the Messiah-King of the Jews was lately born, would scruple for one moment to sacrifice a few obscure infants in order to make sure of the death of a future rival to himself, or his dynasty, is wholly incredible. Herod, we may be sure, would not have hesitated to sacrifice, if need be, a thousand such children in order to insure his own stability or that of his house upon the throne of Judæa.

A suggested mythical explanation of the narrative—that it is "simply a detail in the universal sun-myth of the attempted slaying of the child sun-god, the disappearance of the stars at morning suggesting a massacre, from which the sun-child escapes" (*Christianity and Mythology*, pp. 322 and 323) is too fanciful to merit any serious notice. A really clever person can find analogues in the sun-myth to almost anything and everything that happens upon the surface of the earth. But this fact has no necessary bearing upon the historicity or non-historicity of the event in question.[1]

The Discourse with the Doctors of the Law

This incident has been correlated with a story of the young Bodhisat, who, it is said, at the age of eight years, was sent to the "Hall of Learning" to be instructed by the erudite Visvamitra. The child so astonished the

---

[1] An important point, but one upon which too much stress is often laid by negative critics, is that "Matthew," in describing the return of the Holy Family from Egypt, appears to be ignorant of any previous residence in Galilee. This is the more remarkable because "Matthew," in general, records the Galilean tradition. It is, however, probably due to defective sources of information.

pundit with his command of all the learning then known to India that the latter chanted this song:

> "Whatever arts there are in the world,
> Whatever Sutras and Śasters,
> This (child) is thoroughly acquainted with all
> And is able to teach them to others."[1]

—*The Romantic Legend of Sākhya Buddha*, pp. 67 and 68.

A "Parallel" from Delphi

Mr. J. M. Robertson, on the other hand (*Christianity and Mythology*, p. 334), can find no better "parallel" to the story of Luke than the following anecdote. Strabo, he says, narrates how certain "parents went to Delphi, anxious to learn whether the child which had been exposed [to perish] was still living, while the child itself had gone to the temple of Apollo in the hope of discovering its parents."

It is only necessary to add, in reference to both of these stories, that, if the unbiassed reader will study carefully Luke's narrative and compare it with them, he will see that neither bears the slightest resemblance to it nor shows the remotest connexion. That children, afterwards famous in history, have frequently been reported as displaying precocity at an early period of their lives is quite true. But there all resemblance ends.

According to the rabbi Judah ben-Tema, every Jewish boy at five years of age studied the Hebrew Scriptures, at ten years the Mishna, at thirteen the Gemārā, the two last forming the *Talmud*. Josephus, too, tells us (*Life*, II), that his own progress in learning was so great that at the age of fourteen years he was often consulted by the chief priests, and various other prominent members of the Jewish state, upon difficult points of the law.

---

[1] *Cf.* with this Luke 2 : 46 and 47, and the ridiculous account in the *Gospel of the Infancy*, where the boy discourses upon "physics and metaphysics, hyperphysics and hypophysics."

With examples like these before us we cannot wonder at the wisdom and knowledge which the young Jesus showed at the age of twelve years; the more so that Luke frankly tells us that even he "increased in wisdom as in age, and in favour with God and man."

CHAPTER IV

JESUS. CHRIST. PRE-CHRISTIAN CHRIST AND JESUS-CULTS

Jesus

THE name "Jesus" ('Iησοῦς) is used both in the LXX version and in the N. T. as the equivalent of the Heb. *Jehoshua* (יְהוֹשֻׁעַ) or *Joshua* (original form *Hoshea* הוֹשֵׁעַ, "help," Num. 13 : 8), which is commonly interpreted as meaning "Jah (or Jahveh) is help," or "salvation" (*cf.* Matt. 1 : 21).[1]

[1] Similarly, Philo Judæus (born 20–10 B. C.) explains Joshua (Jesus) as 'Iησοῦς ἑρμενεύεται σωτηρία Κυρίου: "Jesus (Joshua) is interpreted safety of the Lord."

Doctor Cheyne, however, appears to reject this view (see *Hibbert Journal*, April, 1911, pp. 658 and 659). After admitting that "the direct evidence for the divine name Joshua in pre-Christian times is both scanty and disputable," and adding that "if the belief in such a god-man was taken over by the Christists, we are entitled to presume that they did not leave behind the celestial name of the god-man. And that name ought to underlie the popular form Jehoshua, whence the late form Jeshua or Jeshu has come"; he then goes on to urge that this is the case; that the ritual lamentations in the valley of Megiddon were for Hadad-Rimmon, the only or first-born son of the Supreme God, *i. e.*, *Adonis*, and that this name was a compound of the names of two related deities (see Zech. 12 : 10 and 11), referring for details to his *The Two Religions of Israel*, pp. 183 and 213. See also *Crit. Bib.*, p. 191.

He also finds a parallel to this duplication of names in *Jahu-Ishma*, where Jahu is an alternative form for Jahveh and Ishma (=Shema) is short for Ishmael. "The origin of the latter name," he contends, "is as uncertain as that of Yahwè, but at any rate it is a god-name (*Two Religions*, pp. 65 and 400), and does not mean 'God hears' any more than Joshua means 'Yahwè-help.'" Finally, "it appears that Jeshua, or Jeshu, is a corruption of the second part of the cultural divine name Jehu-Ishma[el]."

But, if the whole matter is so uncertain, and the evidence is so "scanty and disputable," how does Doctor Cheyne know all this? Here philology alone is an uncertain basis for both theological and historical theories, and few reputable scholars appear to have indorsed Doctor Cheyne's conclusions.

Moreover, it is a mere surmise that the compound word "Hadad-Rim-

Professor Drews seems to accept this explanation, for he says (*The Witnesses to the Historicity of Jesus*, p. 195): "Joshua, however, means something like 'Jahveh is salvation,' 'Jah-Help,' and corresponds to the German name 'Gotthilf.'"

But he directly afterwards launches out into a number of highly disputable and often erroneous statements as to the connexion of its Hellenistic Greek substitute ("Jesus") with those of various mythical, or semi-mythical, personages in heathen cults. Thus: "The name [Jesus] was fairly common among the Jews, and in this connection it is equivalent among the Hellenistic Jews to the name Jason, or Jasios, which again is merely a Greek version of Jesus (*cf.* II Macc. 4)." He then goes on to say that Jaso (from *iasthai*, "to heal") was the name of the daughter of the saver and physician Asclepios, who "himself was in many places worshipped under the name of Jason in a widely spread cult." Furthermore, this Jason was practically identical with Jasios (=Jasius=Janus Quirinus, Verg., *Æn.*, III, 168). The whole argument, in short, is clearly directed to proving that Jesus and Jason (with its assumed variant forms) were practically one and the same pre-Christian cultual god who was worshipped as the "healer" and "helper" of mankind.

mon" is the name of a deity. Because both Hadad and Tammuz (Adonis) were worshipped in the Phœnician city of Byblus, it has been conjectured that the two deities may have been amalgamated, or confused, so that there was a wailing for a Hadad-Rimmon similar to that for Tammuz. But no evidence for this has so far been adduced. See Baudissin, in *Real-Enc. f. Prot. Th. u. Kir.* (Herzog), VII (1889), *s. v.*

The whole of Doctor Cheyne's theory, indeed,—like that of Professor Drews—is ultimately based upon the assumption that Joshua is a purely mythical character, and not a tribal hero, whose exploits and share in the conquest of Canaan have been, perhaps, magnified by the patriotism of later historians and chroniclers. But Doctor Cheyne at least allows (p. 658) that it is "still possible that [in New Testament times] there was a great teacher and healer bearing the same name who was confounded with that supposed deity"!

But there appears to be a great deal of both reckless assertion and groundless assumption here. In the first place, as regards the identification of Jesus and Jason, the prosaic facts are these. Soon after the time of Alexander Jannæus (d. 78 B. C.) Greek names began to be fashionable among the Jews, especially throughout the upper classes. Thus, a high priest of the period changed his name Ἰησοῦς (יֵשׁוּעַ, Jeshua) to Ἰάσων (Jason), just as a certain Ἰάκιμος (יָקִים, Jākim) called himself Ἀλκιμος (Alcimus), and Σίλας (Silas) was transformed into Σιλουανός (Silvanus).

From that time onward Jason became a common name amongst the Jews. The brother of the above-mentioned Jason, Ὀνίας (חוֹנִיה, Honias) also bestowed upon himself the Greek name Μενέλαος (Menelaus) [see Nöldeke, *Enc. Bib.*, art. "Names," sec. 86].

This practise was no doubt partly suggested by the rough equivalency of healer (in a physical sense) and helper (in, perhaps, both a spiritual and a temporal sense); but there was no *identification* of a Gentile cult-god Jason with a Jewish cult-god Jesus; it was simply a Grecising fashion which had sprung up subsequently to the spread of Greek power and influence in the East, owing to the conquests of Alexander the Great.

Again, the assumed identification of Jason with Jasios (Jasius), or Jasion, is, to say the least of it, highly improbable. It is more likely a case of confusion of different myths. We have not space here for entering into the question in detail, and can only add that Jasios, or Jasion, appears to have been connected with the mysteries of Dēmētēr, and the name is usually derived from ἰάομαι, "to heal"; but the etymology is doubtful. Jason, on the other hand, is the hero of the Medea myth, a wholly different story, it would seem.[1]

[1] Doctor Cheyne, who is, on the whole, kindly disposed to the mythical theory, makes the following admission (*Hibbert Journal*, April, 1911, p. 658)

Once more: the equating of any of the above names with the Roman *Janus* is more than problematical. The Romans themselves thought that Janus and the feminine Jana (= Diana) were the sun and moon, and commonly assimilated the former to the Greek Ζῆν, *i. e.*, Δίην. And the Janiculum (hill of Janus), which was probably the original seat of this worship in Rome, lay on the north, or Etruscan, side of the Tiber, so that an Etruscan origin of the cult is suggested. And as the sun, by its revival after the winter solstice, starts the year, so Janus is the god of opening and beginning; hence January (in later times) the month of opening or beginning of the year. But Janus was no "healer"-god.

We next come to a passage (*The Witnesses to the Historicity of Jesus*, p. 197, note) containing still wilder speculations and more reckless assertion, which, to do him justice, we must first quote almost *verbatim:* "Jes Crishna was the name of the ninth[1] incarnation of Jesnu, or Vishnu, whose animal is the fish, as in the case of Joshua, the son of the fish Nûn. . . . Jes is a title of the sun. . . . The word also occurs in the name of Osiris Jes-iris, or Hes-iris (according to Hellenicus) [and] in Hesus (the name of a Celtic god). . . . The mother of all these gods whose name contains Jes is a virgin (Maya, Mariamma, Maritala, Mariam, etc.); her symbol is the cross, the fish, or the lamb; her feast is the Huli (Jul), from which Cæsar took the name Julus or Julius when he was deified in the temple of Jupiter Ammon; and her

regarding the theory that Joshua means "Saviour"; that he was probably an Ephraimite form of the sun-god; that his name conveys the idea of healer (so Epiphanius), and that it is connected with Jason, or Jasios, the mythical name of a pupil of Cheiron in the art of healing: "I am sorry to say that almost every word of this is contrary to the present decisions of scholarship."

[1] Krishṇa was the *eighth* avatar of Vishnu. The ninth was the Buddha, "the great sceptical philosopher," to delude the Daityas into neglecting the worship of the gods.

history agrees with that of Jesus Christ." [1]   We will now deal with this extraordinary tissue of assertions as fully as our limits of space will allow.

The question of the "virginity" of the various mother-goddesses, and their connexion with the Mary of the Gospels, has been discussed in the first and second chapters of this work, to which the reader is referred. And in the first place let us inquire into the use of the name *Jes*, in the designation "Jes Crishna," leaving the addition "Crishna" to be dealt with later on in the present chapter.

In its fuller form "Jes" is written "Jeseus" ("Jezeus") or "Yeseus." Concerning this appellation the late Professor Max Müller writes (*Trans. of the Vict. Inst.*, vol. XXI, p. 179): "The name Yeseus [Jezeus] was invented, I believe, by Jacolliot,[2] and is a mere corruption of *Yadu*. I answered Jacolliot once;[3] but these books hardly deserve notice."

On the other hand, such eminent Sanscritists as the late Sir Monier Williams, of Oxford, and the late Professor Cowell, of Cambridge, while holding to the spuriousness of "Jes" and "Jeseus" as ancient names of Krishna, think that these appellations may be corruptions of *Isa* ("ruler," "chief"), which properly belongs as a title to Śiva as regent of the northeastern quarter.

The conclusion of the matter, in either case, is that the prefixing of the name Jeseus, or Jes, to Krishna has absolutely no warrant from any ancient Hindu book or custom.

---

[1] Referring here especially to *The Worship of Augustus Cæsar*, by Alexander del Mar (New York, 1900). *Cf.* this passage with one in *Ecce Deus*, W. B. Smith, p. 17, where the argument is similar. Drews appears to accept Del Mar's statements unreservedly.

[2] In his *La Bible dans l'Inde*.

[3] *Cf.* his *Lectures on the Science of Religion* (1884), pp. 24 and 25. Also his *Chips from a German Workshop* (1895), vol. IV, pp. 228 *ff.*

In a similar manner there is no ancient authority for the form "Jes-nu" as a variant of Vishnu.[1]

We will next turn to the attempt to foist the spurious word "Jes," as a divine appellation, into the name of the Egyptian deity Osiris. "The name of Osiris," says Professor Flinders Petrie,[2] "is written with the ⊔, 'the throne,' AS, or, perhaps, in early times IS. The vocalisation of signs varied much, and on Greek authority we know that it was sounded in later times as OS."[3] Ac-

---

[1] Vishnu's connexion with the fish appears only in the later Indian account of the deluge found in the *Bhāgavata Purāṇa*, where the fish is represented as an incarnation of this god. His object in becoming a fish seems to have been to steer the ship. In the earlier account found in the *Śatapatha Brāhmana* (I, 8, 1, 1), the fish was an incarnation of Brahmā.

It may be also added here that there is some doubt as to the meaning of *Nûn*, as the name of the father of Joshua. It may mean a *serpent*, and have, perhaps, a *totemic* signification. Again, it is quite possible that it is a contraction (and corruption) of an Edomite name (see *Enc. Bib.*, *s. v.*).

[2] Extract from a letter to the present writer.

[3] According to Del Mar (*The Worship of Augustus Cæsar*, pp. 88 and 89), the word "Ies-iris" signified "son of God"! And he adds: "Ies-iris (from Hellenicus) is probably correct," adducing as evidence Plutarch, *On Isis and Osiris*, 34. But Plutarch there merely says that "Hellenicus [fifth century B. C.] has recorded that he heard Osiris called *Ysiris* ("Υσιρις) by the priests," which simply indicates a vocalisation of the first sign as US (=OS), not the use of the title of a cult-god, "Jes"!

With regard to the derivation and meaning of the name Osiris, Doctor Budge says (*The Gods of the Egyptians*, vol. II, pp. 113 and 114): "The oldest and simplest form of the name [Osiris] is ⊔, that is to say, it is written by means of two hieroglyphics, the upper of which represents a 'throne' and the lower an 'eye,' but the exact meaning attached to the combination of the two pictures by those who first used them to express the name of the god, and the signification of the name in the minds of those who invented it, cannot be said. In the late dynastic period the first syllable of the name appears to have been pronounced *AUS*, or *US*, and by punning it was made to have the meaning of the word *USR*, 'strength,' 'might,' 'power,' and the like, and there is little doubt that the Egyptians at that time supposed the name of the god to mean something like the 'Strength of the Eye,' *i. e.*, the strength of the sun-god Rā. This meaning may very well have suited their conception of the god Osiris, but it cannot be accepted as the correct signification of the name. For similar reasons the suggestion that the name ÂS-ÂR is connected with the Egyptian word for 'prince,' or 'chief' (*ser*) cannot be entertained. It is probable that the second hieroglyphic in the name ÂS-ÂR is to be understood as referring to the great Eye of Heaven,

cordingly, we see that the first syllable of this compound word (whether written AS or IS, or later US OS) is not a divine *name* prefixed to the main part of the name, but the *vocalisation of a sign denoting a throne*, and its precise meaning here is unknown.

Next, according to Professor Drews, we meet with the cultual divine name, or title, "Jes" in "Hesus," the name of a Celtic god. Now, Hesus, or Esus, has very generally been thought to be radically the same word as the *Aisa*[1] (Αἶσα) of the Greeks, and was the type of an absolutely Supreme Being whose symbol on earth was the oak.

M. Salamon Reinach, however, avers (*Orpheus*, pp. 116 and 117, an English translation) that "We find a divine woodman named Esus associated with the Roman gods Jupiter and Vulcan. This Esus," he continues, "is mentioned by Lucan (circ. A. D. 60), together with Teutates and Taranis; according to the poet they are sanguinary deities who exact human sacrifices. It has been wrongly supposed that these three gods constituted a sort of Celtic trinity; in reality, as the passage in Lucan proves, they were deities venerated by a few tribes to the north of the Loire, among others the Parisii. Esus seems to have been the same word as the Latin *herus*,[2] and perhaps the Indo-Iranian *Asuras*. Teutates was the god of the people, Taranis the god of thunder. The reason for representing Esus as a woodman is not apparent."

Whichever of the above explanations we may adopt, or even if, with Professor Anwyl, we regard Esus merely as "the eponymous god of the Esuvii" (*Celtic Religion*,

i. e., Rā, but the connexion of the first is not so clear, and, as we have no means of knowing what attributes were assigned to the god by his earliest worshippers, the difficulty is hardly likely to be cleared up." See also his *Osiris and the Egyptian Resurrection*, vol. I, chap. 2. Thus, it will seem that Egyptologists lend no support to the theories of Mr. Del Mar and Professor Drews.

[1] Αἶσα, ἡ, like *Moira* (Μοῖρα), the divinity who dispenses to every one his lot or destiny (Lat., *Parca; e. g.*, Hom., *Il.*, XX, 127.

[2] Or *erus* (of the gods), "a master."

p. 33), it is perfectly clear that Esus was not a cult-god of the "saviour" or "healer" type, and therefore in no sense comparable with Jesus as regarded in that light. Indeed, the only connexion is due—as in some other cases—to the accidental resemblance in the sound and spelling of the two names.

Equally wild is the statement that the name "Julius," as borne by Augustus Cæsar, is derivable from "Huli," the feast of "the mother of all those gods." Here, again, the actual historical fact is that Augustus took the name "Julius" on being adopted as his heir by Julius Cæsar, who was a member of the ancient *familia* of the Juli which can be traced back as far as the year 265 A. U. C., when a C. Julius Julus was consul. What Professor Drews means by "her [the goddess-mother's] history agrees with that of Jesus Christ" we confess ourselves unable to understand.

Further, it would appear not improbable that the word Jes, which Professor Drews asserts to be a title of the sun, is really a derivative from the ancient Indo-European, or Aryan, root signifying "to be" or "exist," as applied to the highest deity and means the Existing One.[1] If so, the concept would seem to be quite different from that underlying the various solar and vegetation "saviour" cults.

Finally, Professor Drews sums up his theory as follows (*The Christ Myth*, p. 139): "We can scarcely doubt that the stories in question originally referred to the annual journey of the sun through the twelve signs of the zodiac. Even the names (Iasios, Jason, Joshua, Jesus; *cf.* also Vishnu Jesudu . . .) agree, and their common root is contained also in the name Jao (Jahwe), from which Joshua is derived. Jao, or Jehu, however, was a mys-

---

[1] *Cf.* Sans., *as-mi;* Gr., εἰμι = ἐσ-μί; Lith., *es-mi;* Lat., *sum = es-um;* Slav., *jes-mi;* Old Bulg., *yes-mi.* See also Curtius, *Gk. Etym.*, 564; Max Müller, *Oxford Essays;* and Peile, *Gk. and Lat. Etym.*, p. 151.

tical name of Dionysus among the Greeks, and he, like
Vishnu Jesudu (Krishṇa), Joshua, and Jesus, roamed
about in his capacity of travelling physician and redeemer of the world."

With the above summary we may compare a similar
contribution of Professor W. B. Smith (*Ecce Deus*, p.
17), who says: "The name [Jesus[1]] was closely connected
in form with the divine name IAO, regarded in early
gnostic circles with peculiar reverence. It is not necessary to decide whether this latter is to be regarded as
the equivalent of the tetragram JHVH, or as meaning
Jah-Alpha-Omega (Rev. 1 : 8; 21 : 6; 22 : 13; *cf.* Isaiah
44 : 6). It is enough that in Hellenistic early theosophic
circles the name was in approved use, a favourite designation of deity. In view of all these facts the triumph
of the name Jesus seems entirely natural."

Whether the stories of Iasios and Jason are identical
and originally referred to the annual journey of the sun
through the twelve[2] signs of the zodiac need not be discussed here. Neither is it necessary to inquire whether
the names of the various pagan cult-gods can be traced
to a common root. This is affirmed, but not demonstrated, by Professor Drews. The points to be noted
here are that the *solar* character of both Joshua and
Jesus, and the etymological identity of their names with
those of these cult-gods have not been established, or
even shown to be reasonably probable. In the same
way, the *facile* dogmatism of Professor Drews—which
is wisely avoided by Professor Smith—that *Jao* is identical with Jahveh, a word of very uncertain origin and
meaning,[3] cannot be allowed in the present state of

---

[1] He derives it from the Greek Ἰάομαι, "I heal," which in its Ionic and
epic forms has the future Ἰή-σομαι, and its noun Ιησις (gen., Ἰήσ-εως).

[2] Del Mar, however, states (*op. cit.*, pp. 6 and 298) that originally there
were first only eight and then ten signs in the ancient zodiac.

[3] See art. "Names," in *Encyclopædia Biblica*, secs. 109–113, with notes
appended.

knowledge. It is true that in late Greek Jahveh was variously and loosely transliterated 'Ιαβέ, 'Ιαυέ, 'Ιαουέ, or 'Ιαουαί, and that some Gnostics apparently used 'Ιαώ as an equivalent for Jahveh. Regarding this latter practise, however, Doctor Cheyne writes (*Enc. Bib.*, art. "Names," sec. 110, note 4): "The form Iao, handed down by the Gnostics, may be left out of account. Like all similar forms (*e. g.*, 'Ιευώ in Philo Byblius), it is simply the product of erroneous or misunderstood Jewish statements. On this point *cf.* Baudissin, 'Der Ursprung Gottesnamens Iao,' in his *Studien zur semit. Rel.*, 2, 181 *ff.* (1876)."

Movers, again, remarks: "The forms of the Hebrew sacred name יהוה [JHVH], in heathen writers 'Ιευώ (Philo, *Sanch.*, p. 2) and 'Ιαώ (Diod. Sic., I, 94), are certainly not derived from the tetragrammaton of the Hebrew, but according to the usual confusion of יהוה with Dionysus."

In the preceding paragraph he also says: "This mysterious triliteral, however, 'Ιαώ is manifestly יְהוֹ, the apocopated *Hiphil* of יהוה, 'he makes to live,' formed, as so many names in Hebrew are, in exact correspondence with the tetragrammaton יהוה, apoc. יהו, and with the apocopated forms which appear in the names יִשְׂרָאֵל, יְרוּבַעַל, etc." (see *Phoniz.*, chap. 14, pp. 539–558).

Jao, it is true, was a mystical name of Dionysus among the Greeks; but, as that god had probably an Oriental origin, it was doubtless merely a Greek transliteration of his original name, which was not, it would seem, a form of Jahveh. It has likewise no connexion, etymologically or otherwise, with the names "Joshua" or "Jesus."

Neither can we compare the roaming about of Dionysus as depicted in the various forms of the myth with the traditional work of either Joshua or Jesus. If the accounts are compared the differences are seen to be absolute. *Dionysus* was, perhaps in one sense, a form of

the sun-god, and *Jao* was, it may be, the autumnal
phase of that deity; that either Joshua or Jesus were
solar deities remains, as we have already said, to be
proved. Their stories—especially that of the former—
in their minor details may have collected a few mythical
traits, during the course of transmission, but the historical bases remain unshaken.

Professor Smith's alternative suggestion that *Jao* may
represent the compound name Jah-Alpha-Omega is no
doubt ingenious and plausible, but it rests on no basis
of fact, even if that trigrammaton were (as is probable)
"in Hellenistic early theosophic circles a favourite designation of deity." It is quite as likely, if not more so,
that such interpretation, if current in the earlier Christian centuries (of which, however, we have no proof),
sprang from the special use of Alpha and Omega, the first
and last letters in the Greek alphabet, in the passage of
the Apocalypse to which Smith refers.

Before closing this section of the present chapter, we
may briefly advert to the peculiar mythical theory of
Professor P. Jensen, according to whom the Jesus of the
Gospels is really neither a personified ideal, based upon
pre-Christian Jewish and pagan models (Drews), nor an
anthropomorphised Jewish cult-god (Smith, and mainly
Robertson), but a reproduction, or reflection, of one or
more of the heroes whose exploits are recorded in the
ancient Babylonian Gilgamesh epic. He is to be identified, Jensen thinks, now with Eabani, the man-monster
of the story, now with Xisuthros, the Babylonian Noah,
and now with Gilgamesh himself, the chief hero of the
epic, and the King of Erech (Uruk).[1] In his *Moses,
Jesus, Paulus* (pp. 28–31), he works out a series of (in the
case of Jesus) thirty "parallels," or "correspondences," in

---

[1] See Jensen's *Das Gilgamesch epos in der Weltliteratur* (1906); *Moses,
Jesus, Paulus: drei Varianten des babylonischen gottmenschen Gilgamesch*
(1909); *Hat der Jesus der Evangelien wirklich gelebt?* (1910).

which he thinks the Gospels reproduce the chief episodes of the original myth.   Moses and Paul have a similar derivation.

It will be impossible here to discuss in detail this *theory;* but we may remark briefly that it is *a priori* open to at least two very grave, and indeed insuperable, objections.   In the first place, many of the so-called parallels are very forced and artificial.   As instances of this, two or three examples must suffice.   Sinful humanity and most beasts, including swine, are drowned in the great deluge.   This is paralleled by the drowning of the two thousand demons and swine in the Sea of Galilee. Again, on the Mount of Transfiguration Peter and the two other disciples wish to build tabernacles.   The origin of this episode is traced to Gilgamesh[1] felling some trees before his voyage to Xisuthros, the Chaldean Noah. Many other similar extravagant derivations might be quoted, but these will serve our present purpose.

Secondly, the theory entirely overlooks the numerous incidents in the Gospels to which there are no correspondences in the epic.   Moreover, the highly ethical and spiritual note characteristic of the former is entirely unaccounted for upon this hypothesis.

The theory has received a very slight support upon the Continent, *e. g.*, from Brückner (*Christ. Welt.*, 1907, p. 202) and Beer (*Theol. Jahresber.*, 1906, p. 14); but practically none outside Germany.   The majority of scholars have regarded it as fanciful, and it has even been described by such a frank and outspoken critic as Professor B. W. Bacon (*Hibbert Journal*, July, 1911, p. 739) as "elaborate bosh."   At all events it cannot be regarded as a really serious contribution to the mythical hypothesis.

---

[1] For *Gilgamesh* as a form of *Tammuz*, see *Babylonian Liturgies*, by S. Langdon, p. 20, Rev. 3, and *Rev. d'Assyriologie*, IX, 115, col. 3 : 1.

Christ

The title "Christ"—Greek, Χριστός,[1] substantive form of χριστός, "anointed"—is a translation of the Hebrew, מָשִׁיחַ, *māshiakh*, "Messiah," *i. e.*, "anointed" (Aram., מְשִׁיחָא, *meshiḥā*, more fully *meshiakh Jahveh*, "Jahveh's anointed.")

Christ and Krishna

Following the example of a number of modern writers, Professor Drews, as we have seen, primarily seeks to identify the Christ of the Gospels with the Krishna of the modern Hindu cult-worship.[2] Thus, he speaks of "the Hindu Krishna, who, as saviour, conqueror of dragons, and crucified, is in many respects as like Jesus as one egg is like another" (*The Witnesses to the Historicity of Jesus*, p. 214). As these "many respects" are not detailed here, though elsewhere (*op. cit.*, p. 197), following Mr. Del Mar, he spells the name of the Hindu god "Crishna," we are driven to an examination of the original story of Krishna, and to contrast this with its subsequent additions, as also to ascertain the origin of the variant modern spelling by which it is superficially assimilated to the characteristic Messianic title of Jesus.

The authentic sources for the legend of Krishna are the following Sanscrit works: the *Mahābhārata* (book V), the *Bhāgavata Purāṇa* (book X), the *Bhagavadgītā* (book X), the *Harivaṃśa* (3304 *ff.*), and the *Vishnu Purāṇa* (book V). To these, for the more highly legendary and modern additions, may be added the *Prem Sāgar*, an edition in the vernacular Hindi of that part of the *Bhāgavata* which relates to the life of Krishna. For details the reader is referred to the excellent English

---

[1] The attempt of Professor W. B. Smith (in *Der Vorchristliche Jesus*, 1906) to connect χριστός with χρηστός, χράομαι, "to use" (see Psalm 34 : 5) is quite untenable.

[2] He admits also a subsidiary Buddhist influence.

translations of these books which are now available. It must suffice here to refer to a few main incidents, and to say that we learn from the most ancient and pre-Christian authorities that the mother of Krishṇa was not named "Mariamma," [1] but *Dēvakī;* that she was not a "virgin," but the mother of eight sons, of whom Krishṇa was the last; that her husband's name was not "Jamadagni," a village carpenter, but *Vasudēva*, a descendant of the Lunar line of kings, and, finally, that Krishṇa was not "crucified," [2] but (according to even the *Vishnu Purāṇa*) was shot by a hunter in mistake for a deer. But this by the way.

Further, the legends about his putative father being called away from home "to pay taxes," [3] his "recognition as a god by Magi," his "last supper in company with ten disciples," and similar stories, are all pure fiction and undoubtedly owe their origin to imitators of the Gospel narratives.

Now, the question arises, when did this extraneous matter find its way into the Krishṇa legend and from what sources did it come?

It probably began at an early period. The story of Jesus Christ was carried into India at the latest before the end of the second century A. D. (see Euseb., *H. E.*, V, 10). And, according to Weber's version of a paragraph in the *Mahābhārata*, it was also brought back to India by Brahman travellers. Both Weber and Lassen interpret the passage in question to mean that early in the Christian era three Brahmans visited a community of Chris-

---

[1] This, and the other statements immediately following, are apparently taken from Del Mar's *The Worship of Augustus Cæsar*, pp. 89–92.

[2] The Hindu sculptures of a crucifixion of Krishṇa referred to by Mr. Higgins (*The Hindoo Pantheon*) are unquestionably either representations of Jesus Christ, executed by the early church in India, or later Brahmanical imitations based upon these.

[3] This statement is apparently derived from the A. V. of Luke's Gospel (2 : 3), where ἀπογράφεσθαι ("to be enrolled") is wrongly translated "to be taxed."

tians in the East, and that on their return "they were able to introduce improvements [!] into the hereditary creed, and more especially to make the worship of Krishna Vasudēva the most prominent feature of their system."

An article by an anonymous Sanscritist in the *Athenæum* for August 10, 1867, may also be consulted. In this the writer shows how the Brahmans took from the Gospels such things as suited them and used these extracts in the composition of Krishna episodes which were interpolated into MSS. of the *Mahābhārata*.

Another source of interpolations would seem to be documents of an apocryphal character. Doctor L. D. Barnett, of the British Museum, says (*Hinduism*, 1906, p. 21, note): "A considerable number of the details in the Purānic myths of Krishna's birth and childhood seem to have come from debased Christian sources (apocryphal Gospels and the like) such as were current in the Christian church of Malabar."

But a great deal of interpolation of matter derived from the Bible into Sanscrit works has undoubtedly taken place since the British occupation of India and the revival of Christian missions in that country. In the latter part of the eighteenth century a certain Lieutenant Wilford, of the East India Company's service, was anxious to ascertain whether many prominent Biblical characters were referred to in the Hindu sacred books. Accordingly, he offered rewards for any information which would show this to be the case. Some time afterwards many pundits came forward and placed in his hands copies of Sanscrit MSS. which contained such information as he was seeking. This discovery at the time produced great enthusiasm throughout Europe, and even such experts as Sir William Jones were induced to accept the evidence as trustworthy.

After a time, however, suspicions were aroused, and a critical examination showed that clever forgeries had been committed by means of interpolations of Biblical episodes written in Sanscrit and more or less modified to suit the change. Lieutenant Wilford reluctantly acknowledged that he had been imposed upon; but his *Essays* upon the subject are still quoted by writers who apparently are ignorant of the fraud, as also of the subsequent confession of Lieutenant Wilford that he had been grossly deceived by unscrupulous pundits.[1]

We have now to deal with the question of the variant spelling of Kṛishṇa as " Crishna," " Chrishna," or " Cristna," much affected by some writers, especially those of the mythical school. And we will commence our inquiry by quoting a distinguished modern scholar. " There is no authority," writes Doctor Macdonell,[2] the Boden Professor of Sanscrit at Oxford, " for spelling the name Kṛshṇa (or Kṛishṇa) ' Crishna,' much less ' Cristna.' The initial [letter] is a K, and nothing else. I cannot give you references on this question, as any discussion there may be on it (unknown to me) cannot have any value. On the other hand, it is a fact that in some of the vernacular forms of the word Kṛishṇa (both as an adjective meaning ' black ' and as the name of a river on the southeastern coast) a ' *t* ' often appears. Thus, in Kanarese you have Kṛiṣṇa, Kṛṣṭṇa, Kṛiṣṭṇa, Kṛṣṭa, and Kiṭṭa, for the Sanskrit Kṛṣṇa. The Anglo-Indian form of the name is *Kistna*. In Kanarese and Malayālam, ' Christian ' appears in the form of *Kristiina*, ' Christ ' as *Kristi;* in Tamil, ' Christ ' appears as *Kiristi*."

Similarly, Mr. Blumhardt, university lecturer on the modern Indian dialects at Oxford, writes: " The Bengāli always pronounce *shn* as *sht*, with a nasalisation of the vowel. So Kṛṣṇa becomes *Kristan*. Next ' *r* ' is dropped, and the final inherent ' *a* ' is sounded like ' ö.'

---

[1] See *Chips from a German Workshop*, F. Max Müller, vol. IV, pp. 210–213.

[2] In a letter to the present writer.

Thus we have *Kishton,* which form is perhaps more common than *Krishton.* The similarity of the name with Christ is purely accidental."[1]

From the above-quoted expert information it is quite clear that all theories of the type of Mr. Del Mar's (who appears to be followed blindly by Professor Drews) of a pre-Christian Hindu cult-god "Crishna," equatable with "Christ" (and "Jesus"), are merely unconfirmed guesses with no basis of fact underlying them.

Finally, Krishna, who (as Professor Drews declares) in the oldest Indian literature (the Vedas) appears to be not a sun-god—*i. e.,* an incarnation of Vishnu—but a *demon,* is, only *after* the Christian era, transformed into a divine being through the agency of such comparatively late works as the *Purāṇas.*[2] Hence a later Christian origin of those episodes in the complete Krishna legend which resemble stories found in the Gospels is the most feasible explanation.[3]

[1] It may also be added that the two names have a fundamentally different signification: Christ = "Anointed"; Krishna = "the Black one."

[2] See Jacob's *Manual of Hindu Pantheism,* "The Vedantasāra" (1891), and Weber in the *Indian Antiquary,* II, p. 285. The *Vishnu Purāṇa* dates from about the ninth or tenth century A. D., the *Bhāgavata Purāṇa* from about the thirteenth century A. D.

On this question Mr. J. M. Robertson very lamely remarks (*Christianity and Mythology,* p. 302): "The lateness of Puranic stories in literary form is no argument against their antiquity. Scholars are agreed that late documents often preserve extremely old mythic material." This statement contains a germ of truth; but we may add that the lateness of Gospel stories in literary form is invariably regarded as strong evidence against their antiquity—and this even by Christian critics.

[3] Several other alleged parallels to the Jewish-Christian idea of a Messiah (Christ) have been suggested: *e. g.,* (1) When the Babylonian plague-god Dibbarra attacks the city Erech, chaos reigns in the place and district until after a time the Akkadian will come, overthrow all, and conquer all of them. The anointed saviour who will remedy all this is Hammurabi, who will open up a golden age of peace and prosperity (*Relig. of Bab. and Assyr.,* M. Jastrow, Jr.; *cf.* Mark 13 : 8–12, and Matt. 10 : 21). (2) A Buddhist parallel is also quoted (see Rhys David's Hibb. Lects., 1881, p. 141; *cf.* also Cheyne, *Jewish Religious Life,* p. 101, and *Enc. Bib.,* art. "Messiah," sec. 10).

Pre-Christian Christ and Jesus Cults

"There was . . . not merely a pre-Christian Christ, as Gunkel admits, a belief in the death and resurrection of Christ in Judæo-syncretist circles [refer to Gunkel's *Zum Religionsgeschichtl. Verständnis des Neuen Test.* (1903), p. 82], but there was also a pre-Christian Jesus, as Jesus and Christ were only two different names for the suffering and rising servant of God, the root of David [Jesse] in Isaiah, and the two might be combined when one wished to express the high-priesthood of the Messianic character of Jesus. Jesus was merely the general name of the saviour and redeemer. . . ." Thus writes Professor Drews in his more recent supplementary work, *The Witnesses to the Historicity of Jesus* (1912), p. 200.

Now, if we understand Professor Drews aright, there are two, or rather three, propositions laid down here, all of a highly disputable character. First, it seems to be maintained that there was in pre-Christian times an esoteric *Christ-cult*, of Judaic origin, in which a worship of (or at least a belief in) a divine redeemer was the chief cult-doctrine; secondly, that there was also a similar and contemporaneous *Jesus-cult* (?) of Ephraimitic origin— possibly connected with an old tribal and *solar* god; thirdly, that these two concepts later on became one and the same.[1] Let us proceed to consider this thesis with all due care and impartiality and see upon what basis it rests.

[1] Mr. Robertson (*Christianity and Mythology*, pp. 326 ff.) and Professor Drews (*The Christ Myth*, pp. 79–82) lay great stress upon an alleged pre-Christian twofold idea of a Messiah Ben David and a Messiah Ben Joseph, Drews also (*loc. cit.*) advancing the theory that our Gospels represent "a reconciliation and fusion of the two concepts." The idea of an unsuccessful Ephraimitic Messiah is certainly found highly developed in the *Talmud*, but even its existence in pre-Christian times is problematical (see *Enc. Bib.*, art. "Messiah," sec. 9).

Christ-cults

As regards the pre-Christian Christ, the whole of the valid part of the argument in its favour really turns upon the meaning to be attached to two particular portions of the Old Testament Scriptures—Psalm 22 and Isaiah 53.[1] The two rival interpretations of these documents—both probably referring to the "suffering Servant of Jahveh"—are that the respective writers had in their minds either (1) an individual suffering, dying, and rising "superman," or divine man, or God, or (2) that they (primarily, at least) referred to the collective remnant of Israel and its sufferings during and after the exile and subsequent restoration to God's favour.

Now, it is a remarkable but at the same time indisputable fact that all the extant Jewish literature, both pre and post exilic, apocalyptic and apocryphal alike, and even such notices as we meet with in the greater writing prophets, invariably depict the future Messiah ("Christ") as a triumphant conqueror and prince who will in some way restore the ancient glories of Israel and abase the enemies of God's ancient people.[2] Even for

[1] Gressmann even goes so far as to suggest that chap. 53 is really a hymn belonging to the "mystery" of the Adonis-cult, sung by Jewish *mystæ* on that god's death-day, and celebrating his birth, death, and resurrection. But there are many and great objections to this view: *e. g.*, Adonis is always depicted as a beautiful youth, whereas the "servant" has "no comeliness" and is "despised and rejected of men." There are also other differences. Isaiah 53 : 12 was interpreted by post-Christian (and probably by pre-Christian) Jews of *Moses*, who poured out his soul unto death (Ex. 33 : 32), and was numbered with the transgressors (those who died in the wilderness), and bare the sins of many that he might atone for the sin of the golden calf (*Sōṭāh.*, 14).

[2] The present writer has worked out this view at some length in his *Jesus the Christ: Historical or Mythical?* (1912), chap. 1, to which the reader is referred. Drews, however, claims (*The Christ Myth*, p. 79) that besides Psalm 22 and Isaiah 53, "in Daniel 9 : 26 mention is made of a dying Christ." This is a difficult passage but probably has no true Messianic meaning. Driver quotes Bleek's view of it, as representing that of many

Philo Judæus—a contemporary of Jesus and a man well versed in the mystical interpretation of the Old Testament Scriptures—the Messiah is to be a man of war, who will crush all the foes of Judah.[1] There is no Jewish literature extant—except, possibly, Psalm 22 and Isaiah 53—that lend any support to the theory of a pre-Christian doctrine of a suffering and rising Christ as being in vogue amongst the Jews, and if such a notion were entertained by any Judæo-syncretist circles they have most carefully and successfully refrained from placing their views on record in any literary form.

On the other hand, the interpretation that the Servant meant the faithful remnant who returned from the exile has been the view held by Jewish teachers in all ages and was the universal interpretation in the time of Jesus.

Jesus-cults

The first English writer to urge this hypothesis in any full and systematic manner was Mr. J. M. Robertson,[2] who states his theory as follows: "That Joshua is a purely mythical personage was long ago decided by the historical criticism of the school of Colenso and Kuenen; that he was originally a solar deity can be established at least as satisfactorily as the solar character of Moses, if not as that of Samson. And when we note that in Semitic tradition (which preserves a variety of myths which the Bible-makers, for obvious reasons, suppressed or transformed) Joshua is the son of the mythical Miriam,[3] that is to say, there was probably an ancient Palestinian sun-

modern scholars. For particulars of this, see Driver's *Lit. of the O. T.*, *s. v.* "Daniel," C, 9, and *cf.* the LXX reading of the passage.

[1] καταστρατάρχων καὶ πολεμῶν ἔθνη.

[2] See especially his *Christianity and Mythology* (1900), pp. 82 and 83. He has since been followed by Professor W. B. Smith; see his *Der Vorchristliche Jesus* (1906), *passim.*

[3] Citing Baring Gould, *Legends of O. T. Characters* (1871), II, 138. The statement rests wholly upon a comparatively modern and untrustworthy Arab tradition.

god, Jesus the son of Mary, we are led to surmise that
the elucidation of the Christ-myth is not yet complete."
The inference drawn from this is, of course, that Jesus
Christ was merely a later reflex of the same mythic idea.[1]

It would be, indeed, difficult to meet with a fuller or
more complete tissue of assumptions than we have here.
It is not going too far to state that not a single one of the
above statements has been decided at all.   The whole of
this theory still remains a pure speculation with just sufficient plausibility to render it a debatable proposition.

But let us leave Mr. Robertson and turn to a writer
who is more precise and careful in his presentment of
the case for a pre-Christian Jesus.   Professor W. B.
Smith starts from the statement found in Acts 18 : 25,
that Apollos preached "the things of Jesus" (τὰ περὶ τοῦ
Ἰησοῦ) while he was only acquainted with the baptism
of John.   These "things," he supposes, refer to some
doctrines peculiar to an old cult-god named Jesus, who
was worshipped by the Baptist and his followers.

But the explanation added by the author of the Acts,
when rightly understood, gives the true key to the meaning of this brief expression.   John's baptism was merely
one of repentance as a necessary preliminary to the
recognition and acceptance of the Coming One (ὁ Ἐρχόμενος).   Of the doctrines of this Coming One, and, apparently, even of his identity, John seems to have had very
little definite knowledge.[2]   It is not probable that John
was the head, or representative, of any society, or cult,
or that he had any cult-doctrines to impart.   He seems

[1] Weinel says of this theory of identity (*Ist das liberale Jesusbild wider-
legt?*, p. 91) that any argument based upon the connexion of Jesus with
Joshua is "simply grotesque."   And he carries with him the great mass of
scholars.

[2] It is true that, according to one account (John 1 : 36), the Baptist once
identified Jesus with him; but the synoptists state that just before his
execution John sent to Jesus to ask whether he were really the One or
whether they had still to look for him elsewhere (see Matt. 11 : 3; Luke
7 : 19 and 20).

to have been an individual bearing a certain likeness to
the prophets of old, who felt himself compelled to come
forward to announce the speedy advent of the expected
Messiah, to say that the latter was at hand. And with
this view the Gospels agree. Such doctrines as the
cross, the resurrection, and the gift of the Holy Spirit
were yet to be unfolded.[1] This passage, in fact, affords
no proof, or even presumption, of the existence of an
ancient cult of Jesus-worshippers with peculiar doctrines
which then required (so to speak) bringing up to date.

Another supposed indication of the existence of a pre-
Christian Jesus-cult (or cults) is derived from an obscure
sect called the *Jessaioi*,[2] referred to by Epiphanius (fourth
century A. D., *Hær.*, XXIX), and believed by him to have
been in existence before the time of Christ. Professor
von Soden thinks (*Hat Jesus gelebt?*, English translation, p. 28; *cf.* Isaiah 11 : 1–10; I Sam. 16 : 1; Romans 15 : 12) that their name was derived from Jesse.
"Perhaps," he says, "it was a sect which believed in the
Messiah, and expected him, as the Son of David, to come
of the root of Jesse, or Isai." Professor Drews, on the
other hand, would prefer to think that they were more
probably named after an old cult-god—Jesus.

But we cannot place any confidence here in Epiphanius, who was a prejudiced and credulous man. No other
ancient author even mentions these sectaries amongst
the numerous bodies of heretics.

It is also impossible to draw any conclusions as to a
Jesus-cult from their name; nor can we be even moder-
ately certain that they existed at all in pre-Christian
times. Much the same also may be said of the *Naasenes*,
or *Ophites* (serpent-worshippers), a Gnostic sect whose
chief tenet was belief in a spiritual Christ-æon, who de-

[1] The disciples of John are differentiated in the Acts and elsewhere by
their lack of the pentecostal gifts.
[2] Ἰεσσαῖοι; also "Jessaer," "Jessaes," and "Jessenes."

scended into the material chaos to assist Sophia (Wisdom) in her efforts to emancipate the pre-existing souls of men from the bondage of matter. This Christ-æon for a time tenanted the body of Jesus, entering it at his baptism and leaving it before his crucifixion.

But here, again, the Christian flavour, which is discernible in their doctrines, probably dates from after the time of Jesus. We have no proof whatever that these elements existed among the original tenets of the serpent-worshippers.

A great deal has also recently been made out of the ancient Naasene hymn, preserved by Hippolytus (*Ref. of All Her.*, V, 5). After describing the woes and sufferings of the human soul during its wanderings upon earth,[1] the writer of the hymn continues:

> " But Jesus said: Father, behold
> a war of evils has arisen upon the earth;
> it comes from thy breath, and ever works:
> Man strives to shun this bitter chaos,
> but knows not how he may pass (safely) through it;
> therefore, do thou, O Father, send me:
> bearing thy seals I will descend (to earth);
> throughout the ages I will pass;
> all mysteries I will unfold,
> all forms of godhead I will unveil,
> all secrets of thy holy path
> styled GNOSIS (knowledge) I will impart [to man]."

Now, this hymn—of which the above quotation forms the concluding part—shows clearly that this sect, *after* the time of Christ, professed a theosophical form of Christianity. But we have no evidence to show that they did so before that time, and the identification of the Saviour-æon with Jesus is more likely (in the absence of evidence to the contrary) to be a post-Christian im-

---

[1] Metempsychosis (transmigration) is probably meant here. The hymn in its present form is very corrupt and has been much interpolated.

provement upon an older scheme of pagan Gnosticism.
Moreover, we do not know, even approximately, the date
of this hymn. Professor W. B. Smith cautiously remarks
that it is "old—no one can say how old"—a sufficiently
vague statement. Professor Drews subsequently goes
beyond this, and tells us that it is, "according to all appearances, a pre-Christian hymn." It would be interesting to learn what proofs there are of this; but these
are not vouchsafed to us. The mere fact that these
Naasenes made use of both St. Paul's epistles and the
fourth Gospel certainly suggests very strongly that the
semi-Christian flavour of their system was derived from
post-Christian sources. Moreover, even in the later
form of their doctrines, Jesus is not a "god" in any real
sense of the term—least of all a dying and rising god. He
is merely the temporary embodiment of one of the *æons*
of the *Plerōma*, who comes down to impart divine and
saving knowledge (Γνῶσις) to mankind. This fact, indeed, in itself entirely refutes the theory that the Naasenes worshipped a dying and reviving cult-god of any
kind, as the modern mythicist would have us believe both
the pre- and post-Christian "Jesuists" and "Christists"
did.

But the most plausible argument advanced so far is
found in the document known as the *Parisian Magic
Papyrus*, the date of which is referred to the fourth or
fifth century A. D. In this the following lines occur:

l. 1549. ὁρκιζω σε κατα του μαρπακουριθ' νασααρι.
l. 3119. ὁρκιζω σε κατα του θεου των Εβραιων Ιησου
[Ιαβαιη].

Here νασααρι is identified with *Naṣaria* and made inter-
changeable with του θεου των Εβραιων 'Ιησου, the whole
being understood to mean, "I conjure you by the Protector"; "I conjure you by Jesus the god of the Hebrews"
—these being *formulæ* used in the exorcising of demons.

Here, once more, we have not a shred of evidence to show that these *formulæ* are, in their present shape at least, pre-Christian. It is, indeed, far more probable that the document, if it dates in any form from before the time of Christ, was interpolated with the name Jesus after this had gained repute as a word of power (*cf.* Acts 3 : 6; 4 : 10; 19 : 13 with Mark 9 : 38; Luke 9 : 49). In short, there are no safe indications here either of a pre-Christian cult of any kind.[1] Indeed, Professor Drews seems to be conscious of the weakness of this part of the current mythical hypothesis; for at one of the public discussions, held in Germany during 1910, he was careful to insist that his *thesis* that the Founder of Christianity was a purely mythical character did not depend upon the existence of a pre-Christian cult-god named Jesus, thus differing from both Robertson and Smith, who make it the basis and main support of their respective theories.

Finally, in regard to the statement that the two ideas —a "Christ" and a "Jesus"—might be combined, and that Jesus was merely the general name for the saviour and redeemer, it would be interesting to learn where, in pre-Christian literature, the expected Messiah, or Christ, is, by anticipation, named Jesus,[2] or the expectation itself

[1] As against the cult-god theory, the following passages in the Gospels should be carefully studied: Matt. 16 : 22 *f.*; 20 : 17–19; Mark 8 : 31–33; 9 : 31; 10 : 33; Luke 9 : 22–24. The synoptists unanimously declare that when Jesus announced his resolve to become a sacrifice at Jerusalem his disciples rejected this view of the Messianic office, Luke adding that "they understood none of these things." Had the disciples been members of a cult or brotherhood worshipping a suffering Messiah, or a cult-god named Jesus, as Professor Drews postulates, it would have been at once intelligible to them and they would have been represented as encouraging him in his resolution.

[2] Professor Drews appears to think (*The Witnesses to the Historicity of Jesus*, p. 195) that because "Matthew" says that the Child of Mary was to be called Jesus (1 : 21), and then identifies him with the virgin's son of Isaiah 7 : 14 (Matt. 1 : 23), Immanuel "is also the meaning of Jesus"! This is not so in the sense required by his theory; and, moreover, would be, in any case, *post-* (and not pre-) Christian evidence for that hypothesis. For an analysis and discussion of the Hebrew word *â-lmah*, and its Greek

regarded as in any sense identical with the cultual worship of a god of that name who had previously effected a temporal salvation for the Hebrew people. Until this evidence is forthcoming the theory must remain a mere unsubstantiated speculation.

equivalents, παρθένος and νεᾶνις, see the present writer's *A Critical Examination of the Evidences for the Doctrine of the Virgin Birth*, Appendix E (1908).

CHAPTER V

Bethlehem

IT is, perhaps, somewhat remarkable, in view of modern controversies respecting the birth of Jesus, that there should be in Palestine two places bearing the name of Bethlehem. The less famous of these, now represented by the little village called *Beit Lahm*, is situated about seven miles northwest of the present town of Nazareth. It is mentioned in the book of Joshua (19 : 15), where it is stated to be a portion of "the inheritance of the children of Zebulun." [1]

The other Bethlehem—about six miles from Jerusalem —often distinguished from the former by the addition of the word "Judah" (Judges 17 : 8 and 9; 19 : 18; Ruth 1 : 1), or "Ephratah" (Micah 5 : 2), is generally supposed to have derived the latter appellation from being situated in a district so named (I Sam. 17 : 12). *Bēthlehem Ephratāh* (בֵּית־לֶחֶם אֶפְרָתָה) is the reading of the Massoretic text in Micah 5 : 2, though here the LXX has "Bethlehem house of Ephratah" (Βηθλεὲμ οἶκος [τοῦ] Ἐφραθά), which doubtless has suggested to Professor G. A. Smith the omission of *-lehem* and the writing of the word "Beth-Ephratah." The usual interpretation of Bethlehem, "house of bread," and of Ephratah, "fruitful," are no doubt allusions to the former fertility of the district. A doubtful proposal, however, has recently been made to find in Bethlehem the name of the

[1] In the *Talmud* it is termed צריה, commonly regarded as a corruption of נצרייה, "of Nazareth."

89

god *Lakhmu,* which is known to us from the opening
of the Babylonian creation epic. But here Professor
König protests (*Expository Times,* September, 1913, p.
547): "Are we to suppose," he asks, "that even David
worshipped Lachmu in Bethlehem?" And he points
out that the prefix "Beth- also occurs in combination
with many other words which do not designate any god,
as, for instance, in Beth Diblathayim."[1]

Now, since many modern scholars, including the vast
majority of German critics, while holding to the historicity of Jesus, reject the traditional place of his birth for
one which they would place in Galilee, it might be worth
while to consider whether there has been, either before
or subsequent to the time of Christ, any confusion between these two Bethlehems. If the Messiah really were
ever said to have been, or to be destined to be, born
in Galilee, according to some Ephraimitic or northern
tradition now lost, then the Bethlehem Zebulun—if that
place were named either in tradition or prophecy—
might possibly have been changed by the compilers of
the two birth-stories to Bethlehem-Judah (Ephratah),
in order to fulfil the prophecy recorded in our present
text of the book of Micah.[2] Such a theory, however,
would seem to have very little, if any, evidence to support it.

Turning now to the views of the present-day mythicists, we find Professor Drews asserting a theory somewhat similar. The Messiah of the *Israelite*-myth was,
he says (*The Christ Myth,* p. 81), to be undoubtedly a
Galilean by birth; but the authors of the birth-narra-
tives "invented the abstruse story of the journey of his
parents to Bethlehem" in order to connect Jesus with

[1] Professor Sayce, however, says (*Patriarchal Palestine,* p. 82): "Mr.
Tomkins is probably right in seeing even in Bethlehem the name of the
primeval Chaldean deity *Lakhmu*" (later *Anu; cf.* also *op. cit.,* p. 260).

[2] Or, perchance, altered previously in the text of Micah by the Massoretic redactors?

the House of David, from which the southern, or *Judah-ite*, mythical Messiah was to be descended (Micah 5 : 2).

Mr. J. M. Robertson, on the other hand, has a rather different explanation of the choice of Bethlehem. It was selected purely for mythical reasons. "The cave of Bethlehem," he asserts (*Christianity and Mythology*, p. 329), "had been from time immemorial a place of worship in the cult of Tammuz, as it actually was in the time of Jerome; and, as the quasi-historic David bore the name of the sun-god Daoud, or Dodo (Sayce, Hibb. Lects., pp. 56 and 57), who was identical with Tammuz, it was not improbable on that account that Bethlehem was traditionally the city of David, and therefore, no doubt, was deemed by the New Testament myth-makers the most suitable place for the birth of Jesus,[1] the mythical descendant of that quasi-historical monarch and the pseudo-historical embodiment of the god Tammuz, or Adonis." We will take Mr. Robertson's view of the matter first of all.

The statement that Bethlehem had been "from time immemorial a place of worship in the cult of Tammuz" has no historical foundation. The emperor Hadrian, it is said, to annoy the Jews, set up an image of Venus (the mother of Adonis) on the site of the temple at Jerusalem, while the Christians were similarly punished by the devastation of Bethlehem and the planting of a grove dedicated to Adonis upon the spot (Jerome, *Ep. ad Paul.*, 58, 3). Whether the cult of the latter god had ever been previously carried on in that place is wholly unknown (see Frazer, *Adonis, Attis, Osiris*, 3d ed., vol. I, p. 257). As regards his further speculation that Bethlehem was probably called "the city of David," because the king thus designated "bore the name of the

---

[1] *Cf.* the extraordinary statement in the *Jerusalem Talmud* (Berakhoth, f. 5, 1) that the Messiah was born at Bethlehem on the day of the destruction of Jerusalem, but carried off from his mother by a strong gale!

sun-god Daoud, or Dodo," who was worshipped there,
Doctor Sayce (quoted by Mr. Robertson) also points
out that while Tammuz bore the epithet (not name)
Dōd ("beloved"), the same word is also used of Jahveh,
who is addressed as *Dōdi* ("my beloved," Isaiah 5 : 1),
and he truly adds: "We can easily understand how a
name of this kind, with such a signification, should have
been transferred by popular affection from the deity
[Jahveh] to the king, of whom it is said that 'all Israel
and Judah loved him' (I Sam. 18 : 6)."

There can be little doubt, therefore, that Bethlehem
was called the city of David, not from a local worship of
Adonis carried on there, but because all Hebrew tradition unanimously declared that the beloved king was the
son of a great sheep-master of Bethlehem and was born
and spent his early youth in that place.[1]

Thus Mr. Robertson's hypothesis, all through, is, to
say the least of it, purely speculative and improbable.

Professor Drews's theory of an abstruse story of a journey to Bethlehem, invented to secure for Jesus a place
in the pedigree of the Davidic, or southern, Messiah,
can now be most satisfactorily met by showing that the
story referred to is neither so entirely abstruse nor necessarily such a pure invention as it was somewhat hastily
decided to be by Strauss and later mythicists. The recent researches of Sir W. M. Ramsay have now at least
practically settled two much-disputed historical points
in connexion with the birth-story, viz.: (1) that Quirinus was, as Luke states, governing Syria about the
time of the first census (9–8 B. C.) ordered by Augustus,
and (2) the fact that all persons residing out of their
own proper *nomes* had to return thither for registration
therein.[2] In view of these important facts, so long con-

---

[1] David has been explained as meaning either (1) "beloved," (2) "pa-
ternal uncle" (pron. דוֹד), or (3) as an abbreviation of *Dōdijah*, "Jahveh
is patron" (= *Dodai*)—best of all.

[2] See Appendix A (1).

tested, it is for Professor Drews to demonstrate more
clearly that this particular journey must have been a
pure invention and wholly contrary to established customs.   Moreover, that simple and unsophisticated writers
like the synoptists, in telling this straightforward story,
made such an elaborate and artificial selection from alleged rival and conflicting Messianic expectations, and invented the stories, is in the highest degree unlikely. Such
a view demands considerably greater proof than has been
adduced so far.

Nazareth

Professor Drews is extremely doubtful about the very
existence of Nazareth in pre-Christian times (*The Christ
Myth*, p. 59; *cf. The Witnesses to the Historicity of Jesus*,
p. 200). His chief reason for this doubt is: "Such a place
is not mentioned either in the Old Testament or in the
Talmud, which, however, mentions more than sixty Galilean towns, nor again by the Jewish historian Josephus,
nor in the Apocrypha."

This seems, at first sight, a formidable array of adverse
evidence, though only of a negative type. But when we
look further into the matter such testimony is by no
means convincing. That a small and insignificant village (*cf*. John 1 : 46), buried miles away in the remote
Galilean hills, should not be mentioned in our extant
Jewish records is in no way remarkable. Why should it
be referred to? Nothing ever happened there. It had—
in pre-Christian days and from the point of view of the
writers of the Old Testament and the Apocrypha, as also
from that of Josephus—no importance whatever. The
compilers of the Talmud, too, which is believed to have
begun to take a written form towards the end of the
second century, must have at least known of its existence in the fourth century, and for some time previously,
although they do not refer to it; for Epiphanius ob-

serves (*Hær.*, I, 136) that *until* the time of Constantine it was inhabited only by Jews, while Jerome refers (*Ep.* 86) to Paula passing through it in his time. Accordingly, if before the fourth century A. D. there was a village of that name peopled exclusively by Jews, it is clear that the place did not, at a comparatively late date, owe its origin and name to mythical Christian tradition and piety, while it is also probable that it must have existed there for some time before the reign of Constantine. We cannot, of course, absolutely prove this, owing to the paucity of records; but it is, nevertheless, the most likely explanation of the facts of the case as these are known to us.[1]

Again, in replying to the argument of Weiss that it "cannot be denied that it was firmly believed by the Christians of the first century that Jesus came from Nazareth," Drews can merely say that this statement "is based on the unproved assumption that the Gospels already existed then in their present form."

It is true that here, again, owing to the literary barrenness of the first century, we have little evidence of an external character as to the dates of the canonical Gospels. Still, there is a great mass of internal evidence,

[1] *The Jewish Encyclopædia*, art. "Nazareth," says that "Eleazir Kalir (eighth and ninth centuries A. D.), in the elegy 'Ekah Yashebah,' mentions the priestly class of Nazareth (נצרה = 'Mishmeret'), doubtless on the basis of some ancient authority." Doctor Cheyne's latest views on Nazareth are expressed in his *Fresh Voyages in Unfrequented Waters* (1914): Nazareth is an old synonym for Gālil, *i. e.*, the southern Galilee. The old form of the synonym is Resin or Rezon. But this, again, is a corruption of Bar-Sin, and Bar-Sin is a shortened form of Arab-Sibon, which is Arabian Ishmael, which is—Jeraḥme'el! The ending of Nazareth, however (*-eth*), shows that it was really the name of a goddess, not of a town. Finally, "the original form of the gracious deity's name was Yarḥu-Asshur-Rabṣinath" —a remarkable genealogy!

Paul Haupt regards Nazareth as the new name of the old city Hinnatuni (Hinnathon, Joshua 19 : 44; Hethlon [?], Ezek. 47 : 15. *The Open Court*, April, 1909, p. 198). Their common meaning is supposed to be "defense"; but this and the identifications are very doubtful.

chiefly appreciable by scholars and impossible to detail here, which goes a very long way to establish that conclusion. And even to the ordinary reader it is very obvious that the synoptic Gospels, at least, differ wholly in their literary style and phraseology, as well as in matter, from all extant documents of the second and third, and later, centuries. The ideas which they contain, the references and local colour, no less than the ethical and spiritual standpoint, all belong undoubtedly to the first century A. D. And these facts, amongst others, are at any rate very strong proofs of a relative, if not absolute, character in their favour.

Nazoraean

For an explanation of this designation of Jesus the modern mythicist usually pins his faith to a critical theory advanced by Professor W. B. Smith in his *Der Vorchristliche Jesus* (1906) and repeated in *Ecce Deus* (1912). According to this hypothesis, Jesus derived it from being the cult-god of a sect who were known as Nazoraeans (Ναζωραῖοι),[1] and had existed in pre-Christian times (see Epiphanius, *Hær.*, XXIX, 6).

Professor Smith's derivation of the title and its meaning may be summarised as follows (*Der Vorchristliche Jesus*, pp. 142 *ff.*; *cf.* 36 *f.*; also *The Monist*, 1905, "The Meaning of the Epithet Nazorean," pp. 25 *ff.*). It comes, he says, from an old Hebrew root NṢR [or NZR], which has the meaning of "guardian," "protector," or

---

[1] The chief codices vary between Ναζωραῖος, Ναζορᾶος, Ναζαραῖος, Νασαραῖος, and Ναζαρηνός, the last-mentioned being very frequent in the MSS. generally, but the first-named now appears uniformly in critical texts. Similarly, the town is commonly written Ναζαρέθ or Ναζαρέτ; Ναζαρά is also found in some MSS., and Keim (*Jesus of Nazara*) argues strongly in favour of this reading, and regards Ναζαρηνός (Nazarene) as a true derivative from it. When the common readings have been corrected, and Jesus appears as the "Nazoraean," there are yet six passages left (Mark 1 : 9; Matt. 2 : 23; 21 : 11; Luke 2 : 4; John 1 : 45 and 46; also Acts 10 : 38) where Nazareth appears as a place.

"keeper." This view is adopted by Drews, who adds (*The Witnesses to the Historicity of Jesus*, p. 202): "In his [Smith's] opinion the name can be traced to the ancient root N-Z-R, which means something like watcher, protector, guardian, saviour. Hence Jesus the Nazoraean, or Nazarene, was Jesus the protector, just as Jahveh (Psalm 121 : 5) or the archangel Michael, the angel-prince, who often takes the place of the Messiah, is known as the 'protector of Israel,'[1] its spokesman with God, and its deliverer from all its cares (Daniel 19 : 13; 12 : 1; Gen. 48 : 16); the rabbinical Metatron also plays this part of protector and supporter of the Jewish people, and is regarded as the angel of redemption, especially of the damned suffering in hell. The followers of Jesus will, therefore, have called themselves Nazoraeans[2] because they primarily conceived the expected Messiah in the sense of a Michael or Metatron, a protector; that is, at all events, more probable than that they took their name from the place Nazareth, with which they had no close connection. It is not at all improbable that the place Nazareth took its name from the sect of the Nazoraeans, instead of the reverse, as is admitted by so distinguished a scholar as W. Nestle."[3]

---

[1] It is claimed that in the *nomen restaurationis* of Marcus (Irenæus, *Adv. Hær.*, I, 21, 3) Jesus has this surname (*Nazaria*); further, that in the *Parisian Magical Papyrus* (l. 1548), a god of that name is mentioned (see chap. 3, p. 36). In the former Jesus Nazaria is taken as Jesus *Nazar-jah, i. e.*, "Jesus (the) Protector Jah."

In reply to any objection that Jahveh as protector is described by the psalmist as *shomēr* (שֹׁמֵר), and not as *noṣēr* (נֹצֵר), Drew urges that "we are concerned here not with the word itself but its meaning." But the main point in Smith's argument seems to be the special connexion of the root NZR with divine beings as "protectors of men." The reference to Psalm 121, therefore, falls somewhat flat, as it would be more to the point to quote a case where Jahveh had the latter designation.

[2] Smith further maintains: "They were close to the Jessaioi (or Jessees), who adored the same god as *Saviour*, or *Jesus*, who were themselves nearly related to the more Hellenic Gnostics, who worshipped the same god as *Sōtēr*, or *Saviour*" (*The Open Court*, January, 1910, p. 15).

[3] Citing *Südwestdeutsche Schulblätter* (1910), Heft 4 and 5, p. 163.

This explanation of Professor Smith's is sharply criticised by Doctor Cheyne, who declares that his view of the word is impossible. "Need I remark," he writes (*Hibbert Journal*, 1911, p. 892), "that in Hebrew the guardian would be *ha-noṣer*, not *ha-noṣri?*"[1]

Professor Smith's reply to this question will be found in his *Ecce Deus* (pp. 320 and 321): "Inasmuch as three pages of *Der Vorchristliche Jesus* (47–50) are given to the consideration of this point, the answer would seem to be that one need not.[2]

"But when it is said that surely neither Hannathon nor Nazareth means *defense*, it must be said that authorities seem to differ. Professor Cheyne refers to 'Hannathon' and 'Nazareth' in the *Encyclopædia Biblica*. One may read the nine lines on 'Hannathon' and the interesting article on 'Nazareth' repeatedly without finding any reason for the statement just quoted. Professor Haupt declares: 'Both Hittalon and Ḥinnathon mean protection'—a judgment, so far as Ḥinnatuni is concerned, confirmed by other most eminent Assyriologists. As to Nazareth, the force of the termination may be uncertain, *even as the termination itself is*, but hardly the stem Nazar, which appears in the older form Nasaraioi; and about the Hebrew *Naṣar* (to guard) there is no doubt." . . . "Nasaree was a religious term or designation; it expressed some religious peculiarity of the sect that bore it; and when the multiplied conceits of linguistic ingenuity are all finally laid to rest, the obvious

---

[1] The Hebrew letter *Tsādē* (צ) is variously transliterated as *ts*, *ç*, *tz*, *ss*, and *ṣ*; also, commonly by Professor Smith (in *Naṣar*), as *z*; *e. g.*, *Nazar*. Modern Hebraists generally write *Naṣar* and *Naṣoraean* for Nazoraean.

[2] The Talmudic name of Jesus, *Jeshu Ha-noṣri* (יֵשׁוּ הַנּוֹצְרִי), Sanh. 43, a, etc.), seems to be strong evidence against Smith's theory. Similarly, *Noṣrim* (נוֹצְרִים) cannot be the "protectors." Smith's contention, however, is that either *Ha-noṣri* = *Ha-noṣer* (הַנּוֹצֵר) or it is a rabbinical disguise of that term, or, again, more probably, an abbreviation of N Ṣ R I H, "keeper of Jahveh," or "Jahveh, the keeper."

reference will be seen to be to the perfectly familiar and apparent Hebrew stem *naṣar* (to guard). As Winckler has so well expressed it: 'From the concept *neçer* [or *neṣer*] is named the religion of those who believe on the "Saviour"; Nazarene Christians and Nazairier. Nazareth, as the home of Jesus, forms only a confirmation of his saviour nature in the symbolising play of words.' The notions of guardian and saviour are so closely akin that *servator* and *salvator* are used almost interchangeably as applied to the Jesus."

It is extremely difficult—not to say hazardous—for any one who is not a specialist in Hebrew[1] to pronounce definitely upon the point at issue here. Nevertheless, it seems to the present writer that, so far, the balance of evidence lies with the Hebraists as against the mythicists.

Professor Smith lays great stress upon the evidence afforded by Epiphanius in favour of his theory—that "careful and erudite heresiograph," as he calls him (*The Open Court*, January, 1910, p. 14). Epiphanius says: "All men called the Christians Nazoraeans"—that is, in his time. And again: "The heresy of the Nazarees was before Christ, and knew not Christ."[2]

"There!" exclaims Smith, "the cat is out of the bag." But is it? Let us examine into the matter a little more carefully.

Beginning with the statements of Epiphanius, we have: "The heresy of the Nazarees was before Christ, *and knew not Christ.*" Surely, if this means anything, it is that Jesus Christ was not a cult-god of this sect! Further, Epi-

---

[1] Drews affirms (*The Witnesses to the Historicity of Jesus*, p. 202, note 2) that "Schmiedel has recently maintained against Weinel, in the *Protestantenblatt* (1910, no. 17, p. 438), that Smith's hypothesis is philologically admissible. Hence the charge of 'gross ignorance of the Semitic languages,' which Weinel brings against Smith, is quite unjustified."

[2] *Hær.*, XXIX, 6, ἦν γὰρ ἡ αἵρεσις τῶν Νασαραίων πρὸ Χριστοῦ, καὶ Χριστὸν οὐκ ᾔδει. Ἀλλὰ καὶ πάντες ἄνθρωποι τοὺς Χριστιανοὺς Ναζωραίους ἐκάλουν. . . .

phanius gives a very confused account of them, and seems
to think that, while the Nazoraeans were Christians, the
Nazaraeans (Nazarees) were Jews.[1] Indeed, his statements about them all through are both careless and un-
critical, and this fact alone detracts greatly from their
value as really serious evidence in the case.

Again, Marcus, who is called in as witness (p. 96, note
1), was a *second*-century heretic, and the statement that
the invocation of Jesus Nazaria "goes back very obviously and probably to the remotest antiquity" has no
historical evidence to back it. Neither has it been shown
that the Νασααρι of the Paris magical formula is connected with the Ναζωραῖος of the New Testament. And,
even if it be considered as proved that Nazoraean means
"guardian," it still remains to be shown that this word
is practically identical in meaning with Jesus, and still
more that either Jesus or Nazoraios was a pre-Christian
cult-god.

As a matter of fact, however, from the stem N Z R (נצר)
comes also the substantive *nēzĕr*, or *nēṣĕr* (נֵצֶר), "shoot,"
"branch"—and, figuratively, "scion" (*cf*. Isaiah 9 : 21;
60 : 21). And in 11 : 1 the prophet promises that a
"branch" (or "scion") of the stem of Jesse shall be
born; it seems, therefore, most probable that this is
what is referred to by Matthew when he says that it was
predicted by prophets that Jesus should be called a
Nazoraean.[2] He plays (so to say) upon the similarity
between the two words *as regards their three root letters*,
and declares in effect that the *N*(a)*z*(o)*r*-aean represents

---

[1] See Meyboom, "Jezus de Nazoraer," *Theol. Tijdschrift*. (1905), pp.
529 *ff*. *Cf*. Lepsius, *Zur Quellenkritik des Epiphanios* (1865), pp. 130 *ff*.

[2] " 'Ναζωραῖος κληθήσεται' summarises the prophecies referred to. Isaiah
11 : 1 had called the Messiah (so Targ.) נצר = branch; Jer. 23 : 5; 33 : 15
had called him צמה branch, and Isaiah 4 : 2, צמה (Targ. has 'Messiah')."
Archdeacon Allen on St. Matthew *in loco*. The Arabic name for Christians
(*Nasārā, Koran*, Sura V) has been derived from *nasara*, "to help," but this
is doubtful.

the N(e)z(e)r-æan,[1] whose coming was foretold in prophecy, not any "watchman-god" or "guardian-god" of some
ancient cult-idea.

Finally—and Doctor Cheyne's explanation of the origin and meaning of "Nazareth" supports the conclusion
—it is also probable that *The Nazōraean*, or *Naṣoraean*
means simply "The Galilean," a name by which Jesus,
especially later on, was known, and particularly by pagan
writers. The present-day Mohammedan designation of
Christians as Nazarenes (*i. e.*, Naṣoraeans) is merely the
equivalent of Galileans, as the Emperor Julian always
insisted on their being called, *i. e.*, followers of the Prophet
from Galilee.[2]

After references to Isaiah 41 : 25; 9 : 1, 2, 3, 6, and 7
as having, in the eyes of at least many of the Jews of
the time of Christ, a Messianic significance, Professor
Drews proceeds as follows (*The Witnesses to the Historicity of Jesus*, pp. 210 and 211 and note 1):

Galilee

"It is the word of the prophet [Isaiah], not a hard
fact of history, that demands the birth of the Saviour.
Then Nazareth, with its relation to *nazar*, occurred at
once as the proper birthplace of Jesus, as soon as men
began to conceive the episode historically. Astral considerations may have co-operated. Galilee, from *gālīl*,
circle, connects with the zodiacal circle,[3] which the sun
traverses; even in the prophet the Saviour is associated
with the sun.[4] The people that walk in darkness and
that 'dwell in the land of the shadow' might easily be
identified with the 'familiar spirits' of whom Isaiah

---

[1] Ancient Hebrew was written originally without the vowel-pointing in
MSS. "Nezoraeans" would mean "Disciples of the Branch."

[2] Doctor Cheyne also notes (*Enc. Bib.*, art. "Joseph," sec. 9) that the Aramaic *n'sar* (Heb. נָשַׁר) means *to saw;* so that "Jesus the Nazarene," or (?)
"Nasarene," might merely mean "Jesus the carpenter" (*cf.* Mark 6 : 3).

[3] *Cf.* also *The Christ Myth*, p. 240.

[4] Isaiah merely compares him to the sun.

speaks (8 : 19), in whom there is no light, who 'pass through' the land 'hardly bestead and hungry; and it shall come to pass that when they shall be hungry, they shall fret themselves and curse their king and their god, and look upward; and they shall look into the earth, and behold trouble and darkness, dimness of anguish, and they shall be driven to darkness.' They suggest," he continues, "the souls in the nether world, the stars in their course below the celestial equator which rejoice at the birth of the 'great light' at the winter solstice, and are led to their time of brilliancy.[1] On this view, Galilee of the Gentiles (*Gālīl ha-goim*) coincides with the lower half of the 'water region' of the zodiac, in which are found the aquatic signs of the Southern Fish, Aquarius, the Fishes, the Whale, and Eridanus." In a note to the above he further adds: "In truth, Zebulun, according to Gen. 49, relates to the sign of the zodiac *Capricorn* and Naphtali to *Aries*, both of which belong to the water region of the zodiac, the dark part of the year (*cf.* A. Jeremias, *Das Alte Testament im Lichte des alten Orients*, p. 398). According to M. Müller, *gālīl* means, in a derivative from the Coptic, the 'water-wheel.' A water-wheel might (according to Fuhrmann) be traced in the constellation Orion, the spokes being represented by the four chief stars and the axis by the stars of the belt, the wheel being set in motion by the falling water of the Milky Way.[2] In so far as Orion is

[1] It would be interesting to know what evidence there is for the mythical interpretation of these "spirits of the dead" (*ōbōth*) as equivalent here either to the people that dwell in darkness (= distressed Israelites) or to stars "below the celestial equator"! The words here have merely a plain literal meaning. The prophet is denouncing the use of necromancy, as a means of prying into the future, and what it may bring forth, by a suffering people, and he means nothing more than this. Any such mythical interpretation would be purely modern and fanciful.

[2] Is not Professor Drews here confusing the *Milky Way* with the constellation *Eridanus?* The Chinese, however, seem to have called the Milky Way the Celestial River (*tien ho*). And the Egyptians (later) regarded the

the Hanging Figure of the 22d Psalm, we may note that the latter is a *gālīl* (Galilean), and as the constellation Orion is, as we saw,[1] astrally related to the *nazar* (the Hyades), the birth of the Saviour in Nazareth might be deduced from this (see Niemojewski, *Gott Jesus*, pp. 161 and 193)."

But to return to the text. "We thus," he continues, "understand why Galilee, 'the way to the sea, the land by the Jordan,'[2] plays so great a part in the story of Jesus; it was bound to be recognised in a Messianic age. Hence this watery region of the sky is the chief theatre of the Saviour's life; hence in the Gospels the 'Sea of Galilee,' the Sea of Gennesaret, and the many names of places in the district. For the Greeks and Romans they had no ulterior [*i. e.*, mythical] significance, and were mere names, but much like the names of places in Homer or Vergil, or the description of the voyage of the *Argonaut* by Apollonius of Rhodes. It is incredible that von Soden should seek a proof of the historicity of the Gospel narrative in these names."

Again (p. 212), he further seems to attack even the geographical existence of one of the chief towns of Galilee at that time: "It may be the same with other supposed names of places. In regard to the most important of them all, Capernaum, Steudel has called attention to Zech. 13 : 1, where it is said: 'In that day there shall be a fountain opened to the house of David and to the inhabitants of Jerusalem for sin and for uncleanness,'

Milky Way as the Heavenly Nile. Elsewhere Professor Drews speaks of it as the celestial form of the *world-tree!* And this, again, is equated with the *cross!*

[1] Note, pp. 203 and 204: "Possibly *nazar* has also an astral significance as the *Hyades* in Taurus have the form of a branch [*nazar* (? *nezer*); in Zechariah *ṣemaḥ*]; and Orion, in which we have already suspected the Baptist, seems to bring the twig (Fuhrmann)."

[2] On the next page he says that the Jordan has an astral significance in the Gospels and corresponds to the celestial *Eridanus* (Egypt., *iero*, or *iera*, "the river," see chap. 5, p. 107).

and reminds us that in his *Jewish Wars* (III, 10, 8) Josephus mentions 'a very strong' and fertilising spring 'which is called Capharnaum by the inhabitants of the district.' When we read in Josephus the description of the fish-abounding sea of Gennesaret and the country about it, with its beauty and charm, its palms, nuts and olives, and fruit-trees of all kinds, we feel that no other knowledge of the locality was needed in order to invent the whole regional background of the life of Jesus with the aid of these indications."

Now, in Isaiah 9 : 1–7 we have, in the first place, an historic reference to the northern districts of Israel, which had been ravaged by Assyria in 734 B. C. (II Kings 15 : 29), followed by a prediction that a "great light" would shine upon the desolate land and its despairing inhabitants. This relief is to come through a Davidic king, though how he is to exercise authority over a separate kingdom of Israel is not clear. Probably the text of this prophecy is corrupt, or we have not the whole of the original, or, again, the prophet perhaps contemplates a reunion by conquest, or agreement, of the two kingdoms as a part of the mission of this Messiah-prince. In 41 : 25—the work of another "Isaiah"—the deliverer, who will be raised up by God, is to be a great warrior from the northeast, *i. e.*, *Cyrus* (vs. 2), who will restore "Israel" to his own land. This is a later view of the contemplated restoration. In 11 : 1 the deliverer is to be (as in chap. 9) a Davidic prince, more definitely a "branch" (נֵצֶר) of the stock of Jesse. And here we come again to the main point in this part of Professor Drews's *thesis*. This *nēzer*, or *nēṣer* ("branch"), has *suggested to the Gospel writers a pseudo-historical Nazareth as the birthplace of this deliverer* (Jesus), *as soon as the idea came to be historicised.*[1]

[1] Similarly, Doctor Winckler (*Ex oriente lux*, Band II, 1906, p. 59, note): "From the word *neçer* comes the religion of those who believe in the

But this is just what did *not* happen! Christian tradition, as we have already pointed out, uniformly connects the *birth* of Jesus, not with Nazareth, but with Bethlehem. The Nazareth-birth is a modern critical theory and opposed to all tradition both documentary and oral. And whatever may be the origin of the place Nazareth and its relation to Jesus—it is difficult to believe that almost contemporary writers would be so foolish as to link him with a then non-existent village —we would maintain that it is more probable that (as Matthew seems to say) an actual Jesus was called the *Nazōr-aean* (*i. e., Nēzĕr-aean*) and his disciples the *Nazōr-aeans*, through a punning upon the identity of the consonants in both words, which are derived from the same Hebrew root (N Z R or N Ṣ R), than that he was a mere pseudo-embodiment of a supposed "guardian-god" which was worshipped by a sect hypothetically existent in pre-Christian days. The play upon the words is a good one in Hebrew, since the ideas of both the branch of prophecy and the domicile (Galilee) of the youth and early manhood of Jesus are combined and expressed under the same term.[1]

We will now turn, in conclusion, to the astral considerations brought forward by Professor Drews. It is very evident to a careful and thoughtful reader that, to a great extent underlying the whole conception of a mythical Jesus, there is an *a priori* astral and zodiacal theory which is *assumed* to have been current in Palestine at that time. Into this preconceived and underly-

Saviour—the Nazarene Christians, or Nazaraeans. Nazareth as the home of Jesus is *merely a confirmation of his character as Saviour for the symbolising tendency.*" (Italics ours.)

[1] *Cf.* the expression קֶדֶשׁ בַּגָּלִיל ("Kedesh in Galilee"). The view taken by Doctor E. A. Abbott, in *Miscellanea Evangelica* (1), is that "Nazarene" and "Nazoraean" are not different forms of the same adjective, but that, while the former means "man of Nazareth," the latter means the *neṣer*, or "Rod of Jesse" of Isaiah; and that the people, recognising Jesus as the life-giving healer, called him the "Nazoraean" instead of the "Nazarene."

ing framework the mythicist literally forces—as we will
see from time to time—all (or nearly all) the Gospel
narrative, whether it bears reference to persons, events,
or even places. Let us take, first of all, the term "Galilee."

The word *gālīl*, "circle," "circuit," is used in the
Bible in reference to a region containing twenty small
towns grouped round the city Kedesh,[1] inhabited mainly
by Gentile races, and hence means nothing more than district. It is so used in the lists of Tiglath-Pileser's conquests (II Kings 15 : 29; *cf.* I Kings 9 : 11) and also in
Isaiah 9 : 1 (A. V.). In the LXX we find it in the same
sense, Γαλιλαία ἀλλοφύλων, "Galilee of the Gentiles" (I
Macc. 5 : 15), and ἡ Γαλιλαία simply occurs often in I
Maccabees with the same meaning. But Professor Drews
asks us to believe that in the Gospels it has simply an
"astral" (or mystical) sense; that, in fact, Galilee represents merely the lower half, the water region, of the
zodiac. Now, what proof does he offer for this mystical
interpretation of what is, on the surface at least, a plain
historical narrative? He instances several zodiacal signs
which, he avers, find their counterparts (so to speak) in
Galilee. Let us examine these severally. *Zebulun*, he
says, relates to the sign *Capricornus* (he-goat), referring to
Gen. 49 : 13.

Now, in the "Blessing of Jacob," the dying patriarch
is made to predict mainly that the tribe will, in the future, dwell along some coast-line and engage in some kind
of maritime business (*cf.* Deut. 33 : 18 and 19). There is
certainly no reference to *Capricornus* here and no mystical meaning involved! According to Josephus (*Ant.*,
V, 1, 22), the Zebulunites were settled in the north as
far as the coast of Gennesaret and perhaps touched
the Mediterranean shores. Again, *Naphtali* is described
(Gen. 49 : 21, A. V. and R. V., *cf.* Deut. 33 : 23) as

[1] See also *Nazareth and the Beginnings of Christianity*, by C. Burrage.

"a hind (אַיָּלָה, *ăjjālāh*) let loose." This, we presume, has
suggested the zodiacal *Aries* (Ram).[1] But, unfortunately,
the Hebrew word never means a "ram" (though a word
slightly resembling it [אַיִל, *ăjil*] has that signification).
It means a "female deer," or, according to some authorities, perhaps a "wild she-goat." Moreover, the text
here is probably corrupt; for in the LXX we have in
place of the Massoretic reading N. στέλεχος ἀνειμένον ἐπι-
διδοὺς ἐν τῷ γεννήματι κάλλος ("N. [is] a growing stem
producing beauty by its budding"). Instead of אַיָּלָה,
"hind," many scholars read אֵילָה, a "spreading tere-
binth" (which seems to be implied by στέλεχος above).
The following clause, "giveth goodly words," makes no
sense with either reading. Two emendations have, therefore, been proposed as alternatives, אִמְרֵי, "producing
goodly shoots," and אִמְּרֵי, "yielding goodly lambs." This
latter would give a slight support to the theory of some
connexion with *Aries*; but it cannot have been the
original reading, since אִמֵּר, "lamb," is not Hebrew,
though it is found in Assyrian, Phœnician, Aramaic, and
Armenian. There is, in any case, here no reference to
the zodiacal *Aries*, or the dark part of the solar year,
and such exegesis can only be termed fanciful.

The connexion of the zodiacal signs mentioned by
Professor Drews with the mythical scheme seems very
vague; perhaps *Aquarius* might represent the source of
the Jordan and *Pisces* might then stand for the numerous fish to be found in Gennesaret. But, going outside
the zodiac, Professor Drews contrives to bring in several
other and southern signs.

---

[1] Mr. J. F. Blake, in his scheme of identifications of the patriarchs with
the zodiacal signs, makes *Zebulun = Pisces* and *Naphtali = Capricornus*
(*Astronomical Myths*, 1877, p. 106). Others, again, have traced the names
of the heads of the tribes to a *totemic* origin. See Professor Smith's article
on the personal totem names in the *Enc. Bib.*; Doctor H. J. D. Astley's art.
on "Totemism in the O. T.," in *The Quest* for April, 1912.

Eridanus is, of course, represented by the Jordan, its earthly reflection. The most important, however, of these signs, external to the zodiac, is the great constellation *Orion*. This seems to play a variety of parts in the astral scheme.

First, it may, we are told, be regarded as somewhat resembling a water-wheel. This, of course, fits in with the idea of *gālīl*, "a circle," and Galilee as the zodiac. But *Orion* is outside of the zodiac and therefore does not seem to have any particular significance in this sense. Neither does it seem, from inquiries made by the present writer, to suggest to any one the slightest resemblance to a wheel of any kind. True, Eridanus comes up to the left foot and the Milky Way up to the right hand of Orion, as the stream of water does to the mill-wheel which it turns. Here, therefore, a parallel of a sort might be drawn.

But Professor Drews sees something still more important signified by Orion, viz., the "Hanging Figure" of the 22d Psalm interpreted in a Messianic sense.[1] This, however, does not seem to have suggested itself to any pre-Christian Jews. The picture drawn by the psalmist is also rather that of a solitary and exhausted man (signifying probably the pious portion of Israel) ringed in by armed enemies. These are graphically compared to a pack of pariah dogs (Cheyne reads "lions") and a herd of wild oxen which "pierce his hands and feet" with their teeth and horns.

The applicability of this psalm to the suffering Jesus was an afterthought of Christian interpreters and suggested probably by the quotation from it included in the "Seven Words" from the cross and the obvious similarity of some of the verses to the description of the crucifixion scene.

Furthermore, it is probable that Orion had to the Jews—and early Christians—another and quite differ-

[1] See Appendix C.

ent signification. It is generally regarded as the Kĕsīl, or "Fool," who rebelled against God (Amos 5 : 8; *cf.* Job 9 : 1; 38 : 31).[1]

The constellation certainly suggests the figure of a gigantic man armed with a sword at his side rather than any hanging figure or wheel. Even if we imagined the four stars of the (roughly) rectangular figure to represent the hands and feet of a man stretched upon an X-shaped cross, the belt would be all awry. The further suggestion (taken from Fuhrmann)—that the star group known as the *Hyades*, which, along with the *Pleiades* (above it), are situated in the head of *Taurus* (Bull), have the form of, and represent, the "branch" (*nēṣer*) brought by John the Baptist (Orion)—is fanciful in the extreme. They are a small cluster of stars having the form of nothing in particular, and *Orion* has generally been regarded as holding in his left hand a skin, or shield, while with his *right*[2] he is striking with a club the charging Bull. But we have so many suggested identifications associated with this great constellation and zodiacal sign—a water-wheel, the "Hanging Figure" of the 22d Psalm, and, lastly, John the Baptist—that we may well pause and ask ourselves whether, according to this method of interpretation, it be not possible to make the various zodiacal signs and constellations mean almost anybody and anything, according to the exuberant wit and fancy of the critic or the needs of the critical theory! What proof is there—we ask once more—that the people, the mystics even, of two thousand or more years ago read all this into the heavens; that they regarded the various divisions and towns, and the river and the name of Galilee, as mystical and earthly reflexes of these celestial phenomena?

---

[1] So also in Arabian and Semitic literature generally. Later writers refer to a Persian identification with Nimrod.

[2] The view, it must be remembered, is from the *inside* of a sphere.

With regard to *Capernaum*,[1] the most important of the supposed names of places, Professor Drews would seem to regard the town as wholly imaginary, though he refers to the spring Capharnaum mentioned by Josephus. He would rather connect the latter with the mystical fountain spoken of in Zech. 13 : 1. Here, however, Zechariah is certainly thinking of some *person* of transcendent spiritual powers and goodness, while the writers of the Gospel state plainly that they mean by Capernaum a *town* where such a person lived and exercised his beneficent powers for the good of his countrymen and all mankind. The town, no doubt, was destroyed in the great war with Rome, but it is, perhaps, still to be identified with the ruins known as *Khirbet el-Minyeh* on the northern shore of the lake.[2]

Bearing in mind all these various facts detailed above, we think there is little need for wonder that Professor von Soden should, in part, base the historicity of the general Gospel narratives on the various documentary references to Galilean places which we find throughout the records of the evangelists. These were written while the various towns were (recently) existent and while the events referred to were yet comparatively fresh in the minds of men. And if their statements are not to be taken in their natural and historic sense, then we must hold that in ancient literature it is more than doubtful whether writers ever mean precisely what they say.

[1] City of Nahum (? the prophet).
[2] Macalister affirms (*A Hist. of Civilization in Palestine*, 1912) that *Tell Ḥum* is the correct site.

CHAPTER VI

THE BAPTISM

IT is exactly one hundred and twenty-one years since C. F. Dupuis published his once famous book, *L'Origine de tous les Cultes, ou la Réligion Universelle* (Paris, 1795), in which he asserted (vol. III, pp. 619 *ff.* and 683) that John the Baptist was a purely mythical personage and identified his name with that of the Babylonian fish-god of Berossus, *Oannes*, or *Iannes;* the Ea (Aa, Ae) of the more ancient Sumerians. This theory, which depends chiefly upon an alleged identity of names, has of late years been dragged forth by Professor Drews and others from the obscurity and neglect into which both it and Dupuis's clever but superficial and inaccurate[1] work had long fallen, and used by the former scholar as one of the main props of his mythical theory of Christianity. We will, however, defer its discussion until we come to the consideration of the more modern form, and meanwhile pass on directly to the criticism of D. F. Strauss.

Strauss attacks (*Life of Jesus*, 1835, vol. II, sec. 48, pp. 49–51) the narrative of the baptism from an entirely opposite standpoint to that of Drews. He makes great capital out of the practical difficulties in which he thinks the story is involved. Thus he remarks: "First, if we suppose that for a divine being to descend on the earth the heavens were opened to allow a passage from his

---

[1] Mr. E. Walter Maunder, F.R.A.S., late of Greenwich Observatory, states, in a letter to the present writer, that "Dupuis dated the constellations, as designed, at the very time when the unmapped space in the south was farthest removed from a position having its centre at the south pole of the time. In other words, he was between twelve and thirteen thousand years wrong"!

habitual residence, we adopt an opinion which belongs
to a time when people fancied that God dwelt above
the sky. Besides," he continues, "the Holy Ghost is,
according to just ideas, the divine energy which fills the
universe; how, then, can we conceive that it would move
from one place to another, like a finite being, and even
metamorphose itself into a dove? And, lastly, to imagine that God pronounced certain words in human language has been considered, and with good reason, highly
extravagant."

The above criticism, of the "common-sense order," is,
superficially at least, very acute and, in a sense, reasonable; but in the next paragraph Strauss very justly modifies it considerably with worthier views of spiritual phenomena. We will also quote this passage *in extenso:*

"In the ancient church the most reflective amongst
the fathers considered that the celestial Voice of the Old
Testament was not, like an ordinary voice, produced by
a vibration of the air and apparent to the organs of
sense, but an internal impression which God produced
in those with whom he desired to communicate;[1] and
it is in this way that Origen and Theodore of Mopsuete
have maintained previously that the apparition at the
time of the baptism of Jesus was a vision and not a material reality. Simple people, says Origen, in their simplicity, think it a light matter for the universe to be put
in motion or for the heavens to be rent asunder; but
those who think more profoundly on these matters see
in these superior revelations how it is that chosen people
believe, in their watchings, and more particularly in their
dreams, that they have had evidence by their corporeal
senses, while it has simply been a movement of their
minds. It is necessary, therefore, to conceive all the scene
of the baptism, not as an exterior reality, but as an internal vision operated by God; and it is in this way

[1] See also *The Transfiguration*, chap. 8, p. 163.

that most modern theologians have considered the subject."

We might, perhaps, take exception to the particular use of the phrase, "an exterior reality," as here practically equivalent to a material phenomenon; otherwise Strauss's quotation and comments are, in the main, very just and true. Had Strauss, however, lived in an age of psychical research, like our own, he would have seen and grasped all these facts still more clearly.

The *spiritual* view (if we may so term it) of the phenomena he then discusses in greater detail. "This mode of explanation," he goes on to say, "is also supported by certain expressions in the First and Fourth Gospels; as, for instance, 'the heavens were opened *unto him*,' '*I* saw,' and others, which appear to give the scene the character of an internal vision; and it is in this sense that Theodore of Mopsuete has said that the descent of the Holy Ghost was not seen by all the assistants, but that by a certain spiritual contemplation it was seen by John alone; but, according to Mark, it was seen by Jesus as well."

So far, Strauss writes intelligibly and consistently. But at this point he seems to drop the clew which has carried him along safely thus far, for he continues: "In Luke, on the contrary, the expressions employed carry a totally different meaning, such, for instance, as 'the heaven *was opened*,' 'the Holy Ghost descended *in a bodily shape*'! This," he avers, "is decidedly exterior and objective; consequently, if the complete truth of all the evangelical recitals be contended for, it will be necessary, since the recital of Luke is quite precise, to interpret all the others, which are less so, by it and to suppose that the scene they relate was not confined to John the Baptist and Jesus. Olshausen had good reason, then, for admitting by concession to the recital of Luke that a crowd of people were present at the scene and

both heard and saw something; but he stops there, and
says that this something was undetermined and incomprehensible. According to this mode of interpretation,
though on one side the theologian leaves the ground of
subjective visions and passes to that of objective apparitions, still, on the other side, he assures us that the dove
which appeared was not visible to the physical eye but
to the spiritual eye, and that the Voice was not heard by
the external ear but by the internal perception. We do
not," he adds, "comprehend this pneumatology of Olshausen in which sensible realities are placed above the
senses; we shall, therefore, leave this obscure interpretation and pass to the more lucid one which says simply that the scene was undoubtedly exterior but purely
natural."

Here Strauss diverges to the views of such rationalists
as Paulus, who explained the opening of the heavens by
a sudden dispersion of the clouds or by a flash of lightning, the appearance of the "dove" by the advent of a
material bird of that species, and the Voice by a clap of
thunder, and so forth.

Now, at this point it will be seen that Strauss, through
a materialised rendering of the narrative of Luke, entirely drops the suggestion of immaterial phenomena of
a symbolical character, expressing some actual spiritual
reality, in which he seemed, at the outset, more or less
inclined to acquiesce. Luke, he thinks, narrates the
scene both as objective and material, therefore we must,
for consistency's sake, take all the other narratives in a
similar sense.

But there are two great assumptions implied in this
view of the matter: first, that what is subjectively apprehended, without the active co-operation of the normal
senses, as in ordinary perception, is of necessity wholly
non-objective in character, and this because the said
senses do not testify to it as a material existence; and,

secondly, that the use of language, ordinarily applied to sensational phenomena, implies in the mind of the writer materiality in the phenomenon.

But does Luke describe mere material phenomena as occurring after the baptism? Or, again, does he ever represent these phenomena as being seen and heard by all the people who were present? We very much question both of these assumptions. His narrative, no doubt, can be forced into this sense, but not naturally, we think. Luke, for instance, speaks of the "Spirit" as having a "bodily shape," or "form" (σωματικῷ εἴδει), which was "*like* (ὡς) a dove." But there is really no materialising here; even a *spirit* may be conceived as having, symbolically, a "form," or "shape" (εἶδος), relatively to the observer; but this does not necessarily imply materiality, and the next word (ὡς) distinctly implies that it was not a "real dove" of any kind.[1] It is difficult to see how the spiritual can be expressed in human speech except in words that have ordinarily a material signification! Luke certainly does not say specifically (or, it would seem, imply) that all the people saw the dove or heard the "Voice." The Voice, too, it should be noted, is addressed solely to Jesus: "*Thou art* [not here, "This is"] my beloved son," etc. On the whole, there is very decided evidence to show that Luke had not in his mind a material body and an audible normal voice when writing his account of this scene.[2] As for the necessity of bringing the other accounts into line with that of Luke, Strauss lived in days of, for the most part, a very mechanical and unintelligent theory of inspiration and exegesis, and when orthodoxy was

[1] *Cf.* Acts 2 : 3. ὡσεὶ πυρὸς is analogous to ὡς περιστεράν.

[2] De Loosten says (*Jesus Christus vom Standpunkt des Psychiaters*, 1905) that the phenomena attending the baptism were "a case of combined optical and auditory hallucinations." So also W. Hirsch, *Religion und Zivilisation vom Standpunkte des Psychiaters*, and Binet-Sanglé, *La folie de Jésus* (1910–11).

lamentably wanting in imagination. Certainly, if Luke
were, as tradition avers, a physician, we might expect
his mind to have a materialistic bias, or at least his accounts of spiritual phenomena to be couched in materialistic terms. But, in any case, the version of Mark is
prior in point of time and preferable in point of diction
and simplicity, so we may take it as the typical and
original account of this event and decline to adapt its
interpretation in any detailed sense to those of other
narratives.

We now come to the recent and important *critique*
of Professor Drews, who has dealt with the subject of
the baptism more fully than any other mythicist and
takes up the thread of the story where it was dropped
by Dupuis. He attacks these narratives, however, upon
historical as well as upon mythical grounds. We will
deal first of all with his historical objections.

He says (*The Christ Myth*, p. 121): "John the Baptist, as we meet him in the Gospels, was not an historical personage. Apart from the Gospels he is mentioned
by Josephus, and this passage, although it was known to
Origen (second century, *Cont. Cels.*, I, 47) in early days,
is exposed to a strong suspicion of being a forgery by
some Christian hand." In a foot-note to this page he
quotes as his authority Graetz, who designates it (*Gesch.
d. Juden*, 1888, III, p. 278) "a shameless interpolation";
but he offers no proof of this statement.

Again, Drews further continues (*The Witnesses to the
Historicity of Jesus*, 1912, pp. 192 and 193): "It is useless
to oppose to this [mythical] conception of John the familiar passage of Josephus[1] as proving the historicity

---

[1] "Now, some of the Jews thought that the destruction of Herod's army
[by Aretas, King of Arabia] came from God, and that very justly as a punishment for what he did against John who was surnamed the Baptist
(Ἰωάννου τοῦ ἐπικαλουμένου Βαπτιστοῦ).

"For Herod slew him, who was a good man and commanded the Jews to
exercise virtue both as to righteousness towards one another, and piety

of the Baptist. The genuineness of the passage is just as doubtful as that of the two references in Josephus to Jesus. Not only does the way in which it interrupts the narrative show it to be an interpolation, but the chronology of the Jewish historian in regard to John is in irreconcilable contradiction to that of the Gospels. According to the Gospels, the appearance or the death of John must have taken place in the year 28 or 29 [A. D.]; whereas the war of Herod with the Nabatæan Aretas, the unfortunate result of which was, according to Josephus [?], to be regarded as a punishment for the execution of John, falls in the years 35 and 36 of the present era. Moreover, the complaints against Herod Antipas, on account of his incestuous marriage with his brother's wife, which are supposed to have occasioned the death of John, cannot have been made before then.[1] In fine, John might be an historical personality without there being any historical truth in what the Gospels say of him. His connexion with the story of Jesus is certainly due to astral considerations and the passage we quoted [p. 184] from Isaiah 40 : 3–5.

"We have, therefore, no reason to regard it as historical." Let us now take account of these objections.

Our knowledge with regard to the two chief dates (the birth and death) in the life of Jesus has, up to now, unfortunately, been very uncertain. During quite recent years, however, owing to the researches of Sir W. M. Ramsay, Lieutenant-Colonel Mackinlay, and others, this uncertainty has, to a very great extent, been cleared up, and we may now affirm, with a close approximation to certainty, that Jesus was born in B. C. 8 and was

towards God, and so come to baptism; for that the washing [with water] would be acceptable to him, not for the putting away of some sins [only], but for the purification of the body, supposing still that the soul was thoroughly purified beforehand by righteousness (*Ant.*, XVIII, 5, 2)."

[1] See Professor Lake's article on "The Date of Herod's Marriage and the Chronology of the Gospels" (*The Expositor*, November, 1912).

crucified in A. D. 29. Now, assuming, as is most probable, a three years' ministry,[1] the baptism must have
taken place in A. D. 26. It was probably in this year
that Herod Antipas divorced his wife (the daughter of
Aretas) for Herodias. His war with his wife's father,
on the other hand, could well have begun in A. D. 28,
and, indeed, it lasted some six or seven years before
coming to a decisive issue. Accordingly, there was a
sufficient period of time between A. D. 26 and 28 for
John's rebuke to be administered and his imprisonment
and execution to take place before the death of Jesus in
A. D. 29. Hence, so far as this objection goes, there is
no case whatever against the historicity of the Gospel
narrative.

As regards Drews's two other arguments, it will suffice
here to say that the passage occurs very naturally and
appropriately in an historical digression relating to the
affairs of the Herod family, and the very fact that
the reason there given by Josephus for the execution of
John differs from the statement in the Gospels (*cf. Ant.*,
XVIII, 5, 2 with Mark 6 : 17–27) is the strongest possible evidence against the former being a Christian interpolation. If it had been concocted at a later period—
after Josephus wrote—in order to bolster up the account
given in the Gospels, the writer would have been careful to make it agree with them on this important point.
But it does not. Josephus, of course, may have been
better informed than Mark; but this is not likely, as he

---

[1] For the arguments in support of a one-year ministry see Keim, *Jesus
of Nazara*, II, p. 398; for a two years' see Turner's article in Hastings's
Dict. of Bible; for a three years' see Andrews's *The Life of Our Lord*, 2d ed.
(1892). For patristic views see Hastings's *Dict. of Bible*, I, 410. The ministry of only one year's duration is always assumed by the modern mythicist
and, indeed, is essential to his theory. *Cf.* Sepp., *Heident. und dess. Bedeut.
für das Christ* (1883), I, 168 *f.*; also Winckler, *Die Babylon. Geisteskult.*, 89
and 100 *f.* It is the mythological year of the sun's course through the watery region in January and February until the complete exhaustion of its
strength in December.

wrote some thirty years later, and Mark probably got his information directly from some of the disciples of John who had joined the Apostolic Church. We may, therefore, without the least hesitation, indorse the emphatic verdict of the learned and judicious Keim, who pronounced it (*Jesus of Nazara*, I, p. 16) "a splendid and unassailable account," worthy in every sense of being accepted as authentic history.[1]

But here Professor Drews, as though anticipating this conclusion, shifts his ground, and urges that, even if John be an historical personality, there "might" be no historical truth in the Gospel story of his life. "His connexion with the story of Jesus," he says, "is certainly due to astral considerations"—in other words, it is entirely mythical. This view is set forth in detail in the following words (*The Christ Myth*, p. 122): "Under the name John, which in Hebrew means 'pleasing to God,' is concealed the Babylonian water-god Oannes (Eâ). Baptism is connected with this worship, and the baptism of Jesus in the Jordan represents *the reflection upon earth of what originally took place among the stars.*[2] That is to say, the sun begins its yearly course with a baptism, entering as it does immediately after its birth the constellations of the Water-carrier [*Aquarius*] and the Fishes [*Pisces*]. But this celestial water-kingdom, in which each year the day-star [sun] is purified and born again, is the Eridanus, the heavenly Jordan, or Year-stream (Egyptian, *iaro*, or *ïero*, the river), wherein the original baptism of the Divine Saviour of the world took place."

Before going any further into his detailed statements of the theory, let us carefully consider the above points.

Now, in ancient Babylonia, the home of astrology

---

[1] John the Baptist was believed by the Jews to have been born in a πόλις Ἰούδα (according to rabbinical tradition at Hebron, but according to a modern ingenious interpretation of the phrase at Jutta) in the beginning of the second half of the year 749 A. U. C. (4 B. C.).

[2] Italics ours.

and zodiacal mythology, the eleventh month of the year (approximately our January) found the sun, at that period, in the sign *Aquarius*,[1] the Water-bearer, out of whose jar is poured forth the Heavenly Stream (*Eridanus*), one of the extra-zodiacal and southern constellations.

In this month, too, the sun-god revived from his (partial) death at the winter solstice (circ. December 25) and once more started upon his annual journey through the sky. The resurrection of the vegetation-spirit (or god), on the other hand, took place in most cases some weeks later, at the commencement of spring. And, if we may believe Doctor Drews, this celestial phenomenon —the baptism of the young (revived) sun-god in the waters of Eridanus, while that luminary was in the sign *Aquarius*, from which it emerged into the succeeding sign *Pisces*—had its reflection upon earth as Jesus (historically representing the sun-spirit) being baptised in the Jordan, from whence he emerged as the divine fish (Eâ or Oannes), and, passing through the other zodiacal signs, reached the height of his power, and from that time onward steadily declined until his death by crucifixion.[2]

The latter portion of this theory we will defer dealing with until we come to Chap. 12, "The Crucifixion"; meanwhile, we will say generally that Professor Drews's theory —viz., that the earliest Christians saw in these natural phenomena occurring annually in the heavens a kind of prophecy, or forecast, of what was to happen on earth afterwards—is a very great and unwarranted assumption; it is, indeed, the πρῶτον ψεῦδος of the whole mythical theory. But let us first review the actual facts a little more carefully.

The Babylonians (like the Egyptians) lived beside a

---

[1] In the Gilgamesh epic it is marked on the tablet by the story of the deluge told by the "Chaldean Noah" to Gilgamesh, which comes in quite fittingly, when the sun is passing through the Watery Sign.

[2] See further, Chap. 11, "Barabbas."

great river, which powerfully affected (for good and evil)
their whole lives and fortunes. Both of the months,
December and January, were marked by great rains,
and floods caused by the overflowing of the Euphrates,
with the concomitant effects of sickness and destruction
far and wide. Vegetation, too, was seemingly dead, and
the sun was at the *nadir* of its powers of stimulating
reproduction in nature. And the question arose: What
was the cause of all this—what did it mean? The soothsayer (or astrologer) accordingly lifted his eyes to the
heavens and very naturally tried to discover a parallel
there to what he saw occurring upon earth. And his
imagination soon enabled him to find one. Out of a few
conspicuous stars he depicted a man-like figure carrying
a water-pot; a straggling line of stars extending onward
suggested a stream of water issuing from the jar—the
heavenly Euphrates (*Eridanus*). This river would then
suggest fish and a connexion with the fish-god (Eâ).
In such an imaginative way there would spring up and
gradually develop heavenly duplicates of the chief natural phenomena occurring upon earth. These were reflected in the heaven, as it were. Later on, no doubt,
when the more abiding nature of the heavenly phenomena
was noted, the process would be reversed, and the earthly
duplicates then came to be regarded as reflexions of the
heavenly.

But all this referred to the phenomena of nature only.
The myth proper is an explanation of some occurrence
in nature—not in history, which deals chiefly with legend in its early stages. The personifications which take
place in myths, however, help to link nature with history and to parallel events and persons in history with
the phenomena of nature. Thus legendary, and even
historical, stories often became paralleled, and even confused, with mythical ones. Such a process, however, in
no way detracts from the historicity of persons whose

lives and exploits have become regarded as analogues of natural phenomena. This fact is clearly shown by the many instances occurring during recent years, where kings and others, formerly regarded as wholly mythical, have been found to be real figures of living men who had become confused with mythical personifications of natural phenomena.[1]

In this way it is probable that John (and in a certain sense, as we shall see later, Jesus also) became analogues of personified natural phenomena. To the modern and European mind this process obscures and weakens the historical character of the human counterpart; to the ancient and Oriental mind it merely added vividness and reality to his picture.

We now come to the most important point in Drews's theory of the mythical nature of both Jesus and John, viz., that both represent different phases of the sun in its two great periods of ascent and descent in the heavens between two winter solstices. Thus, according to this view, John will be the sun-god from July to December, after the advent of Jesus ("he [Jesus] must increase whilst I must decrease," John 3 : 30), while Jesus represents the god from January to June.[2] This view he further supports by, *inter alia*, a number of questionable etymologies and identities, etc., which we will summarise below.

(1) Jesus is called by the author of the Fourth Gospel "the true light" (τὸ φῶς τὸ ἀληθινόν, 1 : 9); whilst Jesus calls John (5 : 35) the "lamp (λύχνος) that burneth and shineth." (2) John is said (Luke 1 : 26) to have been born six months before Jesus. This indicates the solar

---

[1] Many examples could be given of this: *e. g.*, Minos, King of Crete, and (probably) Melchisedek, Priest-King of Salem, etc.

[2] So, again, in the case of Barabbas and Jesus (Chap. 13); the former, he says, represents the sun ascending to the summer solstice (circ. June 25); the latter, the sun descending to the winter solstice, when it "dies" (see Chap. 11).

and duplex character of both. (3) John wears a cloak of camel's hair with a leathern belt (Matt. 3 : 4). This is supposed to equate him with Elijah (II Kings 1 : 8; cf. Matt. 11 : 14); and Elijah is a form of the sun-god transferred to history; and, further, the latter is the same as the Greek *Helios* ($^{\circ}$Ηλιος), the German *Heljas*, and the Ossetic *Ilia*. This statement, however, Drews modifies directly after making it by saying that "at any rate characteristics of this god *have been transferred to the figure of the prophet*" [1] (cf. Nork, *Realwörterbuch*, I, 451 ff.) —a very different thing.

Now, (4) in his subsidiary work (*The Witnesses to the Historicity of Jesus*, p. 190) we find a few further touches added to his theory of the identification of John with Oannes (Eâ), and, moreover, of both with the zodiacal sign *Aquarius*. He says: "Possibly, however, he [Oannes] was originally *Aquarius*, as this constellation is depicted as a fish-man in the old Oriental sphere, and the constellation of the Fishes was afterwards detached from it" (see Creuzer, *Symbolik und Mythologie der Alten Völker*, 1820, II, p. 78). And, again (5): "We have a reminiscence of this primitive astral significance of John in the fact that we still celebrate his festival *on the day of the solstice*[2] when the constellation of the Southern Fishes rises as the sun sets and disappears as the sun rises." And also (6): "The newly baptised Christians used to be called 'fishes' (*pisciculi*, in Tertullian), and the baptismal font is still called the *piscina*, or 'fish-pond.'"

But the identification of Oannes-John-Jesus with *Aquarius* is, after all, insufficient for the theory, and, standing by itself, would in reality be damaging to it; so a further identification becomes necessary. Accordingly, we find the following convenient one (*The Witnesses to the Historicity of Jesus*, pp. 191–193) ready to hand: (7)

---

[1] Italics ours.   [2] Italics ours.

"As the one who *indicates the solstices and divides the year*,[1] Oannes becomes *identical with the sun itself* [1] as a rising and setting star. In this way he entered the myth-group of Joshua, Jason, and Jesus, and, indeed, corresponds to the Old Testament Caleb as representative of the summer solstice, when the dog-star (Sirius) sets in the month of the Lion, or of the autumnal equinox, which is the division of the year equivalent to the former, when the sun descends below the celestial equator into the land of winter. Joshua (Jesus), on the other hand, represented the *winter solstice*,[1] at which the days begin to grow longer, or the *vernal equinox*,[2] when the sun again advances beyond the equator and enters victoriously the 'Promised Land' beyond the Jordan (or the Milky Way) of the heavenly Eridanus, the watery region of the heavens, in which the zodiacal signs of Aquarius and Pisces predominate."

The remaining portion of Doctor Drews's theory must be briefly summarised. There is also (8) a further identification of the Baptist with *Orion*, "near which the sun is found at the vernal equinox." Orion stands in the celestial Eridanus, in the Milky Way, at Bethabara (John 1 : 28), "the place of setting,"[3] *i. e.*, near the spot where the sun crosses the Milky Way in the zodiac. "With one foot it [Orion] emerges from Eridanus, which connects with the Milky Way and seems to draw water from it with the right hand, at the same time raising the left as if blessing—really a very vivid astral figure of the Baptist: we have also the three stars of Orion's belt in the (leathern) girdle which the Gospels give to the Baptist, and the people are seen in the constellations about Orion,[4] and, according to Babylonian ideas, a meeting of

---

[1] Italics ours.   [2] Italics ours.
[3] Bethabara means "house," or "place, of the ford"!
[4] "I borrow this indication of the connection of the Baptist with the constellation Orion from Fuhrmann's work, *Der Astralmythos von Christus.*"

the gods takes place at the vernal equinox, when the sun
has run its course through the zodiac."

Finally, referring again to the phenomena attending
the baptism of Jesus, Drews says of the "dove" (*The
Christ Myth*, p. 118, note 3): (9) "Phereda, or Pheredet, the dove, is the Chaldaic root of the name Aphrodite,
as the goddess in the car drawn by two doves was called
among the Greeks. In the whole of Nearer Asia the cult
of doves was connected with that of the mother-goddess." [1]

We will now deal with the above points (1–9) *seriatim*
and as concisely as possible.

(1) The term "true light," as applied to Jesus by the
fourth evangelist, and "the lamp," which Jesus is said
by the latter writer to have applied to John, have a much
simpler source than the astral-mythical origin proposed
by Doctor Drews. Light was everywhere associated in
ancient religions with God and goodness, just as the reverse of these terms was identified with darkness in both
a literal and a figurative sense. In the Aryan *Rig-Veda*,
Mitra was the representative of the heaven of day, as
yet expressly distinguished from the sun. Later Mithraism identified him with the sun as both the god of
light and goodness. Among the Semitic Hebrews we
find a similar use of light as, at least, emblematic and
symbolical of God and his attributes. Thus, the Psalmist says (27 : 1): "Jahveh is my *light* and my salvation"; and, again (118 : 27): "Jahveh who hath showed

---

Also see, as to the astral features of the Baptist, Niemojewski's *Bog Jezus*
(1909), a book which rests on the astral-mythical theories of Dupuis and of
the modern school of Winckler.

[1] In *The Witnesses to the Historicity of Jesus*, p. 214, note 1, he says:
"Jesus . . . seems originally to have had a dove for a mother, as the baptism in the Jordan was, according to some, the act of the birth of the Saviour;
and the Holy Ghost, who descended on him in fire and flame [!] in the
form of a dove, was represented in certain Gnostic sects as the mother of
Jesus." The real explanation here is that certain Gnostic sects adapted
the story—with fanciful additions—to their own theosophical speculations.

us *light.*" Here God is expressly separated from the
light, which is merely manifested by him, as in the case
of the Shekinah.

Again, and especially in Isaiah 60 : 1, 3, 19, and 20,
we find light used figuratively of God and his revelation of himself. We cannot be surprised, therefore, that
the author of the Fourth Gospel should describe Jesus,
whom he regards as a special manifestation of God, as
"the true light." Neither can we wonder that it should
be recorded that Jesus had spoken of John, who "prepared the way before him," as "the lamp that burneth
and shineth," and thereby dispelled the mists of prejudice and error. It is no doubt possible to force these
and similar expressions into supports for the hypothesis
which would make Jesus and John coequal half-yearly
phases, or aspects, of the ascending or declining sun.
But this is not their original and simpler signification.
We may, therefore, follow here the philosophical maxim
and adopt the simpler and nearer explanation in preference to the more recondite and remote.

(2) As regards the births of Jesus and John,[1] modern
research has practically shown that these events cannot
have represented solstitial solar phenomena, as maintained by Drews and his school. There is very good reason, as we have seen, for believing that Jesus was born
in the month of October; in that case, John must have
been born in the preceding April (Luke 1 : 36). These
dates also do not coincide with the equinoxes. The reasonable conclusion, therefore, is that the events in question never represented an "historisation" of either solar

[1] Mr. J. M. Robertson thinks (*Christianity and Mythology*, 1900, p. 257)
that "the late Christian myth of the synchronous (!) birth of the Christ's
cousin John the Baptist is reasonably to be traced to the Buddhist myth
of the synchronous birth of the Buddha's cousin Ananda (Bigandet's *Life
of Gaudama*, Trübner's ed., I, 36) rather than to the Krishṇaite motive of
Arjuna or Bala Rama." The latter is probably later and has even less
likeness to the Lucan story.

or vegetal phenomena. In any case, it is clear that the mere fact of the two births occurring at intervals of six months, though exceedingly convenient for this theory, is a very slender and speculative basis to build upon, and it is, to say the least, much more probable that it has no special significance whatever.

(3) John's cloak of camel's-hair cloth and his leathern belt are stated (Zech. 13 : 4) to have been the regular garb of the itinerant prophet or religious teacher in the East. The assumption that Elijah (with whom John is compared) is a form of the sun-god transferred to history is once more convenient but, at the same time, rests upon very slender evidence. Indeed, the known facts seem directly to negative such a supposition. For the name Elijah, i. e., *Elijjahu* (אֵלִיָּ֫הוּ) = "My God is Jahu (Jahveh)," tells against it. In the story, as recorded in the book of Kings, Elijah acts on Jahveh's behalf against the Sidonian Ba'al, who was probably a solar member of the Ba'alim group rather than one of the Canaanitish gods of fertility. It is true that Jahveh was once regarded by a few German scholars as a *fire-god* (Daumer, *Der Feuer-und Moloch-dienst*, pp. 18–22; Ghillany, *Die Menschenopfer*, pp. 278–298; *cf.* also Kuenen, *Tübinger Theol. Jahrb.*, 1842, p. 473) and therefore might be regarded as representing the sun, the central fire of the solar system. But this view of his nature has not found general acceptance. It is more in accordance with known fact to assert that Jahveh was said often to manifest his presence *by means of* fire, as at Sinai and Horeb. In the latter case, however, we are expressly told by the chronicler that "Jahveh was not in the fire." Neither has Elijah's name the least etymological affinity, as Drews seems to maintain, with Helios, Heljas, and Ilia, though its shortened form *Elias* has a superficial resemblance to these words. *Helios* (Ἥλιος and Ἡέλιος) is connected by Curtius (*Gr. Etym.*, 612)

with the Aryan root US, the original form being αὐ(σ)έ-λιος. The ν then either fell out altogether (as in the common Greek form ἀέλιος) or hardened itself into β (as in Cretan ἀβέλιος). And its meaning is the "burning one."

Bearing all these and similar facts in mind, it is difficult to maintain the solar character of either John or Elias. Still more outrageous are such derivations and statements as the following: "Elijah (Eli-scha) and Jeho-scha (Joshua, Jesus) agree even in their names [!], so that on this ground alone it would not have been strange if the prophet of the Old Testament had served as a prototype of his evangelical namesake" (see Matt. 9 : 11 f.; 15 : 1 ff., 11 and 20; 28 : 18). (*The Christ Myth*, p. 238.)

(4) The identification of John with Eâ or Aa (Ae) is in the highest degree precarious, especially if John is considered to be a form of the sun-god. Eâ was one of the great triad of Sumerian deities, Anna (Anu), Enlil (Bel), and Enki (Eâ), who were respectively the gods of heaven, earth, and *the abyss of waters beneath the earth*. Eâ is said to have emerged daily in a fish form (or clad in a garb of fish-skins) from the waters of the Persian Gulf, in order to teach the early inhabitants of Babylonia the arts of civilisation. The Chaldean priest Berossus, who flourished in the time of Alexander the Great, calls this god, in his Greek narrative, Ōannēs (Ὠάννης), or Iannēs (Ἰάννης).

Now, Ἰωάννης ("John") is the Hellenistic Greek form of the Hebrew, יוֹחָנָן (a shorter form of יְהוֹחָנָן, *Jehohanan*), which means "Jahveh (Jeho) is gracious" (*not* "pleasing to God"). This word is undoubtedly quite different, both in meaning and etymology, to Eâ, which Doctor Pinches thinks (*Babylonian and Assyrian Religion*, p. 51) may mean, in the form Aa, "waters," or, if read Eâ, "house of water." Indeed, in any case, Jahveh is a god of *heaven*, while Eâ rules over the abyss, which is connected with the waters of the sea. There is, therefore, no relation here except the accidental similarity in the Greek names *Jōhannēs* and *Ōannēs*, which, of course, proves nothing.

Doctor Eisler, in a learned and instructive article on "John-Jonah-Oannes" (*The Quest*, April, 1912, pp. 474–495), shows that in two places the MSS. would allow us to read Ἰωάννης instead of Ὠάννης, and he regards the former word as "a possible rendering" of the form *Eakhan* ("Ea the fish"), which was believed by Lenormant to be the original form of Berossus's enigmatical Greek word. This, however—whether it be the case or not—does not lend any support to Drews's mythical theory. For, in the first place, it is very problematical whether Lenormant was right in his conjecture, and, in the second, a (later) assimilation by copyists of Ὠάννης and Ἰωάννης would almost certainly take place occasionally, for the latter form, being a common name in Hellenistic Greek, would be better known to many scribes.

In like manner, the attempt to identify *Jonah* (יוֹנָה, Ἰωνᾶς, "a dove")—a name which Robertson Smith thought (*Jour. Phil.*, IX, 85) was connected with *totemism*—with Ὠάννης or Ἰωάννης (or both) is probably rendered invalid by the difference in derivation and meaning. Jonah, Cheyne thinks, is possibly due to a corruption from הונתן, a word which we find in יוֹנָתָן, "Jahveh gives"; but the whole subject is extremely obscure, and where little is known it is dangerous to theorise dogmatically.

Furthermore, the characters and functions of these three beings—whether they be historical or mythical—appear to be quite separate and distinct, and the alleged identities seem, for the most part, to be merely due to a play upon similarly sounding names. Professor Drews's further supposition that Ōannēs (or Eâ) was perhaps originally *Aquarius*, "as this constellation is depicted as a fish-man," seems to rest upon one of the many wild theories of Creuzer, whose fanciful hypotheses were severely criticised by Lobeck in his *Aglaophamus*. The sign *Aquarius* was represented in Babylonian zodiacal symbolism by the god *Ramman*, crowned with a tiara and pouring water from a vase, much as it is depicted at the present time. More frequently, however, the vase and water alone were used. The eleventh month of the year, with which the sign was associated, was known at Babylon as that of "want and rain," hence the water and jar, and (sometimes) the figure of Ramman, the atmospheric god of rain and storms.

(5) The *festival* of St. John the Baptist is celebrated in the Western church on the 24th of June, but in the Eastern church it is held on January 7. It was probably not observed at all anywhere before 300 A. D., since it is not mentioned earlier than Maximus, Bishop of Turin (400 A. D.), and in several homilies of St. Augustine. The date (24th of June) was probably chosen by the Western church when the birthday of Christ was officially fixed by Pope Julius I (in 354 A. D.) on December 25, in order to assimilate it to the pagan festival of the birth of the sun-god, observed annually at the time of the winter solstice.

(6) It is quite natural that the newly baptised Christians should be popularly termed "little fishes" (*pisciculi*), seeing that they were actually brought up out of the water at baptism. Such a ceremony would inevitably suggest the analogy of fishing to every witness of the scene.

Professor Drews, however, is in error in regarding the *piscina* as the name of the baptismal font. The *piscina* is the basin-like cavity in the wall (generally) found near the altar, in which the priest performed the ablutions after the celebration of the eucharist.

(7) But it now becomes necessary to identify Ōannēs with the sun. From being the god of the abyss and the waters (super- as well as subterranean), he must be identified with the god of heaven. This is cleverly managed by means of the argument that Ōannēs "indicates the solstices" and thereby "divides the year" into two equal parts, just as the sun does by ascending and descending the ecliptic. But where is the proof that Ōannēs was even thus used or recognised as a "year-divider"? Certainly he was said to have instructed mankind; but this item of knowledge does not seem to have been included among the "arts" of life. We doubt very much whether Eâ was ever regarded by the Babylonians in any such capacity. Their time-measurers were the sun and moon, and, though no doubt they would observe the various constellations and stars, which appeared, disappeared, and reappeared at fixed intervals, the sun and moon were practically their sole (and sufficient) guides in these matters.

There is no evidence either to show that Eâ ever entered the "myth-group of Joshua, Jason, and Jesus," whose alleged connexion with the sun also in each case still awaits proof.

(8) The next identification is that of John with the constellation *Orion*—"near which the sun is at the vernal equinox." This is even more fanciful than the preceding identifications. The sun, it is true, two thousand years ago, was rather near Orion at the vernal equinox. And the latter constellation certainly "stands with one foot in the heavenly Eridanus; but how Professor Drews makes out that he seems to draw water from it with the right hand, at the same time blessing with the left,"[1] it would be extremely difficult to say. Really, he is generally supposed to be holding in his left hand the characteristic lion's skin, perhaps as a kind of shield, while

---

[1] This should be "right," as it is viewed from the interior of a sphere.

with his right he brandishes the club and threatens the bull, who is charging down upon him. Furthermore, there is no question of a "blessing," which, if given with the left hand, would have been regarded as of very sinister effect.

To this may be added the fact that the true reading in John 1 : 28 is not Bηθαβαρᾷ ("house of the ford") but Bηθανίᾳ ("Bethany"), as shown by Westcott and Hort (*cf.* Judges 7 : 24). The reading "Betharaba" is due to a conjecture of Origen, who could find no traces of any place named Bethany "beyond" Jordan in his day. Orion, again, like the Baptist, certainly has a "belt," but there is no reference in the leathern girdle of the latter to the three belt stars of the former; and to see in the "figures" (nearly all animals!) of the constellations round about Orion any expression of the meeting of the Babylonian gods at the vernal equinox is to let the imagination run to an excess of riot. Moreover, as we have pointed out, all this occurs in the zodiac, not at the vernal equinox, but at the summer solstice.

(9) Lastly, we have to consider the use which Professor Drews makes of the "dove." It does not seem certain that the root of the Greek Aphrodite is to be found in the "Chaldaic" word *Phereda* (or *Pheredet*). The common derivation is, of course, from ἀφρός, "foam" (Liddell and Scott, *Gr. Lex.*, *s. v.*). The goddess was said by the Greeks to be *Aphrogeneia*, "foam-born," [1] and in a moral sense she was the patroness of light love, though there are (? earlier) indications of a chaster view.

But even if it be so, that fact by no means establishes his case. The cult of the dove was, it is true, connected with the worship of the great mother-goddess all through

---

[1] See Hesiod, *Theog.*, 187–206. It would seem probable, however, that her common by-name of worship, Οὐρανία ("the heavenly one"), is an older term, which would connect her ultimately with the Semitic *Astarte* (Ištar).

Asia Minor, *except amongst the Jews,* with whom that bird had only a partially sacrosanct and symbolical character. Its gentle and affectionate disposition was suggestive of those endearing qualities in human nature and even in the nature of God. The connexion of the dove with the Virgin Mary is merely a conceit of the artists of the Renaissance period, who drew their inspiration and concepts largely from pagan sources; for the evangelists are careful, as we have seen, to regard the Virgin Mary purely as a woman.

Finally, we may conclude with a "parallel" (and "origin") of the baptism which has been found in India. Professor Seydel tells us (*Das Evangelium von Jesu,* etc., 1882, S. 155 and 156) that, according to the *Rgya tcher rol pa,*[1] while the future Buddha was bathing, "thousands of the sons of the gods, wishing to render offerings to the Bodhisat, strewed divine aloes and sandal powder and celestial essences and flowers of all colours over the water, so that, in this moment, the great river Nairanjana flowed on full of divine perfumes and flowers."

It would be, indeed, difficult to meet with a more impossible "parallel" than this; the two stories are absolutely and completely dissimilar, and neither suggests or implies the other.

[1] The Tibetan recension of the *Lalita vistāra.*

CHAPTER VII

THE TEMPTATION

The Temptation of Jesus

It will be fitting to commence our study of the temptation with the view of it which was taken by "the father of modern mythical criticism," D. F. Strauss. His explanation of the matter, which at least has the merits of sanity and moderation, takes the following form (*Leben Jesu*, 1835, English translation, II, sec. 54, pp. 84–87).

The first temptation of Jesus in both of the fuller synoptic accounts was, he notes, that of *hunger*. This was predetermined for the early Christian imagination by two facts well known to them. "The people of Israel had been particularly tried by hunger in the desert." And, "in the same way, among the different temptations to which, according to the rabbis, Abraham was exposed, hunger is enumerated." There are, however, he admits, many other examples of voluntary abstinence from food in the Old Testament, so that it is by no means clear why the example of Israel, or even of Moses, should be so suggestive to the early Christian mind. "But," Strauss continues, "one temptation was not sufficient; according to the rabbis, Abraham was subjected to ten." This number, he thinks, was too many for a dramatic exposition such as we have in the two longer Gospel records. A smaller number must be selected if a real effect were to be produced. And, if so, that number would surely be the sacred number three. That number, indeed, frequently recurs in various connexions in the Gospels: thus, three times does Jesus withdraw to pray in Gethsemane; three times did Peter deny his Master; and three times did Jesus test the love which Peter bore towards him.

Again, this sacred number reappears "in the rabbinical passage where the devil personally tempts Abraham; the patriarch endures three assaults";[1] the parallel is still further heightened and strengthened by the fact that the attacks and repulses are accompanied in every case by quotations from the Old Testament.

The second temptation, in the Matthæan order, that Jesus should throw himself from a pinnacle of the temple, Strauss says, "appears suddenly, and the choice seems fortuitous and arbitrary." But this, again, is to be explained in a similar way; "it is borrowed from the conduct of the Jewish people in the desert (Deut. 6 : 16; Num. 21 : 4 *ff.*), the people tempted the Lord."

The third temptation, "that of worshipping the devil," Strauss admits, is not manifestly got from any definite Old Testament instance. He remarks, however, that one of the sins into which the Israelites fell in the desert was idolatry (I Cor. 10 : 7). This, he adds, was "attributed to the suggestion of Satan; and later Jews regarded idolatry as the worship of the devil."

It may be remarked here that Strauss is not very happy in his "parallel" for the last temptation. Israel did fall into idolatry; but this fact seems to have been put down, at least by the earlier Israelites themselves, to their natural "stiff-neckedness" rather than to the wiles of a personal arch-tempter, which was a later conception altogether. Even in the post-exilic book of Job Satan is one of the servants of Jahveh, not a seducer to sin in antagonism to God, and the worship of the devil

---

[1] Strauss does consider the question of the date of the rabbinical stories, which are undoubtedly post-Christian! For late rabbinical parallels of Satan tempting Abraham, Moses, and Israel, see Gforer, *Jahrhundert d. Heils.*, part 2, pp. 379 *ff. Cf.* also the temptations of Adam and Job.

was unknown amongst the Jews both before and after the close of the Old Testament canon.

Finally, Strauss thinks that the ministry of angels, after the temptation was over, recorded by Matthew and Mark, has its type in and was suggested by the angel who brought food to Elijah after his long fast (I Kings 19 : 5 and 6), helped out, he further supposes, by the fact that the manna of the wilderness was called angels' food (Psalm 78 : 25; *cf.* Wisd. 16 : 20) and would suggest itself to the Christian narrator as suitable in such a case.

It is quite true that in the Old Testament the servants and messengers of God are represented as fasting as well as often being severely tested by trials of various kinds during the discharge of their appointed missions and duties. But it would be difficult to establish that such a view of the Messiah who was expected by the Jews had ever prevailed amongst the latter people. In Isaiah 53 and in Psalm 22 we read of the trials and sufferings of the "Servant of Jahveh"; but whether any *pre*-Christian Jews ever applied these pictures to the Messianic life is more than doubtful.[1] It is clear that the Messianic concepts of the Jews, before the time of Christ, were embodied in the picture of a victorious and successful temporal Prince, or Deliverer, who should free the nation from their bondage and punish all the foes of Israel. The notes of suffering and trial of a passive kind, as tests of fitness for the office, are conspicuously absent in the Messianic literature. There seems to be, therefore, no probability even that the contemporary biographers of Jesus should deliberately insert into their narratives a story setting forth a series of grave disciplinary trials as having been undergone by Jesus before entering upon his Messianic career among men.

These difficulties in the way of accepting the explanation offered by Strauss of the genesis of the temptation-

[1] *Enc. Bib.*, art. "Messiah," sec. 9.

myth have evidently been felt by succeeding mythicists, for we find that the derivation of it from Old Testament analogies has been practically abandoned by them. In its stead we have now offered to us a succession of pagan parallels which, it is supposed, suggested the idea and, perhaps, even some of the detailed matter in the narratives. This is the view taken, for example, by Mr. J. M. Robertson (*Christianity and Mythology*, 1900, pp. 343–356). "The temptation of the God," he says, "is a myth of a specifically Oriental stamp"; but, he adds, it is "not to be found in that form in Hellenistic mythology before the rise of Christism. The latter myth, however, turns out to be at bottom only a variant of the former, different as the stories are; and the proof is reached through certain Hellenic myths of which the origin has not hitherto been traced."

The Christian form of the temptation-story is, he thinks, a fairly close analogue of the temptation of the Buddha; and it has a remoter parallel in the temptation of Zarathustra.[1] But, at the same time, he holds that "there are decisive reasons for concluding that the Christian story was evolved on another line." The first clew to its origin he finds in the detail of the exceeding high mountain of the First and Third Gospels, which has a "marked parallel in a minor Greek myth."[2] This turns out to be contained in a story of Ennius preserved by Lactantius (*Div. Inst.*, I, 11), where Pan is said to lead Jupiter to the mountain called the "Pillar of Heaven";

---

[1] These temptations have been traced by M. Darmsteter (*Ormuzd et Ahriman*, pp. 195–203) to the account of the cows of Indra, which, when stolen by the Panis (evil demons), the dog Saramā (Indra's messenger) is sent to bring back again (see *Rig-Veda*, X, 108). A far-fetched derivation, it would seem.

[2] It has more marked parallels in *Semitic myth* (*cf.* the Bab. "mountain of the gods"); also in Hebrew prophecy and Jewish and Christian apocalyptic. See Ezek. 28 : 16; 40 : 2; Rev. 21 : 10, with Herm., *Simil.*, IX, 1, 1, etc.; also Apoc. Bar. 76 : 8. And, indeed, transport (in body or spirit merely) to a hilltop is a marked peculiarity of Jewish apocalyptic.

this hill Jupiter ascended after offering a sacrifice, and "looked up to heaven, as we now call it." This myth, Mr. Robertson thinks, "taken as a starting-point," would suffice, "when represented either dramatically or in art, to give the Christists the basis for their story."

Further, Pan, he believes, since he was furnished with horns and hoofs and a tail, "represents the devil as conceived by Christians from time immemorial." And "Satan showing Jesus all the kingdoms of the world, and asking to be worshipped, is thus merely *an ethical adaptation of the Greek story*" [1] (!). And then follows a passage which expresses so characteristically Mr. Robertson's line of thought and argument that we will transcribe it in full so as to avoid all risk of misrepresenting him: "Any representation of that [scene] would show the young god [Jupiter] standing by the demon [Pan] and the altar on the mountain top; and to a Christian eye this could only mean that the devil was asking to be worshipped in return for the kingdoms of the earth to which he was pointing;[2] though, for a pagan, Pan was in his natural place as the god of mountains (Homeric *Hymn to Pan*). The oddest aspect of the Christian story is the *naïf* recognition of Satan's complete dominion over the earth, another of the many illustrations of the perpetual lapse of Semitic and other ancient monotheism into dualism. But, as such an extreme conception of the power of Satan is not normally present in the Gospels, the episode in question is the *more likely to have been fortuitously introduced*." [3]

Limits of space will prevent us from making more than a brief reference to the remainder of Mr. Robertson's imaginative and interesting sketch of early Christian development as applied to the temptation-narratives.

---

[1] Italics ours.
[2] In the story he is not said to be "pointing" at anything!
[3] Italics ours.

He further suggests, however, that there is also a link here with the zodiacal astrology of the period. In this Jesus would naturally be associated at the outset of his career with the sign of *Capricorn*, which "'leads the sun from the lower places (*ab inferis partibus*),' and, in virtue of the goat nature, proceeds always 'from low places to the highest rocks' (Macrobius, *Sat.*, I, 21, end)." With *Capricorn*, too, Pan "the goat-god" was primarily associated through his goat legs, and is further directly associated in the myth, where he assists Jupiter in his fight with the Titans. He also works out an imaginative connexion between Satan and the Hebrew demon *Azazel*, said to be "identified" with the goat (in Lev. 16 : 8, A. V., and R. V., margin), and a variant of the Babylonian goat-god *Azaga-suga*, which in turn goes back to the Akkadian sacred goat, which was at once a god and the *Capricorn* of the zodiac.

Any criticism of this imaginative hypothesis of Mr. Robertson must, primarily at least, take the form of pointing out the numerous assumptions and inaccuracies which it contains throughout. When these have been marked off and removed it would be time enough to see what remains of solid value.

And, first of all, Mr. Robertson's idea of "the devil as conceived by Christians from time immemorial" makes us wonder greatly with what type of Christians his lot has been cast! It is true that among the crude religious concepts of ignorant and illiterate folk, and especially during the darkness of the Middle Ages, Satan was largely figured in the popular imagination as furnished with horns and also hoofs and a tail. It would be difficult, though, to establish this concept as being that of, at least, the early Christian writers. Moreover, there is no identity whatever between the demon *Azazel* and the Hebrew *Satan*.[1]

[1] Mr. Robertson here quite misunderstands his references. *Azazel* is not "identified with the goat" (see *Enc. Bib.*, art. "Azazel," sec. 1). Two goats

Few people either would see the slightest parallel between Jupiter "looking up to heaven" (even with Pan at his side) and "Satan showing Jesus all the kingdoms of the world and asking to be worshipped," unless Mr. Robertson here supposes that Pan was seeking the adoration of Jupiter. There is no fasting either in the heathen story, and, above all, no temptation. And how the Christian narrative can, by any stretch of imagination, be regarded as an *ethical adaptation of the myth* passes all comprehension. Myths were notoriously *un*ethical and personal morals were wholly negligible factors in all pagan religions.

Furthermore, the Christian story nowhere recognises "Satan's complete dominion over the earth." Such a view prevails neither in the Gospels generally (as Mr. Robertson practically admits) nor in this story. The Christian view is, and ever has been, that Satan, once a spiritual servant and agent of God, has lapsed into a position of revolt against his authority, and that God, in his wisdom, and for some sufficient and good reason—perhaps the discipline of mankind—is permitting this, for a time, in the sphere of this world.

Neither is there in the evangelist's story any illustration of a lapse from monotheism into dualism. The latter admits two co-ordinate and almost eternal powers, one good and the other evil. This is exemplified only in one *Aryan* religion, the faith founded by Zarathustra. Semitic monotheistic religious systems are wholly exempt from it, as witness the case of Mohammedanism to-day. Mr. Robertson's pagan Satan (Pan), too, is here a power not adverse to, but in accord with, Jupiter—a concept

---

were set apart, *one* for Jahveh, *one* for Azazel, who was a fallen angel, one of the sons of Elohim, evil in character, but not altogether unfriendly to man. See *Enoch* 6 : 6 *f.*; 8 : 1, and especially 10 : 4–8; 13 : 1. The reader may also be referred to a very illuminative article on "The Scapegoat in Bab. Rel.," *Expository Times*, October, 1912, pp. 9–13.

wholly unlike that of both the Hebrew and Christian Satan.

In short, it is only by drawing a caricature of the Christian system, and adopting the popular and cruder presentations of that religion, that he can make out a case at all. His other mythical and astrological clews we cannot deal with here in detail. We would, however, point out, before concluding, that in all probability the exceeding high mountain was not a part of, at least, the original tradition as recorded by Mark. In Mark Jesus was merely in the "wilderness," that is, one of the broken and stony deserts to the south or east of Judæa (the resort of ascetics in all ages), "forty days tempted (*i. e.*, tried) of Satan." Even in the narrative of Matthew only one of the trials takes place on a mountain; the last temptation takes place upon a pinnacle of the temple.[1] A mountain has, indeed, but little, if anything, to do with the story; for, as we will see presently, Jesus being taken to either mountain top or pinnacle of the temple is, without doubt, merely a symbolic expression. He was —*in propria personâ*—in the wilderness throughout it all.

And now we may turn to Professor Drews. Robertson's elaborate hypothesis is practically passed over by him. He merely says (*The Christ Myth*, English translation, p. 236): "The account of the temptation of Jesus sounds very much like the temptation of Buddha, so far as it is not derived from the temptation of Zarathustra by Ahriman, or the temptation of Moses by the devil,

---

[1] A fragment of doubtful source and connexion, preserved by Origen (*Comm. in Johan*, III, 63) and supposed to be from the *Gospel according to the Hebrews*, speaks of Jesus being conveyed by his "mother, the Holy Spirit," to the mountain Tabor. Hilgenfeld says (*Nov. Test. extra Can. Recept.*, IV, 23) that this passage is commonly referred to the *Temptation*, but that Baur (*Manichäisches Religionssystem*, 485) rightly assigns it to the *Transfiguration*. The mountain, in any case, as Cheyne says, was later probably supposed to be the old mythical earth's centre, or navel of the Hebrew paradise (Ezek. 28 : 16, etc.), and this, he thinks, was placed by early tradition in the Jerahmeelite Negeb (*cf.* Isaiah 28 : 16).

of which the rabbis told." We will, therefore, turn to the first two of these narratives and give them here as fully as our space-limits will admit.

The Temptation of Zarathustra

In the temptation of Zarathustra[1] the scene is opened by the rush from the regions of the north[2] of Angra Mainyu,[3] the daêva of the daêvas, who orders a fiend[4] (*drug*) to destroy Zarathustra. But the attack of the daêva was repulsed by the chanting of the Ahuna Vairya[5] by Zarathustra, and the fiend returned to report his ill success.

Meanwhile, Zarathustra, who "saw (all this) from within his soul" (or, in modern phraseology, subconsciously) started forward swinging large stones "as big as a house," obtained from Ahura Mazda,[6] with which he threatens Angra Mainyu and the daêvas. The former begs Zarathustra not to harm his creatures, and, changing his tactics, promises him a "great boon" if he will renounce the "good law of the worshippers of Mazda" (*cf.* Matt. 4: 8 and 9). This Zarathustra emphatically refuses to do, and the arch-fiend then asks what weapons he has that will avail in a fight. To this Zarathustra replies that his weapons are the *haoma*[7] and the words taught by

[1] For the English translation of the full text of this narrative, see *The Zend-Avesta*, Vendidad, Fargad XIX (*Sacred Books of the East*), by Jas. Darmsteter, pp. 204–207 and 217–219.

[2] *I. e.*, from hell, which lies in the north (*cf.* XIX, 2; Yt., XXII, 25).

[3] The "hostile" or destroying spirit; afterwards contracted to Ahriman. In the *Vedas* the daêvas are good spirits.

[4] This fiend is said to have propounded "malignant riddles," after the manner of Œdipus and the Sphinx.

[5] A prayer formula considered to have great (magic) power.

[6] "Lord all-wise," afterwards contracted to Ormazd (Ormuz) = the good spirit.

[7] The *soma* of the *Vedas*, an intoxicating drink used at certain sacrifices and regarded as conveying spiritual inspiration from the gods.

Mazda (*i. e.*, the sacred magical *formulæ* for compelling evil spirits), the Ahuna Vairya, and again he chants this aloud.

Then Zarathustra applies to Ahura Mazda for a revelation of "the law." He is taught how the fiend may be still more effectually repelled, how the creation of Mazda is to be worshipped, how uncleanness is to be washed away, and what becomes of the soul after death. The narrative next describes the rout of Angra Mainyu and his host.

Angra Mainyu next tries to rally his daêvas, and orders them to "gather together at the head of Arezūra"[1] for a fresh attack. Upon which, we are told, the "evil-doing daêvas" run away, casting the evil eye. "Let us gather together," they say, "at the head of Arezūra." But they refuse, after all, to attack Zarathustra again. "How can we procure his death?" they urge by way of remonstrance with their leader. "He is the stroke that fells the fiends; he is a counter-fiend; he is a drug of the drugs." The task is an impossible one; and so, finally, "they rush away, the wicked, evil-doing daêvas, into the depths of the dark, horrid world of hell," and the temptation of the holy Zarathustra is at an end.

The Temptation of Gautama

We will now turn to the corresponding trial of Gautama,[2] which is properly prefaced by the "Great Renunciation." In this he leaves his father's palace, and a life of ease and pleasure, and rides forth into the world to discover the great secrets of all being and happiness. His father had ordered the city gates to be shut against his egress; "but the angel residing at the gate opened it." At the very moment of leaving the city, however,

[1] The gate of hell.
[2] For the complete narrative in the *Nidānakathā*, see *Buddhist Birth Stories*, by T. W. Rhys Davids, pp. 83–84, 96–101, and 106 *ff*.

Māra[1] appeared and endeavoured to stay the Bodhisat.
Standing in the air before him, he exclaimed: "Depart
not, O my lord! In seven days from now the wheel of
empire will appear and will make you sovereign over
the four continents and the two thousand adjacent
isles; stop, O my lord!" (*Cf.* Matt. 4 : 8 and 9.) The
Bodhisat informs the evil spirit that he does not desire
sovereignty over the world, but wishes to become a
Buddha,[2] and by so becoming achieve something greater
than earthly sovereignty; he will thereby "make the ten
thousand world systems shout for joy." Thereupon the
fiend resolves to follow Gautama and watch for any
thought of lust or anger or malice in his heart; and so,
the account proceeds, he followed, "ever watching for
some slip as closely as a shadow which never leaves its
object."

We have next the journey to the Bo-tree and the "temptation" thereunder to abandon his aspirations to Buddha-
hood and complete enlightenment, of which the following
is an abstract:

The Bodhisat seated himself with his back to the
trunk of the Bo-tree,[3] and resolved never to move from
his seat there until he had attained to "complete insight." Then, we are told, the army of Māra advanced
against him in due order. It stretched "twelve leagues
before him," and as many on either side, while behind
him it reached to the rocky limits of the world; above
him it was nine leagues in height, and the sound of its
war-cry was heard twelve leagues away, "like the sound
of a great earthquake." At the head of this host rode
"Māra the Angel," upon an elephant two hundred and

---

[1] The evil spirit. Sansc., √ *mṛi*, "to cause to die," "to kill." *Cf.* Hebrew,
Sātān, "adversary."

[2] An enlightened person.

[3] The older *Pāli* texts refer to Māra as the adversary of the Buddha but
are silent as to the "great temptation" under the Bo-tree, of which the
later legend, as we have it, has so much to say.

fifty leagues high. And he had "created for himself a thousand arms and seized all kinds of weapons." With these he and his army "went on to overwhelm the great being." On the other hand, the good angels of "the ten thousand world systems," who are described as ranged on the side of the Buddha, are said to have been meanwhile speaking his praises; and their King Sakka blew upon his great trumpet, which was one hundred and twenty cubits long and which gave forth a blast that resounded for four months. But, on the approach of Māra and his host, they all pusillanimously turned and fled, and the Buddha was left alone.

Thereupon the arch-fiend and his satellites commenced their onset from behind Gautama, and the latter, looking all around and seeing that he was wholly deserted even by the "gods," reflected: "No father is here, nor mother, nor any other relative to help me. But those Ten Cardinal virtues have long been to me as retainers fed from my store. So, making the virtues my shield, I must strike this host with the sword of virtue and thus overwhelm it. And so he sat meditating on the Ten Perfections."

Then Māra began his attack with a great whirlwind from all the four corners of the earth, with the intent to drive away Gautama from his seat; but he failed to do so. The whirlwind was succeeded by a great rain from hundreds and thousands of immense clouds, and the great flood thereby caused overtopped the trees of the forest; but it was unable to wet even the robe of the Buddha.

After this, then, followed a great shower of rocks— "mighty mountain peaks came hurtling through the air" upon Gautama. But all these changed into bouquets of heavenly flowers when they reached the Bo-tree. These, again, were succeeded by volleys of deadly weapons—swords, spears, and arrows; but these, likewise, became flowers when they struck the Buddha. Storms of red-hot charcoal, hot ashes, sand, and mud next came successively "flaming through the air"; but they fell at the Buddha's feet as heavenly perfume. Finally, there fell upon him a thick darkness; but this also disappeared on reaching the Bo-tree.

Then Māra, mounting upon the "Mountain Girded,"[1] ordered Gautama to get up and surrender to him the seat beneath the Bo-tree. "Get up, Siddhatta, from that seat!" he cried. "It is meant for me!" But Gautama reminded Māra that he had not perfected the ten cardinal virtues; he had not sacrificed himself in the five great acts of self-renunciation and the salvation of the world and the attainment of wisdom. The seat did not belong to him, but to the Buddha.

Thereupon Māra threw at him the great sceptre-javelin which he carried; but this became a garland of flowers, which remained as a canopy over him; also the fresh masses of rock hurled by the host became bouquets at his feet, though the angels had now given him up for lost.

The tempter's next move was to accuse Gautama of not having given alms. But the latter, raising his right hand from beneath his robe, called upon the earth to bear him witness of "the seven-hundred-fold great gift" he had made in his former birth as Wessantara; and the earth gave reply: "I am witness to thee of that."

And then the great elephant of Māra fell down upon his knees when he realised the generosity of Wessantara; and the army of Māra "fled this way and that way, so that not even two were left together; throwing off their clothes and their turbans, they fled each one straight on before him. But the heavenly host, when they saw that the army of Māra had fled, cried out: "The tempter is overcome! Siddhatta the prince has prevailed! Come, let us honour the victor," etc.

[1] The name of Māra's great elephant.

The baffled arch-fiend now changed his tactics, and despatched his seductive daughters, among whom were Craving, Discontent, and Lust, to try gentler methods. But their charms were also unavailing. Gautama remained calm and impassive, and, rebuking them for their boldness, forces them to retire discomfited and disgraced.[1]

Before discussing the above narratives, we may briefly mention here another "source" (and, in a certain sense, a "parallel") of the Biblical temptation-story which has been since advanced by Professor Jensen, the distinguished Assyriologist. This is drawn from the Gilgamesh epic of Babylon, which is, he thinks, the basis and real original source of the whole story of Jesus as related in the Gospels and Epistles.[2]

In this myth Eabani, a monster specially created by the goddess *Aruru*, is held by Jensen to be a mythical "parallel" of Jesus,[3] and the alleged correspondences to the temptation-narrative are worked out by him as follows. Eabani, after visiting Gilgamesh at the city of Erech, flees to the steppe. In like manner, after his baptism, Jesus flees into the wilderness. Then the sun-god (*Shamash*) calls from heaven to Eabani in the desert with kind words, and speaks to him of delicious food, of loaves of bread, and of his feet being kissed by the kings of the earth. This incident is supposed to appear in the Christian "myth" as "the devil speaking to Jesus about bread, which he is urged to make from stones,"

---

[1] In the *Khadirangara Jātaka* ("Birth Stories"), pp. 334–337, there is another so-called "temptation" of the Bodhisat, wherein Māra attempts to put a stop to his almsgiving and destroy him. After this failed Māra went away to the place where he dwelt, and the Bodhisat, "standing on the lotus [flower], preached the law to the people in praise of charity and righteousness, and then returned to his house surrounded by the multitude."

[2] *Moses, Jesus, Paulus: drei varianten des babylonischen gottmenschen Gilgamesch.* (1909), pp. 27–30.

[3] Other prototypes of Jesus in this myth are said to be Xisuthros and Gilgamesh himself.

and about "Jesus ruling all the kingdoms of the earth if he would kiss the devil's feet." Finally, Eabani returns from the steppe to Erech and lives there with Gilgamesh once more. Similarly, Jesus returns from the wilderness to his native place.

In reviewing the temptation-narratives of both Zarathustra and the Buddha, the first thing that strikes the reader is the exaggerated use in both of hyperbole and symbolism. To treat these stories as being ever regarded by any one as historical, in our Western and modern sense of the term, seems to the present writer wholly to misunderstand their entire purport and meaning. They are, it is quite evident, highly, if not wholly, symbolic and must be interpreted from that point of view. But, after the usual Oriental fashion, the symbolism is characterised by exaggeration of the grossest and most absurd kind; this, however, is ever the Eastern manner whenever the "supernatural" is in question.

Again, there can be no doubt that both of these stories, in their primitive form at least, are older than the corresponding Gospel narratives and have undergone considerable development and elaboration. The Gospel stories, on the other hand, are moderate in their symbolism, and even prosaic by comparison, and if borrowed from these—even as regards *ideas*—must have undergone much pruning and toning down. That they have not done this, however, is pretty clear from the older and simpler form of the temptation-narrative in Mark, and also from the fact that myths never lose their elaboration by passing into the literature of other peoples, though they often change the modes of expression. All this tells strongly against any theory of borrowing by the evangelists, whether of the details or of the ideas embodied in the story. Moreover, there is, as we have seen, only one temptation which they have in common with the fuller Gospel narratives—that of the bribe of earthly sovereignty. Everything else is wholly different, and even that temptation differs greatly from the one recorded in the Gospels. In the Buddhist story Gautama is to have a world empire if he will stay at home and renounce all aspirations to enlightenment, while Zarathustra is somewhat vaguely promised a "great boon" if he will abjure the "good law of the worshippers of Mazda." On the other hand, Jesus is offered the sovereignty of the world if he will "worship Satan," which we may take to mean, aspire to an earthly and temporal Messianic kingdom such as the Jews dreamt of instead of that kingdom which was not of this world. The physical violence offered to both Zarathustra and Gautama, as well as the malignant riddles of the demon, together with all the exuberant flights of fancy found in both the pagan stories, are likewise conspicuously absent from the Gospels and, above all, from the chaste and subdued narrative of Mark.

We may, therefore, take it as certain that there has been no Zoroastrian or Buddhist influence directly at work in the composition of the narratives of any of the evangelists. That the spiritual concepts of the age have coloured the fuller presentments by Matthew and Luke is more than probable; such a colouration would, in any circumstances, be unavoidable. These points are freely admitted by Doctor Cheyne, who says most distinctly (*Enc. Bib.*, art. "Temptation of Jesus," sec. 14) that the mythic elements in the temptation of Jesus cannot be traced to imitations of either of the two parallel stories, and adds: "So far as we know as yet, it is only in the Apocryphal Gospels (150–700 A. D.) that Buddhist influence can be traced." This is also the view of the great majority of competent authorities on Buddhism. Professor Oldenberg says emphatically (*Buddha sein Leben, seine Lehre, seine Gemeinde*, S. 118): "Influences of the Buddhist tradition on the Christian are not to be thought of." It is unnecessary to multiply cases of such expert opinion.[1]

Comment upon such a scheme of "parallels" as those drawn from the Gilgamesh epic seems really unnecessary even when they are advanced by so brilliant a scholar as Doctor Jensen. Still we may, perhaps, point out that the so-called "temptation" is no temptation at all. It is merely an assurance of Shamash the sun-god that his wants will be provided for. Eabani had grown restive under the restraints of civilisation in Erech, and the sun-god practically asks him why he longed for his former wild life amongst the animals of the desert. Had not Gilgamesh supplied him with food and clothing, and would he not give him an easy seat on his right hand and oblige the kings of the earth to kiss his feet? And then we read that at daybreak "the words of Shamash the mighty loosed the bands of Eabani and his furious heart came to rest." The whole argument is, however, in reality absurd; and it is difficult even to take Professor Jensen seriously.

But, it may be justly observed, all this is so far mere destructive criticism; what can we put in its place? The Biblical story is evidently not history in the modern sense; what, then, is its origin and meaning? This is a fair question, and we will endeavour to answer it frankly.

The story of the temptation of Jesus is, we believe, a symbolic narrative expressive of one of those psychical experiences which affect the innermost core of our spiritual being.[2] It was customary in the East for all founders

[1] For an able and modern article on supposed Buddhist parallels and influences, see M. L. de la Vallee Poussin's "History of the Religions of India in Its Bearings on Christian Apologetics" (*Revue des Sciences Philosophiques et Theologiques*, July, 1912).

[2] *Cf.* with this scene "The Transfiguration," chap. 8. The same may be said of the experiences ascribed to Zarathustra and Gautama, assuming them to have been historical characters, as seems more than probable. In their case, however, the descriptive narratives have been so loaded with extravagant hyperbole and exaggerated symbolism as to place them beyond all

and reformers of religion, as well as prophets, to retire for a while to the broken and desolate country in their respective neighbourhoods and there, by means of a course of fasting and severe mental introspection, to prepare themselves for the mission which they felt called upon to undertake. Here, in places firmly believed to be the special haunts of spirits, chiefly evil or mischievous,[1] as well as wild beasts (*cf.* Mark 1 : 13), inward doubts and questions, and visions, often hallucinatory in character, as a rule, speedily supervened. These experiences, whether hallucinatory or veridical, in a spiritual sense were sometimes recorded in highly symbolical language for the edification and warning of mankind. Doctor Cheyne thinks that all temptation-stories in general originated in the mythical conflict between the light-god and the storm-spirit. This is no doubt true in a sense; but we must remember that the light-god and the storm-spirit themselves were but symbols of spiritual powers by whom men were ultimately controlled and to whom obedience or resistance was due. For there can be no temptation to reject the good and choose the evil, even in the most rudimentary sense of the term, unless there is a spiritual and ethical note in the experience.

Now, Jesus must, at the outset of his earthly career, have been beset by three great temptations, affecting, respectively, body, soul, and spirit, to employ the conventional divisions in general use.[2] He was tempted, no

comparison with those of the evangelists. Binet-Sanglé finds (*La folie de Jésus*, pp. 356 *ff.*) in the narrative of the Temptation seven hallucinations, two purely optical and five which were at once optical and *auditives verbales*. He attributes them to the combined influence of excitement, night, loneliness, and abstinence. See chap. 6, p. 114, note 2.

[1] Such as, especially, the Hebrew, שֵׁדִים ("violent ones"), and שְׂעִירִים ("hairy ones," Isaiah 13 : 21; 34 : 14, etc.); *cf.* the Arab., *Jinns*, Assyr., *Utukkus*, etc., and the Greek, δαίμονες, δαιμόνια ("demons"), etc.

[2] The order of Luke is preferable as giving them in the natural sequence —from lowest to highest.

doubt, to choose the life of greater bodily ease and comfort instead of that path wherein he was often an hungered and had not where to lay his head. Further, there was the temptation to accept the national ideal of a successful earthly monarch and to rule over a greater kingdom than that of Solomon. And, lastly, he would be tempted to mistrust the good-will and support of his Father in heaven, especially in hours of bodily weakness and depression. Ought he not, therefore, to test ("tempt") this in some way at the outset, in order to assure himself that the mission was in truth his Father's will and no mere dream of his own mind? Through all these successive temptations he must have passed one by one; and they would doubtless be related by him afterwards to at least the innermost group of his disciples. And these trials of faith were recorded *more Orientali,* in the language of symbol and hyperbole, by the two later synoptists. As a modern scholar very truly writes: "He was made like to his brethren; he was touched with the feelings of our infirmities; he was able to sympathise (δυμνάμενον συμπαθῆται), for he was tempted in all respects like us. In the Gospel as it is handed down to us the Temptation of Christ is summed up in three episodes set at the beginning of the story, and told in a symbolic form, which may or may not have been given to them by Jesus himself." [1]

Finally, there remains for our consideration one more point which is frequently regarded as of vital importance in such questions as these. Had these spiritual experiences, as described, the objective reality which the narratives seem to imply? Above all, was there an actual arch-spirit of evil in person testing the fitness of the future Messiah? Or were they, severally and collectively, merely the questionings and strivings of that

[1] Mr. T. R. Glover, *The Conflict of Religions in the Early Roman Empire,* p. 127.

mysterious superconsciousness which ever lies at the back of all our normal mental activities and which seems as yet to be called into activity only by extraordinary exigencies in the life of man? The present writer will endeavour, in compliance with his promise, to deal frankly with the reader upon this point also.

The question asked is a difficult if not an impossible one to answer, even partially, at the present time. To put it in other words, it is practically to inquire how, in all such cases, the merely subjective and hallucinatory is to be separated and distinguished from the spiritually objective and veridical. This important problem of the future is now engaging the serious attention of psychical research. Modern orthodox psychology has, it is true, discouraged such inquiries and in some cases even denied the objectivity and independent reality of spiritual phenomena no less than the existence of the indwelling soul which experiences them;[1] but at the same time it has certainly not established the entire subjectivity of either. Neither can the existence or non-existence of an unfriendly spirit, or spirits, be proved or disproved to-day. At the same time the diabolical character of much of the evil in the world seems hard to reconcile with the theory of neuroses. External influences of a demoniacal nature are, it is true, out of fashion just now; but they might any day be discovered to have some elements of fact in them.[2] The true attitude for the moment, therefore, is one of suspended judgment.

But even if it be ultimately established that all the

[1] *E. g.*, "Souls are out of fashion" (William James at Oxford in 1910). See, however, the more recent work, *Body and Mind*, by Professor William McDougall, of Oxford, who reaffirms, from the scientific standpoint, the highly probable objective reality of the spiritual element in man and its experiences. The reader is also referred to the researches found in the modern works on psychical research.

[2] See *Daemon Possession in China and Allied Themes*, by Doctor J. L. Naevius (1896), and *Daemonic Possession*, by Doctor W. M. Alexander (1902).

temptations and sins incident to man are the outcome of subjective stirrings and impulses of a lower type, even if man were proved to be "his own devil," the spiritual *value* of each experience would still remain. The lower self, with all its tendencies and strivings to what is base and earthly, would still need to be conquered by the higher self, with all its nobler aims and aspirations. After all, it matters but little whether evil thoughts and temptations are injected *ab extra* by a personal power or engendered by internal causes and movements. The result in either case is the same. The higher self, strengthened and sustained by powers and energies of spiritual origin, and emanating from the source of all spiritual life and energy, must ever grapple with and strive against the lower self, until the tempter is finally overcome and man enters upon that spiritual inheritance where, we are assured, there is no more temptation and from whence sin and pain and sorrow will have for ever fled away.

CHAPTER VIII

THE TRANSFIGURATION

WE may once more conveniently open our discussion of this event in the life of Jesus with a short summary of the view of it taken by D. F. Strauss, which may be quoted as a fair sample of what we have termed the "common-sense" type of mythical criticism. He comments upon it (*Life of Jesus*, III, pp. 247 and 248) as follows:

"To comprehend how such a narrative could be formed by the legend, we should examine, in the first place, the peculiarity to the essence of which the other peculiarities most readily attach themselves, viz., the brilliance which rendered the face of Jesus like the sun and the bright light with which even his garments were invested. For the Orientals, and in particular for the Hebrews, the fine and majestic is almost always connected with something luminous. Solomon in his Songs compares his beloved to the morning, to the noon, to the sun (6 : 10); pious men sustained by the divine blessing are compared to the sun in his glory (Judges 5 : 31); and especially the future life of the blessed is compared to the brilliance of the firmament (Daniel 13 : 3; Matt. 13 : 43). In consequence, not only does God appear in a burst of light, and the angels with luminous countenances and shining garments (Psalm 50 : 2 and 3; Daniel 7 : 9; 10 : 5 and 6; Luke 24 : 4; Rev. 1 : 13–16), but also the pious individuals of Jewish antiquity. . . .

"In the same way the Jewish posterior legend endowed

154

of burnished cloth of gold on the body of the Blessed One,
lo! it seemed as if they had lost their splendour.' "

Thereupon the Buddha explained the mystery: "On
the night, Ananda, on which a *Tathāgata*[1] attains to the
supreme and perfect insight, and on the night in which
he passes finally away, in that utter passing away which
leaves nothing whatever remaining, on these occasions
the colour of the skin of the Tathāgata becomes clear
and exceeding bright."

There is some resemblance here, but only of a very
general character, which certainly does not suggest borrowing of any kind either way.   And, in any case, that
hypothesis opens up a number of complex and difficult
problems both here and elsewhere, each of which would
require a settlement before any definite conclusion could
be reached; *e. g.*: (1) Does the *Sutta*, in which this story is
preserved, date, *in its present form*, from before the time
of Christ?[2] (2) Can any literary borrowing between
Palestine and India *before* that period be shown to be
even probable? (3) If borrowing of idea there be here,
could not the early Christian compilers have got the
idea more readily and directly from the Old Testament,
as Strauss thought? After making every allowance, the
theory of a Buddhist source seems, to say the least of it,
highly improbable; and undoubtedly similar ideas and
stories frequently spring up simultaneously in different
countries and places, so there is probably no connexion
whatever between the two narratives. This is also the
view of Lester, who says (*The Historic Jesus*, 1912): "The

---

[1] De Bunsen thinks (*Angel Messiah of Buddhists, Essenes, and Christians*,
1880) that this = the Jewish Messianic title *Habbā* (ὁ Ἐρχόμενος), "the
Coming One." But it is a derivative from the Sansc., *tathā*, "so," and
either *gata*, "gone," or *agata*, "come," and accordingly means "so gone" or
"so come." Burnouf (*Hist. du Buddh. Ind.*, pp. 75 and 76) says that the
Tibetan scholar Csoma thought it meant "the One who has gone through
his career like his predecessors" (the previous Buddhas).

[2] Rhys Davids thinks that the *Suttanta* date from about the fourth century B. C. But Indian dates are proverbially very uncertain. And there
is the question of interpolation.

details for the story were abundantly supplied in the legend of Moses (Ex. 25). The six days, the three favoured friends, the light of the divine glory were all to be found in that ancient tale; while the whiteness of the garments, surpassing the brightness of the sun and the whiteness of snow, came from the *Apocalypse of Enoch* (see *The Secrets of Enoch* 22 : 8–10)."

We will now turn to Professor Drews, who, as we might expect, links up the event with ancient astral-mythic ideas that had been long current in other parts of Asia Minor and, further, parallels the details of the story with those of the baptism. On the basis of the theory that the synoptists represent the public career of Jesus as occupying only one year (instead of three, as commonly supposed)—a precarious hypothesis—he proceeds as follows [*The Christ Myth*, English translation, pp. 126 and 127]: "As at the baptism, so here, too, Jesus was proclaimed by a heavenly voice as the Son or beloved of God, or rather of the Holy Spirit. As the latter is in Hebrew of feminine gender,[1] it consequently appears that in this passage we have before us a parallel to the baptism of Jesus in the Jordan. The incident is generally looked upon as though by it was emphasised the higher significance of Jesus in comparison with the two chief representatives of the old order and as though Jesus was extolled before Moses and Elijah by the transfiguration. Here, too, however, the sun-god Helios is obviously concealed beneath the form of the Israelite Elijah. On this account Christianity changed the old places of worship of Zeus and Helios [? Zeus-Herakles] upon eminences into chapels of Elijah; and Moses is no other than the moon-god,[2] the Men of Asia Minor. And

---

[1] The Hebrew word for spirit is *generally* feminine. But the Hebrews had no feminine principle in the godhead.

[2] Moses, however (p. 89, note), "is to be looked upon as an offshoot of Jahwe and Tammuz"!

he has been introduced into the story because the divine lawgivers in almost all mythologies are the same as the moon, the measurer of time and regulator of all that happens (*cf.* Manu among the Indians, Minos among the Greeks, Men [Min] among the Egyptians)," adding in a note (p. 127): "The horns (crescent) which he also shares with Jahwe, as the Syrian Hadah shows, recalls to mind the moon-nature of Moses."

And, lastly, he sums up as follows (p. 127): "Accordingly, we have before us in the story of the transfiguration in the Gospels only another view of the story of the birth of the light-god, or fire-god, such as lies at the root of the story of the baptism of the Christian Saviour. And with the thought of the new birth of the Saviour is associated that of the baptism of Jesus, and particularly that of the fire baptism of which the sun partakes at the height of its power."

It will be convenient to discuss first of all Doctor Drews's derivations.

"Moses is, as regards his name [$\sqrt{ma}$, *mo*], the 'water-drawer'" (p. 127, note). Now, in the Old Testament the name appears as מֹשֶׁה (*Mōsheh*), and, if this be the correct form, its meaning would be "deliverer" ($\sqrt{משה}$, "to draw out," *cf.* II Sam. 22 : 17; Psalm 18 : 17). But this view is open to doubt, and Lepsius (*Chronologie*, 326) has suggested a derivation from the Egyptian *mes* (or *mesu;* W. H. Müller writes it *mose*), meaning child, which occurs as a name by itself and also as part of a theophorous name (*e. g.*, Thothmes, etc., see *Enc. Bib.*, art. "Moses," sec. 2). With this derivation Doctor Sayce agrees (*Fresh Light from the Ancient Monuments*, pp. 64 and 65), and Dillmann holds (Ex.-Lev. 16) that Moses (=Mesu) was the original name. The chief objection to this theory, that the Hebrews would not have accepted a name for their hero from their Egyptian oppressors, is not a valid one. Moses was believed by the former to be of Hebrew birth, and a very slight change in the spelling of his name would give the Hebraic word for "deliverer," a most suitable appellation in their view.

In order to connect Moses with the Asiatic moon-god, Drews lays great stress upon "the horns (crescent), which he also shares with Jahwe, as the Syrian Hadah shows" (p. 127, note)—another very dubious support to his hypothesis. Horns, in Eastern countries, were symbolical of power and were commonly an adjunct to the head-dresses of gods and kings. In Ex. 34 : 29 it is stated in the Massoretic text that when Moses came down from the mount his face "emitted rays," "shone" (קָרַן). The LXX, in the Vatican text, reads δεδόξασται, "was endowed with glory," "shone"; but in the Latin Vulgate we find *cornuta esset*, "was horned." This result is attained by reading קרן as קֶרֶן, instead of קָרַן, and Jerome states that Aquila, in his version of the LXX, followed this reading.[1] Cheyne thinks that this reading, or perhaps the *idea* upon which it is based, may be traced to the two horns of Am(m)on (Amun), the god of Thebes, which Alexander the Great affixed to the effigy of himself on coins, and from which he was later styled "the two-horned king" in the *Koran* (Sur. 18 : 85). "The original reading," he thinks, "must have been not קֶרֶן but בְּרַק" (*bārak*, "lightened"; *cf.* Phœn., *bărca*), and he adds: "It would be going too far off to compare the horns [crescent] of the moon-god *Sin*, whose emblem was a crown or mitre adorned with horns" (*Enc. Bib.*, art. "Horn"). That Moses represents the Semitic moon-god is a mere speculation due to the ingenuity of Winckler, and the alleged affinity of his name to *Manu*, *Minos* (so pressed by Drews), is probably due only to the mere alliteration in the words. It is highly probable, indeed, that the name Minos is only a variant of an original *Manva*, *i. e.*,

[1] Gesenius, in his *Hebrew Lexicon* (1833), comments thus: "Ridicule Aqu. et Vulg. cornuta esset."

"(the being) endowed with thinking," as we see in the Hindu *Manu* and the German *Mann*. In any case, if Manu and Minos are astral deities, they must be forms of the *sun*-god and not connected with the moon at all; for, *inter alia*, the wife of Minos is Pasiphaë, the moon-goddess. *Åmsu*, or *Min* (Men), is also a personification of the male reproductive powers of nature and was identified with Pan by the Greeks. In short, we have here, in Doctor Drews's book, a mere mass of unverified and loose speculation upon which no sound hypothesis can be raised.

Again, with regard to Elijah, surely he cannot mean to equate Elijah[1] (*Elijahu*) with Helios and (above all) with Jesus.[2] Elijah means "Jah is my God," while Helios is derived, according to Peile (*Gk. and Lat. Etym.*, p. 152), from $\sqrt{us}$, "to burn," with an original form $a\dot{v}(\sigma)\acute{\epsilon}\lambda\iota o s$, $\dot{a}\acute{\epsilon}\lambda\iota o s$, with Cretan $\dot{a}\beta\epsilon\lambda\iota o s$ (see also Curtius, *Gr. Etym.*, no. 162).[3]

By no possible process can we legitimately find Helios concealed beneath the form of the Israelite Elijah, and no sound theory of identification can be built upon the similarity of certain forms of their names or the functions assigned to each of them.

Lastly, Drews's view that the transfiguration represents the sun-god undergoing his baptism of fire at the highest and turning-point of his annual career is disposed of by this simple fact alone that, as we have already seen (chap. 4), a careful examination of the name Jesus, and of the circumstances of his career, shows that he was not in any sense of the word a sun-god at all.

[1] Also written *Helias* (IV Esd. 7 : 30). This form offers a great temptation to identify the name with Helios (Helius) the sun!

[2] For "Elijah (*Eli-scha*) and Jeho-schua (Joshua, Jesus) agrees even in their names"! (*The Christ Myth*, p. 238).

[3] From this Aryan root comes the old Etruscan solar-god *Usil*, "the burning one," identified subsequently by the Greeks with Apollo (*cf.* Roman, *Sol*). But Jahveh was almost certainly not a *sun*-god.

We will now turn to the Greek text of the narratives of this event and see what light a careful examination of them will throw upon the matter.

In describing the change which all three synoptists state came over Jesus, Mark and Matthew use exactly the same phrase—καὶ μεταμορφώσθη ἔμπροσθεν αὐτῶν ("and he underwent a change in their presence")—which, no doubt, in each case points to a quotation from a common source. Luke, however, adopts a verbally different phrase, and perhaps describes the change in his own words—ἐγένετο . . . τὸ εἶδος τοῦ προσώπου αὐτοῦ ἕτερὸν ("the form [or expression] of his countenance became different," or "changed")—a general equivalent of the former phrase. All three also note that this change appeared to extend to the clothing; the raiment became white. Now the verb μεταμορφόομαι is used of a *spiritual* change in Romans 12 : 2, and also in II Cor. 3 : 18, with apparently a reference to this scene, for a comparison with the case of Moses (Ex. 34 : 16) is instituted. This event seems also to be referred to in II Peter 1 : 16 and perhaps in John 1 : 14.

Now, it is evident that the evangelists here are trying to describe what they regard rather as spiritual phenomena than as physical. Indeed, Matthew appears to say so distinctly. Jesus afterwards told them, he adds, to tell the vision (ὅραμα[1]) to no one. No doubt ὅραμα can also be taken to mean some object or other presented to the ordinary normal sight; but it can also, and does frequently, mean the higher vision of the spiritual nature, as it seems to do in this case.[2] And herein lies the answer to the chief difficulty felt by Strauss and prob-

---

[1] ὀπτασία is the regular technical word for immaterial phenomena. But this cannot be pressed.

[2] *Cf.* the case of Stephen (Acts 6 : 15), where Luke, it may be noted, again avoids the word μεταμορφόομαι and compares the spiritualisation of Stephen's face to the expression of an "angel."

ably by many other readers. The brilliance which he failed to understand, and mistook for a physical light, is not intended to be taken as a mere physical phenomenon. The writers are endeavouring to describe phenomena of an abnormal, superphysical—a spiritual—character in terminology, which is really only adapted to normal and purely physical occurrences (*cf.* Acts 2 : 4, etc.), and therefore must fail to describe them adequately owing to the insufficiency of language itself.

A similar criticism will apply to the "voice" (φωνή), which is also mentioned[1] and regarded by the mythicists as a further mark of pseudo-historicity. But the subjective character of such voices, as regards the merely bodily senses, was recognised at least as far back as the fourth century. "What is meant," writes Basil the Great (*Hom. in Ps.* 28, "by the voice of the Lord? Are we to understand thereby a disturbance caused in the air by the vocal organs? Is it not rather a lively image, a clear and sensible vision imprinted on the mind of those to whom God wishes to communicate his thought, a vision[2] analogous to what is imprinted on the mind when we dream."

Now, it would be a great error to suppose hastily, as no doubt many readers will do, that all such experiences as these may, after all, be referred merely to the imagi-

---

[1] Jensen identifies this "voice" (*Moses, Jesus, Paulus*) with the voice of the invisible Xisuthros, who calls out to his shipmates: "You are to be pious." It is difficult, we repeat, to take such "parallels" seriously.

[2] Schmiedel lays down (*Enc. Bib.*, art. "Res. and Asc. Nar.," sec. 34) the psychological antecedents of a vision (= here *hallucination*) as follows: (1) a high degree of psychical excitement; (2) all the elements which are requisite for the formation of a visionary image, whether it be views or ideas, are previously present in the mind and have engaged its activities."

This, no doubt, is true of hallucinatory experiences self-engendered in the subconsciousness; but it is not so of veridical ones, such as a *picture* or *message* transmitted telepathically from an agent to a recipient through the superconsciousness. The real difficulty lies in distinguishing between the two visions.

nation, perhaps that day-dreaming which belongs to the borderland between waking and sleeping.

Luke, it is true, adds (9 : 32) that the disciples were heavy with sleep ($ὕπνῳ$), but adds directly afterwards that they became fully awake during the vision itself. Probably he refers here to ordinary sleep; but he may be thinking of that hypnotic condition which often closely resembles sleep and which so frequently accompanies manifestations of the superconsciousness. His remark, however, has given critics of the type of Mr. J. M. Robertson the welcome opportunity of saying that the incident cannot be historical because Luke practically admits that they were all asleep and dreamt the whole thing. But similar phenomena have been frequently recorded by credible witnesses as having been manifested by many of the great saints and mystics of various ages. In moments of great spiritual exaltation, and in ecstasies, when the superconscious has come forcibly into play while the ordinary consciousness is, perhaps, not wholly withdrawn as it is in the state of deep trance, such a lighting up of the face, and even of the bodily form, has been put on record. Even dying persons who have lived lives of peculiar piety and benevolence have been observed to undergo a remarkable spiritualisation of features during their last moments.

This view of the transfiguration of Jesus has been recently very ably urged by a well-known modern writer[1] upon these obscure religious phenomena. She regards—and rightly so, we believe—the visual and auditory phenomena of this scene as the outcome of a state of spiritual ecstasy in which all present shared to some extent. "The kernel of this story," she writes, "no doubt elaborated by successive editors, possessed by the passion for the marvellous which Jesus unsparingly condemned, seems to be the account of a great ecstasy experienced

[1] Miss E. Underhill, in *The Mystic Way*, p. 117.

by him in one of these wild and solitary mountain places where the soul of the mystic is so easily snatched up to communion with the supreme reality."

With this view of the matter the modern theologian, especially if he be versed in the psychology of the abnormal and superconscious, may well, in the main at least, agree.

But it must also be borne in mind that the habit of describing experiences of a supersensual and religious type in terms of a vivid and symbolic imagery is deeply rooted in the Eastern mind of all ages. It is to this fact, perhaps, rather than to the passion for the marvellous, that we owe this intensely realistic picture of a great spiritual event.

It was by prayer, too, *i. e.*, by a profound and deliberate absorption into the divine life, Miss Underhill thinks—and we may note that Luke (only) records this (vs. 28)—that Jesus attained to this transfigured state. Hence it was that the disciples, whose minds were uplifted in some degree, shared in the spiritual exaltation of their Master. And the impression thus made on them was, as we might expect, recorded in a symbolic form. To their minds, full of recollections of the past and of similar experiences to that in which they now had a share, Moses and Elijah appeared and talked with their Master, though not with them. And even when the vision faded the three disciples were left with a joint and abiding sense of the reality of their experience—a reality, not in the material and earthly sense, but reality in the higher and spiritual sense, which, unlike earthly realities, does not pass away but abides with us for ever.[1]

---

[1] Certain medical and scientific writers, as, *e. g.*, De Loosten, Hirsch, and Binet-Sanglé, ascribe the visions of Jesus to *paranoia* (a chronic form of insanity developing in a neuropathic constitution and presenting systematised delusions).

But Schweitzer very justly says that their researches have "simply as-

sumed that what for us is strange and unfamiliar is, therefore, morbid."
And, further, that "this identification of the unfamiliar with the morbid,
which we find in the statements of the historical and medical writers here
in view, is not legitimate, according to the standards established by modern psychiatry."

As a matter of fact, a precise line of demarcation between the above and
the really healthy *spiritual* experiences is badly needed and is being dili-
gently sought for by students of psychical research.   Meanwhile, we may
perhaps add that the merely morbid and hallucinatory has—at least as a
rule—no *ethical* note about it.   *Cf.* Strauss, *Das Leben Jesu für das deutsche
Volk bearbeitet* (1864), pp. 631 *ff.*; also O. Holtzmann, *War Jesus Ekstati-
ker?* (1903).

CHAPTER IX

THE ENTRY INTO JERUSALEM AND THE EXPULSION OF THE TRADERS

AMONG the earlier of the recent attacks made upon the historical character of these two narratives, perhaps that of Mr. J. M. Robertson stands out most conspicuously and, at first sight, as the most plausible. He tells us (*Christianity and Mythology*, pp. 310 *ff.*) that these stories contain "not a single item of credible history"; the former, indeed, he avers, is nothing more nor less than an old myth pseudo-historicised.[1]

The Entry into Jerusalem

After rebuking Professor Percy Gardner for "repeating once more the fallacious explanation which has imposed (*sic*) on so many of us," he adds that "a glance at the story of Bacchus [Dionysus] crossing a marsh on two asses" and "at the Greek sign for the constellation Cancer (an ass and its foal) would have shown him that he was dealing with a zodiacal myth."

The basis of Mr. Robertson's authority for the above confident statement (though not quoted by him) is the *Poeticon Astronomicon* of Hyginus (flourished A. D. 4). There we read (book II, "Cancer") that "when Bacchus had come to a certain great marsh, which he was unable to cross, having come across two young asses, *he is said to have caught one of them*,[2] and in this way was carried across so that he did not touch the water at all."

[1] *Cf.* with this treatment that of Renan (*Life of Jesus*, XXIII).

[2] Dicitur *unum* deprendisse eorum. It is obvious, therefore, that even in the myth *two* asses were not ridden.

Now, in the constellation Cancer there are two stars (γ and δ, *Cancri*) in the body of the Crab which were named by the astronomer Ptolemy "the two asses"— τώ ὄνω—(*cf.* Theoc., *Idyl.*, XXII, 21; Arat., 890–898; Theophr., *Sign. Pluv.*, IV, 2; Pliny, XVIII, 20), and the luminous patch (*Præsepe*) seen between these two stars was known as the "Manger" (φάτνη).[1] And the above story of Dionysus has been interpreted to be a symbolical explanation of the astronomical fact that the sun when in the midst of the zodiacal sign Cancer is said, figuratively speaking, to be "riding upon two asses," as the Greek astronomers expressed it, and shortly afterwards reaches the zenith of its power, when its light and heat gradually but steadily decline, until it reaches its death at the hibernal solstice in December. We will study this interesting hypothesis, and its application to Christian historic documents, in some detail.

The twelve signs of the zodiac are, as is generally known, those stellar constellations through which the sun passes in its annual journey across the heavens. At a remote period of past time that orb, when crossing the equator at the vernal equinox, was in the sign *Taurus* (Bull), and the new year was then opened by the sun, conceived as a bull entering upon the great furrow of heaven (the ecliptic) as he ploughed his way through the starry field which forms the sky. Owing, however, to the astronomical phenomenon known as the precession of the equinoxes, the sun each succeeding year entered upon its annual course, at the equinox, at a slightly different point in the heavens, until by the time of Christ it had come to start the year of nature in the sign (or constellation) *Aries*[2] (Ram). The sign of the Crab (*Can-*

---

[1] This figures largely in the Iranian myth of Tiṣtar, "the angel of the rain." The Greeks undoubtedly borrowed many of their astronomical ideas and terms from the Babylonians.

[2] It now starts the year from the sign *Pisces* (Fishes); but the sign for *Aries* (Ram), Ψ, is conventionally used by agreement amongst astronomers

cer) was, therefore, at that period not reached until the time of the summer solstice (end of June).

But if, after the manner of Mr. Robertson, we apply the above astronomical facts to the story of Jesus' entry into Jerusalem we are at once involved in serious discrepancies and difficulties. That entry is clearly stated by all four evangelists to have taken place just before the Passover; that is to say, *about the time of the vernal equinox, when the sun was in Aries.* In other words, the story of Dionysus "riding upon the two asses" (*sic*) could not be the explanation of a vernal phenomenon, because it could only refer to one taking place at midsummer, namely, when the position of the sun was in *Cancer*, at the end of June. Indeed, it happened at quite the wrong time of year to suit any such astronomical explanation. The truth of the matter, however, is that Robertson's theory is entirely dependent upon the version given by Matthew of that event, which, it so happens, erroneously lends itself to this recondite and ridiculous interpretation. Let us, therefore, turn next to the Gospel narratives and see how this error arose.

We will notice, in the first place, that the editor of "Matthew" assures his readers (21 : 4) that this event was a fulfilment of Zechariah's prophecy (9 : 9). The latter, in the Massoretic text, tells us that the future Messianic King was one day to enter his city riding upon (literally)

"An ass, even upon a foal, a son of she-asses."
(עַל־חֲמוֹר וְעַל־עַיִר בֶּן־אֲתֹנוֹת.)

This prophecy is, as prophetic utterances in the Old Testament usually are, expressed in accordance with a

as the astronomical starting-point, or equinox. It takes about 2,200 years for the sun to pass through one sign and enter upon the next and about 26,000 years to pass through the twelve signs and reach the original starting-point.

notable rule of Hebrew poetical composition, namely, in a system of parallelism in the lines, in which the second half of a line, or the second member of a couplet, repeats in different words the idea expressed in the first half of the line or the previous line itself. In such a case the two halves of the line (or the two lines) are frequently coupled together by the conjunction *Vav* (ו), which, ordinarily, has the meaning "and," but in positions of this kind means "even." [1] This is termed by grammarians the epexegetical (explanatory) use of Vav. The Greek equivalent καί has a similar double use and double meaning.

Now, let us turn to the Greek LXX translation of Zechariah (Vat. text), and we will find the following literal rendering of the Massoretic version:

"Riding upon a beast of burden, *even* (καί) a young ass-foal."

(ἐπιβεβηκὼς ἐπὶ ὑποζύγιον καὶ πῶλον νέον.)

Here the conjunction (καί) is epexegetical. It should also be noticed that the preposition ἐπί ("upon") is not repeated after the καί, as it would be if the writer meant, "upon a beast of burden, *and upon* a young ass," *i. e.*, upon two asses, as the A. V. (but not the R. V.) wrongly translates both versions.

But let us turn to the other Gospels and see how far they corroborate this explanation of the matter. Mark (11 : 7) tells us that only *one* ass, and that a young foal, was brought to Jesus:

"They bring the *foal* to Jesus and put their cloaks upon *him*, and he sat upon *him*."

(φέρουσιν τὸν πῶλον πρὸς τὸν Ἰησοῦν καὶ ἐπιβάλλουσιν αὐτῷ τὰ ἱμάτια [αὐτῶν] καὶ ἐκάθισεν ἐπ᾽ αὐτόν.)

---

[1] Some scholars translate it "yea."

Luke (19 : 35) records the matter thus:

"And they brought *him* [the foal] to Jesus, and having thrown their cloaks upon the foal they set Jesus upon *him*."

(καὶ ἤγαγον αὐτὸν πρὸς τὸν Ἰησοῦν καὶ ἐπιρρίψαντες αὐτῶν τὰ ἱμάτια ἐπὶ τὸν πῶλον ἐπεβίβασαν τὸν Ἰησοῦν.)

The Fourth Gospel (John 12 : 14 and 15) agrees with both these synoptists:

"And Jesus having found a young ass sat upon *it*, as it is written:

"Fear not, daughter of Zion:
Behold thy King comes
Sitting upon *a foal* of an ass."

(εὑρὼν δὲ ὁ Ἰησοῦς ὀνάριον ἐκάθισεν ἐπ᾽ αὐτό, καθώς ἐστιν γεγραμμένον·

Μὴ φοβοῦ, Θύγατερ Σιών·
Ἰδού, ὁ βασιλεύς σου ἔρχεται
Καθήμενος ἐπὶ πῶλον ὄνου.)

Turning next to the corresponding Matthæan version of the story, we find it differently stated. In 21 : 2 we read:

"Ye will find an ass tied, *and a foal with her*,"
(εὑρήσετε ὄνον δεδεμμένην καὶ πῶλον μετ᾽αὐτῆς),

i. e., two asses. The καί here, it will be seen, is *not* epexegetical.

Again, in vs. 5, the writer says, professing to translate the prophecy of Zechariah:

"Thy king comes to thee . . . sitting upon an ass, *and upon a foal*, a son of a beast of burden."

(ὁ βασιλεύς σου ἔρχεταί σοι . . . ἐπιβεβηκὼς ἐπὶ ὄνον, καὶ ἐπὶ πῶλον, υἱὸν ὑποζυγίου.)

Again (vs. 7) he further says:

> "And they led the she-ass, *and the foal* [to Jesus],
> and placed their cloaks upon *them*, and he sat upon
> *them*.
>
> (ἤγαγον τὴν ὄνον καὶ τὸν πῶλον, καὶ ἐπέθηκεν ἐπ' αὐτῶν
> τὰ ἱμάτια, καὶ ἐπεκάθισεν ἐπάνω αὐτῶν.)[1]

Here it is very evident that Matthew and (following
him) Mr. Robertson have misunderstood both Zechariah and the LXX. And this primary mistake on the
part of Matthew has led Mr. Robertson on to his error
in identifying the story with that told of Dionysus in
the Greek myth, which, as we have seen, he misquotes.
In short, his explanation breaks down completely for two
main reasons. First, Dionysus riding upon two asses as-
tronomically was a *solstitial* and not an equinoctial phenomenon at, and long before, the time of Christ; and,
secondly, neither the Hebrew prophet nor the LXX, nor
any of the evangelists except Matthew, say that Jesus
rode upon two asses—a statement which, in actual fact at
least, would be a gross and palpable absurdity to every
thoughtful person.

But other writers belonging to this school of interpretation have sought for different sources of this picturesque
and very natural story. Thus, Drews, abandoning for
once a mythical explanation, urges (*The Witnesses to the
Historicity of Jesus*, pp. 207 and 208) that the story might
easily grow up out of the study of such passages as Isaiah
52 : 7 (*cf.* 12 : 6 and 26 : 2) and Zech. 9 : 9. He falls,
however, into the same error as Robertson, translating the
prophecy wrongly as referring to *two asses* and quoting
in support of his interpretation Gen. 49 : 11, "Binding his

---

[1] Zahn and Blass adopt another explanation; the former reads "him"
(αὐτόν) instead of the first "them" (αὐτῶν), and applies it to the foal, referring the second "them" to the cloaks of the people. The latter adopts
a similar correction, but strikes out the second αὐτῶν and seems to overlook the fact that the καί (and the י) is an instance of epexegetical use.

foal unto the vine, *and*[1] his ass's colt unto the choice vine," as being probably in the mind of the evangelist when he recorded the story. But there is no parallel here and no probability even that the evangelist thought of this passage at all. This fact also is brought out more clearly when it is remembered that he is, throughout the Gospel, describing a *suffering* and not a triumphant Messiah.

Equally improbable, again, is the view that Mark's added statement that no man had ever ridden the ass previously is a reflection of Num. 19 : 2 (*cf.* Deut. 21 : 3), which orders that a "faultless *cow*," upon which "never yoke came," shall be brought to Eleazar the priest. There is absolutely no connexion here either in act or thought.

Drews, however, further accuses Matthew of probably misunderstanding the cry "Hosanna" (*Hoschia-na*), "Save now," and making it a cry of joy. This is more reasonable and not altogether unlikely, especially since, as we have seen, Matthew quite misunderstood the prophet's reference to the ass; at the same time it is not quite clear, from the text of his version of the story, that he did so.[2]

It is also possible, if not probable, that the words of Jesus recorded in Luke 19 : 40 were suggested to him by Habakkuk, as they were certainly appropriate to the occasion and readily lent themselves to quotation. But it by no means follows from this fact that the latter's prophecy was the sole or even the principal basis of the whole story. In fine, we can see no reasonable probability that these various quotations from the Old Testament suggested the material for a pseudo-historical story to the writers of the Gospels.

It is much more probable that we have here some four

---

[1] But here, too, the ו and *καί* are probably epexegetical.
[2] And surely our "God save the king!" is a cry of joy and welcome.

more or less independent records of an actual event, the main features and details of which are quite in accord with the times and the place to which they refer.[1]

The Expulsion of the Traders

A more important suggestion has been made by Mr. Butler in an article on "The Greek Mysteries and the Gospels" (*The Nineteenth Century and After*, March, 1905). Starting from the precarious assumption that the public ministry of Jesus lasted only one year, he parallels the public entry of Jesus into Jerusalem with one of the processions which took place during the celebration of the greater mysteries at Eleusis.

On these occasions the *mystæ* ("initiated") were accompanied by great crowds to the temple, where the *mystes* was admitted to the higher grade of *epoptes* ("beholder"). But the act in the ritual of the mysteries upon which Butler lays special stress is that the bearing of a κέρνος[2] by the mystes reappears in the prohibition which Jesus (subsequently) issued (Mark 11 : 16) that none should carry a vessel through the temple.

Mr. Butler, however, has fallen into some error of detail here. The *kernos* was not carried by one of the mystæ. It was borne by a priest or priestess called the κερνοφόρος ("kernos-bearer"), or κερνᾶς, and, moreover, was an item in the procession itself. The prohibition of Jesus, on the other hand, had nothing to do with the procession and was probably directed merely against the

---

[1] Franke thinks (*Deuts. Lit. Ztg.*, 1901, pp. 2758 f.) that this has "correspondencies" with the solemn entry of Buddha Dīpaṅkhara (*Buddhavaṃsa*, II), where it is stated that, "the people swept the pathway, the gods strewed flowers on the road and branches of the coral-tree, the men bore boughs of all manner of trees, and the Bodhisattva Sumedha spread his garments in the mire, and men and gods shouted 'All hail.' "

[2] A large earthenware dish made with wells, or hollows, in the bottom, in which various fruits were offered in the rites of the Corybantes. See Liddell and Scott's *Lex.*, sub. κέρνος. Mark refers to a σκεῦος, "a vessel or implement of any kind."

excessive formalism and irreverence which characterised the Jewish official worship of the day. The two stories, indeed, are utterly unlike except for the reference in each to vessels of some kind.

The "Cursing" of the Fig-Tree

Equally inconclusive, too, is his attempt to explain the incident of the fig-tree recorded in Matt. 21 : 18 and 19.

"At Athens," he continues, "there was a sacred fig-tree at which one of the processions always halted to offer sacrifices and perform certain mystic rites," the fig being one of several trees having especial significance in the cults of Dionysus and the goddess-mother. But the incident mentioned in the Gospel did not occur during a procession; it took place, we are told, on the morning after, as he returned to the city from Bethany, where the night was spent; also there is no trace whatever of any mystic meaning in the circumstance. It was apparently a mere picturesque and vivid way of calling the attention of his disciples to the fact that the whole sacrificial and religious system of the Jews of that time, while making a fair show and great promise of fruit, was, on a closer view, wholly barren and fruitless.

On the other hand, this order concerning the temple vessels and the expulsion of the traders, Drews thinks, was suggested by the Targum translation of Zech. 14 : 21: "Every vessel in Jerusalem will be consecrated to the Lord, etc.; and at that time there will no longer be shopkeepers in the house of the Lord" (*The Christ Myth*, p. 237, note 2). In this prophecy he imagines "there may have been a further inducement for the evangelists to state that Jesus chases the tradesmen from the temple." It would seem much more probable that this prophecy might suggest the act to Jesus himself, who was undoubtedly scandalised at the shameless traffic which had sprung up and flourished in the outer

court of that building.   In the Fourth Gospel (John
2 : 15 and 16) a similar act on the part of Jesus is recorded which, according to some exegetes, refers to the
same event but has been misplaced by the editor.   Here
Jesus is described as making a scourge of small cords
previous to driving out the traders.   This view is open
to some doubt; but it affords Mr. Robertson an opportunity of saying (*Christianity and Mythology*, XII,
p. 358) that "in the Assyrian and Egyptian systems a
scourge-bearing god is a very common thing on the
monuments."   This is true; but that fact, as a modern
writer has justly observed, "not being an historical one,
is apparently supposed here to prove that the story narrated in all four Gospels is also unhistorical—a curious
application," he adds, "of the logical syllogism!"   The
whip, or flail, depicted on ancient monuments as being
often carried by gods—and in particular by Osiris—is,
however, a general symbol of authority and power.[1]
But the Jews were already very familiar with the idea;
the thirteen-thonged whip with which the "forty stripes
save one" (II Cor. 11 : 24; *cf.* Deut. 25 : 3), were inflicted was a well-known institution in the Jewish penal
code.

Finally, we may notice the explanation put forward
by Fries (*Studien zur Odyssea*) that we have in the story
of the entry of Jesus into Jerusalem simply a variant of
the astromythological myth of the spring-god entering
his temple, or of Odysseus the ascetic *bhikshu*.[2]   The
cleansing of the temple also, in his view, represents the
destruction of chaos by the god (Marduk) and the estab-
lishment of a new world.   But it is very difficult to see
how these ancient cosmogonic concepts could suggest to

[1] Mr. Robertson seems rather to imply (*loc. cit.*) that the flail (or whip)
is a "sign" of Osiris as the "Egyptian Christ."   But this sign of power is
also carried by representations of *Ptah*, the creator, and Jesus in using the
whip is certainly not *ipso facto* figuring as a god!

[2] A kind of mendicant friar in India.

the mind of any scribe or compiler such a matter-of-fact story. The whole narrative undoubtedly suggests strongly to every unbiassed reader that it is a plain account of an actual event which occurred at the beginning of the great and final crisis in the life and work of the great Galilean teacher.

CHAPTER X

THE EUCHARIST AND THE MYSTERY-CULTS

The Institution of the Eucharist

WE will commence our necessarily brief examination of this most important subject with a statement of Doctor Drews's fundamental position taken from *The Witnesses to the Historicity of Jesus*, pp. 81–83.

"Historical theology," he says, "generally regards the passage in Corinthians [I Cor. 11 : 23] as the earliest version we have of the words used at the institution of the supper. But a particularly striking reason that prevents us from seeing in St. Paul the oldest tradition of the words at the Last Supper is their obviously liturgical form and the meaning which the apostle puts on the words. It is very remarkable that Paul and Luke alone regard the Lord's Supper as instituted by Jesus in memory of him; Mark and Matthew know nothing of this. They have a much simpler text than the other two. Hence Jülicher, against Weizsäcker and Harnack, rightly doubts whether the supper was founded by Jesus (*Theol. Abhandlungen für C. Weizsäcker*, 1892, p. 232). He did not institute or found anything; that remained for the time when he came into his father's kingdom. He made no provision for his memory; having spoken as he did in Matt. 26 : 29, he had no idea of so long a period of future time (p. 244).

"Paul, therefore," Drews continues, "according to Jülicher, indicates a later stage of the tradition in regard to the first eucharist than Mark and Matthew, and the earliest tradition does not make Jesus show the least

178

sign that he wishes these material actions to be performed in future by his followers (p. 238). If this is so, *the words of the institution were interpolated subsequently in the text of Paul*,[1] as the liturgical use of them in the Pauline sense became established in the church, in order to support them with the authority of the apostle, and the words 'For I have received from the Lord' serve to give further proof of their authentic character; or else the first epistle to the Corinthians was not written by the apostle Paul, as, in spite of Jülicher, it is difficult to believe that Paul could at so early a stage give a version of the Lord's Supper that differed so much from that of the primitive community."

And he finally concludes (p. 83): "The mysticism of the festive supper cannot have been instituted by Jesus, but is *based on the cult of the Christian community and was subsequently put in the mouth of the supposed founder*."[2] Let us examine the chief statements in the above passage *seriatim*.

Doctor Drews asserts here that the Pauline version of the words of institution of the Eucharist are precluded from acceptance as the oldest version by their "obviously liturgical form." Now, this objection would seem to imply that the early church, soon after the end of the first century, possessed in some form or other a set liturgy at least for celebrating the weekly Eucharist. But this is certainly not the view held by liturgiologists, who are agreed that no set form of liturgical words committed to writing was used by the church before the end of the second century. There is, for example, no mention of any ritual books amongst those delivered up by the *traditores* in the persecutions under Diocletian. Indeed, the earliest extrabiblical account of the manner of celebrating the Eucharist is probably that of Justin Martyr (*Apol.*, I, 65 and 66), which, on the whole, appears

---

[1] Italics ours.   [2] Italics ours.

to follow the Lucan form of words for the consecration. The fact, no doubt, is that each church probably repeated the words of institution and consecration from memory, according as they were handed down in their traditions, which naturally, while agreeing in principle, varied in detail as all oral (even the most trustworthy) traditions tend to do.

Neither can we see any grounds here for Doctor Drews's theory of a first-century development—especially in the idea of a *commemoration* in the Eucharist. If this were the case we should expect to find a steady increase in the prominence given to such a memorial aspect of the Eucharist in documents written subsequently to St. Paul's time. But we do not find this. For, taking the later documents in the order agreed upon by a consensus of critical scholars,[1] we have in Mark the *shortest* form of words; in Matthew a *formula* almost identical with that of Mark; while in Luke, who wrote something like a quarter of a century after St. Paul, the "memorial" is only mentioned incidentally after the consecration of the bread. And this some *thirty* years after, as we are told, a liturgical development and a growth of the idea of the "memorial" had sprung up! These facts as we have them do not bear out this hypothesis; for the "development" in A. D. 85 is clearly less than it was in A. D. 55. And the only way out of this difficulty is to postulate hypothetically a much later interpolation in I Cor. 11 : 23, for which there is not the smallest textual or other evidence whatever.

Neither, again, do we find any reference to this liturgical and memorial development in the Acts, *i. e.*, about A. D. 90; nor is it conspicuous later on in the Fourth Gospel, where, according to the theory, it ought, above

---

[1] *I. e.*, I Corinthians, 52–55; Mark, 65–68; Matthew, 70–75; Luke, 80–85; Acts, 85–90; John, 90–95 A. D.

all, to be met with. In the discourse found in the sixth
chapter, following upon the feeding of the five thousand,
a meal with probably eucharistic characteristics,[1] there
is absolutely no direct mention of the memorial view.
We cannot, therefore, regard the mere fact that Mark
and Matthew do not refer to it as a "memorial" as
indicating beyond question that this view of the Eucharist was undeveloped in the original and still earlier
written Pauline letter. We cannot, indeed, draw any
such sweeping conclusions from a mere omission in two
of the records of direct reference to the memorial aspect of the Eucharist. Mark and Matthew are content to emphasise the most important portions of the
formulæ of consecration: "This is my body—this is my
blood." To draw further conclusions, on the ground of
omission, is just as reasonable as to argue that because
Mark (14 : 22) omits the injunction "eat"[2] it was not
customary at first to do more than handle the eucharistic
bread, as was done in the case of some of the *sacra* in
the mysteries. Mark also omits the Matthæan injunction, "drink ye all of it"—*i. e.*, the wine; but he adds,
nevertheless, that "they all drank of it." The truth is,
the argument, from mere omission, is always an unsatisfactory and a dangerous one; but the theory of development is more dangerous still when the *facts* under consideration have to be seriously distorted in order to
justify some preconceived idea, which is certainly the
case here.

There is also, however, a very strong and direct reason
for holding that the idea of a "memorial" (ἀνάμνησις,
Luke 22 : 19) was attached to the Eucharist in the two
earliest Gospels. All three synoptists (correctly or in-

---

[1] It is probable that the Last Supper was not the first, or the only one,
of these consecrated meals.   Whether it is or is not to be identified with the
Passover meal is another question.

[2] Absent in the best codices.

correctly) regard the Last Supper as the Passover meal.[1]
This latter feast was always regarded as a "memorial"
(μνημόσυνον, LXX, Ex. 12 : 14) of a great deliverance.
It is evident, therefore, that by associating the Eucharist itself so closely with what they believed to be the
paschal supper they meant to imply that the former
of these was in like manner a "memorial" of another
deliverance wrought by Jesus, which was a spiritual
analogue of the deliverance from Egypt. Luke, it is
true, uses a different word for the idea—ἀνάμνησις[2] instead
of the μνημόσυνον of the LXX—but the distinction here,
if any, in their meaning is trifling and unimportant and
does not affect the question.[3]

It is, moreover, quite unthinkable that Jesus, even if
he did regard his own teaching merely as an *interimse-
thik*—which has not been demonstrated—did not estab-

---

[1] The author of the Fourth Gospel, as is well known, apparently does
not regard the Last Supper as the Passover. Much has been written on
the question and many attempts have been made to harmonise the two
positions. The following explanation of the difficulty proffered by Doctor S. Krauss, in an article on the "Passover" in the *Jewish Encyclopædia*,
seems to be especially worthy of notice: "Chwolson (*Das Letzte Passamahl
Christi*, St. Petersburg, 1893) has ingeniously suggested that the priests
were guided by the older Halakah, according to which the law of the Passover was regarded as superior to that of the Sabbath, so that the lamb
could be sacrificed even on Friday night [the preparation for the Sabbath];
whereas Jesus and his disciples would seem to have adopted the more
rigorous view of the Pharisees, by which the paschal lamb ought to be
sacrificed on the eve of the 14th of *Nisan* when the 15th coincided with
the Sabbath (see Bacher, in *Jew. Quart. Rev.*, pp. 683–686)." But *cf.* also
Doctor Sanday's opinion in Hastings's *Dictionary of the Bible*, art. "Jesus
Christ." Mr. G. H. Box (*Journ. of Theol. Studies*, III, 357–369) regards
the Last Supper as the weekly *Kiddush*, a service held in the house.

[2] It should be remembered, however, that some authorities (*e. g.*, W. and
H.) regard Luke 22 : 19b and 20 as no part of the original text but due to
a "Western non-interpolation."

[3] According to Liddell and Scott, ἀνάμνησις in classical Greek = the "act
of remembering," whereas μνημόσυνον means a "remembrance" or "memorial" of some thing or person. But these finely drawn distinctions, even
if they were always (?) observed in the classical period, are often quite
set aside in late Greek. Both words here are undoubtedly synonyms.

lish this sacrament and give to it also its memorial aspect. Such a bond of unity and source of power and inspiration would be necessary to keep the body of disciples together and to perpetuate his authority for a period of even a few years. And how much more necessary for a longer period! Hence the idea that the Eucharist was instituted by St. Paul, or in his time, on the analogy of the meals of the mystery-cults is, for this reason alone, quite incredible.

Once more, it is impossible to accept the view of Doctor Jülicher—as against Professors Harnack and Weizsäcker—that Matt. 26 : 29 implies that Jesus had "no idea of so long a period of future time" intervening before he came into his Father's kingdom, and therefore did not institute or found anything and made no provision for his memory. This view is, indeed, negatived by the following facts. In Mark 13 : 32 (cf. Matt. 24 : 36) he expressly states: "Of that day and of that hour knoweth none, not any angel in heaven, *not even the Son*, but the Father." It is true that elsewhere it is stated that upon occasion he once leant to the expectation that it might all come to pass during the lifetime of that generation. But he had no certainty on this point, and, in any case, a period of some years would probably be involved during which some "memorial" of himself and his work would be needed.

And with this view of the matter the words of Matt. 26 : 29 agree. Here Jesus does not say that the *disciples* will not again eat of that bread and drink of that wine before the inauguration of his Father's kingdom, but that he himself will not do so until the day when he would celebrate it in his Father's kingdom. It is the last occasion during the earth life *for him*, but, by implication, it is not the last time for them. This and nothing else is the plain meaning of this passage, which has been either summarily dismissed or perverted in its

meaning in order to support a special theory of eschatology.

In a similar manner Doctor Drews's suggestion that
the words of the institution were interpolated[1] subsequently [to A. D. 55] in the text of St. Paul's letter as
the liturgical use of them (in the Pauline sense) became
established in the church is a mere makeshift hypothesis for bolstering up the view that the mysticism of the
"festive" [!] supper cannot have been instituted by
Jesus, but is based on the cult of the Christian community and was subsequently put in the mouth of its supposed founder. If, as Doctor Drews holds, Jesus Christ
never existed, and Christianity as handed down to us
from the middle of the first century is a system of mere
cult-worship and ritual devised by the Christian community itself, what need is there for maintaining that
St. Paul's version of the institutive words is a development of the older form (?) found in the Gospels of
Mark and Matthew? This seems to come perilously
near to the vicious system of "circular reasoning," for,
if neither St. Paul's version nor those of Mark and
Matthew represent the words of an actual founder,
then all these alike, with the version of Luke, are mere
liturgical *formulæ* used in a pseudo-memorial sense.
But *ex hypothesi* the *formulæ* of Mark and Matthew do
not show this liturgical form and use. The conclusion,
therefore, is irresistible, even from Doctor Drews's own
reasoning, that the words recorded by Mark and Matthew must be those of a personal founder handed down
in a somewhat brief and incomplete form which is often
assumed by early tradition, but which, nevertheless, preserves the most vital portion of the utterances. It is,
indeed, as Doctor Drews himself confesses, difficult to
believe that Paul could at so early a stage give a version of the Lord's Supper that differed so much from

[1] Or else the letter is not Pauline!

that of the primitive community; but this fact—if it be a fact—does not indicate that the community invented the memorial portion and then foisted it on to a supposed founder.   Rather, it shows that the community had treasured up the various slightly differing traditional forms, which St. Paul doubtless learned from the apostles themselves when he met them in council at Antioch (Gal. 2 : 11) and afterwards combined when he wrote his letter to the Corinthian church.   This view of the matter at least has all the facts, as we know them, wholly in its favour.

The Acts and Words of Institution

We will now turn from the fact of the institution of the Eucharist by Jesus to the acts and words by which it was instituted, and in so doing endeavour to approach this great subject in the spirit of, and with the eyes of, the man of the first century.   And to do this we must first of all disembarrass ourselves of all sacramental theories of a metaphysical nature, whether they be those of the Middle Ages or of the sixteenth century and later.

In the view of the men assembled in the upper room in Jerusalem, and others of their age, a being of a heavenly origin such as the Messiah, by virtue of the divine power within him, was a person "charged" (so to speak) with a living, spiritual *energy* ($\Delta \acute{\upsilon} \nu \alpha \mu \iota \varsigma$[1]) which could be, and indeed often was, communicated to others.   Such transfer, too, was commonly made, voluntarily or even involuntarily, by the bodily *touch* or by the spoken *word;* sometimes, and perhaps more effectually in certain cases, by the two combined.

There are numerous examples of this fact recorded in the books of both the Old and New Testaments.   Thus we read (Mark 5 : 30) that when Jesus was on his way

[1] Hebrew, כֹּחַ, "strength," "force" (spiritual).   See Deut. 6 : 5; Isaiah 47 : 9, etc.

to the house of the head of the synagogue he was *touched* by the woman with an issue of blood. He then became conscious that *power* (δύναμις) had gone out of him, and asked: "Who touched me?" (*cf.* Luke 8 : 46). Again, in Luke 6 : 19, we find: "And the whole multitude sought to *touch* him; for there went *power* out of him (δύναμις παρ αὐτοῦ), and it healed them all." Here we have, perhaps, an instance of the involuntary and subconscious transfer of this innate and spiritual life-energy in response to the purposive touch of faith.

Further, we read again in Matt. 8 : 8 of the centurion who besought the help of Jesus for a sick child, saying: "Only speak the *word* (λόγον), and my boy shall be healed." The spoken word is here regarded as the *vehicle* of this mysterious life-giving energy which (so to say) streams, or is projected, from Jesus under certain conditions and in certain circumstances. Instances of this transfer, as we may term it, drawn from the recorded miracles of healing, might easily be multiplied, but it is needless to do so. We will, however, mention just one other by which a combination of these methods is illustrated. In the case of the "raising" of the son of the widow of Nain, it is stated that "he came and *touched* the bier . . . and he *said*, Young man, I say unto thee, arise !"; and the dead man, says the evangelist, sat up and began to speak.[1]

But here it is necessary to enter a *caveat*. This *power*, or spiritual essence, which is thus transferred by *touch* or projected by *word* or transferred by these methods

---

[1] The reader will clearly understand that throughout this exposition we are merely trying to place ourselves in the position of the man of the first century. Modern psychology would doubtless explain the miracles of healing differently; but it is needless to discuss that question here. Doubtless the problem thus stated will call to mind the long discussion carried on between the mesmerists, who postulated a fluidic substance (the *od* or *odylic* force of von Reichenbach), which was transferred from the operator to the subject, and the hypnotists, who explained the effects as entirely due to mental suggestion.

conjointly is not necessarily operative for good or even operative at all. This one test, indeed, separates it wholly from magic *pure et simple*, with which superficial modern readers have frequently confounded it. Magic is always regarded as operative, in accordance with the will of the magician, whatever the state of mind of the victim; that is, unless the latter can bring into play some more powerful counter-magic. Thus we read (Matt. 13 : 5 and 8): "And he did not many works of power (δυνάμεις πολλάς) there *because of their unbelief*." Failure on the part of the recipients to respond to and to utilise the power bestowed rendered the efforts of Jesus nugatory. So also did a want of faith in the agent to whom the power was delegated render him incapable of transferring the gift (*cf.* Matt. 17 : 20; Mark 16 : 14). In short, if we may express the matter in modern scientific terminology, this spiritual power, or energy, when transmitted was usually *in potentiâ;* it had to be transmuted by the recipient through faith into the *kinetic* form before it was really effective for its purpose.

Once more, the power thus transferred was, in certain cases and spiritual states, not only ineffective but positively harmful to the recipient in both a spiritual and a physical sense, even when transmitted through the *medium* of food.[1] Perhaps the most striking Biblical instance of this is the case of Judas. It is not certain whether we are to understand from the records that he was present or not at the institution of the Eucharist. But in any case he was present at the preceding sup-

---

[1] *I. e.*, it was regarded as effective in resisting the entrance of demons and expelling them, or, again, in case of *misuse* of it, of promoting their entrance into the man. An instance of injurious physical effect is related in the *Acts of Thomas* (501): "Now, there was there a young man who had committed a crime [murder], and he came to and partook of the Eucharist, and both of his hands became withered [paralysed], so that he could not move either of them to his mouth." This story (though uncorroborated) may be quite true, and in that case would doubtless be explained by the modern psychologist as the effect of autosuggestion.

per, whether that were paschal or non-paschal. And we read (John 13 : 26) that Jesus explained to the disciples that his betrayer would be the man "for whom I shall dip the sop (ψωμίον) and give to him." Then he dipped and gave it to Judas, "and," adds the writer very significantly, "*after the sop Satan entered into him.*" This passage has been at all times a sore stumbling-block to many who have failed to grasp its real significance— Jesus deliberately handing over Judas to Satan! Not only was no effort made to save the wretched man, but he was even placed in the power of the prince of evil! How shocking! But this view shows a total misapprehension of the idea underlying the whole act. The "sop" (only mentioned in this Gospel [1]) was a special morsel which Jesus took up at this moment and handed to Judas, perhaps in accordance with a common Eastern custom. But it had been touched by Jesus, and consequently was fraught with spiritual power, which, if received with faith and a real desire to resist temptation, would have saved the man. The latter, however, rejected the opportunity and wilfully *perverted* the gift to his own destruction. Jesus intuitively and swiftly realises this, and then adds in an undertone: "What thou doest, do quickly!" No more sympathy can be felt for the man; he had been given and had lost his last opportunity. He must now work out the consequences of his final decision and reap his due reward.

The action of this power, therefore, it will be seen, was not like that of magic generally; it was not that expressed in later times by the scholastic phrase *opus operatum;* it was conditional and dependent as well upon the faith and will of the recipient for its effectiveness for good or evil.

Now, the synoptists all tell us that when instituting the Eucharist after the Last Supper Jesus, after pro-

---

[1] The question of its historicity does not affect the argument.

nouncing a blessing upon it,[1] took bread and brake it.
Then he gave it to the disciples, saying: "Take [eat],
this is my body" (τοῦτό ἐστι τὸ σῶμά μου).[2] Next, repeating the blessing over one or more of the cups of
wine, he said: "This is my blood (τοῦτό ἐστι τὸ αἷμά
μου) of the [new] covenant." Probably all readers are
familiar with the outlines at least of the long and acri-
monious controversy which has raged over the precise
meaning of these words of institution—a controversy
which, by appealing rather to passion and prejudice
than to an intelligent effort to understand the mental
outlook of the first century, has been largely barren of
fruitful results.[3] Viewed from the standpoint of those
assembled in the upper room, we have here the *touch* of
power and the *word* of power, each effectual for the purpose underlying the act. Hence these phrases, though
in a sense symbolic, are not, however, mere symbols, as

[1] The modern Jewish blessing upon the paschal bread and wine runs as
follows: "Blessed art thou, O Lord our God, King of the universe, who
bringest forth bread from the earth. . . . Blessed, etc. . . . who createst the
fruit of the vine." In the *Teaching of the Twelve Apostles*, chaps. 9 *f.*, are
several eucharistic thanksgivings which are probably modifications of ancient Jewish graces. The cup was very likely the third one of the paschal
meal.

[2] The *formula* given by Mark (see p. 181, note 2).

[3] From the linguistic point of view, it must be remembered that Jesus
almost certainly spoke in Aramaic. The *copula* ("is"), in that case, would
probably not be used. Moreover, the verb "to be" in all languages is
used, in a sense, figuratively. Thus, "I am the way," or "the door," etc.,
are equivalent to "I represent the way," "door," etc., that is, "I have the
value of it."

We have no evidence that there was any sacramental partaking of the
body of such gods as Osiris, Adonis, or Attis in their cult feasts. As regards
Dionysus, see *The Asiatic Dionysus*, G. M. N. Davis, p. 232.

So also, speaking of the Babylonians, Doctor Langdon says (*Tammuz
and Ishtar*, pp. 183 and 184): "They failed to evolve a universal and ethical creed of faith in a vicarious martyr, and, so far as I can see, they failed
to institute any real sacrament with elements of grain, liquor, and bread,
which symbolised their own gods."

For evidence of the doctrine of transubstantiation and theophagy amongst
the ancient Mexicans (Aztecs) and the Hindus, see Frazer's *Golden Bough*,
"Spirits of the Corn and of the Wild." vol. II, pp. 89 and 90.

some have hastily concluded, but symbols teeming with the divine life-energy of Jesus, which has (so to speak) flowed into them, and can pass by means of the elements themselves into the soul of the recipient and affect him either for good or ill, or, it may be, not affect him at all, according to the mental and volitional attitude with which he receives them. The ordinary thinkers of the first century, it must be remembered, were all vitalists[1] to a man, and they regarded the body as the habitation of this operative, personal, and spiritual life-energy and the blood as *par excellence* the channel of its distribution therein. And just as the body and blood of the man hold, locked up within them during life, the human vital power, or soul, so, too, did these creatures of bread and wine hold, transferred to and locked up within them, the vivifying divine life-power (δύναμις) of Jesus. There is here, it will be evident, no subtle transmutation of an hypothetical *substantia* of the bread and the wine, whilst the *accidentia* remain;[2] there is no question of simple representation by mere symbols—an almost incomprehensible thought to the men of that period; the elements are thus operative representatives of the Divine Being which discharge the actual divine energy into the soul of the communicant. This idea is, in effect, the highest possible development of a primitive vitalistic animism, which early Christianity, in this greatest of all sacraments, incorporated in its system and raised to its utmost limit of spiritual value. And it is, we repeat, inconceivable that Jesus should have omitted to institute such a necessary and crowning sacrament of his life and work before ceasing to be visibly present amongst men.

[1] This theory (vitalism) has been revived in modern times in an improved form by Doctor Hans Driesch (*The History and Theory of Vitalism*, 1914). See also his Gifford Lectures for 1907. It has for many years been practically replaced by the mechanistic hypothesis of life.

[2] This view is really founded upon an obsolete theory of matter devised in the Middle Ages by Thomas Aquinas and adopted by the Thomist school.

The Common Meal at Eleusis

We will, in the next place, examine Mr. Slade Butler's case for a eucharistic derivation from, or at least
a parallel to, the common meal partaken of by all the
mystæ at Eleusis[1] ("The Greek Mysteries and the Gospels," pp. 492 *ff.*, *The Nineteenth Century and After*,
March, 1905), and quote him *verbatim:* "It was after a
purification on the evening of the fifth or sixth day of
the celebration that the mystæ partook together of a
meal called the κυκεών [*kykeon*], a mixture which was
both food and drink, being a thickened liquid compounded of barley-meal, mint, and water. The partaking of the κυκεών by all the mystæ in common was the
Eleusinian sacramental meal and was an essential and
necessary rite before any mystes could pass to the higher
grade [*epoptes*]. The parallel between the common meal
of the mysteries and the Last Supper of the Gospels is
especially noticeable in Luke's account (22 : 14–20). As
regards the substance of the κυκεών, it seems to have
been a mixture of such consistence as to be considered
either food or drink. Had the writer of John 6 : 55 the
κυκεών in his mind when he represents Christ as saying: 'My flesh is true food, and my blood is true drink'?
for there is nothing in his allusion to the manna in the
wilderness (vs. 49) to suggest the idea of drink,[2] whereas
the κυκεών partook of the nature of both food and drink.

"The next ceremony in the mysteries was the most
solemn of all the rites which preceded the last scene in
the drama, and was known as the παράδοσις τῶν ἱερῶν,
'the handing over of the holy things' or 'the giving

---

[1] The Eleusinian mysteries were sacred to *Dēmētēr*, the earth-mother, and
her daughter *Korē*.

[2] The mere reference to the wilderness, however, where water was very
scarce, would suggest drink with the food (*manna*).

in turn of the consecrated objects.' In this ceremony, which took place after the partaking of the κυκεών in common, 'the mystæ were admitted one by one to touch, to kiss the holy things, to lift them from the cist, and to pronounce the sacred formula' (Ramsay). In Mark we are told (14 : 22), 'And as they were eating he took (λαβών) the bread (or unleavened cake), and, having blessed it, he broke it, and gave (ἔδωκεν) to them and said: Take ye (λάβετε).' In Matthew (26 : 26) the word 'eat' is added after 'take.'

"The sacred formula which was pronounced by each mystes during or immediately after the παράδοσις τῶν ἱερῶν is thus given by Clement of Alexandria: ἐνήστευσα, ἔπιον τὸν κυκεῶνα, ἔλαβον ἐκ κίστης, ἐγγευσάμενος ἀπεθέμην εἰς κάλαθον, καὶ ἐκ καλάθου εἰς κίστην, 'I fasted, I drank the kykeon, I took from the chest, I tasted, I placed in the basket, and from the basket into the chest.' The κίστη was the sacred box or chest in which the ἱερά or 'holy things' wrapped in linen cloths were preserved: ἐγγευσάμενος signifies 'having tasted' the ἱερά, or some of them, such as the sesame-cake and the pomegranate, which seem to be too sacred to be mentioned by name.

"In reference to this formula in which the κυκεών is regarded as a drink and not as a food, we may notice that Luke (22 : 17) says: 'And he received a cup . . . and said, Take this and divide it among yourselves,' where it is plain that the cup of vs. 17 was an earlier cup than that mentioned in vs. 20—'and the cup in like manner after supper saying: This cup is the new covenant'; that is to say, there seems to have been a second παράδοσις, or handing over of the cup by Christ.[1] Now, in some celebrations of the mysteries[2] there was a second παράδοσις τῶν ἱερῶν, which appears to have been preserved

---

[1] See p. 198.
[2] Those of Cybelē (Mā) with Attis, which differed from the Eleusinia, appear to be referred to here.

for the mystæ who proceeded to the highest grade. In these cases something was eaten, not merely tasted, and something was drunk, which was not the κυκεών; this seems clear from the *formula* then used: ἐκ τυμπάνου ἔφαγον, ἐκ κυμβάλου ἔπιον, ἐκερνοφόρησα ὑπο τὸν παστὸν ὑπέδυν, 'I ate from a drum; I drank from a cymbal; I carried the vessel, the κέρνος; I went in under the curtain.' The κέρνος was a large earthenware vessel, or dish, in which was placed the fruit offerings, and the curtain (παστός) was the variegated veil in the temple of Demeter. Only those mystæ or epoptæ who proceeded to the highest grade—probably to the priesthood—of the mysteries performed the ceremonial acts mentioned in this *formula*.

"Now, it seems that, though the essential words of these two *formulæ* of the mysteries appear in the Gospel narrative of the 'handing over' of the bread and the cup—take, eat, drink (Matt. 26 : 26–29)—the word παράδοσις is not used of the ceremony itself; but it is remarkable that the word occurs in the verses immediately preceding the 'handing over' of the bread and cup vss. 21–25) in the form of a verb—'one of you will hand me over'—παραδώσει (vs. 21); 'he that dippeth his hand with me in the dish, this man shall hand me over' (παραδώσει με, vs. 23). For the true meaning of παραδίδωμι is to 'hand over' from one to another, as a torch in the torch-race, προδίδωμι being the usual word to express betrayal; and it is plain that if Christ uttered the words recorded in vs. 21 the Aramaic verb used by him must have been indefinite in meaning, and suggestive of treachery only by reference to subsequent events, otherwise it would have been impossible that all—every one—(vs. 22) of the disciples should have asked: 'Is it I? Am I the traitor?' In Luke, though the order of the narrative is reversed, the connexion between the παράδοσις of the bread and cup and the use of the word παραδίδωμι is quite as close, for (Luke 22 : 21) as Christ hands over the cup to the disciples he breaks off, saying: 'But the hand of him who is handing me over (τοῦ παραδιδόντος με) is with me at the table'; and in I Cor. 11 : 23 the connexion is closer still: 'The Lord Jesus in the night in which he was handed over (παρεδίδοτο) took (ἔλαβεν) bread.' So, again, just as the ἱερά in the mysteries were kissed during the παράδοσις, or while they were being handed over, so we read in Matthew (21 : 48): 'He who handed him over (ὁ παραδιδούς) gave them a sign saying, Whomsoever I shall kiss, that is he.' And in John 20 : 17 we meet with the word 'touch' in the expression 'touch me not,' that is, 'do not hold me now,' for my παράδοσις is over and completed.

"Returning for a moment to the question asked by the disciples, 'Is it I? Am I to hand you over?' it is to be noticed that in the mysteries the ceremony of handing over the holy things was necessarily performed by the mystæ one at a time, 'one by one,' and in Mark (14 : 19), the earliest known Gospel, we find these words occur: 'They began to be sorrowful and to say to him *one by one*, Is it I?' The expression one by one is not to be found in any of the later Gospels—the phrase is changed in Matthew (26 : 22), it is almost gone from Luke (22 : 23), and has quite disappeared from John (13 : 21 and 26). This seems to indicate that the later writers did not recognise the source from whence the words *one by one* came or that they wished to conceal it. The phrase in Mark, εἷς καθ' εἷς, 'one after one,' 'one after the other,' is remarkable for the peculiar use of the word κατά, which seems to be an adverb rather than a preposition. This strange expression seems to indicate that the writer of Mark's Gospel had found the words so written in some Greek note or document which he was using as the foundation of his narrative, a note or document of weight and authority sufficient to induce him to retain the phrase in his own history; for a translator from some Aramaic or Hebrew writing, or a transcriber of oral tradition, would almost certainly have made use of the ordinary and well-known expression καθ' ἕνα. However, the words εἷς καθ' εἷς express in the plainest manner that the question was asked by all in turn, one at a time, that is to say, one following after the other."

We will proceed shortly to examine this somewhat lengthy quotation in as great detail as our limits of space will admit of. But previously another matter.

The Purification in the Mysteries

On the second day of the greater *Eleusinia* at Athens the cry was raised: "῍Αλαδε, μύσται" ("To the sea, mystæ!"). A procession was then formed, and, going to the shore, the candidates underwent a preliminary purification (καθαρμός) by bathing in the sea.[1] This is compared somewhat vaguely by Mr. Butler with the washing of the disciples' feet (John 13 : 4-11). No mention of this, he admits, occurs in the synoptics; but in Mark and Luke, he says, there is the man bearing the pitcher of water, which he rather hastily seems to assume has an indirect reference to this purification.

Now, there is no evidence in the Gospels or elsewhere to show that this washing of the feet occupied in the institution of the Eucharist anything like an analogous position to the preliminary cleansing of the greater mysteries. It is more akin to the purely social usage common to Eastern peoples (Gen. 18 : 4; 19 : 2; 24 : 32, etc.). It is true that Jesus condemned the merely formal hand-washing of the Pharisees; but this stands on a somewhat different footing. Each mystes, too, was ritually clean after his sea bath; but Jesus very significantly

---

[1] According to Plutarch (*Vita Phoc.*, XXVIII), each candidate took down to the sea a young pig and bathed with it. Sacrificer and sacrifice were together purified by the salt water. It was a rite of "riddance" (*cf.* Lev. 16 : 21).

remarks after this ceremony, "Ye are not all clean," doubtless meaning thereby Judas, who was not spiritually cleansed despite the washing. That the ceremony was symbolic of a higher purity is no doubt true; but it had no effect *ex opere operato;* and the personal act of Jesus was primarily an example of true humility (vs. 14).

Again, as regards the mystic meals of the *Eleusinia* and other mysteries, we have little real information on the subject. The Eleusinian *formula* preserved by Clement says: "I fasted; I drank of the *kykeon*." [1] Did the disciples fast before partaking of this Eucharist? Not absolutely, in any case, for they partook of the frugal supper shortly before. The *kykeon* of the mysteries, too, was a kind of thin gruel. In Homer's time (*Il.*, XI, 638 *ff.*) it was commonly made of barley-meal, goat's-milk cheese, and Pramnian wine; to those ingredients Circe added honey and magical herbs (*Od.*, X, 234 *ff.*). But the *kykeon* referred to in the Homeric *Hymn to Demeter* (ll. 208 *f.*)—which was, no doubt, identical with that used in the *Eleusinia*—was made of barley-meal, water, and pennyroyal.

A similar description of the meal partaken of in the mystery-cult of the Great Mother with Attis is recorded by Firmicus Maternus (flourished circ. 374 A. D.). Here the initiate says (*De Errore Prof. Relig.*, XVIII): "I have eaten out of a drum; I have drunk out of a cymbal; I am become a mystes of Attis" (ἐκ τυμπάνου βέβρωκα ἐκ κυμβάλου πέπωκα· γέγονα μύστης Ἄττεως). Here there is a definite eating and drinking—perhaps, in this case, of bread and wine—spoken of. But what did it signify here? Was it anything beyond an identification of the initiate with the Great Mother through the medium of these fruits of the earth, her children?

Again, in the *Eleusinia*, besides the drinking of the *ky-*

---

[1] Equivalent to "I tasted of the first fruits," which were previously under a *tabû* (= forbidden).

keon, Clement of Alexandria also specifies certain of the ritual acts: "I took [the *sacra*] out of the chest (κίστης), and, having tasted, I placed [them] in the basket (κάλα-θον), and from the basket into the chest." What were thus taken out, transferred, and put in again? It will be worth while to quote Clement's description of them, which is all the more valuable because he himself was an initiate in more than one of the various mysteries (Eusebius, *Præp. Evan.*, II, 2, 35). Clement asks: "What are these mystic chests?—for I must expose their sacred things (ἱερά) and disclose a state of affairs not fit for speech." He then interrogatively enumerates these various *sacra* as follows: "Are they not sesame-cakes, and pyramidal cakes, and globular and flat cakes, embossed all over, and lumps of salt, and a serpent, the symbol of Dionysus Bassareus? And, besides these, are there not pomegranates, and branches, and ivy leaves? And, further, round cakes and poppy seeds? In addition to these there are the unmentionable symbols of Themis, marjoram, a lamp, a sword, a woman's comb, which is a euphemism and mystical expression for the *genitalia muliebria*"[1] (κτεὶς γυναικεῖος, ὅ ἐστίν εὐφήμως καὶ μυστικῶς εἰπεῖν, μόριον γυναικεῖον).

Truly an edifying list! And we cannot wonder that the worthy father—liberal-minded and cultured scholar as he was—indignantly adds: "Such are the mysteries of the atheists. And with reason I call those atheists who know not the true God, but pay shameless worship to a boy torn to pieces by the Titans, and to a woman in distress, and to parts of the body which in truth cannot be mentioned for shame. . . ."

[1] The same writer states that the *sacra* in the mysteries of *Dionysus-*[Zagreus] were dice, a ball, a hoop, apples, a top (ῥόμβος, ? "bull-roarer"), a mirror, and a tuft of wool, with which, according to the later myth, the Titans beguiled the youthful Dionysus before they tore him limb from limb. He further describes the mysteries of Dionysus as "wholly inhuman," a conclusion to which we may readily assent.

Now, the problem which lies before us is, What connexion have these cult-meals with the Eucharist as instituted in the early church? And the answer to this,
despite the opinions of some eminent scholars to the
contrary, would seem to be, they have little if, indeed,
any at all. When the primitive Eucharist is closely
and carefully examined it will be seen, we think, that
its affinities are almost wholly with the paschal feast;
it is, in fact, an outgrowth from this, but possessing special characteristics and peculiarities of its own.

The ancient Passover, as described in Ex. *12 : 11 f.*,
soon underwent considerable modifications, and at the
centralisation of all sacrifices at the one sanctuary by the
Deuteronomic code the old spring pastoral feast coalesced
with the (later) agricultural *Maṣṣoth* (Deut. 16 : 1).

In the time of Jesus various additional ceremonies
were observed, the chief of which were: (1) Four cups
of wine mixed with water were drunk at different stages
of the feast; (2) the *Hallel* [1] was sung; (3) the various
articles of food (the lamb and the unleavened cakes)
were not dipped in the sauce of bitter herbs; and (4)
the feast was not eaten standing, but reclining. The
unleavened bread was broken, and this with the wine
in each cup, after being duly blessed, was passed round
to the guests by the head of the household, though this
passing round is nowhere called a παράδοσις and bore
no analogy to that ceremony in the cult-feasts. Mr.
Butler refers to a "second παραδοσις of the cup by
Christ." But there were in all *four* so-called "para-
doses," since there were four cups; and it is probable
that either the third or fourth cup was the one reserved
for the sacrament of the Eucharist. In short, the whole
manner of celebrating this supper and the subsequent
institution of the Eucharist is clearly based upon the

[1] Probably not identical with the *later* Hallel (Psalms 113–118); *cf. Bab.
Talm.*, Pesach. 9 : 3.

contemporary mode of celebrating the paschal feast, and all such practises as the exhibition of carefully preserved *sacra*, whether food or symbolic objects, all handing of these round and kissing of them by the initiates in turn, are altogether absent. In its form, as found in the Gospels, the Eucharist is typically *Jewish* and in no sense pagan, whatever non-Jewish ideas and practises may have crept in during the second century when the church had become flooded with Gentile converts, many of whom were initiates in the mysteries and brought with them, at least to some extent, the habits of thought which were characteristic of their pre-Christian frame of mind.

"Handing Over" or "Betrayal"?

We now come to a passage in Mr. Butler's article in which the "handing over" (παραδοσις) of the various *sacra* in the cult-suppers is deliberately compared by him to the "handing over" of Jesus to the priests by Judas Iscariot. Strictly speaking, of course—as Mr. Butler admits—any such comparison should be with the distribution of the *bread and wine* to each recipient; but, unfortunately for his purpose, these acts are not termed a παράδοσις by the evangelists. At the same time it so happens that Jesus remarked during the supper: "One of you will hand me over" (παραδώσει). Here, Mr. Butler seems to think, we have the link with the παράδοσις of the mysteries. In the Christian "mystery-drama" the handing over is not that of the objects (*sacra*), but that of the Christ, or, as Professor W. B. Smith states it, of the *"Christ-idea"* from the Jews to the Gentiles.

Now, the somewhat elaborate argument by which Mr. Butler supports his case is wholly dependent for its validity upon a distinction, which he introduces and presses vigorously, between the meaning of the Greek verbs παραδίδωμι and προδίδωμι; the former, he argues, *always* means to "hand over," whilst to "betray" is invariably expressed by the latter verb. This question, which is also raised by Professor Smith in connexion with Judas Iscariot, will be fully dealt with under that heading in chap. 13 (pp. 253–256). Here it must suffice to say (1) that the distinction drawn above, and generally (but not invariably) made in classical Greek, does not at all hold good in the popular and post-classical Greek of the first century, as will be shown by examples;[1] (2) that Judas has in one instance (Luke 6 : 16) the term προδότης ("betrayer") applied to him, which shows that his act of "handing over" of Jesus was not regarded by first-century Christians as a mere ritual act in some Jewish or Gentile mystery-drama akin to the Greek *Eleusinia*, but was looked upon as a piece of actual *treachery* on his part. Accordingly, upon the complete breakdown of this alleged distinction in meaning, the analogy which Mr. Butler attempts to draw between the kissing of the *sacra* from the chest and the kiss of the traitor[2] bestowed upon Jesus in Gethsemane loses its entire force.

Again, Mr. Butler's further effort to associate the touching of the various *sacra* in the mysteries with the touch referred to in John 20 : 17, where Jesus forbids Mary Magdalene to *hold* to him (μὴ μου ἅπτου), "for my παράδοσις is over and completed," is a pure fiction of Mr. Butler's own mind. The writer of that Gospel says that Jesus forbade the act because "I have not yet ascended to my Father" (οὔπω γὰρ ἀναβέβηκα πρὸς τὸν πατέρα), a

[1] We may mention here that Liddell and Scott quote, as examples of this, Xen., *Cyr.*, V, 1, 28; iv, 51, etc. Another case occurs in Thucy., VII, 68; but it is not common in classical times. In the LXX and the New Testament προδίδωμι appears to be rarely used at all.

[2] The Gospels vary considerably here in details. While Mark and Matthew say that Judas "kissed him affectionately" (κατεφίλησεν αὐτόν)—a form of salutation more accordant with deliberate Oriental treachery than the formal kiss of a mystery-drama—Luke and John do not mention any kiss at all.

reason which, whatever its precise meaning may be, shows clearly that the author had not Mr. Butler's thought in view when he penned the passage.

Mr. Butler next proceeds to deal with the question, "Is it I?" asked severally by the disciples when Jesus announced his foreknowledge of the coming betrayal, and in so doing lays great stress upon the peculiar (and ungrammatical) expression used by Mark, εἷς καθ᾽ εἷς, "one after one," *i. e.*, "one after the other." "This strange expression," he urges, "seems to indicate that the writer of Mark's Gospel had found the words *so written in some Greek note or document which he was using as the foundation of his narrative*,[1] a note or document of weight or authority sufficient to induce him to retain the phrase in his own history. Otherwise he would have used the ordinary phrase [εἷς] καθ᾽ ἕνα.

If Mr. Butler means by this remark that the above (hypothetical) Greek note or document was, perhaps, a kind of *rubric* attached to some MS. of a mystery-drama in which there was enacted a ceremonial handing over of any sacred things or *sacred person* by any one, or by a succession of initiates, we can only remark here that this is a purely fanciful hypothesis which practically begs the whole question at issue. There is no evidence whatever of such dramas as existent amongst the Jews or early Christians. And, so far as the phrase εἷς καθ᾽ εἷς is concerned, it is merely a late and ungrammatical variant of the classical [εἷς] καθ᾽ ἕνα. So far, too, from being absolutely strange and unusual, it is found elsewhere in at least one passage of the New Testament (John 8 : 1–11), where we read that the scribes and Pharisees "went out one by one (εἷς καθ᾽ εἷς), beginning from the eldest even to the youngest."[2]

A diligent search in the later and popular Greek litera-

---

[1] Italics ours.
[2] This story is expunged from modern critical texts.

ture of Asia Minor, etc., would doubtless reveal many more instances of the use of this unclassical expression.

Lastly, as regards the question itself, its evident meaning is that the disciples apprehended some severe crisis to be at hand, and each misdoubted the firmness of his own courage and resolutions. This view is quite in harmony with the psychology of the occasion, and the reference to it is a characteristic touch thoroughly in accordance with human nature as we find it in all ages.

A Mithraic Parallel

But a prototype of the Christian Eucharist has also been found in the Mithraic mysteries (O. Pfleiderer, *Christusbild*, English translation, pp. 129 *ff*., and Heitmüller, *Taufe*, p. 46). This derivation appears to be largely based upon the fact that bas-reliefs representing the sacred repast in the cult of Mithra have been found in recent years in Bosnia and Rome (see Cumont, *Textes*, I, p. 176; "Notice sur deux bas-reliefs mithriaques," *Revue Archæol.*, 1902, pp. 10 *ff*.). In these two mystæ are shown reclining at a table standing behind a tripod on which small loaves of bread are placed. One of the surrounding figures (? initiates) holds a horn in his hand.[1]

M. Cumont, however, refers this bas-relief to the third century A. D. If this view be correct, the sculpture lends no support to any theory of the derivation of the Eucharist from Mithraic sources; it would, indeed, rather suggest a loan from Christianity to Mithraism.

---

[1] The sculpture perhaps has reference to the banquet which Mithra celebrated along with Helios (the Sun), after his work of rescuing mankind from the great deluge, which was followed by a general conflagration, and before his return to heaven.

In the supper of the fully developed Mithraic mysteries, as depicted on the bas-relief (reverse) found at Heddernheim, Mithra stands behind the slain bull holding a *rhyton* (drinking-horn) and receiving from Helios a bunch of grapes, a symbol of the divine juice into which the blood of the victim was transmuted by celestial alchemy. This is rather an example of a conversion of blood into wine (grape-juice).

As a matter of fact, we have no really complete and authentic description of the Mithraic cult-supper. The brief notice of it given by Justin Martyr, who says (*Apol.*, I, 66) that "the wicked demons (οἱ πονηροὶ δαί-μονες) have imitated [the Eucharist] in the mysteries of Mithra, commanding the same thing to be done," [1] does not carry us very far in our search for "origins." The meal may have had (like the Eucharist) a sacramental character; but there seems to have been nothing about it reminiscent, or commemorative, of a death or sacrifice, which is one chief characteristic of the Christian institution.

The Taurobolia and Criobolia of Asian Mysteries

This last-named objection, however, has been met by Pfleiderer (*op. cit.*, p. 131) with the following argument: "Though there is no parallel in the banquet of Mithras to this blood-symbolism of the Christian sacrament, one is certainly found in the blood-baptism of the *taurobolia* [bull-slaying] and the *criobolia* [ram-slaying] which belongs to the mysteries of Cybelē and *perhaps also to those of Mithras*." [2] In the former of these ceremonies a bull was slain on a latticed platform and its blood was allowed to fall down upon a *mystes* lying in a pit below. This was a very ancient practise in western Asia, and was carried on in the sanctuaries of Mā and Anāhita long before the rise of Mithraism. It was based upon the wide-spread notion among primitive races that the blood is the vehicle of the spiritual life. [3] M. Cumont

---

[1] He says, however, that "bread and a cup of water" were used instead of bread and wine.

[2] Italics ours.

[3] Sham ritual-murder was probably practised in the mysteries of Mithra (see Frazer, *Golden Bough*, 1900, pp. 445 *f.*; Dieterich, *Mithrasliturgie*, pp. 164 *f.*).   Indeed, the Emperor Commodus is said (*Vita Commodi*, IX) to have actually murdered a man at one of the celebrations. It was also probably the case in the mysteries of Dionysus, though generally the victim was an animal, which was torn in pieces and eaten raw.

writes (*The Mysteries of Mithra*, p. 181) of its meaning in Mithraism: "But, under the influence of the Mazdean beliefs regarding the future life, a more profound significance was attributed to this baptism of blood. In taking it the devotees no longer imagined they acquired the strength of the bull; it was no longer a renewal of physical strength that the life-sustaining liquid was now thought to communicate, but a renovation, temporary or even perpetual, of the human soul." But this ceremony was no part of the original Mithraic cult, and it was only introduced in the second century A. D. into that of Cybelē, from whence it passed into the later Mithraic system. And this fact at once precludes all derivation of the Christian sacraments from Mithraism.

A Parallel from Mexico

A "parallel," if not a source, has been found in Mexico by Mr. J. M. Robertson, who says (*Christianity and Mythology*, p. 408) that there the sacred tree was "made into a cross on which was exposed a baked dough image of a saviour-god, and this [image] was, after a time, climbed for, taken down, and sacramentally eaten." This passage at first sight reads very much like a blend of a eucharistic and a crucifixion narrative; but on reference to Mr. H. H. Bancroft's *Native Races of the Pacific States of North America*, from which it is professedly taken,[1] we find it stated in vol. II, p. 321, that at the festival of Huitzilopochtli, the Mexican god of war, a life-sized image of the god was made of wickerwork and covered with dough made of amaranth and other seeds. A paper cap set with plumes was then put upon the head of this idol.

Again, the author says (pp. 330 and 331) that the Tepanecs had a festival in which "a bird of dough" was

[1] Mr. Robertson (1st ed.) gave the reference as pp. 386 and 509. But this was clearly an error.

placed at the top of a huge tree, and then "women dressed in the finest garments, and holding small dough idols in their hands, danced round the pole, while the youths struggled wildly to reach and knock down the dough image." When thus resolved into its two original and constituent parts, and stripped of the imaginative additions—"the sacred tree formed into a cross," etc. —the story loses even its superficial resemblance to the narratives of the crucifixion and institution of the Eucharist. Moreover, it is a far cry from Palestine to Mexico, and the parallel, such as it is, cannot have had any suggestive value for either Jews or early Christians. In addition to this fact, there is really very little likeness and absolutely no correspondence in meaning between these ceremonies and the Gospel events.

The Common Terms

But the great gulf which exists between the Christian scheme and the various mystery-cults, even in their highest and best forms, is still more clearly shown by the difference in meanings attached to the technical terms which are common to both. Thus, the term μυστήριον, "mystery" (pl., μυστήρια), which is found in *Mark* 4 : 11; *Romans* 11 : 25; 16 : 25 and 26; *I Cor.* 2 : 7, etc., is used in the New Testament in the sense of a secret which can only be known through a revelation from God. In the mystery-cults the whole idea underlying the term is merely that of concealment from the uninitiated. Thus the revelation of Jesus Christ as the Saviour of the world is termed (*Romans* 16 : 25) a μυστήριον χρόνοις αἰωνίοις σεσιγμένον, φανερωθὲν δὲ νῦν, while in the *Eleusinia* and kindred systems μυστήρια stands for the knowledge of certain secret rites which have a magical efficacy in promoting man's prosperity in both temporal and spiritual affairs.

Again, in the mysteries a man was pronounced "perfect" (τέλειος) when the ritual ceremonies of his initiations had all been duly performed and he knew the secrets which underlay the whole of the proceedings.

In the Gospels, on the contrary, where each disciple is enjoined to be "perfect" even as his Father in heaven is perfect, the word has an *ethical* content wholly wanting in the former; those Christians only are "perfect" who have duly ordered their lives according to the divine precepts and model as set forth in Jesus Christ (*Romans* 12 : 2).

Once more, in the mystery-cults σωτηρία ("safety," "salvation") was merely a rescuing of the individual from the pressure of such burdens upon the soul as the thought of the brevity of life and the dark shadow of an ever-impending death and the dim prospect beyond the grave. By the mere union of the life essence of the initiate with that of the cult-god he was secured against these things. And this happy result was wholly brought about "*by the exact performance of sacred ceremonies*" (Cumont), and such a union, once obtained, was, in its character and effects, indelible; it could not be blotted out or annulled. This concept of divine union is especially notable from the absence of any high moral ideal or practise. "We have no reason to think," observes Professor Percy Gardner (*The Religious Experiences of St. Paul*, p. 87), "that those who claimed salvation through Isis or Mithras were much better than their neighbours. They felt secure of the help of their patron deity in the affairs of life and the future world, but they did not, therefore, live at a higher level."

In the New Testament use of the word σωτηρία, on the contrary, the term is full of *moral* implications and conditions from which it cannot be detached. Those disciples who have entered upon the state of safety henceforth are debtors (ὀφειλέται) "not to live according to the flesh" (*Romans* 8 : 12; *cf. II Cor.* 5 : 14 and

15); and if they fail wilfully and persistently in this obligation they *ipso facto* cease to continue in that state of safety.

Again, the law of admission to the mysteries of Eleusis required that a man should be "pure and pious and good" (ἁγνὸς καὶ εὐσεβὴς καὶ ἀγαθός; see Foucart, *Associations religieuses*, pp. 146 *ff.*). But what did these words connote among the ancient Greeks and others of that period? Ἁγνός, "pure," or "chaste," merely meant in the mysteries that candidates for initiation must observe continence for a few days and abstain from certain kinds of food. It was rather a *Levitical* than a Christian purity which was demanded.

Yet again, a man was εὐσεβής, "pious," when he had duly performed all the rites of his special cult. Of the *ethical* and *spiritual* implications of the word, so familiar to us in these later days after more than eighteen centuries of Christian teaching, there were absolutely none.

Finally, the term ἀγαθός, "good," was then in common use for describing a man who was, in a civic sense, a good citizen, a man public-spirited and liberal with his wealth or services. If well-born and honourable, too, he was καλοκάγαθός—"a perfect gentleman." This, it will be seen, refers purely to a worldly standard of excellence, desirable enough in its way, but not going very far, falling short, in any case, of what we would now call "goodness." But this was the highest ideal of the pagan.[1]

---

[1] For an excellent and quite recent treatment of the subject of this chapter, see *The Christian Eucharist and the Pagan Cults* (Bohlen Lectures, U. S. A., 1913), by W. M. Groton, S.T.D.

CHAPTER XI

AFTER singing the "hymn" at the conclusion of the
Last Supper, Jesus and his disciples, we are told, left the
upper room and, issuing from the city by the gate of
the valley of Jehoshaphat, which was identical with or
near to the present *Bab Sitti Maryam* (St. Stephen's
Gate), crossed the Kedron valley and entered the groves
at the foot of the Mount of Olives, an enclosed portion
of which is said to have borne the name Gethsemane.

Gethsēmanē

But at this point we are again met by the mythical
critic. Drews says roundly (*The Witnesses to the Historicity of Jesus*, 1912, p. 204): "There was probably no
such place as Gethsemane." And again (*ibid.*, pp. 208
and 209): "Even the name 'Gethsemane,' which is nowhere else found as the name of a place, is, as Smith observes, inspired by Isaiah. . . . Here [63 : 2] we have
a clear relation to the abandonment of Jesus on Gethsemane, and his comforting by an angel (Luke 22 : 43),
and the reference to the blood (Luke 22 : 44) accords.
Jahveh's vengeance on the Gentiles is transformed in
the Gospels into the contrary act of the self-oblation of
Jesus; and, whereas in Isaiah it is the wine of anger and
vengeance that flows from the press, here it is the oil of
healing and salvation that pours from the press (*gath*)
over the peoples"—truly a great and incredible trans-
formation of the prophet's words and meaning!

Professor Smith continues (*Ecce Deus*, 1912, pp. 295 and 296) in a similar strain: "As to the place called Geth-semane, *i. e.*, 'wine-press [?] of olives,' no one knows anything whatever about it, and its topographic real-ity appears highly problematic. The conjecture seems to be close at hand that the name is purely symboli-cal, suggested by the famous passage in Isaiah [63 : 2]: 'Thy garments like him that treadeth in the wine-vat (*gath*).' This latter term means wine-press, and appar-ently never anything but wine-press.[1] The combination of Gathshemani (wine-press of oil, or olives) is singular, and it seems very unlikely as the name of a place. But why may it not mean simply 'wine-press of Olivet'? As Wellhausen well remarks, the word is not Aramaic but Hebrew. Such a name must have descended through centuries, if it was a name at all. This it would hardly have done had it not designated some place of impor-tance, and in that case we should probably have heard of it. It is very unlikely, then, that there was any place named wine-press of olives. The symbolism seems per-fectly obvious. The wine-press is that of Isaiah 63 : 2 —the wine-press of divine suffering. This explanation seems so perfectly satisfying in every way that it ap-pears gratuitous to look further. That the evangelist was thinking of Isaiah seems clear from his separating Jesus at this point from his disciples: 'I have trodden the wine-press alone, and of the people *no man was with me*'; and (the later?) Luke adds, 'Here there appeared to him an angel from heaven, strengthening him,'[2] not human but divine help was needed. Herewith is ex-plained the 'impremonition' of the disciples, which Well-hausen finds so puzzling and inconsistent (*Ev. Matt.*, p.

[1] Professor Smith here adds a note in which the following occurs: "The word *gath* may sometimes have been used inaccurately for the word *bad* (*â*), which regularly means 'olive-press' "!

[2] Vss. 43 and 44 of chap. 22 are not found in some of the oldest and best codices and are therefore considered by many critics an interpolation.

130). The whole scene is designed to *pathetise* the idea of a suffering god and at the same time to fulfil the words of the prophet in a far higher than the prophet's sense. There was need thus to import pathos, for the notion of suffering was naturally so foreign to the idea of God, though native to the idea of man, that the representation ran the risk of appearing unreal, a transparent make-believe. Hence the increasing care with which each succeeding evangelist elaborates the details of the wondrous picture—with sublime success."

Before discussing these two practically identical views as to the meaning of Gethsemane and of the scene depicted in the Gospels as taking place in that garden (grove), we may, perhaps, interpose here a few general remarks bearing upon Isaiah 63, which figures so prominently in the theories of both Drews and Smith. This chapter forms a portion of the latter part of our present book of Isaiah (chaps. 40–66), which has been named by König "The Exiles' Book of Consolation," and consists of a number of sections referring to the sufferings of the ideal "Servant of Jahveh," who is regarded by almost all modern critical scholars as being, primarily at least, the pious section of the Jewish community, suffering undeservedly, as it would seem, through the faults of the idolatrous and degenerate mass of their fellow countrymen in exile. Setting aside this view, which is too intricate for full discussion here, we will now turn, in the first place, to the question of the derivation and meaning of the word "Gethsemane."

Gethsemane is compounded (Lightfoot and others) of גַּת (*gath*), "a press," and שֶׁמֶן (*shĕmĕn*), "oil." Professor Smith appears to hold (*Ecce Deus*, p. 295), that such a press "might be used for various purposes," including, no doubt, the ex-pression of grapes for making wine, his intention (as also that of Drews) being to affiliate the whole scene taking place there with Isaiah 63 : 2 and 3,

where he thinks the agonies of a suffering god are set
forth.

Now, the regular Hebrew word for a wine-press is
פּוּרָה (*purah*, Isaiah 63 : 3, the passage here referred to;
cf. also Hag. 2 : 16), and, although *gath* is used (*cf.* Joel
3 : 13; Neh. 13 : 15; Lam. 1 : 15) absolutely in the
sense of wine-press, the addition here of the word *shemen* shows clearly that a wine-press is *not* meant but a
press for extracting oil from some kind of fruit. In addition to the olive (the principal source of vegetable oil),
there was another tree, עֵץ שֶׁמֶן (*ĕṣ shĕmĕn*), "oleaster"
(?), from the fruit of which an inferior kind of oil was
expressed; but the word *shemen* normally signifies *olive
oil*, as in Gen. 28 and elsewhere.

Further, the oil-press differed considerably in construction and size from the wine-press. The former usually
consisted of a large, circular trough in which the olives
were crushed by a heavy stone wheel, while the latter
was a kind of narrow stone or cemented trough in which
the grapes were often trodden by the feet. It was also,
as a rule, much smaller in size than the oil-press.

Again, the "garden," or enclosure, called Gethsemane
was situated (Luke 22 : 39) in the Kedron valley, probably somewhere near the foot of the Mount of Olives, so
called from the groves of olive-trees which once covered
its western slopes. No grapes were grown there, and a
wine-press, accordingly, would not be found on or near
that spot.

Now, the above-mentioned facts show clearly that it
is quite incorrect (1) to connect Gethsemane with the
wine-vat (or trough) spoken of in Isaiah 63 : 2 and 3,
and (2) to assert that the "topographic reality" of Gethsemane appears highly problematic. Of course, after
the cutting down of all the ancient trees (Jos., *B. J.*,
VI, 1, 1) and the thorough effacement of many ancient
landmarks by the Romans during the great siege of

A. D. 70, any exact identification of the position of this grove is no doubt impracticable. Professor Lucien Gautier, however, says (*Enc. Bib.*, art. "Gethsemane") of the traditional site, that, while its authenticity is not demonstrable, neither is it wholly improbable. That a press for olives would then exist at or near the foot of the hill is almost certain, and that any such enclosure wherein it was situated would, sooner or later, bear the name Gethsemane is equally probable. At the same time, as the spot was not remarkable for anything else, it would in all likelihood not be mentioned in any Jewish historical or topographical literature which has come down to us. Indeed, had not Jesus resorted thither at intervals for the purpose of retirement and prayer, it probably would have remained wholly unchronicled and unknown to succeeding generations after the destruction of the city.[1]

Turning now to the Isaianic prophecy, upon which both Drews and Smith lay so great stress, we find that it seems to have no direct or immediate bearing upon the scene described in the Gospels. "Who is this," asks the prophet, "that cometh from Edom, with dyed garments from Bozrah?" These garments are stained *red* (vs. 2), like the garments of those who have been treading the red grapes in the wine-trough. Here there is certainly no reference to an *oil*-press, where the fruit was crushed by a stone, and where, moreover, the garment of any one stepping into the press would contract not a red but a yellow stain from the oil! The writer of Mark 14 : 51, therefore, cannot have had Isaiah 63 in his mind when he penned the chapter. Neither did the Jews of that or any other preceding period refer this

---

[1] Doctor Cheyne (*Hibbert Journal*, July, 1913, pp. 920 and 921) thinks that "Gethsemane is certainly from Gilead Ishmael," and, moreover, must have been brought (as also the names Golgotha and Gabbatha) by the north Arabians in the great migration and have been preserved by tradition!

chapter to Messianic sufferings, but rather regarded it as descriptive of the sufferings of the faithful remnant who shared in the exile of the unfaithful majority of their fellow countrymen.[1]   That the prophecy was, after the resurrection, seen by the evangelists and others to be very applicable, in a secondary and metaphorical sense, to the sufferings undergone by Jesus is another matter, and beyond dispute.

Neither, again, can we affirm that the prophet here "designed to pathetise a suffering God."   A God pure and simple cannot be conceived as "suffering," though a god-man or an anthropomorphic deity can.   But such sufferings as those undergone by Jesus are rather the pains and sorrows endured by a highly strung and sensitive human nature.   There seems, therefore, no reason to doubt the probability of either the existence of the place called Gethsemane or the historic nature of the scene which is said to have taken place there.

The Agony in the Garden

Another objection, however, raised by both Mr. J. M. Robertson and Professor Drews to the account of the agony in the garden is that the scene, as described, cannot be historical because Jesus is stated by the evangelists to have been *alone* the greater part of the time of his ordeal, and the three disciples are said to have been *asleep*.   The reported words and acts cannot, therefore, have been derived from them.   But this kind of difficulty not unfrequently arises out of a careless reading of the narrative.   The attentive student of Matt. 26 : 36–44 will readily see that (1) Jesus merely went for-

[1] The earliest Jewish references to a suffering Messiah are to be found in the *Talmud*, Sanh. 93b, 96b, 97a, 98a and b (*cf.* Justin Martyr's *Dial. c. Try.*, chaps. 68, 89, and 90).   But these are all second-century A. D. references.   That the idea was unknown to the Jews (*temp. Chr.*) is shown by Matt. 16 : 22; Luke 18 : 34; 24 : 21; John 12 : 34.   It was, later on, forced on the rabbins by Christian polemic.

ward a little (vs. 39) from the disciples; (2) they only heard (and reported) fragments of his prayers and (3) they were twice awoke by him and would, doubtless, on each occasion, make a strong effort to keep awake for some time. In any case, it is evident that they were not all three asleep and out of hearing the whole time. The record, indeed, has just the fragmentary and disjointed character which we would expect it to have under the circumstances.

The Betrayal

In dealing with the betrayal Professor Drews is very emphatic in his criticism. "The thing is historically so improbable," he writes (*The Witnesses to the Historicity of Jesus*, p. 83), "the whole story of the betrayal is so absurd historically and psychologically, that only a few thoughtless Bible readers can accept it with complacency"! We should have thought, on the contrary, that such cases of treachery and bad faith on the part of some disappointed adherent towards his leader were commonplaces in history. Let us look at the facts. Jesus had come to be regarded by all his disciples as the expected Messiah (Mark 8 : 29; Matt. 16 : 16). Their Messianic ideal, however, was, like that of their contemporaries, a temporal one—a conquering monarch and an earthly sovereignty. But Jesus at once repudiated this view as not his mission (Matt. 16 : 20 and 21; *cf*. John 18 : 36). The disciples were disappointed at first, and Peter in particular remonstrated with Jesus (Matt. 16 : 22). Later on, Judas, the record says, went a step further and resolved to give him up to the authorities. Then, he perhaps reasoned with himself, if he really be the Messiah, he will be forced to act; if not, he will pay the penalty of his false pretensions. Or we may go further and hold (as one of the evangelists says plainly) that Judas was an unprincipled and dishonest man who had had his opportunity of redemption and deliberately rejected it. The whole matter is really—under this aspect—so probable, and so natural psychologically, that it seems that every one should easily grasp the situation.

But Professor Drews's sense of justice is also aroused. "Imagine," he says (*ibid.*, p. 83), "the ideal man Jesus knowing that one of his disciples is about to betray him, and thus forfeit his eternal salvation, yet doing nothing to restrain the miserable man, but rather confirming him in it!" How does Professor Drews know all this? In many places in the narrative we are told that Jesus declared he knew what was coming upon him, and he even openly avowed (Matt. 26 : 21–25) that he knew who would bring it about and the consequences to that man of his act (Mark 14 : 20 and 21; Matt. 26 : 23–25). Judas, it is clear, was fairly warned and, for aught we know to the contrary, may have received other intimations that his purpose was no secret. In either case, Jesus, who knew what was in man, no doubt rightly concluded that remonstrance and appeal were vain with a man of the character and temperament of Judas. And do not such cases occur almost every day? Why, for instance, does not God intervene and directly prevent us from falling into some great sin when we are on the point of doing so? This question is equally apposite and the answer is the same: God gives to all of us grace in due measure to resist sin as well as a certain amount of free choice in all our actions. We accept the helping grace and conquer the temptation, or we reject it and perish miserably. And Judas in this instance chose the latter of these two alternatives.

But further: "Imagine a Judas demanding money from the high priest for the betrayal of a man who walks the streets of Jerusalem daily and whose sojourn at night could assuredly be discovered without any treachery!" And he quotes, with approval, Kautsky, who says (*Der Ursprung des Christentums*, 1910, p. 388): "For Judas to have betrayed Jesus is much the same as if the Berlin police were to pay a spy to point out to them the man named Bebel." Let us again look at the facts before indorsing this remark. From the point of view of the Jewish authorities, there was a man named Jesus going about the country who had exhibited hostility towards them. This man seemed to have many adherents[1] how many it was difficult to determine. In any case, he had undoubtedly come to be regarded by many as the promised Messiah, and he himself, it seemed, might also have come to that conclusion. He threatened, therefore, to become a serious danger to them and their authority, and something must evidently be done. But what and how and when? There were, we can well understand, great discussions and dissensions in the Sanhedrin. Lawyers like Gamaliel would be in favour of a waiting policy. Probably Jesus had a few secret sympathisers in the council itself; we hear of one or two in the Gospels (John 3 : 1; 19 : 38 and 39; Mark 15 : 43). And in the midst of all this confusion and indecision one of the man's adherents suddenly offers to place him in their hands secretly and without exciting the public mind. He knows of a quiet spot where the man retires to pray and meditate away from the crowds who throng him in the city and in the fields and on the highways. His terms, too, are very reasonable—thirty shekels[2]—a mere trifle to the rulers of a nation but a considerable amount in the eyes of a poor peasant who had probably never handled so large a sum before. This offer (they would argue) will solve the problem without any great shock to the people, whose temper is uncertain.

[1] *E. g.*, The five hundred; but great crowds everywhere followed him and acclaimed his entry into the city.

[2] About £3, 15s. in English money, or $19.00 in United States currency (*cf.* Ex. 21 : 32).

This, we take it, was the natural attitude and reasoning of the Jewish authorities. They wished, no doubt, when the arrest was made, that there should be no attempt at a rescue, which, if successful, might precipitate a revolution, especially as the Passover was near and the Jews from a distance were already assembling in great numbers. As for Kautsky's criticism, we have no doubt whatever that the Berlin police did pay many spies, not to point out to them the man named Bebel, but to inform them of his acts and words and where they could best lay hands upon him if he were ever wanted by them. There is nothing novel or improbable in the course of action as depicted by the evangelists; it is, in fact, the course pursued in all ages by all authorities and rulers, whether aristocratic or democratic, civil or military, the whole world over. And the sudden acceptance of the offer made by Judas at the eleventh hour was the very natural outcome of the irresolution and divided opinions and the uncertainty in which the chief priests and scribes and Pharisees found themselves.

As regards the further question here about the meaning of the Greek verb *paradidonai* ("to hand over" or "betray") and its relation to the *paredothē* ("was given up" or "betrayed") of Isaiah 53 : 12, the reader is referred to chap. 13, where the verb is discussed.

Finally, Professor Drews concludes that "the whole story of the betrayal is a late invention founded on that passage in the prophet;[1] and Judas is not an historical personality but, as Robertson believes, a representative of the Jewish people, hated by the Christians, who were believed to have caused the death of the Saviour."

We do not know what precise meaning Professor Drews

---

[1] Isaiah 53 : 12. Elsewhere, however (*The Christ Myth*, p. 237), he says: "The account of the betrayal, of the thirty pieces of silver, and of Judas's death have their source in the Old Testament, viz., in the betrayal and death of Ahitophel"! (refs. to II Sam. 17 : 23; *cf.* Zech. 11 : 12 and Psalm 41 : 10).

attaches to the expression "a late invention"; it is certain, however, that the story was put on record[1] (in the Marcan form) by A. D. 65 at the latest, a time when many who well remembered the events of some five and thirty years previously were still alive; and these would certainly know whether Judas no less than Jesus were historical and also whether the betrayal and death of the Saviour were an actual event or a mere supposition. And the simple fact that St. Paul does not mention the details of the betrayal in any of his writings is no adverse argument whatever against the historicity of the matter. To reason thus—as some critics persist in doing—is merely to abuse the dangerous *argumentum e silentio*, which it is too frequently the fashion nowadays to employ in a reckless manner.

Professor Preserved Smith (*Hibbert Journal*, July, 1913, p. 735) sees "a minor though significant contradiction" in the statement that all forsook him and fled (Mark 14 : 50) and "the assertion that Peter followed." We need only remark here that it is clear that Professor Smith has but a small acquaintance with the psychology of impulsive people.

The Arrest and the Young Man Who Fled Away Naked

We next come to another minor but interesting episode in the narrative of the arrest, commonly known as "the young man who fled away naked" (Mark 14 : 51 and 52). And it is upon this that Professor W. B. Smith in particular pours the phials of his critical wrath and

---

[1] The variations amongst the four evangelists with regard to the words spoken and the kiss given at the time of the arrest arise very naturally out of the confusion and terror of the night. The remonstrance of Jesus chronicled by Matthew, Ἑταῖρε, ἐφ᾽ ὃ πάρει, unnatural under the circumstances and almost untranslatable, is thus ingeniously explained by Cheyne: Εταιρε should come after ο παρει and is a corruption of a dittographed ο παρει. The true reading, he believes, is υποκρινει, "thou feignest," "thou actest a part" (*Enc. Bib.*, art. "Judas," sec. 7).

contempt. "For nearly eighteen hundred years," he avers (*Ecce Deus*, pp. 111–113), "this youth has been the despair of exegesis. Wellhausen thinks that he was merely some unknown fellow in the neighbourhood who heard the racket of the arrest, jumped out of bed with only a night-robe around him, and rushed to the scene as young America hastens to a dog fight . . ."!

But, to turn to his criticism: "These verses appear at first sight to be quite inexplicable, and yet they yield their meaning readily enough. We note that the term young man is not frequent in Mark; it occurs only here and in 16 : 5. In both cases it is a 'youth wrapt all about' (περιβεβλημένος); in this case in fine and costly linen cloth (σινδόνα), especially used for cerements; in 16 : 5, in a white robe (στολὴν λευκήν). Even Leibnitz would have admitted the two figures to be almost *indiscernibles*. The garment in both cases is white, and it is the only garment (ἐπὶ γυμνοῦ, 14 : 51; γυμνός, 52). . . . Are they related?[1] . . . It seems, then, that we are dealing with a technical expression for a celestial personage (*cf.* Rev. 19 : 14). . . . The celestial personage is the angel-self of Jewish anthropology, the Persian *ferhouer* (represented on an extant coin as Sapor II, the rival of Julian the Emperor), a kind of astral body that follows along with Jesus,[2] robed in white

[1] Professor Smith refers here to Ezek. 9 : 2; Daniel 10 : 5; 12 : 6 and 7. These references, however, are not to the point. The "six men" (ἓξ ἄνδρες) of Ezekiel and "the man clad in linen cloth" (ἄνθρωπος ἐνεδυσμένος βύσσιν) of Daniel are mere symbolical figures seen in a *vision*, or trance, a fact which differentiates them from the "young man" seen at the sepulchre and the other young man whose arrest was attempted at Gethsemane.

[2] Professor Smith follows the translation of the R. V. But both this and the A. V. appear to be wrong. W. and H. read νεανίσκος τις συνηκολούθει αὐτῷ, and the preposition prefixed to the verb, if it referred to Jesus, would be *repeated* with the αὐτῷ—σὺν αὐτῷ (*cf.* Mark 5 : 37). What Mark's expression really means is that the young man, along with others, followed Jesus. That is to say, he mixed with the crowd, but was seen to be a suspicious person, and when a guard tried to arrest him he broke away, as it is related.

linen to abate its intolerable splendour. The soldiers try to seize it, but it flees away naked, leaving only the linen investiture behind. The fact that such an idea was not strange to the evangelists is clearly witnessed by Matt. 18 : 10 ('Their angels do always behold, *i. e.*, have access unto, the face of my Father'). What does the evangelist mean to say by these perplexing words? Thus far he has represented the Jesus exclusively as a God [!], a being of infinite power; and now this divinity is arrested and carried away to trial, condemnation, and death! Arrest, judge, condemn, execute a God! How can these things be? Apparently the evangelist would give us a hint that he is not to be taken literally. He would whisper to his reader: Of course the God Jesus could not be arrested, but only the garment concealing his divinity, the garment of flesh that he has put on in this symbolical narrative. Hence the repeated use of the word naked both in 51 and 52. Now, 'naked' ($\gamma\nu\mu$-$\nu\acute{o}s$) is the equivalent of disembodied when applied to a spirit, as in II Cor. 5 : 3.[1] Of the exact shade and shape of the evangelist's thought we may not, indeed, be quite sure, but there seems to be no doubt of the general identification of the 'young man' as a supernatural being.. . . . Originally it [the Marcan Gospel] may very well have squinted towards Docetism."

On pages 198–201 we have this theory worked out in greater detail and illustrated from the epistle to the Philippians 2 : 5–11 (*cf.* also Romans 15 : 3, II Cor. 8 : 9, and Col. 2 : 14 and 15). And he concludes by saying: "The doctrine [of the Docetic Gnostics] above set forth [p. 199] may, in its elaborated form, very well be later than the Gospel, but it is manifest, and it is enough,

---

[1] As applied to a human being, however, $\gamma\nu\mu\nu\acute{o}s$ does not, in common *parlance*, mean "naked," but rather "lightly clad." Here (assuming an actual young man) it would signify bereft of all the outer garments. St. Paul certainly employs the word in one place of the disembodied spirit. But it is not the usual Greek word for that concept.

that the central idea is one and the same—namely, that on the cross the true God, the Jesus, laid aside the form of flesh, temporarily assumed, and escaped, whether as a 'naked' (γυμνόν), disembodied spirit or as clothed upon with an ectypal or spiritual body. That the ancient mind shrank from the notion of a naked (bodiless) spirit is seen clearly in I Cor. 15, where the apostle argues so powerfully for a body for spirit as well as a body for soul, and also in II Cor. 5 : 1–4, where he deprecates being found naked (a bodiless spirit)."

With the above theory Doctor Cheyne seems (*Hibbert Journal*, July, 1913, pp. 921 and 922) to be in accord. He writes: "The arguments which he [Professor Smith] has adduced seem to me conclusive. . . . We know that there are celestial bodies and bodies terrestrial (I Cor. 15 : 40), and in the *Book of Adam and Eve*, translated from the Ethiopic by Malan (p. 16), God says: 'I made thee of the light, and I wished to bring out children of the light from thee.' The conception is that of luminous matter; but the body of unveiled heavenly light would have been too dazzling for ordinary human vision. The fine white linen robe was just what was requisite to mitigate the excess of light. But what has the angelic being to do here? The answer is that the Saviour, according to Mark, was a divine manifestation. To have made him, however, go about in a rich white linen robe would have defeated his object, which was, at any rate, quasi-historical. He determined, therefore, before the difficult crucifixion scene, that the true divine Jesus could not be arrested and crucified. . . . The 'young man' is, in fact, very like the fravashi of the Zoroastrians, the heavenly self."

Professor Smith's highly ingenious theory is at first sight extremely plausible. But after a careful consideration of it, as also of the phenomena following upon the resurrection of Jesus (to which he appeals in sup-

port of it), we cannot see any real grounds for its acceptance. Had Mark's narrative alone come down to us,
it might, perhaps, have been more convincing. But let
us, first of all, compare his story with that of the other
evangelists.

Mark says that the women who visited the tomb saw
a "young man" (νεανίσκον) clothed in a white garment
sitting on the right side of it. This apparition is distinctly stated by Matthew (28 : 2) to have been that of
an "angel of the Lord" (ἄγγελος Κυρίου[1]) who had some
time previously descended from heaven and rolled back
the stone from the doorway of the tomb and sat upon
it. Turning next to the Lucan and Johannine versions,
we find some variations. The former authority says
that "two men" [2] (ἄνδρες δύο) appeared suddenly. The
latter, on the other hand, differs considerably here; it
states that Mary Magdalene alone, on her second visit,
stooped and looked into the tomb and saw "two angels
in white" (δύο ἀγγέλους ἐν λευκοῖς) sitting at either end
of the spot where the body had lain.

Now, it will be seen that the apparition which Mark
describes as a "young man" Matthew (who wrote very
closely upon him) defines as an "angel of the Lord."
Similarly, the two men of Luke are described in the
Fourth Gospel as "angels." It is clear, therefore, that
both this young man of Mark and the two men of
Luke were regarded by the Christians of apostolic times

---

[1] There is, unfortunately, some ambiguity about the word Κυρίου ("Lord")
here. Professor Smith would, perhaps, argue that it refers to Jesus and that
the phrase means "the angel (heavenly self) of the Master (Lord)." But the
phrase ἄγγελος Κυρίου means, invariably, "angel (messenger) of Jahveh"
both in the Old and New Testaments. The duplication of the one ἄγγελος
(or ἀνήρ) in the Lucan and Johannine traditions also supports the view that
it does not represent the "heavenly self" of Jesus.

[2] Angels (ἄγγελοι, literally, "messengers") appear to be frequently called
men in the New Testament (cf. Acts 1 : 10, etc). This is probably because
they were regarded as manifesting themselves in human form. A human
agent is also occasionally called an ἄγγελος (Luke 9 : 52; James 2 : 25, etc.).

(including the evangelists themselves) as manifestations of spiritual beings of a higher order of existence and quite distinct from men whether living or dead. In fact, we have to do here, not with a spiritual duplicate of a material and terrestrial self, but with an ordinary *angelophany* similar to those so frequently referred to in the Old and New Testaments and stated therein to be "messengers of the Lord."

Again, Professor Smith appears to be in some error with regard to the *ferhouer* (frohar), or *fravashi*,[1] *i. e.*, "heavenly self" of the Zoroastrians, an idea which Jesus appears to sanction in Matt. 18 : 10 (*cf.* also Acts 12 : 15).

This certainly bears no resemblance to the "astral body" of the ancient or neo-Buddhists and others. The astral body, properly so called, is held to be an ethereal embodiment of the $\psi v\chi\acute{\eta}$, or "lower soul," which is believed to appear occasionally after death and (it would seem) is at times detachable and visible during life in the form of a facsimile (double) of the person of whom it forms a part. It is, perhaps, the equivalent of what is commonly known as the "ghost" of the deceased. The fravashi, on the other hand, bore almost exactly the same relation to the individual to whom it belonged as the celestial 'Ιδέα ("Idea") of Plato bore to its terrestrial and material copy, or counterpart (see M. Haug, *The Language, Writings, and Religion of the Parsis*, pp. 206, 129).[2]

Moreover, the "heavenly self," or spiritual duplicate, was neither embodied in the earthly clay of its copy nor (it would seem) accompanied it, but apparently lived in

---

[1] In Professor Moulton's *Early Zoroastrianism* (Hibb. Lects., 1912) these figures are traced back to a combination of ancestor-worship and the belief in the external soul. See also *Zend-Avesta*, Darmsteter (1883), part 2, p. 179, and Tiele's *Gesch. der Relig. im Alt.* (1896–1903), II, 256, where a different view is taken.

[2] These *frohars*, or *fravashis*, acted as "protectors" or as (in a sense) "guardian angels" of their terrestrial duplicates.

heaven ("in heaven their angels do always behold the face of my Father," *i. e.*, they are continually there, Matt. 18 : 10). At least this seems to have been the Jewish view of the matter. The astral body, on the other hand, is *embodied* in the person on earth, and after death persists upon the "astral plane," an intermediate etheric state of being above the earth plane but below the heavenly (metethereal) condition.

Again, Professor Smith seems to have misunderstood St. Paul (I Cor. 15 : 40 and 44), whose "spiritual body" (σῶμα πνευματικόν) is to be a new and (? final) post-resurrection embodiment of the spirit (πνεῦμα), while his "natural (psychical) body" (σῶμα ψυχικόν) appears to be identical with the body of flesh which forms a man's vehicle, or embodiment, while he is upon earth.[1] This fact, indeed, entirely distinguishes the concept of a spiritual body from both the "heavenly self" (*frohar*, or *fravashi*) of the ancient Persians and the astral body of the Buddhists and modern theosophists.

From these and other considerations which we have not space to particularise here, it seems clear that Mark cannot be referring in this story (14 : 51 and 52) to a duplicate and spiritual or heavenly self of Jesus who attended the material and earthly Jesus, and finally fled from him either when he was arrested in the garden or just before his crucifixion,[2] but that he means some actual

---

[1] Theosophists, however, appear to identify the "psychical body" with an immaterial "double" (astral body) existing in the fleshly (sarcical) body of our present state.

[2] The *Docetæ*, it will be remembered, regarded the spiritual being who left Jesus *at the crucifixion* not exactly as the heavenly self but as the æon *Chris-tus* who had joined himself to Jesus at his baptism. Doctor Cheyne thinks (*Hibbert Journal*, July, 1913, p. 922) that Smith's view of this young man sheds a light upon the "word from the cross" (Mark 15 : 34 and parallel). If so, then 'Ελωΐ (said by Mark to be equivalent to Θεός μου) is wrongly stated. The heavenly self, even if θεῖος in its ultimate nature, was never θεός. Matthew writes 'Ηλΐ = Θεέ μου (27 : 46). Mark, it will be noticed, uses the vernacular Aramaic.

young man who happened to be in Gethsemane at the time of the arrest and fled, as did the disciples themselves, when he was seized by the soldiers.

Finally, we can see no valid historical or other objection to this last-named view of the episode. Matthew and Mark describe a "multitude," or "crowd" (ὄχλος), as coming to arrest Jesus; Luke uses the same term; while John (18 : 3) speaks of a "band" (σπεῖραν[1]). Now, it is most probable that the Jewish authorities were careful to impress upon Pilate the urgency of the matter. Jesus had acknowledged that he was the Messiah and probably a king; consequently, a formidable Messianic insurrection was about to take place. In that case Pilate would undoubtedly send a sufficiently strong force to Gethsemane to insure the arrest of Jesus and to nip in the bud any attempt at rescue or violence on the part of the people.[2] The measured tramp of troops through the streets at so late an hour would attract attention, and doubtless more than one man "jumped out of bed, with only a night-robe around him, and rushed to the scene," as Professor Smith somewhat contemptuously phrases it. He rightly rejects Professor Bacon's paraphrase ("But a certain man was there, who had followed him thither from his bed, having the sheet wrapped around him"), but he is equally wrong in his own interpretation of συνηκολούθει αὐτῷ. The imperfect tense of a verb has not generally the meaning "was habitually" performing an act; neither is there any reference here to the heavenly self in the form of a young man following Jesus about. The verb "was following" here means, as

---

[1] *I. e.*, a manipulus, which consisted at that time of two centuries, or (about) two hundred men. This would probably not include the body of Jewish temple police sent with the Roman force. The alternative marginal translation calls it a cohort (*cf.* Acts 10 : 1), which would mean from five hundred to six hundred men.

[2] This is not directly so stated; but it seems to be implied in the Johannine narrative.

we have pointed out, that the young man—after the disciples had scattered amongst the trees—had mingled with the throng who were escorting Jesus away and was accompanying them to see what further transpired. One or more of the soldiers or the temple guard, however, suspecting that he was probably an accomplice of Jesus, attempted to arrest him also. The tense here indicates action extending over some time, and really unfinished, not merely momentary and completed, as in the case of the aorist. Probably the party had gone a little distance before the presence of a suspicious stranger was noticed.

There is no doubt, on the other hand, that Zahn's identification of the young man with Mark himself is precarious. Still, it is not impossible. The reference of Keim and others (so also, recently, S. Reinach, *Orpheus*, pp. 216 and 217) to Amos 2 : 16 as the source of the "legend" does not, as Smith says, explain the origin of the story. This prophecy was not a very prominent one in Jewish literature, neither had it any suggestive Messianic connexions in after years. Besides this, Mark (unlike Matthew) is not given to seeking "fulfilments" of prophecy in every incident connected with the life or sayings of Jesus. The fact is, the plain, literal sense of this story is perfectly acceptable, much more so, indeed, than any occult interpretation such as Professor Smith here offers.

With regard to the "linen cloth," a wide garment of linen (סָדִין) was worn over the body by all classes, under the over-clothes. This garment is called, in the LXX (Judges 14 : 12 and 13; Prov. 31 : 24), σινδών, the very word used here by the evangelist. Or perhaps we might regard the *sindōn* here as a night-wrapper of fine linen at that time often worn by the inhabitants of Palestine.[1] In either case there is nothing extraordinary in the man

[1] Herodotus, II, 95, speaks of the σινδών as the usual night-dress of the Egyptians.

being abroad in the groves of Gethsemane during a spring
night with only his usual (working) undergarment or perhaps his night-wrapper upon him.[1] The city was at this
time under the influence of the excitement and ferment
of the approaching Passover, and restless or adventurous
spirits would probably not be abed. A further argument
against Professor Smith's *ferhouer* would be the fact, already referred to, that Mark never anywhere else even
hints at a "heavenly self" accompanying Jesus, and the
present Gospel, even if it be (which is doubtful) a revised edition of an older (and ? Aramaic) version, cannot by any stretch of imagination be said to "squint"
even in the smallest degree at Docetism.

---

[1] John 18 : 18, it is true, says that the night was cold.   Still, the man
would be, speaking technically, "naked" if he had his usual day undergarment left when any wrapper put over it was snatched away.

CHAPTER XII

The Trials

AN outstanding difference between the "Christ-myth"
and the myths of all the numerous "suffering saviours"
of cult-worship is the fact that the former has a detailed
description of an impressive trial,[1] while the various
mythic sun-gods, or vegetation-spirits, who have been so
freely designated as "saviours," died, or were put to
death, without any pretense of the kind.

The narrative of the trial, or trials, of Jesus, however,
is regarded by Professor Drews and the other mythicists as a part of the process of quasi-historicising the
myth and as due wholly to the inventive genius of the
early Christians. But it is very evident, at any rate to
the careful reader who is well acquainted with both the
Jewish and Roman judicial systems, that if the trials, as
described by the evangelists, closely agree with Jewish
and Roman methods of procedure in such cases, due
allowance being made for the irregularities and haste
which, under such special circumstances, would be likely
to characterise them, a powerful argument is furnished
for the actual historicity of the whole affair.

Now, the entire procedure, as set forth in the Gospels,
occupies four distinct stages: (1) A preliminary exami-

[1] As a discussion of the historico-legal aspect of the trials of Jesus does
not come within the scope of this work, the reader is referred, for a full
discussion of them, to *The Trial of Jesus Christ: A Legal Monograph*, by
Doctor A. Taylor Innes, and the excellent little book, *The Trial of Jesus
Illustrated from Talmud and Roman Law*, by S. Buss, LL.B.

nation of a semi-private character before Annas (Hanan)
previous to a delivery to the Sanhedrin.   (2) The actual
Jewish trial before the Sanhedrin, as the chief tribunal
of judicial administration (*cf.* Num. 11 : 16; Jos., *Ant.*,
XIV, 9, 2), presided over on this occasion by Caiaphas.[1]
The charges here brought against Jesus may be com-
prised under two heads: (*a*) false teaching and (*b*)
blasphemy.   (3) The examination before the Roman
procurator, together with (according to Luke) an irrregu-
lar interview with Herod Antipas. Jesus was, in the
former of these, accused by the Jews of perverting the
nation by (*a*) forbidding payment of tribute to Cæsar
and (*b*) claiming to be the Messianic King.[2] (4) The subsequent irregular proceedings in which the procurator,
under pressure from a furious mob which had been in-
cited by the priests, yielded to the general clamour for a
sentence of death.

In view of the fact that the records of the former trial
have been pronounced unsatisfactory, as showing errors
in the matter of procedure, etc., we may notice here the
chief infringements of strict Jewish law which it presents.

As the arrest of Jesus was effected during the night,
the legal course would have been to detain the prisoner
in custody, after the preliminary examination by Annas,
until the next day (*cf.* Acts 4 : 3).[3] This was not done;
consequently the whole of the proceedings before the
Sanhedrin were technically irregular and therefore legally
null and void.   Also, according to Luke 23 : 51, Joseph

---

[1] Edersheim says (*Life of Jesus of Nazareth*, II, p. 556) that in great criminal cases or important investigations the high priest always presided.   In
legal and ritual questions the Nasi presided, who, at this time, was Gamaliel
(Acts 5 : 34).   On the confusion in the narrative in the synoptics and John 18
and its explanation, see Blass, *Philology of the Gospels*, pp. 56–59.

[2] This trial (John 18 : 33–38) really ended in an acquittal and was quite
in accordance with Roman law as then administered in the provinces.

[3] *I. e.*, between 6 A. M. and 6 P. M. (Sanh. iv).   The next day, however,
was equally precluded, being the eve of a Sabbath and perhaps the paschal
festival.

of Arimathæa (and possibly Gamaliel and some others)
had been opposed to the proceedings and probably the
verdict. This was another irregularity, as the whole of
the seventy-one members ought to have concurred in a
verdict and sentence of death against a false prophet.
But as the trial ended, after Pilate's examination, in a
sudden outburst of mob-violence, these points were all
ignored[1] and cannot be laid to the charge of the evangelists.[2] And now let us consider the various objections
which have been raised by the advocates of the mythical
hypothesis.

In the first place, Mr. J. M. Robertson assures us
(*Pagan Christs*, p. 197) that these narratives in the Gospels are clearly unhistorical because, it would seem, so
many events are said to have happened all in the space
of one night. This objection is developed still further
by Doctor Anderson in an article, "The Essence of the
Faith," in *The Quest* for April, 1912, where he says:
"The critic . . . will proceed to prove that the stories of
the trial, arrest, and crucifixion are quite understandable
as scenes of a mystery-play but are quite inexplicable
as facts of history. The trial is represented as lasting
through one night, when, as Renan points out, an Eastern city is wrapt in silence and darkness, quite natural
as scenes in a mystery-play but not as actual history."

Let us deal first of all with this latter and more seri-

[1] A similar instance of a trial before the Sanhedrin, irregularly conducted
by the high priest Annas (circ. 63 A. D.), is mentioned by Josephus (*Ant.*,
XX, 9, 1).

[2] Quite recently Professor Goethals (*Mélanges d'Histoire du Christian-
isme*, "III Jesus a Jerusalem," 1912) thinks that Mark's version of the
trial is largely hagiographical. It was, he says, "worked over at Rome after
64 A. D., and aims at showing Jesus as the prototype of confessors and mar-
tyrs." He follows in preference the account given in the *Additamenta*, according to which there was an actual plot formed by one hundred and fifty
of the followers of Jesus to make him a Messianic King. This conspiracy
was revealed to the Sanhedrin, and he was taken before Pilate, tried, and
discharged. Then came the arrest by the Jews and his condemnation by
the Sanhedrin as a false prophet.

ous objection. Had either Renan or Doctor Anderson really thought twice, the former would never have penned these words and the latter would not have quoted them. "*Darkness*," with the paschal moon almost full and in the clear, bright atmosphere of an Eastern sky! Again, "*silence*," with the crowds of foreign Jews arriving hourly, day and night, and the whole city seething with the bustle and excitement of the approaching Passover which began the next day! This excitement may also have been increased by rumours of an intended outbreak and proclamation of a Messianic King; in which case both Romans and Jews would be in a state of expectancy and readiness during the night and day preceding the celebration of the great feast, the one in order to be ready to crush the movement in the bud, the other in order to be ready to give whatever support might be deemed necessary and prudent. Ordinarily, no doubt, an Oriental city is buried in silence and sleep during the night, but not on critical occasions like this.

As regards the number of events happening during the space of one night and the alleged impossibility of crowding them into so small a space of time, we may add that if Jesus were arrested about 1 A. M., as seems probable, and brought before Annas about 2 A. M., the examinations before the Sanhedrin and Pilate, and even the interview with Herod, could all very well have been carried out, as described, during the next five hours, since all these judges would be lodged within a short distance of one another in the temple area and in the adjoining tower of Antonia. And this would allow sufficient time for Jesus to be crucified at 9 o'clock, as one evangelist states.[1]

Turning to Professor Drews, we find that he indorses

[1] Mark 15 : 25. See an article (*Expository Times*, January, 1909, p. 183) by Mrs. M. D. Gibson, who produces evidence to show that Mark is right and that the sixth hour of John 19 : 14 is due to the error of a scribe.

the view of Mr. Robertson, but also finds fault with the narrative of the trial. He says (*The Christ Myth*, pp. 241 and 242): "But where the authors of the Gospel have really found something new, *e. g.*, in the account of Jesus' trial, of the Roman and Jewish procedure, they have worked it out in such an ignorant (*sic*) way, and, to one who knows something about it, betray so significantly the fictitious nature of their account, that here really there is nothing to wonder at except, perhaps, the *naïveté* of those who still consider that account historical and pique themselves a little on their historical exactness and scientific method." [1]

This, however, is not so. An examination of the works above referred to (p. 228, note 1) will show conclusively that the evangelists understood very well what they were writing about and, though mere laymen in legal matters, have given a very generally correct version of the adherence to the chief rules of Jewish procedure and the requirements of Roman law, as also of the effects of mob-violence, which ultimately defeated Pilate's efforts to get a very just Roman verdict carried into effect. We would strongly recommend Doctor Drews to reread carefully the records of the trial in the light of both Jewish and Roman law.

Again, a reference to the evidence of the *Talmud* with regard to the trial must be preceded by a careful consideration of several points of great importance. None of the *Talmud*, as we now possess it, was, in all probability, in writing before 200 A. D.; all contemporary documents, too, must have been destroyed in the sack and burning of Jerusalem in A. D. 70. During this intervening period of one hundred and thirty years or thereabouts the story of Jesus and his trial and execution must have been to the Jews an oral tradition, liable, as such traditions are, to variations in its details as well

[1] Reference here to Brandt, *Die Evangelische Geschichte*, especially 53 *ff.*

as misrepresentation from religious prejudices. Add to these the fact that, when it had been committed by them to writing, the church was rapidly becoming a dominant power in the Roman world. By the fourth century, indeed, or soon afterwards, it had become unsafe even to refer openly to the Man whom the Jews have ever spoken of as the false Messiah. Accordingly, in such Jewish references as we find, there is a great deal of perhaps intentional vagueness of statement and confusion in details. Jesus is not often referred to directly by name, but generally as *Ben Stada* (though sometimes as *Ben Pandera*) and, it would almost seem, purposely confused with some other (actual or supposititious) Jesus who appears to have incurred the displeasure of the Sanhedrin about one hundred years previously and been stoned to death. At all events, we read that Jesus "was tried by the Beth-Din, condemned, and executed at Lud (Lydda)[1] on the eve of the Passover, which was also the eve of the Sabbath. He was stoned and hanged (= crucified) . . . by Pinhas the robber,[2] and was at the time thirty-three years of age." [3] This reference, in spite of the minor errors of fact which it contains, is amply sufficient for purposes of identification.

It has been suggested, however, that in any case the Jewish writers must have derived their information from the Gospels, which, after 200 A. D., were very widely circulated. This view very largely ignores the strength and tenacity of oral tradition in Eastern countries; and it is in the highest degree improbable that the Jews would set aside any religious tradition of their own or adopt any story from the Gospels which had no basis in their own oral records. In short, the evidence of

---

[1] A small town near Joppa.

[2] Pontius Pilate (?), who was afterwards accused of extortion and robbery during his term of office.

[3] See particularly *Pales. Talm.*, Sanh. Tract., III, 25d, and *Bab. Talm.*, Sanh. Tract., 67a.

the *Talmud*, in spite of the obscurity and errors which it contains, confirms indirectly the story of the evangelists, a fact which the Jews of all ages, without a dissentient voice, have always admitted.

Peter

According to Mr. J. M. Robertson (*Christianity and Mythology*, p. 379): "It is one of the many valuable solutions advanced by Dupuis that Peter's legend is substantially constructed on the Roman myth of Janus. Janus, like Peter, bears the keys and the rod; and, as the opener of the year (hence the name of January), he stands at the head of the twelve months as Peter stands at the head of the twelve apostles. . . . Originally Dianus, the sun-god (Macr., *Sat.*, I, 9), as Diana was moon-goddess, he came to hold a subordinate though always popular place in the god-group and was for the later Roman world especially the key-keeper, the opener (*patulcius*) and closer (*clusius*).[1] There could not be a more exact parallel to the Petrine claims. . . .

"As the mythical Peter is a fisherman, so to Janus, on coins, belongs the symbol of a bark, and he is the god of havens. Further, he is the source or deity of wells, rivers, and streams. It is not unlikely, by the way, that a representation of Janus beside Poseidon, in his capacity of sea-regent, may have motived the introduction of Peter into the myth of Jesus walking on the waves, though, as before suggested [p. 358], the rock may have given the idea."

Further, in his *Pagan Christs* (p. 353), Mr. Robertson continues and expands this theory. There he lays great stress upon the two faces of the god, and further seeks to establish an identity between Janus and Jesus, who "has constructively several of the attributes of Proteus-Janus," instancing "I am the door," "I stand

[1] See Ovid, *Fasti*, I, 129 and 130.

at the door and knock," "I am in the Father and the
Father in me" ("Janus with the two faces, old and
young, seated in the midst of the twelve altars"), "I
have the keys of death and Hades." "The function of
Janus as god of war is also associable with the dictum:
'I came not to bring peace but a sword'. . . !'"

Again, he finds the further remarkable coincidence that
in the Egyptian *Book of the Dead* (chap. 68, Doctor
Budge's translation, p. 123) *Petrâ* is the name of the
divine doorkeeper of heaven. This suggests an ancient
connexion between the Egyptian and Asiatic cults. Furthermore, he thinks that certain early Christian sculptures, which represent the story of Jesus and Peter and
the cock-crowing,[1] "suggest that it [the story] originated
as an interpretation of some such sculpture." These
sculptures he further wishes to connect with a Mithraic
source, because in the *Zend-Avesta* (Bundahish XIX and
Vendidad, Farg. XVIII, 2) the cock is mentioned as a
bird symbolic of the sun-god.

Lastly, he thinks (*Christianity and Mythology*, p. 381)
that "the two-faced image of Janus connects alike with
the dual aspect of Mithra, who is two-sexed, and the
myth of Peter's repudiation of Jesus." And this because the term *bifrons* ("two-faced") does not seem to
have become for the Romans, as it is for us, a term signifying treachery or duplicity, doubtless because Janus,
to whom it belonged, was a benign god. "But," he adds,
"in connexion with a new cult which rejected the old
theosophies, nothing could be more natural than the sur-

---

[1] It has been suggested that this incident, connected with Peter's denial
of Jesus (Mark 14 : 68–72), has reference to the restrictions supposed by
the Jews to be laid upon *mazziḳin* (מזיקין), evil spirits, or demons. These
beings, and the similar *jinns* of the Arabs, etc., carried on their practises
of seducing mankind into various sins and errors during the night. But the
moment the cock crew their powers were suspended. See Weber, *Judische
Theologie* (Leipzig, 1897), p. 255. There may be some connexion; but why
did the cock, according to some authorities, crow twice?

mise that the personage with two faces, looking forward
and backward, had been guilty of some act of double
dealing!" We will now deal with these views in some
detail.

Mr. Robertson's statement of the matter, as set forth
above, is characterised by several errors of fact as well
as some confusion of thought. When these are eliminated it will be seen that the Janus-(? Dianus) myth is
anything but an exact parallel to the "myth" of Peter.

Now, in the first place, it is quite wrong to assert that
Janus (as the month January) was "the opener of the
year", and that "he stood at the head of the twelve
months as Peter stands at the head of the twelve apostles." The old Roman year began in *March*, as the names
of the four last months of our present calendar show.
Peter, too, was not the head of the apostolic college.
So far as there was a head, that position was occupied by
James (Acts 12 : 17; 15 : 13 and 19; 21 : 18; Gal. 2 : 9).
Moreover, it is not at all certain that Janus is a derivative of and equivalent to an older Dianus. The later
Romans thought so; but there are several good reasons
for identifying him with the old Etruscan deity *Ani*.

Again, the Roman *as* bore the impression of a ship on
the obverse of the head of Janus, because the latter
was the god presiding over all journeyings, whether by
land or sea, and was regarded by the Romans as the discoverer of the art of ship-building and described as the
husband of the sea-goddess Venilia. This does not in
the least connect him with Peter, whose actual name was
Simon[1] Bar-jonas and who was merely a fisherman on
an inland lake. Neither does the fact of Janus being regarded as the god of wells, rivers, and streams point to
a connexion with Peter, who had nothing whatever to
do with them. The former was connected with these
and indirectly through them with Poseidon (Neptune),

---

[1] ? = snub-nosed. A Greek name common in post-exilic times.

the god of the sea, because the source of all organic life was moisture and especially moving (*vivus*) water. There is here not the remotest connexion with the story of Jesus walking upon the waves.

Further, the connexion of Janus with the door arose from the fact that he was originally a god of the light, who opened the gates of heaven on the sun's going forth in the morning and closed them on his withdrawal at evening. And so, in course of time, he became the god of all going out and coming in, to whom all places of egress and passage, all doors and gates, were holy. Had Jesus been named "the *guardian* of the door," a parallel might have been drawn. But by such phrases as "I am the door," etc., he really means that he is the sole means of spiritual access to the Father, a widely different notion. And the Janus with the "two faces, old and young," is a product of Mr. Robertson's imagination. On the Roman *as*, as he can see on reference to a specimen of that coin, both faces of Janus are duplicates as regards age and appearance, and in later times both were bearded.[1]

Janus, it is true, as the god of doorways, is depicted with the porter's keys and staff, and Peter is also stated by Matthew (16 : 19) to have had intrusted to him the "keys" of the kingdom of heaven. But it may be added here that (1) this commission is not found in the oldest authority (Mark) and *may*, therefore, be a later addition, and (2) "*I* have the keys of death and of Hades" (Rev. 1 : 9) seems to imply that the early church did not consider that these keys had been put in commission absolutely to Peter, who had on occasion been summarily rebuked and set right by Paul, and who, moreover,

[1] According to Servius (a contemporary of Macrobius), Romulus and Tatius, *i. e.*, the Romans and Sabines, when they agreed to coalesce into one people, made an image of Janus Bifrons as a symbol of their union and distinction (*On Æn.*, I, 291).

as we have seen, is invariably mentioned after James. The contrary view certainly sprang up during the second century, possibly at first suggested by the Janus-myth, and was soon welcomed in certain quarters for the support it offered to the growing claims of the bishops of Rome.

Further, Janus was not in any strict sense a "god of war," but was merely let out to the aid of the Romans when on campaign and kept shut up in his temple when Rome was at peace. And the meaning of the saying of Jesus, "I came not to bring peace but a sword," is that the Gospel will, through its rejection by many, also cause grave dissensions in families and communities instead of the peace and harmony which it was intended to bring about.

Once again, the Egyptian god *Petrà* is, according to the *Book of the Dead* (*loc. cit.*), the doorkeeper of heaven; but this fact does not support any philological theory of identification with Peter (Πέτρος). *Petrà* has nothing to do with the Greek *petrā* ("rock"), but means "the seer," "the all-seeing one," [1] and is, no doubt, expressive of the vigilant sight and attentiveness which all door-keepers should exercise. *Petrā*, on the contrary, implies steadfastness of purpose, the possession of which, in Peter's case, is said to have procured for him the title of *Petros* (πέτρος, "stone") from Jesus.[2]

---

[1] Doctor Budge, in a letter to the present writer.

[2] Attempts have been made by several German scholars to identify the twelve disciples with the twelve signs of the zodiac. This idea was advanced over a century ago by Dupuis (*L'origine*, etc., III, 47), who connected the twelve with the angels of the zodiac.

A few specimens of the arguments used will suffice here to illustrate the methods employed.

Winckler (*Forschungen*, II, p. 387), Jeremias (*Babylonisches*, p. 92), and Fiebig (*Babel u. das N. T.*, p. 18) derive *Alphœus* (Mark 3 : 18) from Bab., *Alpu=Taurus*. As this explanation is open to the trifling objection that it was James himself, and not his father, who represents the sign, Fiebig replies that the names of fathers are not always intended in *the genealogical sense*.

Again, Thomas (Heb., תָּאוֹם, Bab., *tuāmu*, Syr., *thāmā*, "a twin") is identi-

Further, Mr. Robertson's interpretation of the early Christian sculptures descriptive of the story of the denials and the cock-crowing is most certainly a direct inversion of facts. These incidents would be likely to suggest the sculptures; but the sculptures would not suggest the incident to any writer, even if the cock were recognised as being a symbol of the sun-god in his earliest morning phase.

Lastly, as regards the origin of the two-faced conception of Janus, the ordinary explanation is that it arose out of the fact that all doors and gates looked both ways (inward and outward). Doctor Budge, however, thinks that the idea was probably suggested by the two-headed god, the Horus-Set of old Egypt. In any case, it cannot have arisen out of the dual aspect of Mithra, "who is two-sexed" [?]. Neither Janus nor "Peter-Jesus" (whom Mr. Robertson appears to regard as a sort of duplex representation [Proteus-Janus] of the sun) could be in any sense termed "two-sexed"! The mythical view of the matter is further weakened by Mr. Robertson's own subsequent admission that the title Janus Bifrons had no sign of duplicity or treachery about it, and consequently the two-faced god cannot have suggested Peter's facing both ways during the period of suspense and stress at the trial. Neither, in point of fact, have we any evidence to show that the concept of Janus, the benign god, was ever changed by the "new cult" into one implying some act of double dealing.

fied with the zodiacal constellation *Gemini* merely because the two words signify nearly the same thing; and so forth.

These several arguments are further enforced in a collective sense by a reference to the saying of Jesus in Matt. 19 : 28; *cf.* Luke 22 : 30, from which it is inferred that there are twelve disciples because there were twelve tribes. From this fact it would seem to follow that the sons of Jacob and the twelve tribes of Israel must also be personifications of the twelve signs of the zodiac (see Gen. 49 : 3–28) as, indeed, they have been pronounced to be. Most readers will agree that such demonstrations are exceedingly unsatisfactory (see *Astronomical Myths*, J. E. Blake, 1877, pp. 106 *ff.*).

Accordingly, Mr. Robertson's entire hypothesis of Peter, as representing a kind of Christianised Roman Janus, or Egyptian Peträ, and as ultimately a mere mythical character derived from a pagan source, is wholly untenable.

Pilate

The semi-mythologising of Pontius Pilate by Professor Drews is really one of the strongest proofs of the radical unsoundness of his whole system of exegesis. The ease with which well-known and undoubtedly historical characters can be made to lend themselves to this kind of treatment, in the hands of an expert at such schemes, is here most clearly exemplified.

We know from history that Pilate was the fifth of the seven procurators who administered the Roman province of Judæa during the period 26–36 A. D. (*cf.* Jos., *Ant.*, XVIII, 4, 2). His *nomen* is suggestive of a connexion with the Samnite Pontii, while his *cognomen* may be derived either from *pileatus*, *i. e.*, wearing the *pileus*, or felt cap, of the manumitted slave, or (more probably) from *pilatus*, the man armed with the javelin, *i. e.*, the legionary soldier. He seems to have been a man of inferior birth and culture and to have treated Jewish customs and idiosyncrasies with more than ordinary Roman contempt. His portrait, however, as sketched by Josephus, is doubtless drawn from a purely Jewish and unfriendly standpoint.[1] Pilate's hostility to the Jews themselves may, perhaps, partly account for his evident desire to be fair, and even sympathetic, towards Jesus until events proved too strong for him; at any rate, the fierce and uncompromising hatred displayed by the priesthood towards the meek and uncomplaining prisoner evidently touched chords of both pity and indig-

---

[1] So also that of Philo Judæus, who says (*Leg. ad Caium*, 38) that Agrippa I described him as τὴν φυσὶν ἀκαμπής.

nation in his breast, which for a time at least prevailed over Roman truculence and indifference to suffering and wrong.

But all this evidence, set forth so naturally and simply by the Gospel writers, is brushed aside by Professor Drews, who prefers (*The Witnesses to the Historicity of Jesus*, pp. 55, 158, and 159) to follow the speculations of Niemojewski[1] to that of ancient and almost contemporary writers and biographers. Accordingly, the Pilate of the Gospels is identified with the constellation *Orion*, who is said to be the "javelin man" (*pilatus*), with the "arrow, or lance constellation" (*sagitta*). This "arrow," or "lance," in the Greek form of the zodiacal myth, is, he says, very long, and the wielder of it appears in "the Christian [apocryphal] legend" as the soldier Longinus who pierces the side of Jesus with a spear (λόγχη, John 19 : 34). To summarise Drews's theory in his own words: "In the astral-myth, the Christ hanging on the cross, or world-tree (*i. e.*, the Milky Way), is killed by the lance of Pilatus." [2]

But we must not hastily conclude from this that Doctor Drews disbelieves in the existence of the historic Pilate. He thinks, with Niemojewski, that the Christian populace told the legend of a javelin-man, a certain Pilatus, who was supposed (*sic*) to have been responsible for the death of the Saviour. "This," he recklessly adds, "wholly sufficed for Tacitus *to recognise in him the procurator in the reign of Tiberius, who must have been known to the Roman historian from the books of Josephus on the 'Jewish War,' which were destined for the imperial house.*" [3]

---

[1] In his *Gott Jesus im Lichte fremder und eigener Forschungen samt Darstellung der evangelischen Astrolstoffe Astralszenen und Astralsysteme* (1910).

[2] See, however, *Appendix C*, where, in the "astral drama" of the crucifixion, *Orion* represents not (as here) the slayer of the Christ but the Christ himself! This is flat self-contradiction.

[3] Italics ours. On p. 158 (*op. cit.*), however, Professor Drews states his theory less dogmatically: "*It is not certain* [italics ours] that we have not

To offer such an explanation of the "Story of the Cross," as told by Tacitus, the "Gibbon of the ancient Roman world," is to credit that great and philosophical historian with a carelessness and lack of judgment, not to say of common sense, which is wholly undeserved by him. Finally, Drews adds: "In point of fact, the procurator Pontius Pilate plays a part in the Gospels so signally opposed to the part of the historical Pilate, as Josephus describes him, that we can very well suspect a later introduction of an historical personage into the quasi-historical narrative."

But the historical Pilate—as we have already remarked —in the reports of the trial, merely plays the part of a Roman official who is personally hostile to and suspicious of the Jewish authorities, as he is described by Josephus to have been. And even the unscrupulousness, which is stated both by Josephus and Philo to have been a fundamental ingredient in his character, is clearly shown by his finally yielding up Jesus to save himself, contrary to a momentary better impulse which had possessed him. In fine, his conduct throughout the trial is entirely consonant with what we know of human nature, where sound principles are lacking.

Lithostrōton-Gabbatha

"Let us now pass on," as Professor W. B. Smith says (*Ecce Deus*, pp. 297 and 298), "to the place called Lithostrōton, but in the Hebrew Gabbatha" (John 19 : 13). "However," he adds, "we need not tarry there long. It is well known that all attempts in all ages, even by the

here an astral-myth in which the Homo Pilatus (the javelin-man Orion) played a part converted into history on the strength of a similarity of name with the Roman procurator Pilate and that the whole story was not on this account placed in the time of the first two Roman emperors." It can, he thinks, be detached from that period without suffering any essential change —a characteristic of myths.

most ingenious and erudite and sympathetic scholars, to locate this stone-strewn spot have failed utterly. Now, at least it has become clear that they have all the while been seeking in the wrong region, in Jerusalem, whereas the pavement glittered only in the fancy of the evangelist."

With this view of the matter Professor Canney (*Enc. Bib.*, art. "Pavement") seems to have some sympathy.[1]

Let us, however, examine this question afresh. And, first of all, we will turn to Josephus, our great and almost sole authority on the topography of ancient Jerusalem. He says (*B. J.*, V, 5, 8): "Now, as regards the tower of Antonia, it was situated at the corner of two cloisters of the court of the temple, of that on the west and that on the north; it was erected upon a rock of fifty cubits in height and was on a great precipice; it was the work of King Herod, wherein he demonstrated his natural magnanimity. In the first place, the rock itself was covered over with smooth pieces of stone, from its foundation, both for ornament and that any one who would either try to get up or to go down it might not be able to maintain his footing upon it." In other words, this rock, whereon the citadel of Jerusalem was built—the Prætorium[2] of the later procuratorial days— was covered over, both sides and flat top, with a layer of smooth slabs of stone. The top of this rock, therefore,

---

[1] Doctor Cheyne, in commenting on this, says (*Hibbert Journal*, July, 1913, p. 921): "Gab in Gabbatha, like the name of the New Testament prophet Agab(us), and that of the great Babylonian banker Egibi, comes ultimately from 'Aḥ'ab' (*i. e.*, Arabian, *Ashḥur*)." Keim, however (*Jesus of Nazara*, VI, p. 86, note 2) derives it from *gib(e)ba*, or *gibba* (*Targ. Rabb.*, Buxt., p. 377), emphatic *gibbata*, Greek, Γαββαθά (ā).

[2] There is some confusion here in Mark 15 : 16 and Matt. 27 : 27. It is not clear whether by the "Prætorium" the hall of the castle Antonia is meant or that of the palace of Herod the Great, on the western hill, which was connected with the eastern, or temple hill, by means of a bridge. On the whole, the former seems more probable, as it was a fortress, and the palace of Herod would most probably be reserved for the use of Herod Antipas.

evidently answers to the descriptive name Λιθόστρωτον, *i. e.*, a pavement "laid with stone."

Again, the Aramaic word גַּבְּתָא ("Gabbatha") means a "height" or "a back ridge," and, as the only important heights in Jerusalem were the adjoining ones, on which Herod's palace and the temple and the tower of Antonia were built, it is a fair inference to regard one of these as the height Josephus speaks of as furnished with an artificial layer of smooth stones.   That is, in effect, *Lithostrōton* is not a translation of Gabbatha (or Gabbatha of Lithostrōton); but the older name of the place was "the height" and the newer Greek appellation, doubtless given after Herod had covered it with a sort of veneer of stone, was "the pavement."

Now, at the time of the Passover, when, owing to the excited and tumultuous state of the city, disturbances were greatly to be feared, the Roman procurator, who ordinarily resided at Cæsarea, came to Jerusalem attended by a strong body of troops and took up his quarters in the citadel of Antonia.   And, at the trial of Jesus, we are told that he was led by Caiaphas to the Prætorium (John 18 : 28) at an early hour of the morning.   The members of the Sanhedrin, however, entered not into the judgment-hall [Prætorium], that they might not be defiled, but might eat the Passover.[1]

Accordingly, Jesus was taken in alone by Roman guards and closely questioned by Pilate as to his Messianic and regal claims.   When he had declared that his kingdom was not of this world, Pilate went outside and offered his famous solution of the difficulty, viz., that Jesus should be released in compliance with a custom generally adopted at that time, just before the Passover (vs. 39).   This offer was rejected by the Jews, and Pilate

---

[1] The *imperators* had a kind of portable mosaic floor, which they often carried about with them and upon which their tribunal was set.   But this is plainly not what the Gospel here refers to.

then went back and further questioned Jesus. Finally, according to John, he brought him out on to the pavement and presented him to the waiting crowd of Jews with the significant but ironical words: Ἴδε ὁ ἄνθρωπος, "Behold the man!"

Now, it would seem that quite unnecessary difficulties have been raised about the names *Lithostrōton* and *Gabbatha*. They are, indeed, not equivalent to one another as regards meaning, but apparently different names for the same spot. And, although the four evangelists give a somewhat confused account and differ a good deal in details in their versions of the trial scenes, and the synoptists do not mention this incident at all, there seems to be no reason whatever to doubt the historicity of the narrative. As a consequence of this conclusion, we cannot see any justification for such a statement as that "probably Lithostrōton-Gabbatha existed as a definite locality only in the mind of the author." At the same time we can well understand that the relegation of the place to the category of imagination is a great help to the theory that the entire story of Jesus is wholly unhistorical. The evidence for this hypothesis must necessarily be presented in a detailed and cumulative form, and every little incident that can be disposed of as mythical goes a long way towards helping out the case.

Annas and Caiaphas

Doctor Drews tells us (*The Witnesses to the Historicity of Jesus*, p. 212 and note) that "Many names of supposed historical persons seem to have been originally of an astral character and to have been later pressed into the historical scheme; such are Herod,[1] the high priests Annas and Caiaphas, and Pilate."

[1] An interesting and able study of Herod and his connexion with the trial of Jesus, by the late Professor A. W. Verrall, will be found in the *Jour. of Theo. Studies*, April, 1909.

Annas is said to be "identical in name with the prophetess Anna (Sib-Zi-Anna of the Babylonians, Anna Perenna of the Romans) and, according to Niemojewski, corresponds to the star γ in *Gemini*, but, according to Fuhrmann, to the constellation *Cassiopeia*, which 'dwells in the temple' or at the highest point of the Milky Way. Caiaphas is clearly, in that case, the constellation *Cepheus*, near Cassiopeia; and the two names were subsequently applied to the Jewish high priests on account of the similarity. The *Talmud* enumerates the names of the principal men who directed the Sanhedrin from Antigonas (B. C. 250) until the destruction of the temple; a Caiaphas is not to be found among the number. He was high priest for eighteen years; but this also is not mentioned in the *Talmud*, although it gives the names of all who have been high priests for ten years or more."

It is really difficult to understand the force of the above-quoted remarks. *Annas* (called by Josephus Ἄνανος), or *Hanan*, "gracious," is the masculine form of the name *Anna* (Ἄννα), or *Hannah* (*cf.* I Sam. 1 : 2 with Luke 2 : 36). He was appointed high priest by Quirinus and held the office for seven years (A. D. 7–14). See Jos., *Ant.*, XVIII, 2, 1.

Caiaphas[1] was appointed high priest by Valerius Gratus (the predecessor of Pilate) in A. D. 25 and was deposed by Vitellius in A. D. 36. Josephus says (*Ant.*, XVIII, 2, 2) that after the deposition of Eleazer, the son of Annas by Gratus, the high-priesthood was conferred upon Simon the son of Camithus, and "when he had possessed that dignity no longer than a year Joseph Caiaphas was made his successor." [2]

---

[1] Aram., קַיָּפָא. Buxt., *Lex. Chald.*, 1076. Perhaps from Arab., *Ḳa'if*, "soothsayer," *cf.* John 18 : 33–38. According to Josephus (*Ant.* VI, 6, 3), the high priest was generally regarded as having prophetic powers; *cf.* Philo, *De Creat. Princ.*, VIII (ed. Mangey, II, p. 367).

[2] Ἰώσηπος ὁ καὶ Καϊάφας διάδοχος ἦν αὐτῷ, *cf.* XVIII, 4. Ἰώσηπον τὸν καὶ Καϊάφαν ἐπικαλούμενον, "J., who was surnamed Caiaphas."

In the face of this plain historical testimony such guess-work mythical identifications as that of Annas with the "Sib-Zi-Anna of the Babylonians" and the "Anna Perenna of the Romans," who "corresponds to the star γ in Gemini," or to "the constellation Cassiopeia, or, again, that of Caiaphas with "the constellation Cepheus," are worthless. If the name of Caiaphas does not occur in the extant Talmudic list of the high priests, that fact need not prove anything but the faultiness of that record.[1] Perhaps he was better known as Joseph simply; or is it that we have here another instance of "Christian interpolation" in Josephus, the common and final argument when none other is forthcoming?

[1] Caiaphas seems to have earned unpopularity amongst the Jews, perhaps as an intruder into the high-priesthood.

CHAPTER XIII

Judas Iscariot

THE name Judas Iscariot presents a great puzzle to the modern critical scholar. Its traditional interpretation, "Judas, man of Kerioth" (אִשׁ קְרִיּוֹת, *ish Kerijjoth*), has of late years been much questioned, especially by critics of avowedly mythical views. The chief objections raised to this explanation of the name are: (1) It is doubtful whether the initial syllable "Is-" really represents the Heb., אִשׁ (*ish* = man), the 's,' perhaps, belonging rather to the latter word (*cf*. Syr., *skariota*), though this conclusion is at least uncertain. (2) Kerioth (Karioth) seems not to be a place, but to refer to a district, or rather a group of towns (*cf*. Joshua 15 : 25, but see Jer. 48 : 24 and 41, where a Kerioth in Moab is mentioned). (3) Had Judas come from any such place, or even district, we would expect his designation to be I. ἀπο Κεριωθ.

Now, there is, as Doctor Cheyne noted (*Enc. Bib.*, art. "Judas Iscariot," 1899), "a well-supported reading in John, ἀπο καρυωτου, which, according to Zahn and Nestle, confirms the view that it is derived from the *Heb.*, אִשׁ קְרִיּוֹת." Doctor Cheyne, however, thought it more probable that the name may have been incorrectly transmitted to us, and suggested (*loc. cit*.) that Judas's true appellation may have been Ἰεριχωτής, "man of Jericho." Subsequently, in the light of further inquiry, he seems to have decided (*Hibbert Journal*, July, 1911, p. 891, and July, 1913, pp. 919 and 920) that "Iscariot comes from

248

Ashharti, which is practically equivalent to Ashḥurite (northern Arabia), a family surname." [1]

It is perhaps too early as yet to pronounce definitely upon this last-mentioned suggestion. Professor Smith, however (*Ecce Deus*, pp. 319 and 320), admits that it is a "most ingenious hypothesis," though he doubts whether it will hold good; meanwhile, he asks for evidence in support of it, and points out that Cheyne elsewhere admits that Jesus was not betrayed, or even handed over, to the Jewish authorities by "Judas" or any one else; further, that he says: "the twelve apostles are to me as unhistorical as the seventy disciples," a somewhat effective retort in the circumstances of the case.

The various etymological difficulties which are encountered in the derivation of this word, however, cannot be used, even indirectly, in any proper sense of the term, as an argument against the actual existence of Judas as a man. Names, like numbers, are readily open to serious misunderstanding and corruption in ancient MSS., and it is quite possible, if not probable, that the name has been incorrectly transmitted to us.

At the same time it can be affirmed that there is no absolute and insuperable objection to "man from Kerioth (Karioth)," a view which is still held by some competent scholars (*e. g.*, Holtzmann, *Hand-commentar*, I, p. 97); and Keim (1867–72) even went so far as to assert (*Jesus of Nazara*, III, p. 276) that "undoubtedly Judas Iscariot means man of Kariot," and he identifies the place as "most probably the Kerijot (Josephus, Koreae, Korea) on the northern boundary of Judæa, half a league north of Shiloh, and now *Kuriut*." He further suggests that perhaps Judas's father had migrated to Galilee from Judæa.

---

[1] It may also be noted here that in the Fourth Gospel Judas is twice designated (6 : 71; 12 : 4) "son of Simon," to whom (6 : 71) in many old MSS. the appellation "Iscariot" is transferred.

But we have of recent years passed from the verbal difficulties and doubts engendered by etymology to those which find their origin in history and myth. In the year 1900 Mr. J. M. Robertson inaugurated a fresh attack upon the historical character of Judas Iscariot, and urged with great vigour that he was but a mere *dramatis persona* in a primitive "mystery play," or "ritual drama," such as was enacted in the Eleusinian and other mysteries. "In the *Gospel of Peter*," he writes (*Christianity and Mythology*, p. 385), "the Jews figure as equivalent factors with Herod and Pilate in the crucifixion, and in a ritual drama written for an audience so prepared unnamed Jews would figure as the god's enemies and captors. At a later period the anti-Jewish *animus* which led to the presentment of the whole twelve in the Gospel story as deserting their Lord at the supreme moment would easily develop into the idea of the actual treachery of one of the twelve, and to him would be allotted the part of the leading captor, who to start with had been simply Ioudaios, 'a Jew.' A bag to hold the reward would be a natural stage accessory. In this way would arise the further myth that the traitor who carried the bag was treasurer of the group and a miser and a thief at that; while out of the Ioudaios would grow the name Judas." [1]

It will be readily seen from the above quotation that Mr. Robertson's whole case practically rests upon the hypothetical existence in the first century A. D., and perhaps previously, of certain mystery-dramas amongst the early Christians, whether Gentile or Jewish. Now, we know that during the Middle Ages the Gospel narratives were dramatised chiefly for the better instruction of the "masses"; but for the existence of any similar presentation of the tenets of Christianity in the first cen-

---

[1] Elsewhere he connects Jesus with a pre-Christian Ephraimitic sun-god Joshua (Jesus).

tury there is absolutely no evidence whatever. Even
W. B. Smith's "Jesus-cults," [1] and the supposed worship
of a pre-Christian god named "Jesus," fall short of what
is presupposed in the above imaginative sketch. It is
true that many peoples of Asia Minor, as also the Greeks
and the Egyptians, had at that time, and long previously, their "mysteries," in which the cosmic processes
of birth and death, and rebirth and reproduction, in nature, and life after death, were mythicised and set forth
dramatically at Eleusis and elsewhere. But of any mysteries even remotely resembling those among the Jews of
that period, or among the early Christians, we are absolutely ignorant. The former people had long been sat-
urated with the spirit of a post-exilic Mosaic legalism
and held all kinds of idolatry, however artistically represented, in the greatest abhorrence, whilst, as regards the
Christians, we have abundant evidence to show that, both
as individuals and as a body, they shrank from all participation in such pagan mysteries and even from any intercourse with their initiates and devotees.

Neither can the theory that Judas is merely a dramatised and personified form of Ioudaios be sustained.
Judas is the Hellenistic form of Judah, which name had
been, for many years before the time of Christ, not only
a tribal or national designation, but also a common and
very popular personal, or circumcision, name amongst
the Jews. In short, Mr. Robertson's picture of the development of the ideal Jew into Judas, and the evolution of
the money-bag, together with the appellations of "miser"
and "thief" and "villain," are purely imaginative con-
structions of history, clever, no doubt, but not facts in
any true sense of that term.

Again, practically the same view of Judas is taken by
Professor Drews (*The Witnesses to the Historicity of Jesus,*

[1] This question is treated somewhat fully in the present writer's *Jesus
the Christ : Historical or Mythical ?* chap. 7.

1912, English translation, p. 83), who says: "Judas is not an historical personality, but, as Mr. Robertson believes, a representative of the Jewish people, hated by the Christians, who [*i. e.*, the Jews] were believed to have caused the death of the Saviour." It will be observed, however, from the above statement, that during the last dozen years no conclusive evidence in support of this *thesis* has been forthcoming; we must, therefore, infer that it still rests upon the same purely hypothetical basis as when Robertson first advocated it.

Professor W. B. Smith, on the other hand, had in the previous year put forth another defense of the mythical hypothesis (*Hibbert Journal*, April, 1911, pp. 529–544). After discussing at some length the variant forms (I)skariot(h), Iskariotes (Mark 14 : 43), Kariotes (א John 6 : 71, etc.), and Skariotes (D. Matt. 10 : 4, etc.), he dismisses the traditional view of the meaning of the name. "For every reason," he writes, "we must reject the accepted interpretation 'man of Kerioth.'" Wellhausen also, he says, rejects the interpretation and wisely inclines to regard it as a "name of reproach like Bandit (*Sicarius*)."

He further refers to in passing, but does not adopt, the suggestion of the Honorable Willis Brown (*The Open Court*, August, 1909) that the name is connected with the Hebrew root שׂכר (S K R) and means "hired" (*cf.* Matt. 28 : 9 with Zech. 11 : 12); but Mark (probably an older authority than Matthew) omits any mention of hire.

There is, however, he continues, another Hebrew root of very nearly the same letters, סכר (Ṣ K R), which appears once (Isaiah 14 : 4) in exactly the sense which is needed in this story. At the same time he admits that this latter stem, as a rule, means "shut up" in Hebrew, Aramaic, and Syriac, and *may* be rendered thus here (Cheyne); and that in another passage (Ezek. 30 : 12), the initial ס (ṣ) may be an error for מ (m), as many

scholars think. But neither of these facts, in his view,
materially affect the question, and the translation of
v' sikkarti (וְסִכַּרְתִּי, Isaiah 19 : 4) by the LXX version as
καὶ παραδώσω, "and I will deliver up," corresponds exactly to the words of Matt. 26 : 15.

Accordingly, he infers that since the Greek verb here
(παραδίδοναι) means strictly "to hand over," or "surrender," rather than "to betray" (in the bad sense),
"Iscariot means merely 'the deliverer up'—*not* 'the
traitor.' [1] In that case, Iscariot is precisely what Wellhausen felt it must be, a 'Schimpfname,' a *sobriquet*, an
opprobrious nickname, the most appropriate and even
unavoidable."

Finally, the conclusion which he draws is stated thus:
"I suspect that the oldest thought was one of *the surrender of the great idea of the Jesus of the Jesus-cult by
the Jews to the heathen*.[2] This, in fact, was the supreme,
the astounding fact of early Christian history and engaged intensely the minds of men." Further: "That
Judas Iscariot typifies the Jewish people in its rejection
of the Jesus-cult seems so obvious, it seems to meet us
so close to the threshold of the inner sense of the New
Testament, that it may move our wonder that any one
should overlook it."

This critical theory, put forward by Professor Smith,
is argued with so much scholarship and persuasive power
that even the critically minded reader is disposed on
first reading to adopt it. But on a closer inspection it
will not do. Let us examine it carefully and in detail.

Now, the foundation of the whole hypothesis is the hard
and fast distinction which Professor Smith attempts to
draw between the compound Greek verbs προδίδωμι and

[1] Mr. Slade Butler also draws ("The Greek Mysteries and the Gospels,"
The Nineteenth Century and After, March, 1905, pp. 494 and 495) a similar
distinction between the use of παραδίδωμι and προδίδωμι. See chap. 10,
pp. 199–200.

[2] Italics ours.

παραδίδωμι. The former, he says, means "to betray"; the latter always means merely "*to hand over*" (in a neutral sense). This is true as a broad general statement expressing a grammarian's rule, but it is not true absolutely and as regards the practise of writers in Greek. An examination of several authoritative Greek lexicons will reveal the fact that παραδίδωμι has also a well-established and subsidiary meaning of "to hand over," with a collateral notion of treachery; in other words, "to betray." Liddell and Scott, *e. g.*, give, as examples of this secondary meaning, Xen., *Cyr.*, V, 1, 28; V, 4, 51, etc. To these may be added Xen., *Hell.*, VII, 3, 8, and Ceb., *Tab.*, IX, in the latter of which the two verbs occur close to each other in practically a similar sense. A more searching examination would undoubtedly reveal many other instances in classical writers.

But let us now turn to the LXX version and the Greek Testament. In the former an example of the sinister use of παραδίδωμι occurs in I Chron. 12 : 17, where David refers to the possibility that certain men of Judah had joined his band with a view to handing him over (= betraying him) to his enemies. Turning next to the New Testament, we find many instances of its use, in the greater number of which the verb *can* be translated "hand over"; but it would be difficult to maintain that the sinister shade of meaning is wanting in all of them. Thus, in Matt. 24 : 10, "They shall hand over (= betray, παραδώσουσι) one another," there is a decided meaning of treachery implicit in the verb. Compare with this the parallels, where παραδώσει (Mark 13 : 12) and παραδωθησεσθε (Luke 21 : 16) have a similar sinister note. We have so far purposely omitted the passages referring specifically to the conduct of Judas,[1] because

---

[1] The chief are Matt. 10 : 4; 17 : 22; 20 : 18; 26 : 16, 21, 24, 46, and 48; Mark 3 : 19; 14 : 11, 18, 21, 41, 42, and 44; Luke 22 : 4, 6, 21, 22, and 48; John 12 : 4; 13 : 21; 18 : 2 and 5. In each of these cases the verb is παραδίδωμι.

in these, if they are taken out of the context, it is possible to translate the word used "hand over." But the other sense is equally—and even more—suitable, if we take the whole context of the passage into consideration. The fact is that in the New Testament the word προδίδωμι, with its allied noun προδότης ("a betrayer"), are but seldom used, the chief examples being Luke 6 : 16; Acts 7 : 52; and II Tim. 3 : 4. Luke, however, does once apply the stronger term to Judas (6 : 16), "Judas Iscariot, who became a *traitor*" (προδότης)—not simply "a deliverer up" (*cf.* ὃς καὶ παρέδωκεν αὐτόν [Mark] and ὁ καὶ παραδοὺς αὐτόν [Matthew]).

We may also allow largely for the unwillingness of the New Testament writers to use the stronger term to Judas. His conduct is never alluded to in a spirit of harshness, but rather with a feeling of sorrow and sympathy for the unhappy man who had fallen so far below his former estate. The only (apparent) exception to this occurs in John 6 : 70. Here the writer reports Jesus as saying: "Did I not choose you twelve, and one of you is a διάβολος?" This last word is rendered, in both A. V. and R. V., "devil." But it is a very doubtful translation, making every allowance for the wide-spread demonism of the age. Διάβολος is literally "slanderer," and hence "adversary" (Σατανᾶς, Σατᾶν), and in that *rôle* even Peter once figured (Mark 8 : 33 and Matt. 16 : 23). It is preferable, therefore, here to render the word "adversary," in the malevolent sense of spy or traitor, as Judas afterwards proved himself to be.

In short, Professor Smith has not proved his primary contention. He has no real warrant for the hard and fast distinction which he draws, nor for the implication that Judas is never called "*a traitor*" (προδότης) but always merely "a deliverer up." And, since such is the case, the whole foundation of his argument for the non-historicity of Judas falls to the ground. It was possibly the fact of this general distinction between παραδίδωμι and προδίδωμι which also led De Quincey to frame his famous apology for Judas. The latter, he said, merely handed over Jesus to the Jewish authorities, not with the idea of betraying him to his death, but in order to force his hand—to compel him to come forward as the Messiah. It was time (he thought) to put an end to the timidity and hesitation which was hindering that desired result.

This theory, however, has not received any assent from scholars. It is unnecessary to attempt to free παραδίδωμι from its not unfrequent sinister shade of meaning. And, in any case, before we could accept any mythical explanation of Judas Iscariot it would be necessary to show that Jesus himself was unhistorical. This has not yet been accomplished; indeed, it is still very far from having been done.

Finally, with regard to the theory that Iscariot is a mere *sobriquet*, or nickname, expressive of contempt, Doctor Cheyne asserts (*op. cit., supra*) that "a more thorough examination of the names and surnames of the early disciples should convince any one that they were never either opprobrious or nicknames."

We may, therefore, conclude this inquiry by saying that Professor Smith has neither established his views regarding Judas nor advanced any sound arguments which render such a view even probable.[1]

[? Jesus] Barabbas

M. Salomon Reinach reminds us (*Orpheus*, pp. 229 and 230, English translation, 1909) that "at the so-called

[1] In the *Jewish Quarterly Review* (September, 1913, pp. 197–207) Doctor E. Krauss, of Vienna, shows, as against Professor Smith and also Wellhausen, that there is no philological reason against the explanation of Iscariot as "man (or citizen) of Karioth." He also rejects the theory, which he calls a "methodological error," that Judas was meant to typify the Jewish people.

feast of the *Sacaea,* in Babylonia and Persia, there was a triumphant procession of a condemned criminal dressed as a king; at the end of the festival he was stripped of his fine raiment, scourged, hanged [? impaled], or crucified." Further: "We know from Philo that the populace of Alexandria gave the name Karabas to one of these improvised kings, who was overwhelmed with mock honours and afterwards ill treated.

"But Karabas," he continues, "has no meaning either in Aramaic or Greek. It must be emended to read Barabbas, which means, in Aramaic, 'son of the father.' In the Gospels we see Jesus called the King of the Jews, crowned with thorns, and given a reed for a sceptre (Matt. 27 : 26–31); he was, therefore, treated exactly like a Barabbas.

"But what are we then to believe of the incident of the seditious Barabbas and of the choice given to the populace between Jesus and Barabbas? In addition to all this, we learn that about the year 250 [A. D.] Origen read in a very ancient MS. of St. Matthew's Gospel that Barabbas was called 'Jesus Barabbas.' By comparing these various statements we are led to the conclusion that Jesus was put to death, not *instead* of Barabbas, but *in the character of a Barabbas*. The evangelists neither understood the ceremony they described nor the nature of the derisive honours bestowed on Jesus; they made a myth of what was palpably a rite. If there is an historic fact embedded in the narrative it is so overlaid with legend that it is impossible to disengage it."

The question of these mock-kings and their alleged connexion with the passion of Jesus will be dealt with directly. We will, meanwhile, proceed to an examination of this interesting extract from M. Reinach's work.

It is unfortunate that the distinguished author of *Orpheus* should have made no less than four distinct errors and misstatements in the space of a single paragraph; but such, nevertheless, is the case. Let us, however, in the first place, see what Philo himself says.

At the time of King Agrippa's entry into Alexandria, "there was," he says (*Works*, "Against Flaccus," VI, Yonge's translation, vol. IV, pp. 68 and 69), "a certain madman named Carabbas[1] (Καραβᾶς), afflicted, not with a wild, savage, and dangerous madness (for that comes on in fits, without being expected either by the patient or by the bystanders), but with an intermittent and more gentle kind. This man spent all his days and nights naked (γυμνός) in the roads, minding neither cold nor heat, the sport of idle children and wanton youths; and they [the mob of Alexandria], driving the poor wretch as far as the public gymnasium, and setting him up there on high, that he might be seen by everybody, flattened out a leaf of papyrus and put it on his head instead of a diadem, and clothed the rest of his body with a common door-mat instead of a cloak, and instead of a sceptre they put in his hand a small stick of the native papyrus, which they found lying by the wayside and gave to him; and when, like the actors in theatrical spectacles, he had received all the *insignia* of royal authority, and had been dressed and adorned like a king, the young men, bearing sticks on their shoulders, stood on each side of him instead of spear-bearers, in imitation of the body-guards, and then others came up, some as if to salute him, and others making as though they wished to plead their causes before him, and others pretending to consult with him about the affairs of the state.

"Then, from the multitude of those who were standing around, there arose a wonderful shout of men calling out 'Maris.' Now, this is the name by which it is said they call the kings among the Syrians; for they knew that Agrippa was by birth a Syrian and also that he was possessed of a great district of Syria of which he was the

[1] Mr. Yonge has also altered the spelling.

sovereign. When Flaccus[1] heard, or rather when he saw,
this he would have done right if he had apprehended the
maniac and put him in prison, that he might not give
to those who reviled him [Agrippa] an opportunity or
excuse for insulting their superiors, and if he had chas-
tised those who dressed him up, for having dared both
openly and disguisedly, both with words and actions, to
insult a king, and a friend of Cæsar, and one who had
been honoured by the Roman Senate with imperial authority; but he not only did not punish them, he did
not think fit even to check them, but gave complete
license and impunity to all those who designed ill, and
who were disposed to show their enmity and spite to the
king, pretending not to see what he did see and not to
hear what he did hear."

Now, it is perfectly clear from a comparison of this
statement of Philo with that of M. Reinach that (1) the
mob did not bestow the name Karabas upon this man.
His name was Karabas (whatever that may mean) beforehand. It cannot, therefore, have been the name of
a character in a drama or carnival, as the latter supposes. (2) This Karabas, we find, was not ill treated and
put to death afterwards by the mob, as the mock-kings
in the spring carnivals are said to have been, but allowed
to go his way unharmed after the jest was over. Again,
we find (3) in the oldest account (Mark's) it is stated
that when the multitude asked Pilate to release the
prisoner of their choice, in accordance with his custom,
he replied by offering Jesus. Only Matthew represents
him as giving the choice between Jesus and Barabbas.
The mob, however, at the instigation of the priests, riot-
ously demanded Barabbas instead, and Pilate ultimately
gave way to avoid a tumult. (4) Furthermore, Jesus is
nowhere, in the story, said to have been put to death
instead of Barabbas. Neither has it been shown that he

---

[1] Appointed viceroy of Alexandria by Tiberius Cæsar.

was executed *in the character of* a Barabbas. The priests dexterously twisted his avowed claim to be the Messianic king into a charge of treason against Cæsar. Indeed, as Monsignor Batiffol has very justly remarked (*The Credibility of the Gospel*, 1912, pp. 213 and 214): "Salomon Reinach has taken an incident for a custom, an improvised jest for an annual festival, and has never suspected, perhaps from not rereading his Philo, that the students of Alexandria, anti-Semitic and seditious, were that day mocking at the Jews as being friendly to Cæsar."

Again, with reference to the name Karabas, M. Reinach makes one or two rather hasty statements. Karabas, he urges, has no meaning either in Aramaic or Greek; *ergo* it must be emended to Barabbas. We do not follow this reasoning. To do so will, no doubt, be very convenient for the mythical theory, but logically it is a *non sequitur*.[1] On the other hand, Lagrange has pointed out (*Quelques Remarques*, pp. 34 and 48) that a Palmyrene inscription has the word קרבא (*Ḳeraba*, "war," "battle") as the name of a female, and remarks that it would be more fitting to a man.[2] Certainly it would be very suitable to Barabbas, who was doubtless one of the fanatical body known as Zealots (ζηλωταί), or Assassins (*Sicarii*), that waged such constant and relentless warfare with the Romans. The meaning of the name Barabbas M. Reinach also assumes to be "son of a father." This is the ordinary explanation; but it does not seem to be established beyond all doubt. It has been regarded (so Monsignor Batiffol) as signifying "son of a rabbi" (*Bar Rabbān*), and Jerome states (*Comm. in Matt.*, XXVI, 16) that it was translated "Filius magistri eorum" in the

---

[1] To quote Monsignor Batiffol again, this is "a twofold fault of criticism, an inexact reading, and an arbitrary correction" (Karabas = Barabas = Barabbas).

[2] *E. g.*, we might get *Bar Ḳeraba(s)*, "son of war."

Gospel According to the Hebrews. Mr. Nicholson, however, affirms that there is next to no authority in the New Testament for doubling the *r*, though this form is met with in the Harklean Syriac (fifth century) and it is the regular form found in the *Acta Pilati.*[1]

Let us now turn to Professor Drews. He, in the main, follows Reinach, and alters *Karabas* to *Barabbas*, of which he thinks it is probably a corruption. He then proceeds, in some detail, to link up the story of the Passion with the two pagan festivals, closely allied (he thinks) with one another, the Babylonian Sacaea[2] and the Persian feast of "the Beardless One," the former of which he specially identifies with the Roman *Saturnalia.* The Babylonian and Persian festivals, he believes, were blended and adopted by the Jews during the period of their exile, and appeared subsequently in their history as the feast of *Purim*, the origin of which is erroneously stated in the book of Esther. In this last-named festival Drews holds that, while Haman represents the old and dying year, Mordecai is the representative of the new life rising from the dead (*i. e.*, the new year of nature). He says (*The Christ Myth*, English translation, pp. 75 and 76): "While the former was put to death at the Purim feast, the latter, a criminal chosen by lot, was given his freedom on this occasion, clothed with the *insignia* of the dead man, and honoured as the representative of Mor-

---

[1] See, however, *Enc. Bib.*, art. "Barabbas," sec. 2. The word is also found spelt *Barrabas* (Tert., *Marc.*, IV, 42) and abbreviated as *Barba(s)* in the *Talmud.*

[2] Identified by Frazer with the *Zalmuk*, a Babylonian New Year's festival.

Doctor Cheyne also, but less positively, takes this view. He says (*Hibbert Journal*, April, 1911, pp. 661 and 662) that "the Barabbas story may be most simply explained from a Babylonian source"; but he admits that "on occasion of what ceremony this took place does not appear." He adds: "As for the name Barabbas, it is surely a corruption of Karabas (the form in the strange story of Philo), which probably indicates the Arabian origin of this supposed fierce bandit." But why not *Karabas* from *Barabbas ?* It is no more unlikely! But see Cheyne, *Fresh Voyages*, etc., p. 163.

decai rewarded by Ahasuerus [Xerxes] for his services."
And further: "In their account of the last events of the
life of the Messiah, Jesus, the custom at the Jewish
Purim feast, already referred to, passed through the
minds of the evangelists. They described Jesus as the
Haman, Barabbas as the Mordecai of the year, and in
so doing, on account of the symbol of the lamb of sacrifice, they *merged the Purim feast in the feast of Easter,
celebrated a little later*.[1] They, however, transferred the
festive entry into Jerusalem of the Beardless One, his
hostile measures against the shopkeepers and money-
changers, and his being crowned in mockery as 'King of
the Jews,'[2] from Mordecai-Barabbas to Haman-Jesus,
thus anticipating symbolically the occurrences which
should only have been completed on the resurrection of
the Marduk of the new year."

Let us now see what solid facts we can extract from
this tangle of theories and suppositions. Most critical
scholars seem to be agreed that the Purim festival is not
entirely of Jewish origin; further than this they are by
no means in accord. But while there may be in Purim
survivals of former festivals of some kind, whether of a
vegetative or a solar character, there is no evidence to
indicate that the Jews *took over the current interpretation
of these festivals* into the celebration of their new feast.
Neither can there be said to exist any evidence to show
that the various royal "privileges" of the old festivals
were ever attached to Purim. Drews's further sugges-

[1] Italics ours.

[2] Doctors Zimmern and Langdon think that a hymn from the temple service of the city of Isin commemorates certain Semitic kings who played the
part of Tammuz and died for the life of their cities. Doctors Radau and
Sayce, however, think that it refers to Istar's visit to Hades where she
wishes to rest with the deceased kings of Isin. Doctor Sayce says: "I can
find no evidence either in Babylonia or in any other part of the Semitic
world for Sir J. G. Frazer's theory of a king who takes the place of a god
and has to pay the penalty of his divine kingship by being put to death"
(*Expository Times*, August, 1914, p. 521).

tion that the ironical investiture of Jesus with the crown of thorns, and the inscription over the cross, together with the selection of Barabbas, had anything to do with Purim must also, as Professor Jacobs says (*Encyclopædia Britannica*, 11th ed., art. "Purim"), be rejected. "The connexion of the Passion with the Passover rather than Purim," he rightly adds, "would alone be sufficient to nullify the suggestion."

Purim was celebrated on the 14th and 15th of *Adar* (the twelfth month), whilst the Passover was held on the 14th of *Abib* or *Nisan* (the first month), that is to say, in any case, several weeks later.[1] It is most improbable, to say the least, that the Jews, when in Babylonia, should ever have learned to connect the death of a human representative of the vegetation (or solar) spirit with Purim, when a connexion with the Passover would be so much more obvious, especially if the latter festival had originally that kind of signification. And it is still more incredible that the evangelists should commit such a glaring historical error as the merging of the Purim feast in the feast of Easter, celebrated a little later.

Sir James Frazer remarks, *apropos* of Doctor Drews's derivation of the Crucifixion story (*The Golden Bough*, part 6, "The Scapegoat," pp. 414 *f.*), that Jesus may have really perished in the character of Haman; but at the same time he says that the crucifixion occurred at the Passover[2] on the 14th of Nisan, whereas the feast of Purim, at which the "hanging" of Haman would take place, fell exactly a month earlier, on the 14th of Adar. And he adds (note 2) that Professor C. F. Lehmann-Haupt writes to him as follows: "I regard it as out of the

---

[1] Some two months, if a second and intercalary Adar were inserted, as was sometimes necessary.

[2] The paschal lamb is considered by some scholars to be merely a later substitute for a human being (see Frazer's theory, *The Golden Bough*, part 3, "The Dying God," chap. 6, pp. 166–179). *Cf.* John 11 : 50 and 51.

question that Christian tradition shifted the date of the crucifixion by a month. You yourself regard it as improbable; but in my opinion it is impossible. . . . Without the background of the [Passover] festival all that we know of the crucifixion and of what led up to it is totally unintelligible."

Such a proceeding would certainly have made the whole story a confused anachronism, which would at once have been noted by the Jews as unhistorical and untrue. Moreover, we repeat that in most respects the story of Jesus is utterly unlike that of the feast of the *Sacaea*. The license accorded to the condemned criminal in the latter has absolutely no parallel in the case of Jesus,[1] whilst the setting free of Barabbas was clearly not part of a predetermined plan, as in the case of the released man in the Babylonian carnival, but a mere afterthought and desperate expedient of Pilate to evade an issue which he felt unequal to contest. We may, therefore, take it as certain that this story of Jesus and Barabbas has no connexion with either of these feasts, neither does it resemble the story of Karabas in origin or issue; there are, in short, no real parallels in it with any of these events.

We will now proceed to a consideration of the personal or circumcision name of Barabbas. It must have been noticed by every careful reader that in our modern texts, at least, all the evangelists concur in withholding it. Now, this must be due to one or other of three reasons: either (1) they did not know it, not an altogether improbable supposition, or (2) they saw no necessity for its insertion, or (3) they inserted it in the original texts from which it was afterwards removed. As the last-mentioned alternative is the one universally adopted by the mythicists, we will give it a careful and detailed consideration. Professor Drews, indeed, builds upon it one of his proofs

---

[1] See *The Golden Bough*, 1890, vol. I, pp. 226 and 227.

for the mythical character of Jesus. Let us, therefore, hear his statement of the case.

He says (*The Christ Myth*, pp. 75 and 76): "According to an old reading of Matt. 27 : 17 *et seq.*, which, however, has disappeared from our texts since Origen, Barabbas the criminal set against the Saviour is called Jesus Barabbas, that is, Jesus the son of the Father. May an indication of the true state of the facts not lie herein, and may the figure of Jesus Barabbas, the God of the year, corresponding to both halves of the year, that is, of the sun's course both upward and downward, not have separated into two distinct personalities on the occasion of the New Year's feast?" We will, however, turn to the text of the Gospel before adventuring any further on this road.

In Matt. 27 : 16 and 17 five cursive MSS. (together with the Syriac, Armenian, and Jerome's versions) have the reading Jesus Barabbas instead of Barabbas. In addition to this, twenty-one MSS. contain the following marginal note variously ascribed to Chrysostom (who, however, does not refer to the matter in his commentary) and Anastasius of Sinai (end of sixth century A. D.): "In some very ancient MSS. which I came across I found Barabbas himself also called Jesus, so that in these the question of Pilate ran thus, Whether of the twain will ye that I release unto you, Jesus Barabbas or Jesus who is called Christ? For, as it seems, Barabbas, which is interpreted 'teacher's son,' was the robber's sire name."

As a set-off against these facts, none of the existing great (and more ancient) uncial MSS. have this reading in these verses. Neither have the numerous other cursives; even the above-mentioned five do not read Jesus Barabbas *elsewhere*. But a passage in the Latin translation of Origen's *Comm. in Matt.* should also be noted. It runs in literal translation from the Latin (the Greek original being now lost): "In many MSS. it is not con-

tained that Barabbas was also called Jesus, and, perhaps, rightly, so that the name Jesus should not belong
to any sinner." This would seem, at first sight, to imply
that Jesus Barabbas was at that time the reading of
most of the MSS. [uncials] that Origen had met with.[1]
Indeed, the late Mr. Nicholson (*Gospel According to the
Hebrews*, p. 141) pronounced this the heaviest external
evidence in favour of this reading. But its evidence is
by no means conclusive; for (1) it is not certain that the
Latin is an exact equivalent of Origen's Greek, the latter
part of the quotation suggesting the addition of some
translator or copyist; and (2) "many" is a vague term
and probably does not mean here a small minority. In
all probability, too, Origen had not access to a very large
and varied number of MSS.[2]

Furthermore, there are several much simpler and at
least very probable explanations of the intrusion of
"Jesus" into the text of vss. 16 and 17 of Matt. 27.
The best of these is undoubtedly that of Tregelles, who
thinks that it is due to an instance of the error known as
dittography, to which all scribes were very liable. In his
view, the final $\iota\nu$ of $\nu\mu\iota\nu$ was accidentally written twice,
thus:

$$\alpha\pi o\lambda\upsilon\sigma\omega\upsilon\mu\iota\nu\iota\nu\beta\alpha\rho\alpha\beta\beta\alpha\nu. \ \kappa.\tau.\lambda.$$

Now, $\overline{\iota\nu}$ is the usual cursive abbreviation for $\iota\eta\sigma o\upsilon\nu$
("Jesus"), and Tregelles believed that the scribe, on
seeing his error, subsequently *deleted* the superfluous
syllable (underlined above) in the usual way with super-
posed dots, thus: $\ddot{\iota\nu}$. This $\ddot{\iota\nu}$ was then mistaken by a
subsequent scribe (or scribes) for $\overline{\iota\nu}$, the usual cursive

[1] Monsignor Batiffol here very aptly remarks (*op. cit.*, p. 212, note 1):
"If it be true that the full name of Barabbas was Jesus Barabbas, as
Origen thought, the name Barabbas would be all the more the name of
an individual."

[2] It must also be remarked that in the Latin version of Origen's Commentary on Matthew Jesus stands before Barabbas in vs. 17 but *not* in vs. 16.

abbreviation for ιησουν, and this the more readily because βαραββαν in the passage appears to be a patro-
nymic. In this way, then, in the course of a number of
years, a well-established textual reading would originate
and spread especially in a certain group of codices.

Alford explains the matter differently. He thought
that some ignorant scribe, unwilling to concede the
epithet (in the text), επισημον ("notable") to Barabbas,
wrote in the margin ιησουν, and that when the MS. was
recopied this gloss found its way into the text in vs. 16,
and, when once supposed to be a name of Barabbas, from
thence into vs. 17 also. Other arguments, both *pro* and
con, are: "Jesus" was a common and popular Jewish circumcision, or personal, name; it is, therefore, not improbable that Barabbas may have been also so named.
Then "Jesus," in that case, was probably struck out
either from motives of reverence or with the idea that
it was an accidental and superfluous insertion. The
balance of the two clauses also rather suggests that
originally both had personal names. Furthermore, from
vss. 17 to 22 Pilate says: "Jesus who is called Christ."
But a strong counter-argument to this will lie in the fact
that in vs. 20 we read: ἵνα αἰτήσωνται τὸν βαραββᾶν τὸν
δὲ Ἰησοῦν ἀπωλέσωσιν ("In order that they should ask
for Barabbas and destroy Jesus"), where both βαραββᾶν
and Ἰησοῦν, by the article τόν prefixed to each, appear
to indicate that previously he was simply designated
"Barabbas."

Again, another and stronger *contra* argument would lie
in the fact that no MSS. of the other synoptic Gospels
(and above all the older Mark) have any vestige of such
a reading as "Jesus Barabbas."[1] It is, of course, quite
possible that it had been thoroughly eliminated in these,
and only partly so in the MSS. of Matthew, from mis-

---

[1] Mark, however (15 : 7), speaks of the "so-called Barabbas" (ὁ λεγό-
μενος βαραββᾶς).

taken notions of reverence; but it is at least curious, if
this be so, that the sole traces left of the old reading
are to be found in later cursives and in Matthew (in this
place only) of all the Gospels.

On the whole, it would seem that at present a verdict
of "not proven" is alone possible. As, however, the
reader may wish to know the decisions of various eminent modern textual critics, we will conclude this chapter with a brief summary of the more important. Meyer
and Fritzsche defend the insertion of ιησουν here and
think that the copyists erased it from motives of reverence. Tischendorf inserted it in the earlier editions of
his text but omitted it in the later ones. Finally, he concluded that it arose out of Jerome's account of the parallel reading in the *Gospel According to the Hebrews*.

In more recent times Westcott and Hort and Scrive-
ner, and most modern textual editors, omit Jesus from
before Barabbas in these verses, though not, we think,
from motives of reverence. The chief other modern
scholars who favour its retention are Zahn with Burkitt
and Nicholson. At the same time it is rejected by such
an advanced critic as P. Schmiedel, who says (*Enc. Bib.*,
art. "Barabbas"): "In any case, it is remarkable that
in all the MSS. in question Barabbas should have the
name Jesus exclusively in Matthew, and there only in
two verses, while vss. 20 and 26 have simply τὸν βαραββᾶν, with τὸν δὲ Ἰησοῦν, as an antithesis." And he concludes: "Thus we may be tolerably certain that the
name 'Jesus,' as given to Barabbas, has arisen merely
from a mistake."

But even if we admit the reading Jesus Barabbas, the
highly hypothetical though picturesque theory of Professor Drews by no means follows. There can be no doubt
in the mind of any one who has not prejudged the case in
the interests of the mythical hypothesis that the historical explanation best fits the narrative, taken as a whole.

In any case, the Jesus Barabbas of a merely supposed Jewish custom cannot be used as evidence to prop up the theory of a mythical Jesus, which still awaits proof of unequivocal character.

CHAPTER XIV

The Mockery of Jesus

WE have already seen in the last chapter that Professor Drews endeavours to connect the account of the mockery of Jesus after his condemnation to death, as narrated in the first two synoptic Gospels, with the ridicule heaped upon the doomed criminal in the Babylonian feast of the Sacaea and the Persian feast of the Beardless One (*The Christ Myth*, pp. 75 and 76). In these annual solar festivals a malefactor, supposed to be a representative of the declining sun, was, after derision and ill treatment, put to death, while a fellow criminal was set free.

This theory, however, is, as we saw, completely bound up with and dependent upon another—viz., that *two* Jesuses figure here, an hypothesis which, after a careful examination, was found to be unproven. As a consequence, therefore, it will be unnecessary to detail its corollary here (see chap. 13, pp. 261–266).

But another connexion had previously been proposed and worked out in some detail by Mr. Slade Butler ("The Greek Mysteries and the Gospels," *Nineteenth Century and After*, March, 1905, pp. 495 *f.*). He would equate the mockery with the σκώμματα, "jests," and γεφυρισμός, "abuse," practised in the Eleusinian mysteries and supposed to have been reminiscent of the

270

witticisms by means of which the grief of the goddess-mother Dēmētēr for her lost daughter Persephonē was assuaged.[1] "These jestings and revilings," says Mr. Butler, "were not peculiar to the Eleusinian mysteries but seem to have been necessary elements in or adjuncts to all mystical celebrations; thus the τὰ ἐξ ἁμαξῶν, 'the words from wagons,' in the mysteries of Dionysus, and the στήνια in the Thesmophoria, were jibes and sneers of the lowest and grossest character. These extraordinary proceedings, so incongruous with religious worship, originated in very early times, and were probably intended for the purpose of attracting the notice of the populace and by this means inducing them to take some part in the observances and ceremonies which were being celebrated."

. Mr. Butler next refers to the account of the mockery given by Justin Martyr and in the fragment of the apocryphal *Gospel of Peter*. The former says: "The soldiers dragging him about (διασύροντες) made him sit down upon the judgment-seat, and said [to him]: 'Judge us!'" In the latter narrative we find: "But they took the Lord, and pushed him as they ran, and said: 'Let us drag away the son of God, having obtained power over him.' And they clothed him with purple and set him on the seat of judgment, saying: 'Judge righteously, O King of Israel!' And one of them brought a crown of thorns and put it on the head of the Lord. And others stood and spat in his eyes and others smote his cheeks; others pricked him with a reed, and some scourged him, saying: 'With this honour let us honour the son of God.'" "These variations," adds Mr. Butler, "seem to indicate some origin not strictly historical, and to a Greek who had seen the mystes upon the bridge

---

[1] Apollodorus (circ. 140 B. C.) relates that when the goddess came to the house of Metanira, in Attica, her servant Iambē σκώψασα τὴν θεὸν ἐποίησε μειδιᾶσαι, "joked the goddess and made her smile."

at Athens, or before the temple of Dēmētēr, that origin
would plainly appear to be the σκώμματα, or 'mocking
jests' of the mysteries.''

Further, in reference to the additional mockery which
took place whilst Jesus was upon the cross, he continues:
"And must we not attribute to the same source the rail-
ing and reviling in which all classes of the people are
made to indulge (Mark 15 : 29–32)? that is to say, the
people, who less than a fortnight ago had hailed him as a
prophet, now blasphemed him; the priests of God came
down from the temple to jeer at him in his agony; the
criminals heaped insults upon him; and the soldiers, not
content with the acanthine wreath and the crimson robe,
began to mock him again. Is this"—he asks finally—"a
true picture of human nature in the face of death and
undeserved suffering, or is it the γεφυρισμός and the στήνια
of the Greek mysteries?''

Before examining the case presented by Mr. Butler,
we may mention in passing a somewhat similar theory
which would identify this mockery with the coarse wit
and general license which was annually indulged in by
the Romans at the *Saturnalia*, an old feast of Saturn
celebrated just before the winter solstice. All class distinctions were laid aside, schools were closed, and no
punishment was inflicted. The utmost freedom of speech
was allowed to all, gambling with dice, at other times
illegal, was permitted, and gifts were generally exchanged, the commonest being wax tapers and clay
dolls. Varro thought that the last-named represented
original sacrifices of human beings to the infernal god.
There certainly existed a tradition that human sacrifices
were once offered to Saturn, and the Greeks and Romans
gave the name of *Kronos* and *Saturnus* to a particularly
cruel Phœnician Ba'al to whom children were sacrificed,
e. g., at Carthage. It is probable, however, that the
Saturnalia were in their origin a celebration of the new

birth of the sun at the winter solstice and not an equinoctial festival of any kind.

The connexion between the mockery of Jesus and the jests and "abuse" of the mysteries, suggested here by Mr. Butler, will be found to have no really valid evidence in its favour. The latter, like the Saturnalia, occurred at stated intervals and were merely, in later times, opportunities for a general exchange of gross wit and *badinage* during a period of universal license. If Mr. Butler's explanation, that they were intended to arouse the interest of the public in the celebration of the mysteries, be the true one, that fact alone would tend to differentiate them from the mockery of Jesus. The latter proceedings were initiated solely by the Roman soldiers of the garrison and, it would seem—from the absence of any other recorded instances—were not an example of any periodically observed festival. The whole affair seems to have been merely a kind of rough military horse-play, an exhibition of the coarse mental vulgarity so innate in the lower and middle-class Roman of the period. We can, indeed, only regard such occasional outbursts as compensatory relaxations of the iron discipline commonly exacted in the Roman armies, by means of which the man in the ranks was reconciled to the severity of the control in which he was normally kept by his superior officers.

Again, the slightly different versions given by Justin and in the *Gospel of Peter* are not at all suggestive of non-historicity. All accounts of an event by different reporters, however truthful, vary in details, and it is a legal maxim that these minor differences in evidence tend rather to establish the truth of a story than otherwise. The *motif* here, too, is quite different to those in the Mysteries and the Saturnalia. Jesus is mocked and jeered at by the soldiers as a helpless and unsuccessful claimant to royalty, not as a man who is in possession of some (perhaps silly) secret, as in the case of the mystæ.

In reply to the further suggestion that the subsequent jeers and scoffs of both Jews and Romans around the cross are not a true picture of human nature in the face of death and undeserved suffering, it is sufficient to say that Mr. Butler is judging purely from the point of view of the hypersensitive humanitarianism of the present day. Such feelings were entirely unknown to either the average Jew or Roman of that time, as the brutal severity of their criminal codes and daily practises abundantly show.[1] The fickleness of the mob is also proverbial and their reputation for it well deserved. Little value, in short, was set upon either human life or feelings in any case; none whatever when the person concerned was a criminal condemned by the laws of his country.

The Crown of Thorns, the Reed, and the Purple Robe

The historicity of the incident of the crown of thorns is denied by Mr. J. M. Robertson (*Christianity and Mythology*, p. 397) mainly on two grounds: (1) it finds its root motive in the *nimbus* of the sun-god, and (2) because St. Paul makes no reference to it in his letters. Mr. Slade Butler, on the other hand, appears to object to the story chiefly because, according to Mark (15 : 16; *cf.* Matt. 27 : 27), this crowning took place in the paved court of the Prætorium, where there would be some difficulty in obtaining the acanthus and perhaps also the reed for a sceptre; whereas, in Luke 23 : 11 it is said to have occurred in Herod's palace; and, again, in John, Pilate is said to have been present at the scene.

[1] We need not go outside of our own country and comparatively modern times for similar examples. Sir William Wallace, at his trial in London, wore a laurel crown in mockery of his claims, and Athol was murdered by having a red-hot crown forced upon his head! (*Magic and Religion*, A. Lang, 1901, p. 203.)

Mr. Robertson's connexion of the idea of the crown of thorns with the nimbus of the sun-god [1] is certainly far-fetched. The former was, as Doctor Estlin Carpenter observes, "a chaplet of pain" and was bestowed in derision. The nimbus, or wreath of solar rays, on the other hand, was regarded as the glorious diadem of the "Sol Invictus," whose representative was furnished with it as a mark of honour and worship.

Mr. Butler's objections, too, do not present any difficulty. The acanthus here is probably the *nābk*, a prickly shrub with pale green, ivy-shaped leaves which grows freely outside Jerusalem. As regards St. Paul's omission to mention the mockery, that apostle appears systematically to avoid such biographical details in his scattered references to Jesus. He does not profess to give us a *life* of Jesus, and consequently such incidents have no place in his letters to the various churches.

By the "reed" (κάλαμος), used as a sceptre, is probably meant some cane (*Ḳaneh* = Canna) found on the margins of streams in Palestine and no doubt as readily procurable as the nābk in the neighbourhood of Jerusalem. The Romans flogged criminals condemned to the cross with a whip; but lesser offenders were beaten with rods or canes (*cf.* II Cor. 11 : 35). Such rods would doubtless be kept in readiness in the Prætorium, and one of them would admirably serve the purpose of a mock sceptre.

The robe—"purple" in Mark's version, but "scarlet" according to Matthew—apparently has not yet been mythicised. Its historical explanation, however, is that it was probably the *sagum*, or military cloak, of some centurion; "possibly," as Doctor Swete suggests, "a

[1] Elsewhere in the same work he appears to connect this crown with the wisp pad worn by Hēraklēs in his eleventh labour and, again, with the crown of osiers and an iron ring worn by Prometheus (Athenæus, *Deipnosophistae*, XV, 13 and 16) "as a memorial of a sacrifice undergone for the good of mankind."

cast-off and faded rag, but with colour enough left in it to suggest the imperial purple." This robe was also bestowed in ridicule of the kingly pretensions of Jesus.[1]

Simon of Cyrene

In accordance with the usual custom in the case of condemned criminals, Jesus had to bear the horizontal beam (*patibulum*) of his cross to the place of execution. Falling by the way from pain and exhaustion, we are told (Mark 15 : 21) that the soldiers "compel one Simon a Cyrenian, who passed by, coming out of the country, the father of Alexander and Rufus, to bear his cross." Mr. Robertson mythicises this incident as follows (*Christianity and Mythology*, p. 410): Simon is the nearest Greek name form to Samson, who is a sun-god, one of whose exploits was the carrying away of the gate-posts of Gaza. Hēraklēs, too, a Greek form of the sun-god, carried two pillars to Gades. Consequently—it is inferred—Simon the Cyrenian must also be a sun-god, and it would seem, in that case, that we have here portrayed *two* solar heroes each representing the doomed orb!

The reasoning displayed above is remarkable but far from convincing. Moreover, the scenic effect of this portion of the mystery-drama is wholly marred by the introduction of a second solar hero. As regards the etymological side of the argument, the name *Simon* (שִׁימוֹן) has the signification "snub-nosed" and was a common Hebrew and Aramaic name; the latter appellation *Samson* (שִׁימְשׁוֹן, *Shimshon*) means "solar." Perhaps the slight similarity in spelling between the variant form Simeon

---

[1] In Luke 23 : 11 Jesus is said to have been arrayed in "gorgeous apparel" (ἐσθῆτα λαμπρόν) and mocked by Herod and his soldiers. It is uncertain whether the author here regards this as a previous mockery or was misinformed on the point. Doctor Verrall (*Jour. of Theol. Studies*, April, 1909) points out that λαμπρός means "bright" and is frequently used of snow-white cloths. The Hebrew royal colour was *white* (*cf.* Matt. 6 : 28 and 29). Hence white is probably the colour here meant by Luke.

and the more strictly Hebrew Shimshon suggested the proposed identification. But there is no real connexion, etymological or otherwise, between the words. And, while the story of Samson has been regarded as a solar myth[1] (though he is more probably a primitive and local hero around whom some solar-mythic exploits have gathered), there is nothing whatever mythical about Simon of Cyrene,[2] whose sons, Alexander and Rufus, appear to have been well known in Marcan circles of the early church about the middle of the first century. A mythologist constructing a mystery-drama of the passion of a god would never have thought of introducing so human and characteristic a touch as this.

Golgotha and the Phallic Cones

"The Gospel," says Professor Drews (*The Christ Myth*, p. 186), "was in origin nothing but a Judaised and spiritualised Adonis-cult."[3] This view he further works out in detail in a foot-note to the same page as follows: " 'I am A and Ω, the beginning and the end,' the revelation of John makes the Messiah say (1 : 8). Is there not at the same time in this a concealed reference to Adonis? The Alpha and the Omega, the first and last letters of the Greek alphabet, form together the name of Adonis, AŌ (Aoos), as the old Dorians called the god, whence Cilicia is also called Aoa. A son of Adonis and Aphro-

---

[1] Wellhausen, *e. g.* (*Composition des Hexateuchs*), rejects this view but regards him as unhistorical.

[2] The Basilidian Gnostics believed that he died on the cross in the place of Jesus.

[3] In *The Witnesses to the Historicity of Jesus*, however (pp. 215 and 216), he asserts that it originated in Gnosticism. "The Gnostic sects from which Christianity originated," he says, "knew at first only an astral Jesus, whose mythic history was composed of passages from the prophets, Isaiah, the Twenty-second Psalm, and Wisdom." These questions have been dealt with in detail in their proper place. Here we need only remark that Jesus is not mentioned at all in pre-Christian Gnosticism but was merely a post-Christian *graft* upon the older scheme of Gnosis.

dite (Maia) is said (*Schol. on Theoc.*, XV, 100) to have been called *Golgos*. His name is connected with the phallic cones (Greek, *golgoi*), as they were erected on heights in honour of the mother-divinities of western Asia, who were themselves, probably on this account, called *golgoi* and *golgōn anassai* (queens of the *golgoi*), and is *the same as the Hebraic plural Golgotha*[1] (Sepp, *Heidenthum*, I, 157 *ff.*).

"Finally, was the place of skulls an old Jebusite place of worship of Adonis under the name of Golgos, and was the cone of rock, on which a statue of Venus was erected in the time of Hadrian,[2] selected for the place of execution of the Christian Saviour because it was connected with the real sacrifice of a man in the *rôle* of Adonis (Tammuz)?" Let us, first of all, put this theory into other and simpler words.

He appears to think that on the summit of some hill (thereafter named Golgotha), just outside Jerusalem, there was held in ancient times a kind of cult-worship of the vegetation spirit Adonis, and that on this very spot a *phallic cone*, symbolical of the procreative powers of the god (*numen*), had been set up, and that subsequently a ritual drama consisting of the mock sacrifice and death of his image—originally, perhaps, a real man was slain—was enacted, and that this image, possibly by some juggling process, was, after lamentation by women and burial, produced "alive" to the people. Our gospels, in short, contain a literary *résumé* and presentment of this symbolic nature drama expressed in pseudo-historic terms.

[1] Italics ours.

[2] Renan says of this (*Life of Jesus*, p. 286): "The erection of the temple of Venus on Golgotha proves little. Eusebius (*Vit. Const.*, III, 26), Socrates (*H. F.*, I, 17), Sozomen (*H. E.*, II, 1), Jerome (*Ep.*, XLIX, *Ad Paul.*) say, indeed, that there was a sanctuary of Venus on the site which they *imagined* to be that of the holy tomb; but it is not certain that Hadrian erected it, or that he erected it in a place which was in his time called 'Golgotha,' or that he had intended to erect it at the place where Jesus suffered death."

We will now see what real grounds there are for taking this view of the matter.

In the pre-exilic days we read of various kinds of idolatries as being prevalent in Israel and Judah; but there is little mention of any native cult of Tammuz (Adonis).[1] Had any such worship existed in Judah the writing prophets and historians would certainly have mentioned it along with the various forms of idolatry which are chronicled by them. We read in our extant records, in connexion with the many Ba'al-cults, of certain *ashērīm* (wooden posts or trunks of trees) and *maṣṣēbōth* (upright stones) set up beside the altars of the Ba'alim (and even of Jahveh) upon the hilltops of Canaan.[2] Oort (*Worship of the Baalim*), Movers (*De Phonizier*), and Collins (*Proc. Soc. Bib. Archæol.*, XI, p. 291) think that these were phallic emblems sacred to Ba'al; but the latest modern scholarship rejects this view.[3] Perhaps the ashērāh was a conventionalised aniconic representation of the vegetation spirit, while the stone pillars may have served some pur-

---

[1] Isaiah 17 : 11 contains references to "Gardens of Adonis," which show that the northern kingdom was tainted at times with the Adonis-cult. Ezek. 8 : 14 and 18 also refers to a case of men worshipping the sun (? Mithra-cult), but neither they nor any other prophet or chronicler mention "phallic cones" nor indicate any systematic Adonis-cult in either kingdom.

[2] Any single sacred stone, as an object of reverence, or as a sepulchral *stēlē*, or boundary stone, was usually called *a maṣṣēbāh*. The ashērāh was probably a conventional representation of the "holy tree" (Assyr., *Asher*), or "tree of life."

[3] See *Enc. Bib.*, art. "Baal," and W. R. Smith (*Rel. of the Sem.*, p. 457, etc.). The latter says: "Indeed, the whole phallic theory seems to be wrecked upon the fact that the *maṣṣēbāh* represents male and female deities indifferently." The chief evidence in its favour is found in Herod., II, 106, and Lucian, *De Dea Syr.*, XVI (but see XXVIII). Movers also cites (I, 680) Arnobius, *Adv. Gent.*, V, 19, as supporting that view. A great deal of nonsense, however, has been written on phallicism, *e. g.*, *Sex Worship, the Phallic Origin of Religion*, by Clifford Howard (1908), which tries to base all religion ultimately on phallic worship; *Ancient Faiths Embodied in Ancient Names*, by Thomas Inman (1872), which insists upon the universality of phallicism. This is gross exaggeration. Phallicism is only prevalent among peoples of a decadent type, whether civilised or savage.

pose in solar-worship, *e. g.*, indicating the time of the solstices and equinoxes. This is all very problematical, however, and the real meaning and use of both is unknown.

Turning next to the New Testament, Professor Drews's exposition of the phrase "I am Alpha and Omega," etc., is certainly open to the gravest objection. A and Ω, though they are the first and last letters of the Greek alphabet, are not the first and last letters of Aoos (? = Aō) alleged by him to be a Greek [Doric] name for Adonis. Cilicia, the land of the dawn, or East, was sometimes called *Āōa* (*Ēōa*) by the Greeks; but this fact appears to have no connexion whatever with Adonis as a vegetation spirit, but to be derived from the goddess *Ēōs* (*Āōs*), who was said to be a daughter of the Titan Hyperīon and Theia. It is very improbable that the Dorian Greeks applied the same name, Aō(s) = Ēō(s), to the male spirit of vegetation (Adonis) and to the goddess of the dawn. Moreover, Adonis was not really the name of the god.[1] The Greeks had heard the Syrian women bewailing his fate and addressing him as Adōni ("my Lord"). This they hastily assumed to be his name (Ἄδωνις).

The alleged connexion between *Golgotha* and *Golgos*, too, and the precise signification of the latter word, is—at least as worked out by Professor Drews—highly problematical. In Theocritus, *Idylls*, XV, 100, Γολγώς (Γολγοί) is coupled with Ἰδάλιον and is obviously a *town* and not a "phallic cone," the two places being famous seats of the worship of the Cyprian Aphrodite. The scholiast on the passage may, perhaps, mean that the people of

---

[1] He was a variant of the Sumerian *dumu-zi*, "the faithful son" of the great earth-goddess, who also appears under many variant names and characters (*Tammuz and Ishtar*, Langdon, 1914). He also thinks (p. 8) that "the original name of the divine son appears to have been *ab-û*, 'the father of plants and vegetation.'" See Doctor J. C. Ball on "Tammur the Swine-God" (*Proc. Soc. Bib. Arch.*, vol. XVI, pp. 198–200) for a discussion on the origin and meaning of Tammuz.

the former place claimed descent from an eponymous ancestor Golgōs (possibly a son of the goddess), and in consequence may have called themselves Golgoi; but this, if it be so, does not support any argument for a connexion with Golgotha.

Golgotha, on the other hand, said by the evangelists to mean "the place of a skull" (not skulls; it does not appear to be plural), has been variously derived from the Hebrew, gŭ(u)lgolet (√galal, "to roll"), and gol goatha (Jer. 31 : 39) (?), "hill of dying"; but the actual origin and meaning of the word are still unknown.[1] Even the latter of these derivations, if it be correct, does not necessarily support Doctor Drews's theory, since it may indicate merely that the spot had been a place of execution for criminals before the time of Christ.[2]

There is, however, another possible clew to the origin and signification of Golgotha which may be worthy of consideration. All students of the Old Testament are familiar with the various local centres of ancient Canaanite worship known as "gilgals" (גִּלְגָּל, τα γαλγαλα, "a circle").[3] These consisted of rings of sacred stones similar to those called by modern archæologists "cromlechs." They were probably once very numerous in Palestine; but during and after the religious reformation of Josiah they were mostly destroyed. These stones were, no doubt, originally regarded as the *habitats* of the local nature spirits (*numina*, (?) early Elohim). It seems

---

[1] Cheyne derives *Gülgoleth* from *Galuth*, a form of Gilead (see *Hibbert Journal*, July, 1913, p. 921).

[2] A Jewish tradition as early as the second century identifies it with the place of execution mentioned in the *Talmud* (Mishnah, Sanh., vol. VI, 1). Luke translates it κρανιον, "skull."

[3] Ex. 24 : 4 refers to an interesting example of one of these circles which Moses himself is said to have erected alongside of (or around) an altar which he "builded" to Jahveh. The chief gilgal where Samuel and Saul sacrificed (I Sam. 10 : 8, etc.), where prophets dwelt (II Kings 4 : 38), and where also the worship of (? aniconic) idols was practised (Judges 3 : 19; Hosea 4 : 15; Amos 5 : 5) was in historic times a town or village.

possible, therefore, that a connexion of some kind between a gilgal and a golgotha may exist which will throw
some light upon the origin and meaning of the latter
name.[1]

The Cross and Its Astral Significance

Not only Professor Drews and Mr. J. M. Robertson,
but also almost all writers of the mythical school labour
hard—and for the most part quite unnecessarily—to
prove that the cross is a pre-Christian symbol.

Mr. Robertson, for instance, finds evidence of its use in
both ancient Mexico and Central America. In support
of the former he cites Mr. Bancroft as stating in his
Native Races of the Pacific States of North America (1875),
vol. II, p. 386, that "the sacred tree" was there made into
a cross (*Christianity and Mythology*, p. 408). A careful
examination of that work, however, has failed to verify
either the reference or the statement.

His other quotation is from Mr. Stephens's *Central
America* (1842), vol. II, p. 346, where the author states
that in an ancient ruin in Yucatan he found a stone tablet with an inscribed cross upon it, surmounted by a bird,

---

[1] The following points are to be noted in connexion with the two names.
We have the three Hebrew words: גלגל, *gilgal*, "a circle"; גלגלת, *gŭlgoleth*,
"skull," "head" (in the Rabb. כֶּסֶף הַגֻּלְגֹלֶת = "a poll-tax"), with its corresponding Aram., גולגלתא (see *Targ. Onk.* on Ex. 16 : 16).

In the Greek transliteration the second ל of the original word has generally been dropped to facilitate pronunciation.

In the MSS. of the LXX version we find a variety of renderings of גִלְגָל,
the chief of which are γαλγαλα, γαλγαλ, and even (BA. Deut. 11 : 30) γολγολ
[Eusebius writes γολγωλ] and (F) γολγο. Here we come very near to γολ-
γοθα for γολγολθα (*gŭlgo(l)tha*).

The stones in these *gilgals*, however, were certainly not phallic cones, but
were doubtless originally regarded as abodes of the various local *numina*,
who promoted the fertility and the prosperity of the neighbourhood, and
were anointed with oil, etc. (See Robertson Smith, *Religion of the Semites*,
"Sacred Pillars," pp. 203 and 456.) A conical stone (depicted on coins as
resting upon an altar) was the emblem of *Elagabal*, originally a god of fertility, who by the third century had become a solar deity, partially identified
with Apollo.

and with two human figures [males?], one on either side. This Mr. Robertson would like to consider a representation of a crucifixion scene. But there is no figure on the cross, and Mr. Stephens wisely contents himself with remarking that the cross was known and had a symbolical meaning among ancient nations long before it was established as the emblem of the Christian faith.

Again, Professor Drews also asserts that "in all private associations and secret cults of later antiquity the members have made use of a secret sign of recognition or union. . . . Among these signs was the cross, and it was usually described under the name of 'Tau,' after the letter of the old Phœnician alphabet." Such an application of the cross to mystic or religious ends, he thinks, reaches back "into grey antiquity" (*The Christ Myth*, p. 149).

This statement—the latter portion of it, at least—is true. Amongst the numerous examples of the fact we find its use in ancient Egypt, especially in the cult of Isis and her son Horus. It was also worn by both kings and priests in Assyria and Persia. Among the Greeks it was placed upon the images of such gods as Apollo, Artemis, and Dēmētēr, while in Rome it was used partly as an ornament by the vestal virgins.

Among the Norsemen, again, it appears in Runic inscriptions and, in the form of the *crux commissa*, as Thor's hammer. Imaginative persons have also detected its use in the mystic mark made in blood by the ancient Israelites on the door-posts of their houses before eating the Passover, and even in the attitude of Moses when he stood with outstretched arms upon the hilltop watching the battle between Israel and Amalek.

In like manner, M. Salomon Reinach writes (*Orpheus*, p. 77): "A chapel in the palace of Cnossus contained an equilateral cross in marble, a token of the religious character of this symbol more than fifteen centuries before

Christ. Another form of cross, known as the gamma-dion, or *svastika*[1] (a Sanskrit word), is frequent at Troy (on votive objects) and at Cyprus. It reappears on Greek pottery about the year 800, then on archaic coins, and becomes rare in the classic period, to show itself again in the Christian era in the catacombs of Rome and on the funeral *stelae* of Asia Minor. The *svastika* is also frequently employed in the Buddhist art of India and China." He further thinks that this mystic sign, "to which Indian literature attributed a magic power," may perhaps have been formed by "the conventionalisation of the image of a large bird like the stork"—an origin, it would seem, to say the least of it, improbable.

The attempt sometimes made to identify the Hebrew תָּו (Tau) with the Greek σταυρός, as meaning "cross," has been emphatically condemned by Doctor Cheyne, who remarks: "Unfortunately, the sense of 'cross' (σταυρός) for תָּו is justified neither by its etymology (see *Ges-Buhl*)[2] nor by usage. *Taw* means properly a tribal or religious sign, and is used in Ezek. 9 : 46[3] for a mark of religious import on the forehead and in Job 31 : 35 (if the text is right) for a signature. No Jews would have used תָּו for σταυρός, though the *crux commissa*, being in the shape of a T, the cross is often referred to by early

---

[1] *I. e.*, a hooked cross (卐), said by Beal (*The Romantic Legend of Sakhya Buddha*, p. 59, note 1) to be "the symbol of the sun's apparent movement from left to right." But see *Buddhism*, Monier Williams, pp. 522 and 523.

[2] The mythical school is generally very insistent on the fact that σταυρός merely meant *a stake* and not a cross!

[3] We read here of the marking of the forehead of the faithful Judahites with a *Tau*, the symbol of life (*cf.* the Egyptian ☥ '*nḫ*, "life," with ☥, the Phœnician form of the letter *Tau* found in the older variant of the language, *e. g.*, on the Moabite stone and in the Siloam inscription), to save them from slaughter. See also Rev. 7 : 3 *f.* ; 13 : 16 *f.* ; 20 : 4, and perhaps Gal. 6 : 17. "The magic virtue ascribed to the cross has, doubtless, a non-Christian origin" (Cheyne). With regard to the '*nḫ* (*ànkh*) Doctor Budge writes: "The object which is represented by this amulet is unknown, and of all the suggestions which have been made none is more unlikely than that which would give it a phallic origin" (*Egyptian Magic*, 1901, p. 58).

writers as the mystical Tau" (*Enc. Bib.*, art. "Cross," sec. 7).

But the real question, after all, is, what has this to do with the specific use of the cross in Christian symbolism? And the answer thereto would seem to be, little or nothing, except in so far as its appropriateness was suggested to the Christians of the first and later centuries by the fact of the crucifixion of Jesus. There is no proof whatever that it was used by them as a secret society symbol during the lifetime of Jesus or that the alleged pre-Christian cults of Jesus and Christ ever employed it. Its use, too, amongst the earlier Jews, legalists or mystics, is unproven and at least doubtful. As for its mystical and perhaps religious uses in various parts of the world, an ample justification is found in the fact that it is a symbol easily drawn and remembered, and commonly used everywhere, not only in religion, but as a brief memorandum of matters pertaining to daily life. Some writers have regarded it as an ancient symbol deriving its origin from astral worship and expressive of the sun crossing the equatorial line twice yearly, at the vernal and autumnal equinoxes. This is quite possible, as we know that these periods, as also the solstices, were important festivals in all forms of sun-worship. But, whether or not it was primarily suggested to the first Christians by ancient usage, it is quite certain that its adoption was sanctioned chiefly by their firm conviction that it was the instrument by which their Master suffered death, and that it was, in addition, a fitting symbol of the Christian life of tribulation in this present world.[1]

---

[1] Mr. J. M. Robertson refers—without offering proof—to "the phallic significance of the cross"—as he terms it.

We may presume that he is thinking of the Egyptian *ankh*, or handled cross, carried by certain gods and used as a symbol of enduring life. But this is quite different from the phallus, which was only used in the coarser ethnic nature-cults as a symbol of *reproductive energy*.

The Crucifixion

Professor Drews calls into serious question (*The Christ Myth*, pp. 146 *ff.*) not merely the fact of the crucifixion of Jesus, but even the correctness in detail of the description of that event as given by the several evangelists. We will deal first with the latter of these objections and state his *thesis* in his own words:

"In the whole of Christendom it passes as a settled matter that Jesus died upon the cross; but this has the shape, as it is usually represented among painters, of the so-called Latin cross, in which the horizontal crosspiece is shorter than the vertical beam. On what, then, does the opinion rest that the cross is the gibbet? The evangelists themselves give us no information on this point. The Jews described the instrument which they made use of in executions by the expression "wood" [ξύλον], or "tree" [δένδρον, arbor]. Under this description it often occurs in the Greek translation of the Old Testament, in which the gibbet is rendered by *xûlon*, the same expression being also found in the Gospels. Usually, however, the gibbet is described as *stauros* [σταυρός], *i. e.*, "stake," so much so that *stauros* and *xûlon* pass for synonyms. The Latin translation of both these words is *crux* ["cross"]. By this the Romans understood any apparatus for the execution of men generally, without thinking, however, as a rule, of anything else than a stake or gallows (*patibulum, stipes*), upon which, as Livy tells us[1] (I, 26), the delinquent was bound with chains or ropes and so delivered over to death.

"That the method of execution in Palestine differed in any way from this is not in any way shown. Among the Jews also the condemned used to be hanged upon a simple stake or beam and exposed to a lingering death from heat, hunger, and thirst, as well as from the natural

[1] *Cf.* Cic., *Pro Rab.*, 4, etc.

tension of his muscles. 'To fasten to the cross' (*stauroun, affigere cruci*), accordingly, *does not mean either in East or West to crucify in our sense,*[1] but at first simply 'to torture' or 'martyr[ise],' and later to hang upon a stake or gallows. . . ." As there are many errors contained in the above statement, we will now submit it to a close examination.

In the earlier Roman times capital punishment appears to have been inflicted by tying the offender to the *furca* (a heavy wooden instrument shaped liked the Greek letter Λ) or to the *patibulum* (supposed to have the form of the Greek Π). He was then either flogged to death or allowed to die of the combined effects of the flogging and exposure.[2] Contact with the East, however, introduced what Lipsius (*De Cruce*, I, 5–9) and Gretzer (*De Cruce Christi*, I, 1) call the *crux simplex, i. e.*, a single upright stake, similar to that used in Eastern countries for the purpose of impalement, to which the criminal was tied.

But during the second Punic war the Romans became acquainted with the *crux composita*, or true cross, to which the Carthaginians were accustomed to affix the condemned man by means of nails driven through the hands and feet, leaving him to die of pain and exhaustion. To both of these instruments of death the term σταυρός (*crux*) was applied.

In the case of Jews the earliest and authorised form of capital punishment was stoning (Lev. 20 : 20; Deut. 13 : 10); but in post-exilic times a limited use of the *crux simplex*, or stake, grew up. To this stake the offender was fastened and either strangled or left to perish from exposure. During the reign of Alexander Jannæus (reigned 104–79 B. C.) true crucifixion was, perhaps, used, and according to Josephus (*Ant.*, XIII, 14, 2) many Pharisees perished in this way.

---

[1] Italics ours. The *Das Kreuz Christi* of Zöckler should be consulted here.
[2] *Cf.* Livy, I, 26, *sub furca vinctus inter verbera et cruciatus.*

Turning next to the Greek terms employed in the LXX version and the New Testament, we find in the former work a general use of κρεμμάννμι (Heb., תָּלָה, tālāh), "to suspend" or "hang." There are several classical examples of this in the book of Esther (2 : 23; 5 : 14; 6 : 4; 7 : 10; 8 : 7; 9 : 13). In 7 : 9, however, we find σταυρηθήτω, and it would seem that the meaning here in each case is suspension from a post and not impalement.

Taking the New Testament, we find in the four *loci classici* (Mark 15 : 25; Matt. 28 : 35; Luke 23 : 33; John 19 : 19) the verb σταυρόω used, and the real question is in what sense it is to be taken. In *earlier* times it would probably have meant merely bound to a stake; but in the first century A. D. it undoubtedly means, for reasons given above, crucifixion in its *later* sense, *i. e.*, a literal nailing to the cross and nothing else.[1] And the mere fact that the old term κρεμμάννμι ("hang") is still employed is no argument to the contrary; for a man nailed to a cross and "lifted up" may just as fitly be said to *hang* there.[2]

But Professor Drews seems to dispute this conclusion. He continues (*op. cit.*, p. 147): "And in this connexion it appears that the piercing of hands and feet with nails, at least at the time at which the execution of Jesus is said to have occurred, was something quite unusual, *if it was ever employed at all*.[3] The expressions *prospassa-*

---

[1] *Cf.* also Acts 2 : 36; 4 : 10; I Cor. 1 : 13 and 23; 2 : 2 and 8; Gal. 3 : 1; Rev. 11 : 8.

[2] On p. 498 of his article, referred to above, Mr. Butler (in support of a theory that the tomb of John 19 : 41 was merely a "memorial place") urges that the verb σταυρόω never signified, in true classical Greek, "to crucify," but "to impalisade" or "fence off." This is true; but the Gospels were written neither in classical Greek nor in classical times, and words had frequently acquired a new meaning in the days of the Roman supremacy. Consequently, his rendering of both ἐσταυρώθη and μνημεῖον in the above passage of the Fourth Gospel is untenable, and there is no analogy, as he supposes, between the tomb and the mystical σηκός of Dēmētēr.

[3] Italics ours.

leuein and *proseloun*, moreover, usually signify only "to fasten," "to hang upon a nail," but not at all "to nail to" in the special sense required.

"There is not, then," he adds, "the least occasion for assuming that according to original Christian views an exception to this mode of proceeding was made at the execution of Jesus. The only place in the Gospels where there is any mention of the "marks of the nails" (viz., John 20 : 25) belongs, as does the whole Gospel, to a relatively later time, and appears, as does much in John, as a mere strengthening and exaggeration of the original story. For example, Luke 24 : 39, upon which John is based, does not speak at all of nail-marks, but merely of the marks of the wounds which the condemned must naturally have received as a consequence of being fastened to the stake. Accordingly, the idea that Christ was 'nailed' to the cross was in the earliest Christianity by no means the ruling one."

If Doctor Drews means in the above passage that nails were not usually employed by the Romans as early as, and even earlier than, A. D. 30 to affix criminals to the cross, he certainly cannot have consulted the Latin writers. Thus, Plautus, who died as early as B. C. 184, refers (*Most.*, II, 1, 13) to a man condemned to the cross who seeks a substitute, humorously promising a reward on the condition that "they [the nails] are driven twice into the feet and twice into the arms,"[1] an expression not in any way suggestive of roping or chaining, but plainly meaning that each foot and hand should be severally affixed by means of a nail. This view is also supported by Jewish evidence (*Hor. Heb.*, p. 57, Lightfoot),

---

[1] *Offigantur bis pedes, bis brachia.* A nail from the cross was also used in certain magical ceremonies (Apuleius, *Metamorphoses*, book III, Bohn's translation, p. 59; Pliny, *H. N.*, XXVIII, 11). In Col. 2 : 14 we have the phrase προσηλώσας αὐτὸ τῷ σταυρῷ, "nailing it to his (lit., the) cross," referring to an ancient method of cancelling bonds by driving a nail through them.

and Josephus tells us (*Life*, 75) that out of three friends whom he had once rescued from the cross only one survived, though they were most carefully tended by a physician. This again points strongly to death from actual wounds rather than from exposure or any preliminary flogging which they may have received.

Further, although the evidence of John 20 : 25, with its reference to the nail-holes in the feet and hands, is late and, therefore, perhaps inconclusive, the statement in Luke 24 : 39 undoubtedly means that the wounds were caused by the piercing of the limbs and were not mere abrasions caused by ropes or chains, which would cause much less severe injuries.

But Doctor Drews's object in bringing into the discussion the Greek word προσπασσαλεύειν is not clear, since the word does not occur in the New Testament; and προσελοῦν, which is seldom used, could not here mean, as he urges, to "hang upon a nail," because the *cruciarii* were never hung upon nails, but either tied to the cross itself or, in the case of slaves and persons convicted of treason (*perduellio*), literally nailed to the wood, as is abundantly testified by ancient writers.[1]

M. Salomon Reinach, to whom we will turn next, appears to waver in his view of the origin of the idea of the crucifixion of Jesus. At one time (*Orpheus*, p. 32) he quotes, "They pierced my hands and my feet" (Psalm 22 : 17), and says: "We must admit that this verse in the Psalms may be the origin of the tradition that Jesus was crucified." But at another time he appears to re-

---

[1] The whole scene of a Roman crucifixion is, indeed, most carefully and accurately described by the evangelists. We have the preliminary *flogging* of the *cruciarius*, who generally carried his αἰτία ("charge") suspended round his neck to the place of execution. Soldiers were set to watch him and a stupefying draught was offered (*cf. Bab. Talm.*, Sanh. Tract., *f*. 43, 1) to lull the pain caused by the nails. The breaking of the legs (*crurifragium*) was also distinctively a Roman practise, especially in the case of slaves (Seneca, *De Ira*, III, 32; Suet., *Aug.*, 67; Tert., *Ap.* 21).

gard the story as an "orphic projection made through
the lens of a passage in Plato's *Republic* about the impalement of the perfectly just man who should happen
to stray into, or turn up in, a community of unjust men"
(J. Rendel Harris).

In a similar manner Professor W. B. Smith (*Ecce Deus*,
p. 142) lays a great stress upon this ill treatment of the
"just man." He says: "The notion of the impalement
of the righteous man found its classical and immortal
expression in the second book of *The Republic* in a context of matchless moral sublimity.   Glaucon, putting
Socrates on his mettle, draws the liveliest possible picture of the sufferings of the just who is thought unjust:
'He will be scourged, will be racked, will be bound, will
have his eyes burned out, (and) at last, having suffered
every ill, he will be crucified (361 D).'

"The last verb (ἀνασχινδυλεύω) is commonly rendered
by 'impale' and is rare; but it is the exact equivalent of
ἀνασκολοπίζω, which, again, is exactly the same as ἀνασταυρόω (as in Philo, I, 237 and 687), which appears in
Heb. 6 : 6 (where it has been falsely rendered 'crucify
again') and is the regular Greek word for 'crucify,'
shortened also into σταυρόω, the New Testament term.
The ἀνα means 'up' and not 'again.' "

Dealing first of all with the former suggestion of M.
Reinach, we would reply that the passage in the Psalms
is undoubtedly corrupt and the reading here rendered
"pierced" consequently uncertain.   But, in any case,
כָּאֲרִי (ka-ari) does not mean "pierced" as in a crucifixion.
It refers here rather to the biting of wild animals of some
kind (see Appendix C).

As to the passage from *The Republic* of Plato, the late
Professor Jowett (*The Dialogues of Plato*, vol. III, p. 41)
translates the verb ἀνασχινδυλεύω, "impaled," and not
"crucified."   Turning to the lexicon of Liddell and Scott,
we find that the verbs ἀνασκολοπίζω and ἀνασταυρόω be-

came practically synonymous in *later* Greek; but they certainly were not so in Plato's time. Therefore, we have no authority for treating ἀνασχινδυλεύω as the equivalent of ἀνασταυρόω and translating the former verb (as used by Plato) "crucified."

As a matter of fact, true crucifixion was unknown to the Greeks of Plato's day and was not at that time practised in western Asia. The force of ἀνα in composition, we may add, according to Liddell and Scott, is frequently that of *repetition*—as well as "up." Hence the rendering "crucify afresh" or "again," in Heb. 6 : 6, cannot be termed "false." As it makes the better sense, too, with the context, it is probably the correct one.

Orpheus, in the myth, is merely one of the many representatives of the god torn to pieces every year by the envious powers of nature, a ceremony which was enacted by the *Bacchae* in earlier times with a man, but afterwards with a bull who represented the god. The god of all these nature-myths is ever a manifestation of the reproductive power of nature, and how it could in any way be syncretised with the ethical "just man" of Plato, or the ethical and spiritual figure of Jesus, is not explained and, moreover, is impossible to understand.

Finally, Mr. J. M. Robertson endeavours (*Pagan Christs*, 1911, pp. 108 *f.*) to explain the idea of the story from a custom which formerly prevailed among the Khonds of India. The victim was garlanded with flowers and worshipped. He was then inserted into the trunk of a tree in such a manner that he and the tree formed a cross. His arms and legs were then broken and he was made insensible with opium, or datura, and finally put to death.[1]

There is some very vague resemblance here to the story of the crucifixion; but it is not explained how this came

---

[1] See Frazer's *Golden Bough*, "The Dying God," 3d ed., p. 139. On Odin as the "hanged god," see *Adonis, Attis, Osiris*, 3d ed., pp. 288 *ff.*

to be adopted by the earliest Christians, who were bitterly hostile to all heathen ideas and practises. It would seem that any such theory of origins must be the last resource of some desperate anthropologist.[1]

The Two Thieves

In his article, "Die Kreuzigung Jesu," in the *Zeitschrift für die neutestamentliche Wissenschaft*, II (1901), pp. 339-341, Doctor W. R. Paton has hazarded the opinion that the crucifixion of Jesus between the two robbers had a ritual significance "as an expiatory sacrifice to a triple god." It seems that a Persian martyr, St. Hiztibouzit, is said to have been crucified between two malefactors on a hilltop opposite the sun (see *The Apology and Acts of Apollonius and Other Monuments of Early Christianity*, 1894, by F. C. Conybeare, pp. 257 *ff.*). The narrator, however, does not attach any religious significance to the triple execution, and we may readily agree with Sir James Frazer that "the grounds for the conjecture are somewhat slender" ("The Scapegoat," p. 413, note 2).

Professor Drews, again (*The Christ Myth*, pp. 82 and 83), finds another explanation of the two criminals who were crucified with Jesus.

"The story," he writes, "of the two fellow prisoners of Joseph, the baker and the cup-bearer of Pharaoh, one of whom, as Joseph foretold, was hanged, while the other was received into favour by the king, was transformed by them [*i. e.*, the evangelists] into the story of the two robbers who were executed at the same time as Jesus, one of whom mocked the Saviour, while the other be-

---

[1] Fiebig says of the "darkness" which is said to have occurred at the time of the crucifixion that it is "certainly mythical." But σκότος (Matt. 27 : 45) also means "gloom," and Humboldt relates in his *Cosmos* that "in the year 358, before the earthquake of Numidia, the darkness was very intense for two or three hours." According to vs. 51 there was an earthquake on this occasion also.

sought him to remember him when he entered into his heavenly kingdom."

The two stories, it must be pointed out, are utterly unlike, and it is inconceivable that either of them should suggest the other. But, setting this fact aside, Professor Drews's dogmatic statement raises a number of recondite and difficult questions. In the first place, was Joseph a divine being, the representative, like the various solar heroes, and (Doctor Drews would add) Jesus, of the sun?[1] It is impossible to dogmatise here, but any theory based upon such assumptions is precarious in the highest degree.

Again, Mr. Robertson (*Pagan Christs*, 1911, pp. 108 *f.*) explains the origin of this incident as follows: In former ages a king's son was sacrificed; later, when criminals were substituted, one of them was represented as a king by having two others in their real character as evil-doers set up by his side. But where is the proof of this? None is offered, and as the statement stands in the book it is mere fanciful assertion. Without specific examples of such a custom these "explanations" explain nothing. On the other hand, the story of the evangelists is quite as consistent with actual Roman practise as it is with unregenerate human nature at all times and in all places.

The Seamless Tunic

The idea of providing a pseudo-historical Jesus with a seamless coat was, if we may credit Mr. J. M. Robertson (*Christianity and Mythology*, pp. 414 and 415), derived from the story of the *chiton* woven for Apollo or the shawl woven for Here at Elis. These garments have, he says (ostensibly quoting Plutarch), a mystical significance,

---

[1] The name *Joseph* may be taken as Jo-SePh (Ja-SePh), "Jahveh add to me another son," Gen. 30 : 24). In vs. 23 it is explained as "God has taken away (a-SaPh) my reproach. See Sayce, Hibb. Lects. (1887), pp. 50–52; also *The Higher Criticism and the Monuments*, pp. 337–339.

since they represent "the robe of the solar Osiris, which is one and indivisible, that robe being the universal light."

The reference here is evidently to the *De Iside et Osiride*, 78, where Plutarch writes: "That [vestment] of Osiris has no shadow nor variation, but is one, simple, the image of light." The quotation, it will be observed, is inaccurate and the inference drawn inexact.

We need not, however, depart from plain, sober history here. Jewish tunics, as a rule, consisted of two separate parts which were held together by clasps; but Josephus tells us (*Ant.*, III, 7, 4) that a single seamless tunic was habitually worn by the high priests. It is clear, therefore, that single tunics were in some cases woven all in one without any seam.[1]

The writer of the Fourth Gospel, it is true, lays some stress upon the seamlessness of the garment. He seems to find in it a mystical meaning, perhaps that of indicating that Jesus acted as his own high priest in the sacrifice of himself. But this, in any case, does not affect the question at issue.

The Last Words of Jesus

Here we must again quote Mr. Slade Butler (*Art. cit.*, p. 496): "After the illumination or consecration of the mystes was completed," he says, "a sacred formula was uttered to show that the ceremony was over. What that formula was does not seem to be known, though it has been said by some to have been the words κόγξ ὄμπαξ

---

[1] Seydel (*Evangelium*, etc., pp. 282 and 299; *cf. Buddha Legende*, p. 123, refers the story of the division of the clothes of Jesus (John 19 : 23 *f*.) to one told in the *Mahāparinibbāna Sutta*, VI, 51 *ff*.) of a quarrel over the relics of the defunct Buddha, which is finally settled by a Brahman. It is unnecessary here to say more than that the two stories are totally unlike and that the clothes of a condemned man have ever been the perquisite of the executioner.

There arises also the question of priority of the narratives.

or κογξ ὁμοίως πὰξ,[1] the first word denoting the sound made by the voting pebble as it fell into the urn, and so 'the vote is cast,' the other words meaning 'likewise enough,' the formula, therefore, signifying 'all is over.' Now, the last saying, or utterance, on the cross is, in the Fourth Gospel (John 19 : 30), represented by the word τετέλεσται, which in one sense means 'it is finished'; but τελέω, 'to perform,' has in the passive a further meaning, viz., 'to be initiated' or 'consecrated' in the mysteries—and more particularly in the last or highest grade of the Eleusinian mysteries—just as τελετή means 'the end' as well as 'the rite of initiation.' To a Greek —and especially one who had passed through the mysteries—the word τετέλεσται would have the double meaning 'all is over' and 'the consecration is complete.'

"It is to be noticed that the words of the last utterance on the cross are omitted in Mark (15 : 37) and in Matthew (28 : 50), as though they were not known or were too sacred to be reproduced in writing."

Mr. Butler's attempt to equate the final τετέλεσται ("It is finished") of the Fourth Gospel with the mysterious *formula* used as the final benediction of the hierophant of Eleusis is a very precarious essay in criticism. The *konx om pax* of the latter has absolutely no meaning in its Greek form, and is generally believed to have been derived from the East, where perhaps it had a mystical sense attached to it. Wilford gives the words a Sanscrit origin and explains them as follows: *konx* from *kansha* = the object of strongest desire; *om* from *oum* (*aum*) = the soul of Brahma; *pax* from *pasha* = turn, change, cycle. This apparently meaningless jumble of words, he concludes, signifies: "May thy desires be fulfilled; return to the universal soul!"

But this interpretation is doubtful in the extreme, and it is practically certain that the real meaning of the Eleu-

---

[1] *Konx ompax* or *konx homoiōs pax.*

sinian *formula* is lost. One thing, however, may safely be taken as fact; whatever it may mean it does not signify "It is finished" ($\tau\epsilon\tau\epsilon\lambda\epsilon\sigma\tau\alpha\iota$).

The last "word from the cross" is the final exclamation of a weary man who has just fought and finished a long and bitter fight and feels that at last he has come off conqueror. It is in no sense a benediction either; the final benediction of Jesus upon his murderers and their wretched tools was fitly expressed in that other "word" recorded in Luke 23 : 34: "Father, forgive them; for they know not what they do." [1]

The Lance Wound and the Breaking of the Legs

"The transfixing of the victim with the holy lance," writes Professor Drews (*The Christ Myth*, p. 97, note 3), "as we meet it in John 19 : 34, appears to be a very old sacrificial custom which is found among the most different races. For example, [it is met with] both among the Scythian tribes in Albania, in the worship of Astarte (Strabo), and in Salamis, in the island of Cyprus, in that of Moloch (Eusebius, *Præp. Evang.*, IV, 16). 'The lance thrust,' says Ghillany, with reference to the death of Jesus, was not given with the object of testing whether the sufferer was still alive, but was in order to correspond

---

[1] On p. 497 of the same article we also find: "There are also other details in the Gospel narrative in which a Greek might see allusions to the mysteries just as a Jew might recognise in the same words a reference to his prophets; thus in the words, 'but he held his peace and answered nothing' (Mark 14 : 61; Matt. 26 : 63) 'and he gave him no answer, not even to one word' (Matt. 27 : 14), a Greek would recognise the closed, sealed lips of the mystes, while a Jew might think that he saw in them a reference to the writings." The very vague analogies to the mysteries pointed out here really prove nothing; and the mere fact that to the Jew they had quite a different meaning shows this very clearly. Jesus held his peace when a false charge was preferred against him and when he knew that his death had been predetermined by the Jewish authorities. No purpose was served by making any answer. The mystes, on the other hand, was *mute* because a secret had been confided to him in initiation which he must not divulge.

The two cases are poles apart and all comparison between them is fanciful and unreal.

with the old method of sacrificing. The legs were not broken because the victim could not be mutilated. In the evening the corpse had to be taken down, just as Joshua only allowed the kings sacrificed to the sun to remain until the evening on the cross.' "

The learned German writer above cited is apparently under a misapprehension as to the meaning of the author of the Fourth Gospel. The latter does not say, or imply, that the soldier thought Jesus might be alive, for in vs. 32 it is distinctly stated that they saw that he was dead already. But the "holy lance," as used in early times in the sacrifices of nomadic races, was certainly employed for the slaying of the victim whatever the later import of the act may have been. Had the Gospel writer intended to illustrate any such later custom here he would probably have inserted the incident earlier in the chapter or else omitted vs. 32. As matters stand, his object in mentioning the incident is clear to any one whose mind is not obsessed by some other and *a priori* theory. He states that he was an eye-witness of the scene. He saw the soldiers set about the *crurifragium*, and noticed the exemption accorded to Jesus, for the reason which he gives. But a sudden and irrational impulse *to stab* the body with his spear seized one of the soldiers. Both these events struck the writer as being unconscious and involuntary fulfilments of two scriptures[1]—not as ancient sacrificial customs. He was struck also with what appeared to him as blood and water flowing from the spear wound.[2] This, on reflection, appeared to have a spiritual significance (*cf.* I John 5 : 6), as symbolical of

[1] (1) Ex. 12 : 46. This rule is commonly laid down in the ritual of all religious sacrifices. The victims must be *perfect*. (2) Psalm 22 : 16 and 17. This quotation is not apposite. The Hebrew word used means "to gnaw," or "bite," like a dog or lion. See Appendix C.

[2] A book has been written (*A Treatise on the Physical Cause of the Death of Christ*, by W. Stroud, M.D., 1st ed., 1847) explaining the death of Jesus as due to rupture of the heart, the blood in which, the author thinks, may

the work of redemption (by blood, Lev. 4 : 6) and regeneration (by water, Num. 8 : 7). There is not a shadow of reason to suppose here that the writer is, consciously or unconsciously, perpetrating on his readers a mere pseudo-historisation of an ancient custom, though it may happen that this incident has some affinity with the Jewish sacrificial rules, of which he was evidently thinking at the time of writing. Moreover, had the evangelist regarded the scene he describes as merely a sacrificial drama he would have probably included the thieves also, whose legs in that case, like those of the chief victim, would have remained unbroken.

Doctor Ghillany's assumption that the five kings hanged on stakes (Joshua 10 : 26) were a sacrifice to the sun-god is a mere begging of the question. *Makkedah* ("place of shepherds," *Ges. Lex.*) has no apparent connexion with any solar cult. The war in which they are said to have lost their lives seems to have been one of those semi-barbarous contests, on a small scale, in which a subsequent massacre of important prisoners is a common feature. And the reason for their burial at sundown (as also for the taking down of Jesus and the two malefactors)—"that the land be not defiled"—was part of an old criminal code afterwards embodied in Deut. 21 : 23.

The Burial in the New Tomb

This event, as recorded in the Gospel narratives, is traced to Greek mystical sources by Mr. Slade Butler. He says in the article already quoted: "In the mysteries we are told that 'some kind of memento of the ceremony

---

have escaped into the pericardium, where it separated into a mass of clotted red corpuscles and serum, which was set free by the spear piercing the sac. This theory has been adversely criticised by Doctor Creighton (*Enc. Bib.*, art. "Cross," sec. 6). The most probable explanation is that death ensued from syncope; but the witness observing the blood mingled with the death sweat (often copious before a painful death) incorrectly assumed that *both* issued from the spear wound.

(the παράδοσις τῶν ἱερῶν) was given by the priests to the
votaries, which a believer used to keep in a linen cloth.'
In Mark (15 : 46) we read of Joseph of Arimathæa, 'who
also himself was Jesus' disciple,' that 'he bought a linen
cloth and, taking him down, wound him in the linen cloth,
and laid him in a memorial place (μνημείῳ) which had
been hewn out of a rock.' Why is this word μνημεῖον
used to signify 'a tomb' instead of the usual and ordinary word τάφος? Μνημεῖον (μιμνήσκομαι, 'to bear in
mind'; μάω, 'to desire') means 'remembrance,' then 'a
memorial,' and so 'a monument' raised in memory of
the dead [a cenotaph], but not the tomb in which the
dead body was laid; yet in the Gospels the word seems
to be intended to signify 'tomb' as well as 'remembrance'—a 'tomb of memory.' The reason for this use
of the word μνημεῖον in place of and with the meaning
of τάφος cannot be explained by the suggestion that the
word τάφος had fallen into disuse, for in Matthew's account, which was written some time after Mark's Gospel
was compiled, we find that the word τάφος appears exactly as many times—four times—as μνημεῖον is used, as
though the writer had some apprehension that the word
μνημεῖον, which he had taken and adapted from Mark (or
the source of information used by Mark), might be misunderstood."

In this *thesis* presented by Mr. Butler the whole stress
of his argument is laid upon the use of the word μνημεῖον
instead of τάφος. Now, undoubtedly, the earliest and
general Greek prose word for grave, after the time of
Homer, was τάφος. But in later and post-classical times,
as the stones which were set over or before graves became more and more elaborate, and served more and
more the purposes of memorials, especially in the case
of notable men, the term τάφος, though still used, largely
gave place to the word μνημεῖον (μνῆμα), by which the
burying-place of the dead man was kept in mind by suc-

ceeding generations. And in the New Testament period this later word was often used in Greece and elsewhere almost exclusively for τάφος in such cases.

But let us turn to the LXX version and see how far that work supports this view. In Gen. 23 we readily find four examples (vss. 6, 9, 20 twice). In three of these μνημεῖον is undoubtedly used where a tomb containing a body is meant. In vs. 20, however, this is first named a τάφος, and then, in the same verse, called a μνημεῖον. Other examples in the LXX version, taken at random, are Ex. 14 : 11, where μνῆμα means a grave, not a cenotaph or mere memorial place; Num. 11 : 34 and 35; 19 : 16; and Ezek. 33 : 23. Another example occurs in Josephus, *Ant.*, XIII, 6, 6. In the face of these facts—which might be multiplied considerably—it is impossible to maintain that μνημεῖον in *later* times invariably meant a *cenotaph*, or other mere memorial of a dead person, and never a tomb which was the actual grave of the deceased.

This conclusion is further borne out by the New Testament use of the word. The present writer, in making a by no means exhaustive list, has found therein nineteen examples of μνημεῖον (with three of μνῆμα), as opposed to four cases of τάφος in Matthew. Some of these undoubtedly refer to actual graves, *e. g.*, Matt. 8 : 28, where the allusion is to the rock tombs by the side of the lake Gennesaret, the abode of the demoniacs who dwelt among the bodies of the dead.

As for the subsidiary details, Mr. Butler surely cannot mean to compare the *memento*, wrapped in linen cloth, given to initiates in the higher mysteries, with the body of Jesus wound in linen bands by Joseph of Arimathæa! A *corpse* was not wrapt in linen and given to any one as a *memento* of initiation! Neither is Joseph himself supposed to be keeping it as a memorial. And linen cloths have served to enwrap many other things besides bodies and *mementos*.

CHAPTER XV

The Descension to Hades

THE theological tradition of the descent of Jesus to the
nether world, which forms a separate article of the faith
in the so-called Apostles' Creed (though it was omitted
in the symbol of Nicæa), is largely based upon the well-
known passage in I Peter 3 : 19[1] (*cf.* Eph. 8 : 9).

It has been the practise of many scholars for some
years past to trace this tradition back to the mythological conceptions of various races and nations—Mandae-
ans, Babylonians, Greeks, Persians, etc. Even Buddhist
eschatology has been drawn upon in the search for "origins" or at least "parallels." We will now examine the
chief of these and see how far they can be said to correspond with Christian ideas and teaching.

Perhaps the oldest extant story of this kind is that of
the now well-known "Descent of Ištar" to the underworld—"the land of no return," [2] as it is pathetically

---

[1] It is doubtful here, however, whether the preacher is Christ or Enoch.
Doctor Rendel Harris reads ἐν ᾧ καὶ Ἐνώχ (*Expositor*, April, 1901), which
is a plausible correction, as a copyist might easily omit Ἐνώχ after ἐν ᾧ. It
is also uncertain whether the "spirits in prison" are not the rebel angels
spoken of in the book of Enoch.

Other passages more or less definitely referring to the descent, or perhaps
throwing light upon it, are: Matt. 12 : 40; Luke 23 : 43; Acts 2 : 24, 27,
and 31; Romans 10 : 7 (on Deut. 30 : 13), but note alteration in text of the
LXX version here; Eph. 4 : 9; Rev. 1 : 18. See also Wisd. (Latin text)
24 : 32, where "Penetrabo omnes inferiores partes terrae, et inspiciam omnes
dormientes et illuminabo omnes sperantes in Domino" has been deemed an
influence towards formulating the doctrine.

[2] The ghost (*utukku*) of Eabani, the man-monster of the Gilgamesh Epic,
however, returns when summoned, and appears to Gilgamesh for a brief

termed—preserved in a Babylonian poem probably based
upon Sumerian materials.   The goddess visits the abode
of the dead, the city of Arallū—

"the house of gloom, the dwelling of Irkalla,
  the house from which those who enter depart not. . . .
  the house where those who enter are deprived of light;
  a place where dust is their nourishment, clay their food;
  . . . in thick darkness they dwell;
  they are clad like bats in a garb of wings;
  on door and bolt the dust is laid"—

in order that she might find Tammuz, the husband of her
youth, and give him to drink of the waters of life which
gushed up under the throne of the spirits of the earth,
and so bring him once more back to the light and life
of earth.   This myth has been commonly interpreted as
a version of the ubiquitous story of the mutual wooing
of the sun-god and the earth-goddess (or of the latter
by the spirit of vegetation) in order that the earth may
bring forth its fruits in the following spring.

In the Mandaean story of Hibil Ziva's[1] descent into
the underworld we have the Babylonian myth raised to
a higher level ethically and spiritually.   He was commis-
sioned by the "great ones"[2] to go and wage a successful
war with the king of darkness (*Ahriman*), and to liberate
the souls of the righteous detained there and to restore
them to the world of light.   The story, it will be seen,
has now assimilated some of the elements of Persian dual-

---

space.   Notable men, or heroes, it was thought, could be recalled to earth
for a little while in order to be consulted (*cf.* I Sam. 28 : 7–21; Hom., *Od.*,
II, 488 *ff.*).   Hence some scholars derive Sheōl from Assyr., *Siâlu* (?), and
interpret its meaning as "the place where oracles may be obtained."

[1] A divine hero, son of Mandā d' Hajjē (see Brandt, *Mandäische Schrif-
ten*, pp. 138 *ff.*; *Mand. Relig.*, pp. 182–184; Gunkel, *Schöpfung und Chaos*,
pp. 364 and 382.

[2] Are these equivalents of the (original) Hebrew *Elohim*?

ism. "The representation of the hero as fighting with the powers of darkness," says Doctor Cheyne (*Bib. Probs.*, p. 104), "seems at first sight to fill a gap in the Biblical myth. The Christ, as one might think, must have had to fight with these potentates before he could quit the city of death as a victor." And he thinks it very probable that "the Jews had a Messiah story (now lost) which agreed with the Mandaean in this respect."

A Zoroastrian "parallel," or at least a story containing a similar idea, which has "arisen out of the same need" (noted by Tiele, *Geschichte*, II, pp. 267 *f.*) has been found in the *Avesta*, Vendidad Fargad, II, 42, where, in reply to the question, "Who propagated there the Mazdayasnian religion in these enclosures which Yima made?" Ahura Mazda makes reply: "The bird Karshipta, O Spitama Zarathustra!" [1]

Ancient Greek and Roman literature, moreover, abound, comparatively speaking, in stories of legendary "descents" to Hades. For example, there is the descent of Hēraklēs to bring up Cerberus; that of Dionysus to bring back his mother Semelē and carry her to heaven; of Orpheus to recover his beloved wife; of Æneas, the Trojan hero, to consult his father Anchises; of Hermes, sent by Zeus to find the lost Persephonē, etc. All these have at one time or other been suggested as possible "sources" or as, at least in a sense, "parallels" of the *idea* of the descent of Jesus to the nether world of the dead.

But when we come to look closely into these several stories their insufficiency is very obvious. In the cases just quoted the whole object of the journey as well as its mythical framework is totally different. Moreover, in these stories the anthropomorphic hero (or heroine) is generally represented as visiting Hades in his (her) lifetime, not after death. There is, in short, no possible comparison to be made.

---

[1] *I. e.*, Zoroaster.

The Avestan parallel, again, is also unlike for similar reasons. It is not the after-death visit of a man. Jesus is thought to have fulfilled this part of his mission during the "three days" immediately succeeding his death. It is worth noting also that Zoroaster's teaching (*Khordah Avesta*, XXII) is that the soul of a deceased man remains near the head of the corpse for three days and nights; after this it goes to "its own place." A similar Jewish rabbinical belief held that it stayed near the body for that period of time in the hope of being able to return to it; but on the fourth day the face became so changed that it realised the impossibility of reanimation (*cf.* John 11 : 39 and *The Rest of the Words of Baruch*, IX, 7–13). This belief would seem to preclude the idea of such a journey arising in the early Christian mind from Zoroastrian or Jewish sources.

As compared with the Mandaean story, in the case of Jesus there is no "war" with the powers of darkness or evil. Doctor Cheyne, as we have seen, suggests that, in the Jewish Messianic cycle of ideas this part has been dropped, and that "evidently the Christian instinct was against it"; and this because "the New Testament writers, as a rule, prefer to represent the battle between Jesus Christ and the demons as having taken place in his earthly lifetime" (Matt. 12 : 29; Luke 10 : 18; John 12 : 31; 14 : 30; 16 : 11). But these examples do not refer to "battles" with demons. The latter are invariably expelled with a *word!* And in Rev. 12 : 7–11 we are told that the divine armies which overcome Satan are led by the archangel Michael. This, it is true, has been unsatisfactorily explained by saying that Michael represents Jesus Christ in his relation to the angels![1] But why should not the simpler explanation suffice, viz., that in the "descent" of Jesus no battle at all, with an al-

[1] In vs. 11 Michael and Jesus ("the Lamb") appear to be regarded as different persons.

most coequal power (as in the view of Mazdeism) was
thought of?

But we have still to consider the Buddhist "parallels."
The first of these is recommended by Mr. J. M. Robertson, who says (*Christianity and Mythology*, p. 257): "The
motive of the descent into hell [Hades] may have been
taken by the Christists from the [Chinese] Buddhists'
fable of Buddha's expedition to preach, like all former
Buddhas, to his mother[1] in the upper world of Tawa-
deintha" (*cf*. Bigandet's *Life of Gaudama*, I, pp. 219–
225).

Setting aside the fact that this story is not found in
early Buddhist scriptures, and is not improbably derived
from corrupt Christian sources, the whole *motif* is different to that in the story of Jesus, who does not go during his earthly lifetime to the "*upper* world" to preach
either to his mother or to the gods, as another version
puts it, but, it is said, to proclaim his message to "the
spirits in ward, who formerly disobeyed, when the long-
suffering of God waited in the days of Noë"—that is,
perhaps, in other words, to the generations preceding his
advent into the world.

Another Buddhist story, regarded apparently as in
some sense a "parallel" by Doctor Van den Bergh Van
Eysinga (*Einflüsse*, pp. 87 *f*.), is the one referred to by
the late Professor Cowell as "The Northern Buddhist
Legend of Avalokiteswara's Descent into the Hell Avichi"
(*Jour. of Philology*, vol. VI, 1876, pp. 222 *ff*.). He says:
"The name and attributes of Avalokiteswara[2] are entirely

---

[1] In the Tibetan version the preaching is to the *gods*. There is an allusion to a visit to hell of the Buddha in the *Lalita vistāra*, 2 Gatha, 8, trad.
pour Foucaux, I, 14; *cf*. Lefmann, *Lalita vistāra*, I (1874), p. 98, which is
declared by Seydel (*Evangelium*, etc., 183, 267 *f*., and *Buddha-Legende*, p.
35) to be a "parallel." But there is no mention in it of preaching or of re-
leasing captives.

[2] In northern India he was regarded as a Bodhisattva (potential Buddha);
but in China he is worshipped, under a female form, as the Buddha's *per-*

unknown to the southern Buddhists and his worship is one of the later additions which have attached themselves to the simpler original system. . . . The two best-known northern works which contain details respecting Avalo-kiteswára are the Káranda-vyúha and the Saddharma-Puṇḍaríka.

"The first few chapters of the former work are occupied with a description of Avalokiteswára's descent into the hell Avichi ['no-joy'] to deliver the souls there held captive by Yama the lord of the lower world. . . . These seem to me to bear a curious resemblance to the Apocryphal *Gospel of Nicodemus*. . . ."

He then sums up the question of priority thus: "Is the resemblance of the two legends accidental, or is it possible that in the Buddhist account we have one of those faint reflections of Christian influence (derived, perhaps, from Persian Christians settled in western and southern India) which Professor Weber has endeavoured to trace in the doctrine of faith as taught in the Bhagavad Gítá and some of the mediæval schools of the Vedanta? Much must depend on the date of the Apocryphal Gospel of Nicodemus. Maury and Cooper would place it as low as the fifth century; but Tischendorf with greater probability would refer it to the second.[1] Even if the present form in which we have the legend is interpolated, much of it must surely be of an early date; and we find direct allusions to events described there in the pseudo-Epi-phanius homily 'in Sepulchrum Christi' and in the fif-teenth sermon of Eusebius of Alexandria.

"At the same time we have no reason to suppose that the Buddhist legend was connected with the earliest worship of Avalokiteswára. It is not alluded to by Chinese

sonified power (see S. Beal, *A Catena of Buddhist Scriptures from the Chinese*, pp. 282, note 2; 383-409).

[1] In more recent times Doctors Harnack and Van Manen have regarded it as "not earlier than the fourth century"; but Doctor Rendel Harris has lately supported the view of the early date.

travellers in India; and the date of the Káraṇḍa-vyúha can only be so far fixed that it seems to have been translated into Tibetan in the ninth century."

There can be little doubt, we think, that the idea contained in this story—whatever its historical value may be—was not *borrowed* by the early Christians from any of the above-mentioned sources. Jesus, as man, would be universally expected to descend at death to the world of the dead; it would also be natural to suppose that his mission to mankind would be extended to that state of being also. The phraseology in which these concepts are expressed is no doubt largely symbolical; but we are, at least in the canonical books, spared the lurid sensationalism which marks the account in the *Gospel of Nicodemus*.

The Three Days

On the subject of the traditional interval between the death and the resurrection, Professor Drews comments as follows (*The Witnesses to the Historicity of Jesus*, pp. 164 and 165): "Whether, *e. g.*, the traditional 'after three days' in the account of the resurrection has been chosen on astral grounds, and is related to the three winter months from the shortest day when the sun dies to the vernal equinox when it triumphs definitely over the winter and so the months are condensed into three days in the myth, or whether the moon has furnished the data for the three days and three nights, as it is invisible for that period, and, as so often happens in myths, the moon and the sun have been blended, we need not consider here. Possibly the number may be explained by the popular belief in Persia and Judæa that the soul remains three days and three nights in the neighbourhood of the body, only departing to its place on the fourth morning. Possibly, again, the number was determined by Hosea 6 : 2, where we read: After two days he will revive us. In any case, where there are so many possible explanations, we have no convincing reasons to regard the account in the Gospels as historical." [1]

In discoursing on this matter in the neighbourhood of Cæsarea Philippi, Jesus is variously reported to have said that "after three days" he would rise again (Mark 8 : 31); be raised again "the third day" (Matt. 16 : 21); and be raised "the third day" (Luke 9 : 22). To these statements may be added the testimony of St. Paul who affirms (I Cor. 15 : 4) that he rose again the third day. [2]

Now, the statement in Mark (which may be taken as the original version, of which the other two are variants) "after three days" is really quite satisfied by the narratives themselves. These all imply that the body lay in the tomb about thirty-six hours, *distributed over three successive days*, which corresponds to the Hebraic expression "on the third day" of II Kings 20 : 5, and Hosea 6 : 2; but *not* to the statement in Jonah 1 : 17, where the analogy is at best only very approximate. This, again, is corroborated by the form used in Matthew and Luke and by St. Paul.

Turning next to Professor Drews's attempt to show that this statement is "unhistorical," we have first the suggestion that what is really in the writer's mind is, perhaps, "the three months from the shortest day, when the sun dies, to the vernal equinox, when it triumphs

---

[1] On p. 77 (*op. cit.*) Doctor Drews refers also to Isaiah 53 and Jonah 2 : 1, and adds: "The story of Jonah itself seems to have been originally only an historical embodiment of the myth of the dead, buried, and risen Saviour; in fact, Jesus refers to the prophet in this sense (Matt. 12 : 40)."

In the next verse, however, Jesus says: "A greater than Jonas is here!" This remark does not harmonise with any view that both were mere historical embodiments of the myth of the dead, buried, and risen Saviour. There is comparison of missions but no identity of persons.

[2] In the Jewish mode of computing time any portion of a day was popularly and loosely spoken of as the whole. And the portion of time beyond a whole day was referred to as "a third day" (*cf.* Gen. 11 : 13; I Sam. 30 : 12; and II Chron. 10 : 5). John says (2 : 19 and 21) ἐν τρισὶν ἡμέραις, "within three days," which is less Hebraic.

definitely over the winter,[1] and so"—he continues—"*the three months are condensed into three days*." But what authority has he for asserting that a definite statement like this, repeated over and over again, may mean three *months?* This is a monstrous and unwarrantable assumption.

No doubt, for the conveniences of the solar-mythical theory the literal three days is quite impossible; hence when a *sun*-myth proves intractable he naturally turns to the *moon*, where there is a *monthly* full three days' obscuration, and consoles himself with the reflection that in myths the sun and moon have been often blended![2] But the moon has never been concerned in this matter, and its introduction here is plainly a makeshift, as is shown directly afterwards by the fact that the Persian and Jewish beliefs about the soul—though these state

---

[1] On p. 95 of *The Christ Myth*, he admits, "it is obvious, however, that the sun can only be regarded from such a tragic standpoint in a land where, and in the myths of a people for whom, it possesses in reality such a decisive significance that there are grounds for lamenting its absence or lack of strength during winter and for an anxious expectation of its return and revival" (see Lobeck, *Aglaophamus*, p. 691, where the whole theory is disputed). From this dilemma Doctor Drews tries to escape by postulating (1) that the people originally came from a more severe climate, and (2) that the *solar* festivals at the solstice became (later) conjoined with *vegetative* festivals at the equinox. "Usually," he adds, . . . " death and reappearance were joined in one single feast, and this was celebrated at the time in spring when day and night were of equal length, when vegetation was at its highest, and in the East the harvest was begun." Dupuis argues in a similar manner (*L'origine de tous les cultes*, p. 152). The cult of Dionysus-Zagreus at least affords a striking exception to this alleged rule. Under the form of a bull he was torn to pieces and eaten raw by women in *the winter time*, and further rites, representing his revival, took place in *the spring!*

[2] In true Semitic mythology (unlike Aryan) the moon, it is true, is a male divinity, and in some cases it is regarded as a different *aspect* (? nightly representative) of the chief, or solar, god. Also there is some relation between the moon-god and Tammuz, as there is also between the sun and Tammuz, who, like most of these vegetation spirits, developed solar and lunar characteristics. This fact is shown *inter alia* by the Osiris variant of the "Dying God" cult. But there is no evidence whatever for the syncretism and confusion postulated by Doctor Drews.

the exact contrary—are drawn upon as another possible source of the idea; and a yet further source is next found in Hosea 6 : 2, where "after two days" has certainly no reference to the experience of Jesus,[1] though both the late Doctor Pusey and many of the fathers have professed to find a mystical reference here.

But the whole *solar-mythical* theory here really breaks down owing to the fact that the sun is never out of sight for three months, or even three days, except in very high latitudes, and in the case of the moon its monthly three days of obscuration are not comparable with the thirty-six hours' sojourn in the tomb, because the latter is exactly only *one-half of three days!* Hence the analogy drawn fails to satisfy the conditions, as also does that relating to the full three days' sojourn of the soul beside the corpse.

The Empty Tomb

Much discussion has also taken place upon the subject of the empty tomb. St. Paul, it is urged, in his (the earliest) account of the resurrection, says nothing about it, and the Gospel accounts are discrepant.[2] But St. Paul asserts that Jesus rose again "on the third day," after being buried, which is another way of stating the same thing! And had his appearances been of an hallucinatory character, as Professor Schmiedel argues in the *Encyclopædia Biblica*, and been regarded as apparitional by St. Paul himself, the latter would not have referred at all to any "rising" on the third day, because a mere phantasmal appearance may be seen any day after death, whether the body is or is not lying in the grave.

[1] Because in the Mass. version of the text the reference is to "us." So also the LXX version reads ἐξαναστησόμεθα. There is, it is true, another possible pointing of the Hebrew, but it does not agree so well with the context as the above rendering.

[2] The present writer has discussed these objections in his *The Resurrection Narratives and Modern Criticism*, chap. 8.

M. Salomon Reinach, on the other hand, revives an old and non-mythical objection when he asserts, with Strauss and Volkmar, that Jesus never had a tomb at all. He remarks (*Orpheus*, p. 255): "The discovery of the empty tomb is the less credible in that Jesus, if he had been executed, would have been thrown by the Roman soldiers into the common grave of malefactors." It is to be feared that the learned French scholar penned this passage hastily and without having previously consulted his authorities! In earlier times it was usual for bodies to be left to decay upon the cross; but, according to Quintilian (*Declam.*, VI), after the time of Augustus, the bodies, if claimed, were given up to the friends for burial.[1]

The First Day of the Week

The *vox universa* of Christian tradition has in all ages asserted definitely and clearly that the first day of the week was held to be a sacred day, in place of the seventh, in commemoration of the resurrection of Jesus from the dead. This tradition has of late years, however, been disputed. Doctor Paul Carus says (*The Monist*, 1906, p. 420): "Sunday was then [*temp. Chr.*] the great festive day of the Mithraists, and the disciples of St. John [Baptist] as well as the Nazarenes celebrated the day by coming together and breaking bread in a common meal. . . . That Sunday was celebrated prior to Christianity is unquestionably proved by the fact that St. Paul visits in several cities those circles of disciples who had neither heard of the Holy Ghost nor believed as yet on Christ Jesus, and they used to break bread in common on the first day of the week."

Doctor Carus here does not state the facts quite fairly. Acts 19 : 1–5 certainly affirms that St. Paul, when at

---

[1] The Jews, too, were careful that they should be buried before sunset (πρὸ δύντος ἡλίου, Josephus).

Ephesus, visited a community of the disciples of John the Baptist, who had not heard of the Holy Ghost or received apostolic baptism.

But the passage does not refer to the breaking of bread by them on any day. The Nazarenes, too, seem to have been the more Jewishly minded of the disciples of Jesus, though the term was also probably often loosely used for all in the apostolic fellowship. They would, therefore, naturally follow the same rule, and possibly observed both days in some degree.

As to the Mithraists, it is true that in the later period of their history at least they observed Sunday, and that in the second and third centuries A. D. their doctrines and practises bore, in some respects, a remarkable resemblance to those of the Christian church. But, owing to the loss of all early Mithraic literature, it is by no means certain, or probable, that this was the case in pre-Christian times. Some of the second-century Christian writers, indeed, accuse the Mithraists of travestying both the sacraments and the doctrines of Christianity. But, whether this be the case or not, it is both wiser and safer to say, with M. Franz Cumont (*The Mysteries of Mithra,* 1910, p. 194): "We cannot presume to unravel to-day a question which divided contemporaries and which will doubtless forever remain insoluble. We are too imperfectly acquainted with the dogmas and liturgies of Roman Mazdeism, as well as the development of primitive Christianity, to say definitely what mutual influences were operative in their simultaneous evolution." This pronouncement in effect amounts to a verdict of "not proven" as against the case presented by Doctor Carus, who would suggest a borrowing of the observance of the first day from the Mithraists. We do not know definitely whether the pre-Christian Mithraists observed the first day of the week; but we do know that the very earliest Christians firmly believed that Jesus rose again on that day, and honoured it in consequence instead of the older Jewish Sabbath, which it henceforward superseded in the church.[1]

The Angelophanies at the Tomb

We have already seen (chap. 11, pp. 218 *ff.*) how Professor W. B. Smith has endeavoured to prove that the "young man" ($\nu\epsilon\alpha\nu\iota\sigma\kappa\acute{o}s$) of Mark 15 : 5 was nothing else than the fravishi (frohar), or "heavenly self," of Jesus. That particular phenomenon, however, we submit, stands on precisely the same footing as the similar figures seen at the tomb and recorded by the other synoptists and in the Fourth Gospel.

These "angelophanies," commonly set aside without examination by "liberal" critics, have been briefly noticed by Fiebig (*Babel.*, p. 7) in the following terms: "In the reports of the resurrection the angelophanies are undoubtedly mythical in character."

But why should this conclusion be thus dogmatically stated? There are other possibilities, *e. g.*, visions of an hallucinatory character. The women may have fancied that they saw these apparitions! Again, there is at least the possibility that these appearances had some objective basis. It is true that (granting this possibility) the dividing line in such matters between what is wholly subjective and hallucinatory and what is (spiritually) objective and, therefore, veridical is one which is extremely difficult to draw. But a careful study of the latest modern literature bearing upon this branch of psychical research will at least prevent any thinking person from hastily forming the opinion that because a phenomenon of the class known as "supernatural" is reported as occurring many years ago, therefore it must certainly be mythical. It is really to a very large extent a question

---

[1] Gunkel thinks (*Verständnis*, pp. 73 *ff.*) that Sunday was already observed by the Jews also; but he offers no proof.

of the intelligence and veracity of the witnesses, and perhaps one of the best proofs of the objectivity of the phenomenon is to be found in the fact that all the witnesses in question relate very similar experiences.[1]

Certain Mythical "Resurrections"

We will now proceed to state and deal with certain alleged parallels to the resurrection of Jesus as found among the chief dying and rising saviours of the ethnic nature-cults.

Osiris

In the case of the Egyptian cult-god Osiris (Bab., *Ašari*, a form of Marduk), whose body was hacked to pieces, the myth relates, by his brother and adversary Set, the idea of resurrection, in the Christian sense, is but imperfectly expressed and even that of identity is somewhat vague. In the developed form of the Osirian religion Osiris becomes identified with the sun[2] of to-day (this year) which rises to-morrow (next year) in the form of his son Horus. Osiris himself is regarded as remaining below as king of the underworld and judge of the dead. The idea of resurrection, or rather revival, was certainly moralised and spiritualised as it never was in Babylon or elsewhere; but the whole concept, even in Egypt, was originally expressed in a mere materialistic form, as is shown by the primitive story told of the *membra disjecta* of his body, which Anubis pieced together, and Isis, assisted by the snake-goddess Ḥeptet and other gods and goddesses,

---

[1] It is not, however, an absolute test; for collective hallucinations do occur under certain conditions. The present writer has discussed fully the phenomena, etc., at the tomb in his *The Resurrection Narratives and Modern Criticism* (1910).

[2] *The Book of the Dead* (Budge's translation), vol. I, pp. 87 and 88. But, doubtless, in earlier times he was a vegetation spirit and a god of fecundity. Later, however, he became identified, or confused, in some degree with Rā as Osiris-Rā.

fanned into life again with her wings,[1] while, according to
one account, Horus by means of various magical ceremonies made him to "stand up" again. Such is the Egyptian
resurrection (see Budge, *Osiris and the Egyptian Resurrection*, vol. I, pp. 72, 74, and 75)! These stories point
merely to the old material life of nature which is simply
revived; hence the practise of mummification, without
which there can be no revivification either for Osiris or
the Osirian.

Adonis

A two days' festival in honour of the death and revival
of Adonis (the Syrian *Tammuz*[2]) was celebrated early in
February by the Phœnician women of Byblus. The first
day was spent in grief and lamentation, the second in
joy and triumph. In Greece, whither the rites were subsequently transferred, the festival took place in summer
and was prolonged to eight days.

According to the anthropomorphic setting of the myth
Adonis was slain by the tusk of a wild boar, whilst hunt-
ing in the mountains of Lebanon, and was revived annually at his festival in the spring or in some places in midsummer.[3] In Ovid's poetical version of the myth (*Metam.*,
X, 735) his return to life would seem to be evidenced by

[1] An image of Osiris was buried in a hollowed-out pine trunk, which was
kept for a year and then usually burned, as was done with the image of Attis
attached to the pine-tree (see below, and Macrobius, *De Err. Prof. Rel.*,
XXVII). The myth should be studied especially in Doctor Budge's *Osiris
and the Egyptian Resurrection* (see also his *Gods of the Egyptians*, vol. II,
131–138, and Frazer's *Adonis, Attis, Osiris* (3d ed.), vol. II, pp. 12 and 13).
Foucart thinks that the drama was enacted at the *Anthesteria*, Mommensen
places it in the following month at the *Lesser Mysteries*.

[2] Doctor Radau states (*The Bab. Exped. of the Univ. of Penn. : Sumerian
Hymns and Prayers to the God Dumuzi, or Bab. Lent. Songs*, 1913) that the
resurrection of Tammuz is never mentioned in the [older] dialectal texts of
southern Sumer.

[3] So Milton in his *Paradise Lost* (book I):

"Thammuz came next behind,
Whose wounds in Lebanon allur'd

the springing up of the red anemone in the place where his blood was spilt.[1]

During the festival, as described by the Greek poet Biōn,[2] on the first day an image[3] of the young lover lying on a couch and dying in the arms of Aphrodite[4] (Astarte) was exhibited. Early on the next day the statue was carried down to the seashore, where its "wounds" were washed by women amid great lamentations. Directly afterwards the drama of his "resurrection" was enacted. This is described by Lucian (*De Dea Syr.*, VI) in a few sarcastic words: "They say mythically that he is alive" (ζώειν τέ μιν μυθολογέουσι).

Attis

The ritual in the cult of Attis,[5] the Phrygian type of the vegetal (-solar?) god, began with the felling of the

> The Syrian damsels to lament his fate
> In amorous ditties all a summer's day."

But Adonis and Attis, unlike most of these cult-gods, remained to the end almost free from solar characteristics (see Frazer, *Adonis, Attis, Osiris*, vol. I, p. 232, note).

[1] *Cf.* also Baudissin, *Adon. und. Eshmun*, p. 169.

[2] See Ahren's *Bucolici Græci*, sub Bionis reliq.

[3] That this part of the ceremonies is based on old Semitic ritual, and is not a later Greek addition, is evidenced by Lampridius, who says (*Heliogab.*, VII): Salambonam (צלם בעל, "image of Ba'al") etiam omni planctu et jactatione Syriaci cultus exhibuit.

Doctor Langdon thinks that in the case of *Dumu-zi* (Tammuz) "a wooden figure of the dying god was probably placed in a skiff and given over to the waters of the Euphrates or the Tigris, precisely as in Egypt the image of Osiris was cast upon the sea. When the figure of the god disappeared beneath the waves he was supposed to pass to the underworld and maintain a peaceful existence after the pain of death" (*Tammuz and Ishtar*, pp. 11 and 12). Dumu-zi figures here as the fertilising spirit of the inundation.

[4] Aphrodite (like Istar) "descends" to Hades to bring up Adonis. There is no "descent" of Mary in the Christian tradition!

[5] Attis = "Father" (Frazer). He was variously said to have bled to death as a consequence of self-mutilation at the foot of a pine-tree and to have been killed (like Adonis) by a wild boar. According to Sir James Frazer he was originally a tree spirit. In one passage Firmicus Maternus states (*De Err. Prof. Relig.*, 27) that a ram was sacrificed in the worship of Attis.

sacred pine-tree into which he was said to have been changed at death. The trunk of this, swathed in bands, like a mummy, with the effigy of a young man attached to it, was taken to the temple where the mourning broke forth. After a period of fasting the tree trunk was solemnly buried, and those present stimulated their emotions by wild dances, during which, like the priests of Ba'al, they gashed themselves with knives till the blood[1] flowed. On the evening of the following day they again met in the temple to celebrate the restoration of Attis to life; the grave was opened, and when a light had been produced the priest anointed the lips of the worshippers with oil, and said: "Be of good cheer, initiates, the god has been saved; thus for you also there shall be salvation from your troubles."[2] The joy of the mystæ was then expressed in a sort of carnival.

Dionysus

The grave of Dionysus,[3] who was said to have been torn in pieces by the Titans, according to one form of the myth, was at Thebes. His "resurrection" (revival) is variously related. According to one version—probably an earlier form (cf. myth of Osiris)—his mother pieced him together and made him young again (Diodorus Siculus, first century A. D., III, 62); in another form it is merely stated that he rose from the dead[4] and ascended

---

[1] The blood, it must be remembered, was both the seat and the *medium* of the life. Hence this act was probably regarded as aiding the development of the new life.

[2] θαρρεῖτε, μύσται τοῦ θεοῦ σεσωσμένου,
ἔσται γὰρ ὑμῶν τῶν πονῶν σωτηρία.
—Firmicus Maternus, *De Err. Prof. Rel.* (Zieg.), p. 57.

[3] Probably = "son of Zeus" (Διός and νῦσος, a Thracian word for "son").

[4] Pomegranates were supposed to have sprung from the blood of Dionysus, as anemones from the blood of Adonis and violets from that of Attis. This points to the conclusion that both Dionysus and the other forms of this annually dying god were originally "Spirits of the Corn and of the Wild" (Frazer) and unconnected with the sun. The oldest (and aniconic) representation of Dionysus was a consecrated post formed from a holy tree.

to heaven (Macrobius, fifth century, *Comm. in Somn. Scip.*, I, 12, 12; *cf.* Origen, *Cont. Cels.*, IV, 17); again, it is related that Zeus swallowed the heart of Dionysus and then begat him afresh by Semelē (Proclus, *Hymn to Minerva*, see Lobeck, *Aglaophamus*, p. 51); finally, we read that his heart was pounded up and given to Semelē, who swallowed it and again conceived him (Hyginus, *Fabulæ*, 167).

It will be observed that the only variant of the myth of the (annual) revival of Dionysus (that of Macrobius) which bears any resemblance to the story of Jesus is a very late one and undoubtedly shows evidence of Christian syncretism. The other, and earlier, forms are utterly unlike throughout.

Mithra

As the Mithra-myth is wholly lost, it is only possible to study it tentatively by means of the Mithraic sculptures which are extant. One of them, in which Mithra is represented as struggling with a bull and plunging a knife into its neck, is commonly supposed to display the god in the *rôle* of a "suffering saviour." So far as the sculpture goes, however, it would seem that it is rather the bull which is suffering. Indeed, the whole meaning of this symbolic representation is doubtful. Doctor St. Clair Tisdall suggests (*Mythic Christs and the True*, pp. 19 and 20) that as the Avestic word *gāus*, besides meaning "bull" is translatable "earth," and since the word *urvan* ("soul") is probably a derivative of the same root as *urvarā* ("plant," "tree"), this sculpture really means that the sun by piercing the earth with its rays (the knife) causes the vegetation to spring up.[1]

[1] Professor Drews, however, explains it differently. He says (*The Christ Myth*, p. 142) that before 800 B. C. the sun, in the shape of the constellation of the Bull, opened the spring equinox and released the world from the power of winter. But why the stabbing of the bull? Mr. H. Stuart Jones holds (*The Quart. Rev.*, July, 1914, p. 119) that we have here one of those legends

Another sculpture shows Mithra issuing from the rock. This has been hastily pronounced by Mr. J. M. Robertson (*Christianity and Mythology*, p. 417) to represent the resurrection of Mithra from the tomb. But there is no extant tradition of Mithra's burial in a tomb or of his issuing from one after death.[1] Doctor St. Clair Tisdall thinks that since the Avestic word *asman* (Ved. Sansc., *aśman*) means, besides "rock," "cloud" and "sky," the reference here is to Mithra (*i. e.*, the sun) as a child of the sky. In both of the above cases dogmatism is impossible, but the explanations suggested by Doctor Tisdall may at least be pronounced very feasible.

The Resurrection of Jesus Christ

It must suffice here to point out that the two main differences between the Christian resurrection and the mythical revivals (incorrectly termed "resurrections") of the cult-gods are: (1) In the case of the nature-cults the revival of the god is merely to a fresh lease of the former type of life and reproductive energy in nature. In the Christian resurrection (as taught by St. Paul in I Cor. 15) both Jesus himself and Christian people rise to a new and wholly different life, in which a "spiritual body" (σῶμα πνευματικόν) replaces the former material or "natural (psychical) body" (σῶμα ψυχικόν).[2] (2) The death

---

invented in order to explain primitive ritual—in this case the sacrifice of a bull (embodying the corn spirit)—in order to promote the fertility of the earth.

[1] Justin Martyr says (*Dial. c. Try.*, LXX): "Those who record the mysteries of Mithra say that he was *begotten* of a rock (ἐκ πέτρας γεγενῆσθαι αὐτόν)." These mysteries were, as a rule, celebrated at the spring equinox (Cumont, *Monuments figurés relatifs aux mystères de Mithra*, vol. I, p. 326). For a description of a Mithræum near Rome, in which they were held, see the London *Athenæum* for October 30 and November 6, 1886.

[2] For a discussion of St. Paul's teaching on the resurrection and the spiritual and natural bodies, see *The Resurrection Narratives and Modern Criticism* (1910), especially chaps. 10 and 11.

and revival of the cult-god is an *annual* matter: Jesus
and the Christian die and are raised from the dead "*once
for all.*"

The Epidauria

But a "source" of the idea has also been found in the
Eleusinian mysteries. In Mr. Slade Butler's article, already quoted, we find the following passage (p. 498):
"The last act of the sacred drama performed within the
temple of Dēmētēr took place on the eighth day, which
appears to have been called Epidauria, in honour of
Æsculapius (Asklepios), the god of returning life. The
ceremony and ritual used on this day are not known,
but "doubtless the thought really lay in this, that Æsculapius was supposed by his wondrous skill to have raised
Iacchus from the dead" (Purser). Iacchus was the son
of Persephoné, the maiden (Koré), but how his death
was enacted has never been ascertained; probably this
ceremony was performed when a mystes, or rather an
epoptes, was admitted to the highest grade of the priesthood, on which occasion the candidate would represent
Iacchus and would symbolically die and be raised to life
again. In any case the ritual would be mystic and dramatic, showing by type and figure the passage through
death to life. The eighth day of the Eleusinian celebration was, in fact, the festival of returning life or resurrection."

It is not in any sense demonstrated by Mr. Butler how
this mystic ceremony, if it be rightly set forth here, could
supply the *idea* of the Christian resurrection, which was
certainly not that of mere "returning life," as we have
seen above. The eighth day of the mysteries, called Epidauria, is said to have been added to the original number of days during which the mysteries were celebrated
because Æsculapius, arriving too late for the ceremonies
of the sixth day, asked for initiation. But the whole idea

here also is very different to the Christian story of the resurrection of Jesus. Æsculapius (who may be an ancient physician, euhemerised) does not himself rise to renewed life, but raises another by his skill in the healing art. Moreover, this takes place not on the third but on the *eighth* day. "It is extremely difficult," says Professor Clemen, "to see any connexion here," and we are compelled to indorse his judgment.

In conclusion, we may add a Buddhist story which has been regarded by some irresponsible writers as a "parallel" to the resurrection of Jesus. It is described by Doctor Edkins (*Chinese Buddhism*, p. 57) as follows: "After the body of the Buddha had been consumed upon the funeral pile, Anuruddha went up to the Tusita heaven to announce these events to Māyā, the mother of the Buddha. Māyā at once came down, and the coffin opened of itself. The honoured one of the world rose up, joined his hands, and said: You have condescended to come down here from your abode far away. Then he said to Ananda: 'You should know that it is for an example to the unfilial of after ages that I have risen from my coffin to address inquiries to my mother.' " [1]

Comment on the above is really superfluous, but, if any be needed, it is sufficient to add that when death came to the Buddha it was, according to the Buddhist scriptures (*cf. Mahāparinibbāna Suttanta*, IV, 57; also III, 20; V, 20, etc., *Sacred Books of the East*, vol. XI), "with that utter passing away in which nothing whatever remains behind." [2]

---

[1] A variant form of this legend is given by Doctor Eitel, *Three Lectures on Buddhism*, p. 13.

[2] The exact meaning of the Buddhistic *Nirvāna* is in dispute. By many scholars it is interpreted as simply *extinction* (so Rhys Davids). Pfungst, however, maintains ("Che è veramente il Nirvāna dei Buddhisti?", *Coenobium*, May–June, 1907) that it is a state of being in which, while *Will* disappears, *Consciousness* remains.

The Ascension to Heaven

We will notice in the first place, in connexion with this event in the story of Jesus, a statement made by the well-known and eminent critic and churchman Doctor T. K. Cheyne, who, quoting the views of Doctor Winckler, says (*Bible Problems*, 1904, pp. 114 and 115): "The same scholar is of opinion that the forty days between the resurrection and the ascension of Christ (Acts 1 : 3) may originally (*i. e.*, in a pre-Christian myth out of which the Jewish and Christian representations grew) have meant the forty days during which, as the ancients well knew, the Pleiades become invisible.

"In this case the forty days of the evangelical tradition were properly the interval between the death and the resurrection of Christ; *i. e.*, from a purely archæological point of view, the resurrection and the ascension were one and the same thing.[1] In fact, the resurrection and ascension of the solar heroes were naturally identical, and the archæological theory here expounded is that myths of solar deities supplied details for the close of the story of the Messiah, which, according to a highly satisfying theory, preceded the appearance of the Christ of history."

And he continues further: "In spite of a churchman's natural inclination to a reverential reticence, I am bound to say that the form of the spiritual truth of Christ's resurrection and ascension can be explained by archæology. Provisionally and tentatively it may be possible to explain the form in each case as a postulate of faith; but in the light of what has been shown to be the probable origin of the form of the belief in the descent we cannot consider this explanation very plausible. That there are mythic parallels for the statement (less emphasised in our documents than we might have expected) of

[1] So Zimmern, *Die Keilinschriften u. d. Alte Test.*[3], p. 389.

the ascension is beyond question. Not to dwell on the
myths of Adonis and Hēraklēs, the Babylonian solar deities who descend (*arâdu*) necessarily ascend (*elû*) afterwards." [1]

The traditional period of the invisibility of the Pleiades
is, as above stated, forty days (*cf.* Hesiod, *Works and
Days*, II, 383–386). At the present time, in latitude 31°,
they set, heliacally, about May 2 and rise, heliacally,
about June 6, thus giving an interval of approximately
five weeks.

In A. D. 29 the Pleiades were invisible for almost exactly forty days, which, so far, would support the suggestion of Winckler. But the real question here does not
depend upon any mere coincidence of this kind. The
point is, what have the Pleiades to do with the matter at
all? Have the Jews, for example, or any other people,
ever regarded this group of stars as the "astral representative" of the sun or connected them in any way with a
cult of this kind? No proof of this has ever been brought

---

[1] The rest of the paragraph deals with the mythic ascensions which are not
preceded by descensions, *e. g.*, those of Mithra, the Babylonian Etana, Enoch,
Elijah, etc. Doctor Langdon admits (*Tammuz and Ishtar*, p. 33) that
"The ascension of the dying god into the far-away upper regions, where he
vanished forever from mortal eyes, does not form any part of the doctrine of
the official liturgies. These adhered from first to last to the traditional view
that the divine son descended into Sheôl, whither his mother and the demons
followed him and whence they fetched him back to the upper world [earth]."
Doctor Budge (*Osiris and the Egyptian Resurrection*, vol. I, pp. 75 *ff.*) thus
describes the ascension of Osiris: "When the body of Osiris was ready to
leave this earth for heaven, some difficulty, it seems, arose in raising him
up to the sky and a ladder was found to be necessary. From the text of
Pepi II (II, 975 *ff.*) we learn the tradition that the wooden sides of the ladder were shaped by an adze wielded by the god Sasha, that the rungs were
made of the strong sinews of Ḳasut, the bull of the sky, and that they were
fashioned in their places on the sides of the ladder with the knotted thongs
made from the hide of the god Utes, the son of Ḥesat (*Pepi II*, II, 975 and
976). This divine ladder was set up from earth to heaven by Horus and Rā,
according to one legend, and, according to another, by Horus and Set. The
text of *Unas* says: Ra setteth up the ladder before Osiris in his going to his
spirit. One of them [standeth] on this side and one of them on that side."
The concepts which are set forth above are very materialistic and crude.

forward in support of this theory. Ordinarily, in classical mythology, the Pleiades were regarded as the seven daughters of Atlas, and their rising and setting merely marked the opening and closing of the sailing season. What particular constellation even the Hebrews identified with the Pleiades is uncertain (*Enc. Bib.*, art. "Stars"). In short, this group of stars seems to have no connexion whatever with the sun, or with the cults of "dying" and "rising" solar or other heroes, and the borrowing from them of the forty days' interval before the ascension has not even a shadow of probability.

But Doctor Cheyne admits that in these ethnic myths the resurrection and the ascension are invariably one and the same event. If so, why were they not in the Christ-myth, if that story were merely another instance of a solar-myth? As a matter of fact, in Christian tradition they have never been regarded as practically synchronous, which fact alone constitutes a strong argument for rejecting any solar or astral origin of the resurrection and ascension[1] narratives. Furthermore, a comparison with the story of the ascension of Adonis, the Syrian god of vegetation, yields results which are very instructive and, no doubt, fairly typical. Lucian, who has preserved the story, tells us that his assembled worshippers, after theatrically pronouncing him to be alive, "send him into the air" (μιν ... ἐς τὸν ἠέρα πέμπουσι), probably by uttering some magic *formula*.[2] In other words, he intimates plainly that the whole scene was a mere make-believe and was not looked upon by any one, even those most

---

[1] Strenuous efforts have been made by some critics to show that the ascension of Jesus is stated by Luke (24 : 50–52) to have taken place *directly after* the resurrection. But Luke's narrative here is clearly condensed; and he (as author of Acts 1 : 2) says definitely that the intervening period was one of forty days. Moreover, the number of appearances of Jesus, as given by all authorities, strongly suggest a considerable interval.

[2] Mr. Bouchier thinks (*Syria as a Roman Province*, p. 264) that at this point in the ceremony an image of Adonis was thrown up into the air.

concerned, as anything more than a kind of magical ceremony to secure the fertility of the land during the following year.[1]

Now, it is impossible to compare a scene of this sort with the story of the ascension of Jesus. Whether the apostles and the other earliest Christians were right or wrong, they certainly believed that they had witnessed the departure of Jesus from this world. If this were not a fact of some order, then we are dealing with a case of hallucination or one of imposture.

Again, in the case of Hēraklēs—who really has no resurrection (cited by Mr. J. M. Robertson, *Christianity and Mythology*, p. 420)—after putting on the robe tinged with the philter of Nessus, and when the venom contained in the latter had begun to consume his flesh, he went to Mount Oeta, where he built a funeral pyre, ascended it, and caused it to be set alight. While the pyre was flaming a thunder-cloud of Zeus is said to have conveyed the sufferer to heaven where he was endowed with immortality.[2]

Here, again, it is impossible to see how a story of this type could have suggested to any reasonable and earnest men, such as the early Christians were, any mere fanciful story of an actual ascension. It is wholly different both in *motif* and in detailed incidents. Even Mr. Robertson

---

[1] The original (pre-Christian) ascension of the dying god was undoubtedly merely from Hades to earth. *Cf.* the story of Tammuz (p. 324, note 1), which goes back at least 5,000 years and is, perhaps, the oldest extant form of the myth. There is an "ascension" to heaven in Babylonian literature by the hero Etana, who mounts thither on the back of an eagle in order to obtain the "plant of begetting" (see Jensen, *Mythen und Epen*, pp. 100–105). With this story may be compared what Doctor Budge (*Osiris*, etc.) indexes as "Osiris ascends to the heaven of Sefert," as related in the pyramid text of Unas. In this the deceased king (Unas), identified with Osiris, mounted on the hawk-headed creature Sefert, who was in charge of portions of the body of Osiris, goes to heaven where he works magic upon or for Rā.

[2] According to another variant of the myth, the god Eshmun-Iolaos restored Hēraklēs to life by giving him a quail to smell at.

himself appears to see the absurdity of such a derivation
of either the story or the *idea* which it contains; for he
remarks (p. 420) that the suggestion of an ascension of
Jesus probably came "from the spectacle of the litten
clouds at sunset." So far as this proposed solution of
the problem is concerned, it may be remarked here that
imaginative persons have often derived many strange
ideas from the spectacle of a gorgeous sunset; but it has
nowhere else been placed on record that any one has
thought that he saw a man ascending out of his sight!
To Mr. Robertson himself the whole scene is, of course,
"obviously a fable born of ignorance. Only," he continues, "in a world living under the primitive delusion of
a flat earth and of a solid, overarching firmament could
such a fable have been framed."

This is, no doubt, a very superior attitude to assume,
and highly satisfying to all of a like mind with Mr. Robertson himself. But before yielding to the attractions of
so *facile* a solution, let us for a few moments examine the
original story a little more closely.

Assuming here, provisionally and for the present purpose, the existence of a spiritual world and the survival
of a spiritual element in man, the question arises whither
does this undying ego depart at death? Now, of course,
it is well known that the concept of a passage from this
lower and mainly material world to a higher and coexist-
ent spiritual universe has, among the higher races, generally been *formulated and depicted in terms of time and
space*—as, in fact, *an ascension in space*.[1]

[1] It may not be inopportune here, in order to show to what degree of folly
the thoughtless adoption of the crude concepts of untrained minds may lead
even a distinguished modern thinker, to quote the following anecdote chronicled by Doctor F. C. Conybeare (*Myth, Magic, and Morals*, pp. 358 and
359). He says: "The Irish mathematician, Sir William Rowan Hamilton,
once allowed himself to be drawn into the speculation of how far out into
space Jesus could proceed in a certain time if he were rising at the moderate
rate which the above passage contemplates. When his calculations revealed
to him that he would not have reached yet the nearest of the fixed stars, he

But such descriptions have always had (except among the ruder peoples and the more uncultured races of mankind) a greater or less degree of symbolical meaning attached to them. And, even in the case of those races and persons who have made considerable advances in culture and the power of thought, there is a convenience in this mode of representation which it would be difficult even now wholly to dispense with. Hence we can understand the use of such concepts by the more backward people of the first century. Probably they did hold to "the primitive delusion of a flat earth" and "a solid, overarching firmament." Almost every one did in those and even later times, and adjusted their ideas of things, spiritual as well as temporal, in accordance with this common error. But this is not really the important point here. What the writer of the Acts is primarily endeavouring to impress upon his readers is that Jesus, as the son of God and man, after his death and resurrection, passed over from this lower and material to a higher and *spiritual mode of existence*, i. e., to the kingdom of heaven or of God. And he expresses this *idea* in the only form in which he himself and his readers, for the most part at least, can grasp it, viz., a temporal and spatial one. And this mode of expression is still necessary to a very large extent even nowadays. But, on the other hand, it is also true that there are in these times an increasing number of persons to whom the cruder symbolisations of spiritual truths are less necessary. Some, at least, will have learned from the immortal work of Kant[1] that both space and time— as we know them—are, perhaps, but mere forms of our sense-perception, chiefly, if not wholly, concerned with the phenomenal world; and we are able dimly to under-

began as a good Christian to recoil from his speculation and relegated the matter as a mystery beyond the reach of human wisdom."

This story is in the highest degree instructive!

[1] *The Kritik of Pure Reason : The Transcendental Æsthetic.*

stand that the passage from a material and phenomenal to a spiritual and real world *cannot be one of actual spatial transition at all*. It must be something different from this: something higher, in a spiritual sense; something which we cannot yet fully grasp and understand. "For," says St. Paul (I Cor. 13 : 12) with great truth and insight, "now we see in (lit., "through") a mirror obscurely (δι' ἐσόπτρου ἐν αἰνίγματι), but then"—when the obscuring veil of the senses is removed—"face to face; now I know in part," he adds, "but then I shall know fully, even as also I was fully known."

APPENDIX A

THE DATES OF THE BIRTH AND DEATH OF JESUS CHRIST

Many readers are well aware of the futility of attempts
of the editors of chronologists to fix the dates of
the above-named events. This fact is sometimes urged
by inquirers as an additional argument in favour of the
non-historicity of the Gospel narratives.

During the last few years, however, some very subtle
and acute researches into both of these questions have
been carried on by Sir William Ramsay and Lieut.-
Colonel G. Mackinlay. The latter gentleman sums up
the results (*The Churchman*, July, 1914, p. 515) as follows: "There is a mass of secular historic evidence in
favour of 3 B. C. and 29 A. D. for the birth of the nativity and the crucifixion respectively. The former date
agrees with the express statement of Tertullian that
Christ was born during the rule of Sentius Saturninus
[in Syria], and the latter date is in accord with the universal testimony of the early Latin fathers that the Lord
suffered under the rule of the Gemini."

We will give here a very brief summary of the grounds
upon which these dates are based.

The Birth. The difficulties in the way of fixing the date
of the birth of Jesus have been largely due to (1) apparent errors in the Lucan narrative; (2) that Quirinus
was connected with the first census held in 4 B.C.; and
(2) that in certain of these enrolments in the eastern province of the empire it was the custom to require that all
should return to their ancestral homes for purposes of
registration. Both of these statements of Luke have
been frequently denied and even defended by St. Luke,
and others who were desirous of impugning the historical
trustworthiness of that writer.

As regards the former of these points, it has now been

APPENDIX A

MOST readers are well aware of the hitherto complete failure of the efforts of chronologists to fix the dates of the above-named events. This fact is sometimes urged by mythicists as an additional argument in favour of the non-historicity of the Gospel narratives.

During the last few years, however, some very acute and useful researches into both of these questions have been carried on by Sir William Ramsay and Lieutenant-Colonel G. Mackinlay. The latter gentleman sums up the results (*The Churchman*, July, 1911, p. 515) as follows: "There is a mass of secular historic evidence in favour of 8 B. C. and 29 A. D. for the dates of the nativity and the crucifixion respectively. The former date agrees with the express statement of Tertullian that Christ was born during the rule of Sentius Saturninus [in Syria], and the latter date is in accord with the universal testimony of the early Latin fathers that the Lord suffered under the rule of the Gemini."

We will give here a very brief summary of the grounds upon which these dates are based.

The Birth. The difficulties in the way of fixing the date of the birth of Jesus have been largely due to two apparent errors in the Lucan narrative: (1) that Quirinus was connected with the first census held in 8 B. C. and (2) that in certain of these enrolments in the eastern provinces of the empire it was the custom to require that all should return to their ancestral homes for purposes of registration. Both of these statements of Luke have been frequently denied and even ridiculed by mythicists and others who were desirous of impugning the historical trustworthiness of that writer.

As regards the former of these points, it has now been

331

definitely shown by Sir William Ramsay,[1] from the indisputable contemporary evidence of inscriptions, that Quirinus was in charge of Syria about 10–7 B. C., and probably in the exact years 9–8 B. C., the period of the first enrolment.

The second point has also now been settled by the discovery and publication of a copy of a similar edict, issued by Gaius Vibius Maximus, eparch of Egypt, A. D. 104. Sir F. G. Kenyon, in an editor's note, writes[2] (p. 124): "It is a rescript from the prefect requiring all persons who were residing out of their *nomes* to return to their homes in view of the approaching census. The analogy between this order and Luke is obvious. The census in question is that of the seventh year of Trajan (A. D. 103–4) and the determining date is the last day of the year. . . . The rescript is accordingly issued in Epeiph, the last month but one, which would give time for the necessary journeys. . . . Edicts requiring persons to return to their own *homes* are contained or mentioned [elsewhere; four documents are cited]; these, however, have no reference to the census but to persons who have left their domiciles to avoid λειτουργία [public duties]."

This perfectly plain and—to all acquainted with Eastern customs—intelligible order, that every man should return home, "each to his own hearthstone" (ἐπανελθεῖν εἰς τὰ ἑαυτῶν ἐφέστια), has, however, been curiously misunderstood by Professor W. B. Smith, who writes ("The Real Question of the Ancestry of Jesus," *The Open Court*, January, 1910, p. 13): "On census day every one should be at his own hearth, surely not in some distant ancestral city!" But this is precisely what is meant here. In ancient law and custom a man who left his own birthplace and that of his forefathers was a vagrant and without any rights in his adopted city or country; he was not

---

[1] In his articles in *The Expositor*, November and December, 1912, which complement and even supersede his former book, *Was Christ Born at Bethlehem?*

[2] *Greek Papyri in the British Museum*, III, 125 (1907), F. G. Kenyon and H. I. Bell; see also Milligan's *Greek Papyri*, p. 73.

even numbered in a census of the population of the latter. The later empire largely changed this old view; but in the East old customs were found to be too deeply rooted and too strong for even Roman officials to override.

A somewhat analogous parallel in modern times is the legal *status* of an alien, that is, a foreigner resident in a country which is not his own and where he has not been naturalised. He remains there on sufferance and is liable at any time to deportation should the exigencies of the state demand it.

The Crucifixion took place, we are told, immediately before a Passover, which was on the 14th day of the first month (Ex. 12 : 6). It was also upon the eve of a Sabbath, *i. e.*, on a Friday. Several dates have been proposed as "historically possible"—A. D. 29, 30, and 33. Colonel Mackinlay maintains that these conditions are best fulfilled in A. D. 29.

An objection to this date has, however, been raised by the Reverend D. R. Fotheringham on the ground that in A. D. 29 the 14th of *Nisan* did not fall on a Friday but on a Saturday, because (he alleges) Nisan 1 *was on March 5, when the new moon was first visible*. Had Nisan 1 fallen on the day previous (March 4), Nisan 14 would also have been a day earlier (viz., Friday), in which case the calendar would have agreed with the supposition that A. D. 29 was the year of the crucifixion.

Now, it will be seen that the whole question of this date practically turns upon whether the new moon, by which the beginning of the month was calculated, *could* have been seen *just after sunset on March 4 in that year*. The young moon was then about *thirteen and a half hours old*, and Colonel Mackinlay maintains that it *could* have been seen and duly reported by the watchers for it to the priests. In proof of this he instances the fact that in the year 1910 "Mr. D. W. Horner, a well-known and careful observer, and three others, saw the new moon [at Tunbridge Wells—about six hundred feet above the sea-level] with the naked eye on February 10 . . . when it was only sixteen hours old." It is true that the particular moon of A. D. 29 was, at the time in question, 2.5 hours younger than Mr. Horner's moon; but Colonel Mackinlay points out that (1) it was placed about as favourably for visibility[1] as Mr. Horner's moon; (2) the atmosphere of Palestine is much clearer than that of England; (3) in the latitude of Jerusalem (31° 47′ N.) darkness comes on after sunset more rapidly than in England, consequently a young moon can be more easily seen in Palestine; (4) Jerusalem is about two thousand six hundred feet above the sea-level, and celestial objects near the horizon can there be seen with greater clearness than from a lower level because there is a less density of air to see through; (5) the Jewish observers were specially trained to search for the new moon with the naked eye; they must have known, too, approximately where to look for it—a most important matter when endeavouring to "pick up" a faint celestial body.

Mr. E. Walter Maunder, F.R.A.S., formerly superintendent of the solar department in the Greenwich Observatory, discusses the question in *The Churchman*, June, 1912, and decides that it was quite possible for the moon to have been observed on March 4, as Colonel Mackinlay contends; but he adds (p. 472) that "in A. D. 29 the new moon of March fell very early, indeed, to be taken as that of Nisan." This objection, however, seems not to be in any sense final, and the date advanced by Colonel Mackinlay remains quite possible and, all things considered, probable.[2]

---

[1] See *The Observatory*, May, 1911, p. 203. The elements for the new moon of March 4, A. D. 29, at sunset were: altitude (about) 6°, difference of azimuth from setting sun 6.5°. For the moon of 1910 they were: altitude 4.5°, difference of azimuth 10°.

[2] For further details the reader should consult the entire discussion in *The Churchman*, which will be found in the numbers for March, 1910, April and July, 1911, and April, June, September, and November, 1912. But see also the article in the *Jour. of Theo. Studies*, October, 1910, vol. XII, p. 120, where the writer contends that the new moon in question was not seen till March 5. In that case the choice of dates would rest between A. D. 30 and 33.

APPENDIX B

AGNI AND AGNUS

DOCTOR DREWS labours very hard to equate *Agni*, as
the old Vedic fire-god, with *Agnus*, the lamb, as sacrificed
at the Jewish Passover, which, later, was regarded by the
primitive Christians as a type of Jesus Christ. He says
(*The Christ Myth*, pp. 144 and 145): "In the church of
the first [?] century, at Easter, a lamb was solemnly
slaughtered upon an altar and its blood collected in a
chalice.[1]

"Accordingly, in the early days of Christianity the
comparison of Christ with the light and the lamb was a
very favourite one. Above all, the Gospel of John makes
the widest use of it. As had already been done in the
Vedic cult of Agni, here, too, were identified with Christ
the creative word of God [*Logos*] that had existed before
the world, the life, the light, and the lamb. And he was
also called 'the light of the world' that came to light up
the darkness ruling upon the earth, as well as 'the Lamb
of God, who bore the sins of the world.' And, indeed,
the Latin expression for lamb (agnus) *also expresses its relation to the ancient fire-god and its sanctity as a sacrificial
animal. For its root is connected with ignis*[2] (Sansc., *agni*,

---

[1] Reference to Doctor Hatch's Hibb. Lects. (1888), *The Influence of
Greek Ideas and Usages upon the Christian Church,*" p. 300. The authority
given by Doctor Hatch is Mabillon, *Com. Præv. ad Ord. Rom.; Musæum Ital.
II.*, XCIV. Mabillon here remarks that the complaint of the Greeks that
the pope offered a lamb on the altar at St. Peter's arose from a mistake; the
lamb had been roasted for eating and was brought for the papal benediction (Migne, *Patrologia Lat.*, LXXVIII, 907, 1044). Pope Nicholas I said
(Hardouin, *Concilia*, V, 309 D) that the story was a lie of the Greeks, and
Æneas, Bishop of Paris (*ibid.*, 318 A), says that "only a fool would believe
it." Doctor Hatch has evidently been misled if he accepts such a palpably
cock-and-bull story as a statement of fact.

[2] Italics ours.

'the purifying fire,' and *yagna*, 'victim'), and also, according to Festus Pompeius, with the Greek *hagnos*, 'pure,' 'consecrated,' and *hagnistes*, 'the expiator.' In this sense *Agnus Dei*, 'the Lamb of God,' as Christ is very frequently called, *is, in fact, nothing else than Agni Deus, since Agnus stands in a certain measure as the Latin translation for Agni* [1] (Burnouf, *La Science des Religions*, 4th ed., 1885, pp. 186 *ff.*)."

Before discussing the main points involved in the above quotation we may be allowed to cite the remarks of Doctor Cheyne—a not altogether unfriendly critic—upon the position taken up here by Doctor Drews (*Hibbert Journal*, April, 1911, p. 660): "One is sorry that the name of Burnouf should be attached to what I may call the Agni-heresy and, in general, that a Burnouf should have set the example of the misuse of the Indian (Vedic) key to religious archæological problems." He consoles himself, however, with the thought that it is not the great Burnouf, but a relative, who has thus disgraced himself.

Now, according to Professor Whitney, the eminent philologist and lexicographer, *agnus*, "lamb," is probably a syncopated form of *avignus* (*avis*, older form of *ovis*, "sheep"). Hence, *agnus* must mean "the sheep-born animal" (*i. e., ovi*(*g*)*natus* for *avi*(*g*)*natus*), the same root appearing in the name for sheep in Sanscrit, *avi*, and in Greek as ὄἴς (= ὄϝις) [see Curtius, *Greek Etymology*, 596].

Agni, on the other hand, is derived from an old Aryan root, *ag*, "to move quickly," which appears in the Latin *agilis*, "agile." Fire was thought by the Vedic Indian to be the manifestation of an active but invisible spirit which had been born in the "fire-stick" and issued from the wood. "Men," says Professor Max Müller (*Lects. on the Orig. of Relig.*, p. 212), "were struck most by his quick movements, his sudden appearances, and so they called him the quick, or agile; in Sanscrit, *agnis*; in Latin, *ignis*."

[1] Italics ours.

The god Agni was regarded by the early Vedic Indians as the carrier to the gods of the volatile essence of the sacrifice, and *in that sense only* he was spoken of as a "mediator" between the latter and mankind.

In the face of the above considerations, therefore, it cannot be said that *Agnus Dei* ("Lamb of God") is "nothing else than *Agni Deus*"; there is really no connexion, etymological or other, between the words.

The lamb was *par excellence* the sacrificial animal of the nomadic Hebrews before their entrance into Canaan, and was so employed, in all probability, long before the institution of the Passover as we know it.

APPENDIX C

THE ASTRAL DRAMA OF THE CRUCIFIXION

A Mythical Exposition of Psalm 22[1]

On the World-tree (the Milky Way), says Professor Drews, *Orion* hangs with his arms and legs outstretched in the form of a cross (✕, *crux decussata*). Above and bearing down upon him, on his left, is the *Bull* and the group of stars known as the *Hyades* (= *nazar*); *Leo* is running up on the right. Behind Orion is the *Unicorn* (Monokerōs), representing the herd of *re'ēmim* (רְאֵמִים), "wild oxen," and about to pierce the hanging figure with its horn. The two *dogs* are near by.

His detailed exposition of the Psalm is as follows:

Vss. 1–5. *The Cry of the Sufferer:* "*My God* (Eli), *my God, why hast thou forsaken me*," etc. The sun is very far away; it is the winter half of the ecliptic; *Orion* (as representing the sun[2]) seems to cry for help against the dangers of the winter, which threaten him with extinction.

Vs. 6. "*I am a worm and no man*," etc. The sun in the winter time is pale and despised and creeps over the earth like a worm. Also, the Milky Way, in which Orion is, stretches like a worm across the sky when Orion sets in the beginning of winter. In the Babylonian myth the Milky Way was *Tiāmat*, described as a "worm" (= reptile), which the sun (= Marduk) split into two halves to form respectively the heavens and the earth.

Vs. 7. "*All that see me laugh me to scorn*," etc. The

[1] See the Appendix to *The Witnesses to the Historicity of Jesus*, A. Drews (1912).

[2] Among the Egyptians Orion, says Doctor Drews, was identified with the sun and moon god (Boll, *Sphæra*, 1903, p. 164; but see p. 344, note 2).

338

various constellations look down on Orion from higher points of the ecliptic,[1] etc.

Vs. 12. *"Many bulls have compassed me,"* etc. The zodiacal sign *Taurus* is charging *Orion*, who is flourishing his club with his right hand, while with his left he thrusts forward the lion's skin (*cf.* Hēraklēs). Professor Drews, however, thinks that he is "blessing" with his uplifted (?) left hand.[2]

Vs. 14. *"I am poured out like water,"* etc. The celestial river *Eridanus* flows beneath the feet of Orion; it seems to flow from his left foot; and the Milky Way, besides being regarded as a tree, may be taken as water (*cf.* Psalm 69 : 2 and 15).

Vs. 16. *"For dogs have compassed me,"* etc. The stars *Sirius* and *Procyon*, in the constellations *Canis Major* and *C. Minor*, are behind and beneath Orion.

"The assembly of evil-doers have enclosed me." These are the constellations *Bull, Dogs, Lepus* (hare), and *Dioscuri*, or *Gemini* (twins), who are described as "wicked" (criminals, robbers) in the astral myth (*cf.* Gen. 49), where they are related to the twins Simeon and Levi, and are called "bull-slayers,"[3] because they drive the zodiacal bull before them and push him out of the heavens.

"Like the lion are my hands and feet" (Massoretic text).
"They pierced my hand and my feet" (LXX version).

---

[1] E. g., the *Twins* (Dioscuri, Gemini) "mock" the sun as it moves heavy and dull on the lowest stretch of its annual path. They may also represent the "two thieves" crucified on either side of Jesus. Niemojewski, however, sees the two evil-doers ("thieves") in the dogs *Sirius* and *Procyon*. Drews remarks of this view: "The difference is not great, as the dogs culminate at the same time as the twins and may, therefore, be substituted for them." *Castor* is regarded as evil on account of his relation to winter; *Pollux*, good, on account of his relation to summer. The twins also appear as the "little boys" who jeered at Elisha (the sun): "Go up, thou baldhead" (II Kings 2 : 23). This means that the sun has lost his "hair" (=heat and light rays) at the lowest point of his course; *cf.* the "solar heroes" Samson and Hēraklēs.

[2] It is the *right*. Moreover, a *left*-handed blessing would be ominous.

[3] Gen. 39 : 33 and 34, however, says that Simeon and Levi were not *twins*, and in 49 : 6 that they "slew a man and *houghed* an ox" [oxen], *i. e.*, in the sack of Shechem (Gen. 34 : 25 and 29; *cf.* Joshua 6 : 21; 11 : 6 and 9).

The former reading, which is undoubtedly corrupt, Drews thinks may mean that the wicked (zodiacal signs) surround the hands and feet of the sufferer, *sicut leo*.

But there may be, he adds, a cryptic reference to the constellation *Leo*, whether because the chief stars in it are distributed as in Orion, and represent a recumbent Orion, or because of the astral relation of Orion to Leo. (He carries the lion's skin of Hēraklēs, who is a form of the sun-god.)

The meaning of the LXX version is explained thus: The (left) hand of Orion, which carries the lion's skin, goes with the arrow of one of the *Twins* (Castor), piercing the hand; and in the period of *Taurus* the constellation of the *Arrow* is in opposition to the arrow of Castor, the latter rising in the east when the former sets in the west.

Vs. 17. "*I may tell all my bones*," etc. These words recall the fact that no other constellation shows as plainly as Orion, on account of the number and distribution of its stars having the shape of a human being with extended limbs.

Vs. 18. "*They part [by lot] my garments*," etc. At the same time the shape of Orion may be regarded as a cup (dice-box) with the three (!) stars of the belt as dice[1] in it. The vesture of Orion is the heavens, which are often conceived as a "starry mantle," and they seem to be distributed among the various constellations.

Or we may take the *Milky Way* as his garment, the "seamless robe," because it runs continually across the sky, which is divided at the Twins into two halves by the passage of the sun.

Vs. 20. "*Deliver my soul from the sword; my darling from the power of the dog.*" The sword is that of Orion, which is drawn up against his body. The dogs are Sirius and Procyon.

Vs. 21. "*Save me from the lion's mouth; yea, even from the horns of the wild oxen thou hast answered me.*" The lion's mouth again refers to the *Hyades*, or to the constellation *Leo*, which seems to be running up from a distance, while

[1] Elsewhere these latter are regarded as the "three" Magi!

the *Unicorn* indicates the herd of *re'ēmim*. The LXX version translates the latter as *monokerōs* (? unicorn). "The real meaning of the passage," says Doctor Drews, "is lost when people learned in philology insist that 'the unicorn was really a buffalo.'"[1]

But now (vs. 22) the situation changes. Jahveh has heard the sufferer's cry. The sun has crossed the equator and the better season (the summer half) of the year has begun. "The meek shall eat and be satisfied." In fervent strains the delivered sings amid the chorus of stars ("the great congregation") the praise of Jahveh. Jahveh once more resumes the lordship of the world and all people gladly praise his name.

Other general features introduced into the drama are: substituting for the "crucified" Orion of the 22d Psalm the two other important crosses, viz., the *vernal* Cross with the *cup* (skull) below it, the *Virgin, Berenice's Hair* (*megaddela* = Mary Magdalene), etc., we have the elements of Niemojewski's annual "astral Via Dolorosa."

When Orion plays the part of the crucified Saviour, the *Pleiades* (the "rain sisters") represent the weeping women around the cross. Electra, the supposed centre of the Pleiades, is the mythical mother of *Jasios* (= Jesus) and is represented with a cloth over her head just as in Christian art the Virgin Mary is. But, as Jasios was also regarded, according to another genealogy, as the son of *Maia*, the mourning Pleiad may also stand for her. Moreover, in early Christian thought the mother of Jesus is a *dove* (*pelias* = Pleiad).

Without going into any detailed criticism of the text or translation, we will note down the following points in relation to the above exposition:

Doctor Cheyne regards the Hebrew text of this psalm as very corrupt, and if his view be correct the "parallels" drawn will, in any case, be considerably discounted. *E. g.*, in vss. 12–16, Cheyne wholly rejects the reading dogs (כְּלָבִים) and reads only "wild oxen" and "lions." Both of these animals, he thinks, are symbols for the op-

[1] See, however, *Enc. Bib.*, art. "Unicorn."

pressors of the Jews, the רְאֵמִים ("wild oxen") suggesting
ירחמאלים, "Jerahmeelites." Lagarde (*Orientalia*, II, 63 *f.*)
goes much further and identifies the several animals with
the rulers of various neighbouring peoples. Thus Tobiah
the Ammonite is referred to as a bull, Geshur the Arabian as a lion, and Sanballat the Samaritan as a dog.
But he accepts the Massoretic text as we have it.

According to the general critical-historical theory the
sufferer is clearly *the ideal community*—the faithful Israel
in the midst of an unfaithful nation in exile, and suffering with them, not an individual.[1]

The conception of the cosmogonic or world-tree, of
which the Scandinavian *Yggdrasil* is the most familiar
example, is very wide-spread. The idea is met with
among the ancient Chaldeans, the Egyptians, the Persians, the Hindus, and the Aryan races of northern Europe as well as in the mythology of China and Japan. It
would, however, be interesting to learn where Professor
Drews found it identified with the Milky Way! This
galaxy of stars is referred to in myth as a road, a river,
and a serpent ("worm"), or dragon, but never, to the
present writer's knowledge, as a *tree*.[2]

The Cry of the Sufferer. Why should Orion seem to be
crying for help at this time? It is then that we see him
dominant in the sky!

Vs. 6. It is scarcely correct to describe the sun as
seeming to be "pale and despised" in the winters of
southern Palestine and Egypt. The diminished heat and
glare is a welcome change from the oppressiveness of
summer.

Vs. 7. If the constellations may be said to "laugh at"
Orion at one time of the year they do so at every other,
for they never change their relative positions and passive
relations to him.

Vs. 16. In vs. 16 "they pierced" (כָּאֲרִי) should be "they
gnawed" (lit., "dug into"). The Hebrew word was

---

[1] A few scholars still hold to the individual interpretation, *e. g.*, Duhm
and Winckler, etc.

[2] It might be added, too, that the world-tree is not a *cross*.

translated "pierced" from a desire for a specific reference here to the crucifixion (Briggs). Professor Drews's
mythical arrangement of the various zodiacal signs is
likewise very strained. He says, *e. g.*, that the *arrow* of
Castor "appears to be piercing the left hand of Orion."
It is certainly drawn on the planisphere in the same
straight line, but a long way off him, and, in the present
writer's copy (at least), the *point* of the arrow is turned
in the opposite direction.

The constellation *Arrow*, too, seems to have no connexion with Orion. It is almost the antipodes of Orion, in
fact, and the Greek myth does not represent *Sagitta* as
a long lance. Ptolemy gives for it only five small stars
close together.

The constant changing about of the interpretation of
Orion, who is (*The Witnesses to the Historicity of Jesus*,
p. 55) now the crucified, now (on the authority of Niemojewski) his slayer, and again the dice-box used in the
division of the garments at the crucifixion, is very unsatisfactory. It seems possible to make it mean anything one chooses.

Vs. 21. Again, it is impossible to see any astral connexion between the *Hyades* and the "lion's mouth."
And, despite all the confident assertions to the contrary,
the "unicorns" (רְאֵמִים) probably refer to the Auroch
(*Bos Primogenius*), called by Cæsar (*B. G.*, VI, 28) *Urus*.
This animal when sketched from the side point of view
appears to have only one horn projecting forward. It
was a larger and fiercer animal than the "fat bulls of
Bashan."

Further, Professor Drews seems to have forgotten that
the constellation *Monokerōs* (Unicorn) was only devised
by Hevelius about 1690 A. D. It was wholly unknown
to the ancients and could not have figured in any astral
scheme ! [1]

For the rest we must protest against the implied iden-

[1] The "astral enemy" of both the *sun* and his stellar reduplication *Orion*
seems to have been the constellational *Scorpion* (see *The Primitive Constellations*, by R. Brown, Jr., 1899, vol. I, pp. 67 *ff.*).

tification of *Pleiades* with *peleiades*. Πλειάδες is probably derived from πλεῖν, "to sail," because these stars
rose at the beginning of the sailing season in the Mediterranean. Πελείας, "a dove," on the other hand, is probably a derivative of πέλειος [ὄρνις], "the dusky [bird]."
The later Greek poets, it is true, lengthened Πλειάδες by
an extra syllable, thus making it Πελειάδες, because they
regarded them as doves (as also the Ὑάδες, *Hyades*, "pig-
lings," both) fleeing before the hunter Orion, whose dog
(Sirius), we may add, was regarded as his master's faithful companion and friend.

The connexion between the asterism *Berenice's Hair*
and Mary Magdalene is very fanciful and forced, depend-
ing, as it does, upon a second-century A. D. and slan-
derous Jewish story that the latter was a dresser of wom-
en's hair and a courtesan.

The *Pleiades* (p. 314, l. 15) is apparently an error for
Hyades, who are "the weepers," because they are connected with the rainy season. *Electra*, moreover, is a
Pleiad. As Eastern women are commonly depicted in
art as covered and veiled, there is no significance in both
the Virgin Mary and Electra being so represented. The
Virgin was sometimes represented by the *symbol* of the
dove; but the dove was never said to be the mother of
Jesus.[1]

Finally, as regards the main points of the astral "parallels," though *Orion* does not well represent the sun on his
annual journey, because he is quite off the latter's path
(the ecliptic), he seems to have been regarded as a celestial reduplication of the sun[2] (*The Primitive Constellations*,
J. R. Brown, Jr., vol. I, p. 92; see also pp. 67 *ff.* and 93).
Also, Orion is, roughly speaking, *dominant* in the heavens
during the period of the sun's depression. He cannot, how-

[1] An early but futile attempt was made to *identify* the Holy Spirit with
the feminine principle of the Gnostic deity.
[2] Doctor Budge says (*The Gods of the Egyptians*, vol. II, pp. 215 and 249)
that the star ["constellation"] *Saḥ* (Orion) was the *abode* of the soul of
Osiris (the sun). But this is hardly identifying Orion with the sun (*cf.*
p. 338, note 2).

ever, be said to " hang on" the Milky Way, for he only just touches the end of it.

Lastly, most of the constellations comprising Niemo-jewski's celestial *Via Dolorosa* are not on the sun's actual path at all. Indeed, the whole astral scheme is fantastic and improbable in the extreme, and no proof is offered that it was ever devised in this form, or interpreted in this sense, before the time of Christ.

INDEX

Abbot, Dr. E. A., on Nazarene and Nazoraean, 104, *n.*

Abhinishkramana Sūtra, 14.

Accidentia and *substantia*, 190.

Acts of Thomas, 187.

Adam and Eve, the *Book of*, 221.

Additamenta, the, 230.

Adonis, 18, 91, 280; ascension of, 325; resurrection of, 316, 317.

Æneas, descent of, to Hades, 304.

Æsculapius, 321.

'Αγαθός, 207.

Aglaophamus, 129.

Agni, 6, 17, 22; birth of, 31, 35, 335, 336, 337; derivation of, 336, 337.

Agni-hotra, 35, *n.*

Agnus, derivation of, 336, 337.

Agony in the Garden, the, 213.

Αἶσα, 69.

Alford, Dean, on the reading of Matthew 27 : 16, 267.

'Almah, 87, *n.*

Alpha and Omega, 280.

Alphæus (= Alpu?), 238, *n.*

Amma (Ma), 8.

Anastasius of Sinai, 265.

'Ανασταυρόω, 291.

'Ανασχινδυλεύω, 291, 292.

Anderson, Dr., on the trial of Jesus, 230, 231.

Angel-self, 219.

Angelophanies at the tomb, the, 222, 314.

Ani, 236.

Ānkh, as representing phallus, 284, *n.*, 285, *n.*

Anna Perenna, 247.

Anna, the prophetess, 44.

Annas and Caiaphas, 245, 246, 247.

Annunciation, 24.

Anonymous Sanscritist, on Christian episodes in Krishna-myth, 77.

Anthesteria, 316, *n.*

Anwyl, Prof., on Esus (Hesus), 69.

Aoa, 280.

Aphrodite, 124, 131, 317.

'Απογράφεσθαι, translation of, 39, *n.*

Apostles as signs of the zodiac, the, 238, 239, *n.*

Apuleius on Isiac cult, 16; on magic, 289; (*Metamorphoses*), 19.

Arallū, 303.

Arrest of Jesus, the, 218.

Ascension, the, of the dying god, 326; to heaven, the, 323, 327, 328.

Ascensions, mythic, 324, *n.*

Ashērīm, 279.

Asita, blessing of, 45.

Ass, the, in myth and symbol, 36, *n.*

Assassins, *see* Zealots.

Astral body, 219, 223, 224.

Atia, 7, *n.*

Attis, burial of image of, 316, *n.*; resurrection of, 318.

Augustus on massacre of children at Bethlehem, 58.

Auroch, the, as the Unicorn, 343.

Avalokiteswara, descent of, to Hades, 307.

Azazel, 138, 139.

Babylonian ascensions, 326, *n.*; liturgies, 13, *n.*

Bacchus (Dionysus), 167.

Bacon, Prof. B. W., on Jensen's theory of Gospel origins, 74; on young man who fled naked, 225.

Balaam and the natal star, 46.

Ball, C. J., on Tammuz, 280.

Bancroft, Mr., on the cross, 282.

Baptism of Jesus, the, 110.

Barnett, Dr., on Christian sources of Krishna-myth, 77.

Bar Rabban, 260.

Bas-reliefs of Mithraic cult-meal, 202.

Basil the Great, 163.

Batiffol, Mgr., on Karabas, 260, 266, *n.*

Battles with demons, 305.

Beal, S., on the *svastika*, 284.

Beardless One, feast of, 261, 270.

Houston Public Library

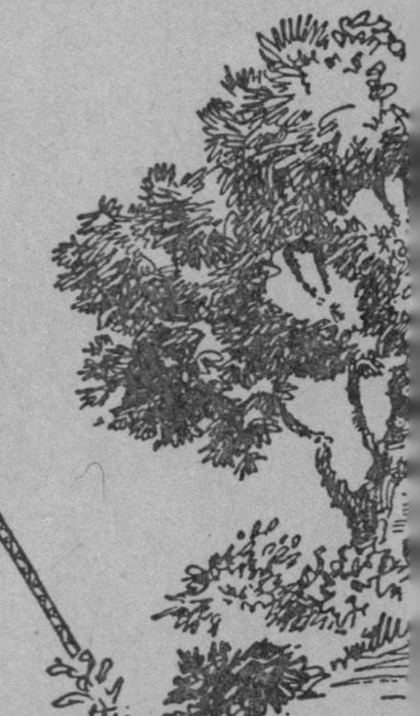